· THE ·
GOURMET
L · I · G · H · T
COOKBOOK

THE
GOURMET
L·I·G·H·T
COOKBOOK

Recipes and Menus for the Health and Calorie-Conscious Cook

By GREER UNDERWOOD

Illustrated by Frank Westerberg

Galahad Books
New York

Published in 1990 by
Galahad Books
A Division of LDAP, Inc.
166 Fifth Avenue
New York, NY 10010

Galahad Books is a registered trademark of LDAP, Inc.
Published by arrangement with The Globe Pequot Press.

Library of Congress Catalog Card Number: 90-80123

ISBN: 0-88365-756-2

Printed in the United States of America.

Acknowledgments

❖

Many thanks to all the people who have helped to make this book possible: To Cary Hull, an expert editor, who unerringly corrected my slip-ups, made the copy consistent, and suggested many changes for the better; this is a better book for you the reader. To Kate Bandos for her persuasive campaigns to get *The Enlightened Gourmet* noticed. To Kevin Lynch and Linda Kennedy for producing a lovely and readable book. To Lissa Tully, who gave me her last bag of black beans when the local store was out. To Nina Simonds and the staff of Al Forno for allowing me to adapt their recipes. To Carolyn Van Dam, who volunteered to take the photos for Frank Westerberg, who drew the clear, simplifying illustrations. To Jelia Witschi, Jane Lavine, Evette Hackman, and Laurie Burrows Grad for taking time from their busy schedules to review this book. To those at the Frances Stern Nutrition Center who figured all the nutrient values. And special thanks to Tripp and Tyler for sharing the computer with Mom, and to Teddy, who took us out when I couldn't cook another thing.

Contents

❖

Introduction:

The Culinary-Conscious '80s

❖

These are exercise-crazed yet food-happy times. Never have so many Americans panted and pumped their way to visions of physical perfection. And never have so many been interested in food and its paraphernalia—an irony peculiar to this running-shoe era. The culinary consciousness of the 1970s, like the national devotion to exercise, has grown more rapidly than a croissant can rise. The challenge of the '80s is to enjoy the one without compromising the other.

Fitness is more than physical, it's a healthy psyche as well as a strong body. It's a vitality of body and spirit that can't be nurtured on an inadequate diet. One too rich in calories or too poor in nutrients defeats all that hard work. As eaters one and all, we have our homework to do. The basics of nutrition are as foreign to most of us as the intricacies of a silicon chip. While we wouldn't try to build a computer without knowing how one works, we often try to build our bodies on a similar lack of knowledge. Of the three classifications of food, proteins, carbohydrates, and fats, which do you think nutritionists recommend should make up the bulk of our daily diet? And the second? Most experts agree carbohydrates should account for slightly more than half (53 percent), fats for a bit more than a third (35 percent), and the proteins the remaining 22 percent.

You may think your daily fat intake is decidedly below that 35 percent figure. Yet in this century, according to the Food and Nutrition Board of the National Academy of Sciences, fat intake has risen from 32 percent to 42 percent of our daily intake, probably due to the excessive use of fats, oils, and to some degree, meat. We have one of the highest fat content diets in the world. It lurks in most everything we eat, from avocados to zwieback, making a 100 percent fat-free diet as impossible as it is unhealthful. With our burgeoning culinary curiosity and fat intake, it makes sense to cut calorie corners where we can—without diluting our pleasure or endangering our health.

Voicing a concern about calories or vitamins was once the province of health food faddists, the type who would forage for wild nuts and berries rather than eat anything a machine had touched. Today, the cook who is unconcerned with overprocessed foodstuffs, nutritionally empty foods, and calories is the rarity. We're learning about the foods we eat even as we begin to hanker for pâté instead of meat loaf. Many are finding it difficult to indulge their love of fine food and maintain a healthy respect for the body. This book will point the way.

Thinking Thin

Is your life a revolving cycle of Spartan restraint followed by hedonistic indulgence? Do you diet successfully for a week or two, denying all pleasures, then binge on goodies? Is a hot fudge sundae your idea of a reward for losing weight?

If you answered yes to all of the above, you're probably still looking for a way to lose weight. The most successful dieters are those who don't. Don't binge diet, that is. They enjoy good food, in moderation, every day. They are aware of calorie counts in common foods. They know that there is no such thing as a skinny food, that only water is calorie-free. And they are active people, not necessarily marathon runners, but people who stand when they can sit, walk instead of ride, climb stairs, and shun elevators. Successful dieters know, at least intuitively, that taking fat off via exercise and semi-starvation is much harder than not eating to begin with.

Consider this: A 120-pound person running an eight-minute mile expends about 82 calories per mile; a 160 pounder will use about 110 calories. That's the calorie equivalent of an apple for the lighter runner, or a glass of low-fat milk for the heavier one. Nutritionists estimate that a pound of fat represents about 3,500 calories your body didn't use. Assuming you can exercise off 100 calories for every mile run, it would take 11 or 12 days to lose a pound of fat running 3 miles every day. Disheartening, isn't it? In light of these figures (and your own), thinking thin is more than a state of mind, it must be a mode of life.

What Gourmet Light is

To be a winner at the weight-loss game means educating yourself about the basics of metabolism and nutrition. It means learning how to eat to satisfy your hunger and learning how to cook to satisfy your appetite. This is a cookbook, an everyday guide to good, healthful eating habits. Many of you don't need to lose a pound, but you are looking for ways to eat well and maintain your happy weight state.

Gourmet Light is for those who enjoy fine food, but keep a calorie-conscious eye peeled. This is a cookbook for people who exercise not only for the sport of it but because it feels good also. This is also a cookbook for people who plan to exercise but can never quite fit it in, people looking for viable ways to trim extra calories from their daily meals. This is for those who like to keep abreast of food trends, from sun-dried tomatoes to shitake mushrooms, and for people who relish a meal not only for what it is, but also for what it is not.

Herein the reader will find information on nutrition, metabolism, the role of fats, proteins, and carbohydrates and, of course, good reduced-calorie recipes. You'll find out what pot to buy for which task, how to store foods, and sources for hard-to-come-by ingredients. There are short soliloquies on everything from how to peel an artichoke to the virtues of extra-virgin olive oil. Because not everyone is a seasoned cook, the recipes are thorough and detailed. If you already know your way around the kitchen, this book will teach you how to reduce calories in many of the dishes you now prepare, as well as give you some new and delicious ideas. When the ten techniques of *Gourmet Light* cooking become as natural to you as boiling water, you'll be able to pare calories from many of your favorite dishes.

This is not meant to be the only cookbook you'll ever need, for there are decidedly occasions when a no-stops, full-calorie-ahead, four-star dinner is in order. This is a way of cooking for everyday sort of use that you can live with happily, for a lifetime. Learn to pare a few superfluous calories from your daily "bread" and those strident days of diet may become a thing of the past.

What it is not

This is not a diet manual. No promise here of pounds lost in two easy weeks, no ersatz ingredients, no forbidden food lists. Avoidance, yes, but you won't have to take the pledge with *Gourmet Light* cooking. Wine, spirits, butter, and beef are all used, but in moderation.

It's tempting when writing a reduced-calorie cookbook to imply that all manner of foods can be prepared in such a way as to render them skinny. Not so. You'll find a Mimosa Sherbet but not ice creams. You'll enjoy Duck Breast with Zinfandel Sauce, but neither the accompanying wild rice, nor the sauce itself, is aswim in butter. Many dishes can be rewritten to remove excessive calories; those that can not simply aren't here. The aim was not to make do but to do well, and if that couldn't be done the recipe wasn't included. There is a place for plenty of fresh unsalted butter, for swirls of whipped cream, and well-marbled beef, but it is not here. Instead, indulge in Sole and Crab Peppers, Chilled Tomato Soup with Tarragon Ice, Turkey Cutlet with Cranberried Apple Sauce, and finish with a smooth Mango Mousse. Here are the techniques of good cooking without excessive use of highly fatty, cholesterol-choked foods.

How it came to be

Internationally, the French have always been acclaimed for turning out the world's best chefs, and it is to them we have turned for decades to decree what's new. When they threw away the flour bin, reaching instead for the stockpot and mounds of butter, we followed (or at least au courant restaurants did). When they threw the vegetables into the food processor creating smooth purees, we did too. When they started undercooking not only beef, but also lamb and fish, we at least agreed the beef should be very rare, and many started enjoying lamb that way, too. If they said "Pirouette!" we obliged like good students. They taught us haute cuisine, they brought us nouvelle cuisine, and they introduced cuisine minceur, the "skinny" cooking of Michel Guerard. One hears little of cuisine minceur these days, mostly because it is time-consuming and expensive to duplicate in the average kitchen, but I would be amiss not to mention what was a large inspiration for this book. I had long believed that good food didn't have to be fattening and that thin food didn't have to be boring, and had worked on ideas to that effect. But it was the international interest in Guerard's cuisine minceur that led me to believe others were looking for good, but not fattening, food. Guerard's cuisine minceur is not for the single-person kitchen or even for the American kitchen, calling for such delicacies as squab and spiny lobster. But it is a volume to which I still go to browse.

Food today in France and the United States has been strongly influenced by nouvelle cuisine as outlined by Guerard, Paul Bocuse, and other French chefs. There are fewer red meats; fish and poultry predominate. There is a greater emphasis on vegetables and how food looks. Sauces are lighter, not to be confused with thinner, for they're enriched with oodles of butter and cream rather than flour. Portions are smaller. The grill is in. Precious and often hard-to-find ingredients such as radicchio, yellow and eggplant-hued peppers, and bonsai (miniaturized) vegetables reign.

In the United States there is a newfound pride in our native foods and chefs, less dependence on the grand masters—a surge of independence. Everyone is talking about the new American cuisine, its dedication to simplicity, homegrown ingredients, and the home-town talent responsible for it. Although when one sees a recipe that typifies the new cuisine such as Chèvre-Stuffed Chicken Breast with Wild Mushroom Sauce I sometimes wonder just who redefined simplicity. Perhaps the crux of the matter is best explained by the French gastronome and cook, Raymond Oliver, who wrote, "To innovate in cooking it is more difficult to attack a boiled egg than a pheasant mousse." Cooks have long known it is easier to elaborate than delineate, easier to pile luxury on excess than improve on the ordinary. Nevertheless, the new American cuisine remains true to its indigenous roots—namely plain food, in the sense of native products such as corn, grits, buckwheat, and maple syrup are coming into their own again. Our chefs are becoming the trendsetters in a field heretofore dominated by Europeans.

Gourmet Light cooking includes a bit of all these trends, for it is a product of our times. Its soul lies in French techniques, lightened in the spirit of the day and using the very freshest and best our native seas and lands have to offer—but always with an eye on the scale. So, enjoy!

RECOMMENDED DAILY DIETARY ALLOWANCES OF SOME NUTRIENTS

Age	Weight	Height	Calories per day	Protein, g	Vit. A, IU**	Vit. C, mg	Thiamin, mg	Vit. B₆	Riboflavin, mg	Calcium, mg*	Phosphorus, mg	Iron, mg	Zinc
Females													
19-22	120	64 in.	2100	44	4,000	60	1.1	2.0	1.3	800	800	18	15
23-50			2000	44	4,000	60	1.0	2.0	1.2	800	800	18	15
51+			1800	44	4,000	60	1.0	2.0	1.2	800	800	10	15
Males													
19-22	154	70 in.	2900	56	5,000	60	1.5	2.2	1.7	800	800	10	15
23-50			2700	56	5,000	60	1.4	2.2	1.6	800	800	10	15
51+			2400	56	5,000	60	1.2	2.2	1.4	800	800	10	15

Carbohydrates and fats: Recommended dietary allowance for carbohydrates and fats has not been established. It is recommended that 30 to 35 percent of the day's total calories come from fats, and 50 to 55 percent from carbohydrates.

Cholesterol: The American Heart Association recommends limiting cholesterol to 300 mg/day.

Sodium: There is no recommended dietary allowance for sodium. An individual's need depends on physical activity and exposure to high temperatures. The estimated safe and adequate intake is between 1.1 to 3.3 grams/day for adults.

*The Food and Nutrition Board may raise this recommendation.
**IU = International Unit

Food & Nutrition Board
National Academy of Sciences, Revised, 1980

About the Recipes

❖

1. For better flavor and to keep the sodium level of a recipe low, I recommend you use unsalted butter whenever butter is called for. Our nutritional analysis of these recipes was based on unsalted butter.
2. To further reduce sodium, use homemade stocks made without salt instead of canned products.
3. Skim milk has 60 percent fewer calories than whole milk. Take advantage of this in your cooking.
4. You can save on calories by using aerosol cooking sprays, but to avoid a possible fire, never spray them near a heat source.
5. Carefully read each recipe before beginning to cook to avoid the disappointment of lacking a necessary ingredient or piece of equipment. If you envision each step as you read it, the actual preparation will be greatly simplified. If you're new to cooking and making more than one recipe at a time, make yourself a brief timetable. I remember one enthusiastic student breezing into cooking class with the proud announcement that he had cooked the previous week's menu for his appreciative wife. "How was it?" we all wanted to know. "Great," he beamed, "the only problem was the flaming bananas were done before the steak, and the potatoes were done after both of them!" Timing is one of the most difficult things for a budding cook to get the hang of. But planning and practice bring results.
6. When possible, instructions have been given for what may be done ahead, and what needs last-minute doing. Freezing information is also given, where feasible.
7. Saute sometimes appears as "saute" for the cook is actually boiling the food in a small amount of liquid rather than frying it in fat.

PART I
GOURMET
L · I · G · H · T
COOKING

Chapter 1
THE PRIMER

The Primer

--- ❖ ---

The Primer is perhaps the most important chapter in this book, for here are the ten techniques of *Gourmet Light* cooking. Once you've mastered them, paring calories from most any recipe will become automatic. Nothing here is tricky or requires culinary expertise; anyone who can separate an egg can cook—deliciously—the thin way. Success rests on your resolve to think thin, always looking for ways to cheat a dish of excessive calories but not at the expense of flavor.

This Primer will teach you how to cut down on the overuse of butter, fats, oils, and calorie-heavy flour thickenings. You'll discover how some readily available and inexpensive kitchen equipment can make you a winner at the calorie game. And you can have some fun testing your calorie IQ.

So hone up those knives, and fill your kitchen with appetizing aromas fat only with flavor and happy cooking!

Getting Started

--- ❖ ---

Not convinced? Think the only way to watch your weight is to go on a celery and water regime for a few days? Perhaps the following tallies will give you pause. The same meal, one prepared the traditional way and one the *Gourmet Light* way. Both are good, but which would you choose?

The Traditional Meal

Gazpacho, made with oil and croutons	157 calories/cup
Sauteed sole (6 oz) with Hollandaise	425 calories
Asparagus Mimosa (1 cup)	115 calories
Mixed-Green Salad with Vinaigrette	135 calories
Apple Pie	404 calories
	TOTAL 1236 calories

The Gourmet Light Meal

Gazpacho (limited oil, no croutons)	90 calories/cup
Steamed sole (6 oz), Reduced-Calorie Hollandaise	229 calories
Asparagus Mimosa (1 cup)	65 calories
Mixed-Green Salad with Herbed French Vinaigrette	50 calories
Hot Apple Tart	145 calories
	TOTAL 579 calories

Cooking the *Gourmet Light* way is no more difficult than any other. It takes only the resolve to want to change a few habits, the knowledge of what to change, and a nodding acquaintance with calorie counts. Why not test your Calorie IQ right now with the quiz below? And then on to the stove! (Or do you have to exercise first?)

Check Your Calorie IQ

You can't play the game until you know how to score. Calorie awareness is the key to weight control. While it's not necessary to carry a pocket calorie guide, it is sensible to have a working knowledge of some basic calorie facts. Check your calorie IQ here.

TRUE or FALSE
1. A glass of soda water and a glass of tonic water have about the same number of calories
2. A handful of Pepperidge Farm Goldfish have roughly the same number of calories as an equal amount of peanuts.
3. Low-fat milk has about half the calories of whole milk.

4. A banana, a half-cup of dried lima beans, and a baked potato have about the same number of calories.
5. A 4-ounce serving of poached salmon has fewer calories than a 4-ounce serving of lean broiled steak.
6. An apple has more calories than a cup of popcorn.
7. A tablespoon of honey has more nutrients and is lower in calories than a tablespoon of sugar.

CIRCLE THE FOOD LOWER IN CALORIES

8. A 5-ounce piece of steamed haddock seasoned with parsley, dill, and lemon or 1 deviled egg.
9. A tablespoon of vegetable oil, margarine, or butter.
10. A cup of cottage cheese or a chocolate-coated ice cream bar.
11. A McDonald's Fillet o'Fish sandwich or a McDonald's hamburger.
12. A veal chop or a piece of pizza.
13. A half-cup serving of chocolate pudding, a cup of New England–style clam chowder, or 1 cup of fruited yogurt.

THE ANSWERS

1. False. Tonic water, which is sweetened, contains about 70 calories in an 8-ounce glass; soda water contains none.
2. False. A half-ounce of Pepperidge Farm Goldfish contains about 59 calories; a half-ounce of oil-roasted peanuts contains about 90 calories.
3. False. One percent low-fat milk contains about 100 calories a cup; whole milk contains about 160. Low-fat milk with 2 percent fat has as much as 145 calories a cup. Skim milk contains about 90 calories per cup.
4. False. The potato and the banana each have about 90 calories; dried lima beans, a half-cup serving, contain as much as 131 calories.
5. True. But the difference is much smaller than you might think. The salmon, a relatively fatty fish, has about 246 calories for 4 ounces; the beef, with visible fat removed, about 272.
6. True. An apple contains about 80 calories; the popcorn, 23 calories, salted but unbuttered.

7. False. A tablespoon of honey has 61 calories; a tablespoon of sugar has 46. Honey does supply a very small amount of potassium.
8. The haddock has about 112 calories in 5 ounces; the egg, made with 1 tablespoon of mayonnaise, has 180 calories.
9. All the same, approximately 100 calories per tablespoon.
10. A 2½-ounce bar of chocolate-coated ice cream has 147; the cottage cheese has 240 calories a cup.
11. The McDonald's burger has 257 calories; the fish sandwich, 407. Although the fish is lower in calories than the beef, the frying and the mayonnaise used in the sandwich make up the extra 150 calories.
12. One-eighth of a 14-inch size, home recipe of a sausage pizza has about 176 calories; a veal chop about 300.
13. The New England–style chowder has 157 calories, the pudding 192, the fruited yogurt about 260.

11–13 correct	highest honors
8-10 correct	honor roll
5-7 correct	passing grade
0-4 correct	it's study time

This is not to suggest that those interested in losing pounds or maintaining their weight should opt for a chocolate-coated ice cream bar instead of cottage cheese, or pizza instead of a veal chop. Its intent is to point out some commonly held misconceptions and myths; fish is *not* automatically low in calories, how it's prepared is essential. There are several vegetables more fattening than potatoes, and butter is not more fattening than margarine. A paperback calorie guide is good reading for anyone interested in weight control.

Here are the ten techniques of *Gourmet Light* cooking. Digest them and say good-by to diets forever.

The Ten Techniques
of Gourmet Light Cooking

❖

1. "Saute" in stocks, broths, and wine instead of fats and oils

When a recipe calls for butter and/or oil for the sauteing of onions, garlic, shallots, and so on, substitute stock, broth, or wine or a combination for calorie-free cooking. Add enough liquid to cover the bottom of the pan by about one-eighth inch, bring to a boil, add food to be "sauteed," cover, and reduce heat to medium. Stir frequently, adding more liquid should it evaporate before the food is cooked.

2. Replace heavy cream with skim or low fat milk

The importance of using milk, either whole, low fat, or skim, is best stressed by the figures (pun intended):

Skim milk made from dry solids	80 calories/cup
Skim milk	90 to 100 calories/cup
Low fat milk with 2 percent nonfat milk solids	130 calories/cup
Whole milk	150 calories/cup
Half-and-half	300 calories/cup
Light cream	480 calories/cup
Heavy cream	800 calories/cup

How many calories you want to save will determine which of these dairy products you use. My recipes specify milk; whether you choose whole, skim, low-fat, or reconstituted from dry solids is your decision. Should you opt for the latter, remember this: Dry milk doesn't have to be chilled for cooking purposes, but reduce cooking temperatures somewhat, for this product scorches more easily than whole milk. A nutritional aside: Cooking with skim or whole milk supplies almost twice the amount of protein found in cream.

3. Reducing and replacing oil in salad dressings

When a skinny bowl of greens is lavished with 2 tablespoons of regular dressing, the result is a caloric avalanche of at least 200 calories. If you eat but 5 salads a week, it will only take 3½ weeks for that dressing to be a pound of fat. Why not reduce or even eliminate much of the oil used in dressings with a skinny alternative? The unlikely but excellent surrogate is chicken stock (the kind you make yourself) or canned beef consomme. Why homemade? Why the consomme and not just canned broth? Both the canned consomme and your own homemade stock contain enough gelatin—one occurring naturally as the collagen in the bones melts, the other added—to somewhat duplicate the natural viscosity of oil. Another very acceptable alternative is enriched commercial broth; instructions may be found on page 18. Stock-based salad dressings are light, flavorful, and nutritious.

4. Thickening with cornstarch and arrowroot instead of flour

Although the current culinary trend, popularized by nouvelle cuisine, is to thicken sauces by reduction (that is, boiling down), it is occasionally necessary to thicken a soup, stew, or classic sauce such as a mornay by means of a starch—either flour, arrowroot, or cornstarch. Note these measures for the *same* thickening ability:

3 teaspoons flour (1 tablespoon)	50 calories
2 teaspoons cornstarch	20 calories
1 teaspoon arrowroot	15 calories

Arrowroot and cornstarch (you may also use potato starch) give a shiny, translucent quality to a sauce, flour gives a more opaque look. Both arrowroot and cornstarch must be dissolved in a little cold liquid before using, and if heated too long or brought to a boil, a sauce thickened with arrowroot or cornstarch may liquefy, a process called hydrolizing. Always keep foods with these starches added to them on moderate heat to avoid this.

5. The magic of crème blanc

Sometime in my early twenties I became aware of the omnipotent presence of the calorie god. Now every morsel I ate and drank seemed to get counted whereas before it had gone unnoticed. As a child, I yearned for the independence of adulthood, only to find it came harnessed with responsibility. Mother didn't make me finish eating

liver anymore, but that didn't mean I was free to eat potato chips for
dinner either. To escape the calorie god's ever watchful eye, I became
a constant calorie counter, being careful not to overindulge. To avoid
the boredom of diet foods, I experimented in the kitchen a great deal,
developing the cooking style you find here. One wonderful way I
found to cheat the calorie god at his own game was crème blanc, a
mixture of cottage cheese and yogurt used in place of sour cream and
sometimes butter, which adds a touch of finesse and variety. You'll
find out how to make it on page 37.

6. Retaining the natural moisture in foods

It may seem redundant to stress the importance of buying fresh foods
in a day when processed foods are as "in" as a beehive hairdo, but
natural flavors are so vital to the success of *Gourmet Light* cooking
that it can't be stressed enough. Second only to buying the best is to
select the cooking method that most retains the natural moisture in
foods, reducing, even eliminating, the need for fats, oils, and rich
sauces. Here are suggestions in no particular order of importance.

a. *Parchment paper, aluminum foil, and wax paper*—By encasing
   the food in an envelope, evaporation is greatly reduced and the
   food stews in its own juices, creating a natural sauce. Lettuce,
   cabbage leaves, and cornhusks may also be used.

b. *Salt-encased cooking*—This very old method of cooking is excellent for roasting large pieces of meat, fish, or poultry to juicy perfection. The food is encased in a paste of coarse salt and water,
   forming an inedible crust that is cracked open and discarded after
   roasting. Oddly the salt doesn't permeate the food; because of the
   salt, the moisture in the food isn't lost.

c. *Poaching*—The term means to immerse a food in a simmering
   liquid. Poaching is generally reserved for poultry, but lamb and
   even beef can be deliciously poached. For oven poaching the food
   is placed in a film of liquid, covered with aluminum foil or wax
   paper, and roasted; it's excellent for chicken breasts.

d. *Steaming*—Using either a cake rack, Chinese bamboo steamer, or
   metal basket with folding sides, the steaming of fish, poultry, and
   vegetables is much used in *Gourmet Light* cooking.

e. *Grilling*—This watchword of the new American cooking is ideal for our purposes, for foods pick up the added flavor of the smoke and cook with a minimum of added fats.

7. Pureeing vegetables

This darling of nouvelle cuisine, which like so many trends is really a revival more than a discovery, is an excellent way to add variety and create a richly satisfying dish without butter. Pureeing vegetables, either alone or in creative combinations, is best accomplished in a food processor, but it can be done using a food mill or ricer.

8. Desserts

Because *Gourmet Light* cooking doesn't use saccharin or other ersatz substitutions, most of the desserts in this book rely on the natural sweetness of fruits. You will find recipes for them poached in wine, iced, or pureed. There are also recipes that use reduced amounts of sugar. But taste was always the deciding factor: If a reduced-sugar recipe tasted like something was missing, it wasn't included here.

9. Presentation

Presentation is important because I've always felt cooking is a little bit of art; its visual appeal is nearly as important to me as its sapidity. But spending precious time carving radish roses and lemon baskets is best left to well-staffed kitchens. Mine, as I suspect yours is, is most often a one-person show. So presentation for me has come to mean simple garnishes, minced fresh parsley, twisted lemon slices, a grating of carrot, or a snippet of chive. It means taking care to wipe away a dribble of sauce and arranging the food on the plate or platter with an eye toward color and order. Nor is presentation an afterthought. It rightly belongs up-front during menu planning when you consider not just what tastes good together, but what looks good together as well. And while considering color contrasts, don't overlook texture, what I call "toothsomeness." Pair something hard with something soft, something crisp with something creamy. The art of cooking doesn't stop at the stove, it is part of both the conception and the presentation, and all the workings in between. Cooking is a pragmatic art, a personal expression that brings pleasure and satisfaction. Do with these recipes as *you* will, your creative input will make them work for you.

10. Equipment for reduced-calorie cooking

The cook who wants to incorporate the *Gourmet Light* way into his or her cooking style may like to investigate the following:

a. *Cooking sprays*—There are a few aerosol sprays on the market that grease a pan while adding only minimal calories. You could probably accomplish the same by dipping a pastry brush or paper towel in oil and rubbing it on the pan surface. Naturally, you won't achieve perfect browning, but foods won't stick if cooked at moderate heat.

b. *Teflon- and Silverstone-coated pans*—Although it is difficult to brown foods in these pots and pans, they do allow high heat searing and cooking without sticking. I recommend owning at least an 8-inch skillet.

c. *Degreaser*—Looking like a measuring cup with the spout coming off the bottom, degreasers have become widely available of late. They are excellent for separating fats from soups, broths, and sauces.

d. *Ice cream maker*—A luxury item useful for creating fruit ices and sherbets.

e. *Parchment paper*—Covered in Technique 6, parchment and wax papers allow food to cook without losing precious juices to evaporation.

f. *Chinese bamboo steamer*—Also covered in Technique 6, this inexpensive and useful contraption allows you to cook a whole meal in one pot.

g. *Immersion blenders*—Immersion blenders are like mechanically powered whisks. They make it possible to whip milk and are advantageous for persons with arthritis.

h. *Grill*—Also listed under Technique 6, indoor or outdoor grills allow for fat-free cooking with maximum flavor.

Chapter 2

THE FOUNDATIONS: STOCKS AND SAUCES

The Foundations

———————————❖———————————

We've covered the ten techniques that can help you to lose or maintain weight loss without depriving yourself the enjoyment of good food. The following are the foundations upon which this cooking style is built: the stocks, or enriched commercial products, reduced-calorie egg sauces—Hollandaise, Béarnaise, and mayonnaise—wine sauce, cheese sauce, basil-walnut sauce, and more.

Taking Stock

———————————❖———————————

Because stocks and broths are used extensively in *Gourmet Light* cooking, you might like to make your own in quantity, freezing this indispensable ingredient in plastic containers for future use. Although making stock is a lengthy process (four hours for chicken, eight hours minimum for beef), it is not time spent entirely over a hot stove. The preparation time is about 20 minutes, cleanup time about the same. Canned broths may be used or enriched with additional bones and/or vegetables if added flavor or thickness is desired. Commercially prepared consomme is an excellent alternative, because the added gelatin nicely equates the natural thickness of a homemade stock.

If you decide to make your own stock, you'll need at least a 12-quart stockpot; making any less is a waste of time in my opinion.

Although a heavy pot is preferable as it will prevent vegetables from scorching on the bottom and ruining the stock, a thin pot is considerably less expensive and fine for a trial run; a lobster steamer is ideal. It's also good to have some old, thin kitchen towels for straining or you'll need to purchase cheesecloth at a hardware store or in the cleaning department of the grocery store.

Because of the high concentration of proteins, homemade stock should be frozen if not used within 48 hours. Fish stock must be frozen if not used within 24 hours of preparation. Always boil stock a minute or so before using, too. Freeze stock in plastic containers, so you can defrost quickly by placing the container in simmering water or under hot water. When the block is loosened, slip it into a saucepan, cover, and turn heat to medium high. Frozen stock will keep without flavor loss for up to one year. If you use a variety of sizes of freezer containers, you can just reach for the size you need, rather than have to thaw more than necessary.

Although the clarity of a stock is simply a matter of aesthetics and won't affect the flavor of a finished dish, here are some tips for producing jewel-clear stocks:

- scrape the scum that rises to the surface in the first hour of cooking
- once the boiling point is reached, reduce the heat so stock just simmers
- don't stir, this makes the stock cloudy (if you are using a thin pot, disregard this advice, better a cloudy stock than a burned one)
- if you add wine to the stock, don't use an aluminum pot or the stock will appear gray
- don't add starchy vegetables such as potatoes or cooked leftovers
    Here are some general hints about stocks:
- tomatoes added to a stock cause it to sour more readily, mushrooms darken it (handy for beef stock), and members of the cabbage family such as parsnips and turnips lend an unpleasant flavor
- keep uncooked beef and chicken bones in plastic bags in the freezer until you have enough to make the stock
- don't treat the stockpot like the garbage disposal, it is not a catchall for leftovers
- add no salt, this is done when seasoning the completed dish

Beef Stock

❖

8 pounds uncooked beef bones, marrow bones
   highly recommended
3 carrots, sliced (no need to peel)
3 small to medium onions, sliced (no need to peel,
   the skins add color)
3 celery stalks, sliced
7 quarts water
1 cup red wine (optional)
a small handful fresh parsley stems, chopped
freshly ground pepper to taste
1 bay leaf
1 garlic clove, halved

1. Put the bones in a large roasting pan with the carrots, onions, and
   celery, and roast about 40–50 minutes in a 400-degree oven, or
   until the bones and vegetables are beginning to brown.
2. Strain away and discard the fat. Put the bones and vegetables in a
   12-quart stockpot, cover with the water, add the wine, and bring
   to a full boil.
3. Reduce heat to a simmer and scrape the scum that rises to the
   surface with a slotted spoon. Repeat scrapings two or three times
   until most of the scum is removed.
4. Add parsley, pepper, bay leaf, and garlic. Half cover the pan and
   simmer about 8 hours, adding more water if the volume falls more
   than a quart below the original.
5. Wring out an old kitchen towel or a piece of cheesecloth in cold
   water and line a strainer with it. Pour or ladle the stock through
   the strainer.
6. If using the stock immediately, pour what you need into a degreaser to complete the defatting, or refrigerate the stock. A pan-

cake of fat will form that is easily scraped off. Freeze stock in plastic containers of various sizes.

Yield: 3½ to 4 quarts
Calories per cup: 18
Protein per cup: 1g

Fat per cup: 0
Carbohydrates per cup: 4g
Sodium per cup: 20mg

Meat Glaze (Glacé de Viande)

❖

Like an expensive perfume, meat glaze is used sparingly — a little goes a long way. Half a teaspoon stirred into sauces or soups boosts the flavor without making its presence known. It is truly a chef's secret. A commercial alternative is meat extract or concentrated beef-flavored broth, usually available in the gourmet section of the supermarket or at specialty food shops. Use half the amount of the commercial as you would the homemade; it tends to be salty.

Simply boil 3 quarts of homemade or bone-enriched commercial beef stock down to 1½ cups of iridescent, deep brown syrup. It should be thick enough to coat a metal spoon.

Meat glaze will keep in the refrigerator in a sterile glass container for about two weeks. After that a harmless mold may form that can be scraped away. Or freeze the glaze in ice cube trays and pop them into plastic bags when frozen. Thaw the cubes in a small, covered saucepan with a tablespoon of water.

Yield: 1½ cups
Calories per tablespoon: 9
Protein per tablespoon: 0

Fat per tablespoon: 0
Carbohydrates per tablespoon: 2g
Sodium per tablespoon: 10mg

Veal Stock

❖

Veal stock is made as beef stock is, simply using veal bones for beef bones. However, it is so difficult for the home cook to obtain veal bones that I don't call for it in this book. Should you have a ready supply of veal bones, you'll find it works wonderfully whenever beef or chicken stock is called for.

Chicken Stock

❖

5–6 pounds uncooked chicken bones (saved from
        boning breasts, or buy wings and backs)
2–3 carrots, sliced (no need to peel)
2 medium onions, sliced
2 celery stalks, sliced
4 quarts water
1 cup dry white wine (optional)
a small handful fresh parsley stems, chopped
freshly ground pepper to taste
1 bay leaf
1 garlic clove, halved

1. A rich, brown chicken stock is made like the beef stock (see page 14), by browning the bones and vegetables in a 400-degree oven for about 40–50 minutes. Strain away and discard the fat. Place the browned bones and vegetables in a stockpot, cover with water, add the wine, and bring to a boil. Continue at Step 3.
2. A "white" stock is made by putting unroasted bones and vegeta-

bles in a 12-quart stockpot, cover with the water, and add the wine. Bring to a boil.

3. Reduce heat to a simmer and scrape the scum that rises to the surface with a slotted spoon. Repeat scrapings two or three times until most of the scum is removed.

4. Add the parsley, pepper, bay leaf, and garlic. Half cover the pan and simmer about 4 hours, adding more water if the volume falls more than a quart below the original.

5. Wring out an old kitchen towel or a piece of cheesecloth in water and line a strainer with it. Pour or ladle the stock through the strainer.

6. If using the stock immediately, pour what you need into a degreaser to complete the defatting, or refrigerate until a pancake of fat forms. Scrape off the fat and freeze the stock in plastic containers of varying sizes.

Yield: About 3 quarts
Calories per cup: 21
Protein per cup: 1g

Fat per cup: 0
Carbohydrates per cup: 4g
Sodium per cup: 20mg

❖ **ICE CUBE STOCK** ❖

Freeze homemade stock in ice cube trays and pop the frozen cubes into a plastic bag. Use when a few tablespoons of broth are called for to "saute" an ingredient.

Enriched Quick Commercial Beef or Chicken Broth

❖

½ pound uncooked beef or chicken bones
3 unpeeled carrots, sliced
1 onion, chopped
1 tablespoon oil (optional)
1 quart canned beef or chicken broth
½ cup red or white wine (optional)
1 bay leaf
1 clove garlic, halved
freshly ground pepper to taste
a small handful fresh parsley stems, chopped

1. If dark color is desired, brown the bones and vegetables in the oil in a covered skillet over high heat for about 6 minutes. Deglaze the skillet with 2 tablespoons wine (from the ½ cup).
2. For a "white" stock simply put all the ingredients in a 2½-quart saucepan, half cover, and simmer 30 minutes.
3. It may be used immediately after straining and discarding bones, vegetables, and herbs.

Yield: 3½ cups
Calories per cup: 126
Protein per cup: 7g

Fat per cup: 6g
Carbohydrates per cup: 12g
Sodium per cup: 923mg

Fish Stock

❖

This delicate stock must be frozen if not used within 24 hours.

> 1 fish rack (skeleton) weighing about 1 1/2 pounds
>   from a white-fleshed, nonoily fish such as
>   haddock or cod, innards removed and rack rinsed
> 6 cups water
> 2 cups dry white wine (optional)
> 1 small onion, chopped
> 1 small carrot, chopped
> 1 bay leaf

1. Put the fish rack (don't shy away from using the head, as it contains lots of collagen, which melts into gelatin) in a heavy pot, preferably nonaluminum if using the wine, and add the water and wine.
2. Bring to a boil, reduce heat so liquid just simmers, and scrape the scum away with a slotted spoon. When most of the scum is removed, add the remaining ingredients and half cover pot. Simmer 40 minutes.
3. Rinse out an old kitchen towel or a piece of cheesecloth in water, line a strainer with it, and pour or ladle stock through. Store in the refrigerator or freezer if not used within 24 hours.

Note: Bottled clam juice is a very acceptable substitute in recipes calling for fish stock. Dilute the bottled product with 1/4 cup dry white wine or vermouth to 8 ounces clam juice, and omit salt from the recipe.

Yield: Approximately 1 quart
Calories per cup: 33
Protein per cup: 1g

Fat per cup: 0
Carbohydrates per cup: 8g
Sodium per cup: 10mg

The Trademarks of Classic Cooking—Sauces

❖

The cynosures of fine cooking are frequently the sauces: lemony Hollandaise ribboning asparagus, rich and pungent Béarnaise complementing a flavorfully steamed fish, the cool richness of crème blanc offsetting a steamy bowl of beet soup. *Gourmet Light* cooking doesn't deny the lover of good food the pleasures of the table. Here, follow the reduced-calorie versions of such classic recipes.

Egg-Based Sauces

Egg-based sauces owe their creamy richness to the emulsion that forms when egg yolks poach in butter and an acid such as lemon juice (Hollandaise), vinegar (Béarnaise), or wine. My thin versions of these classic sauces use chicken stock for the majority of the butter, but are otherwise the same. You'll find them packed with flavor that belies their lightness, and you'll be happy to note that they may be prepared ahead and gently reheated with little danger of curdling or separating.

The *Gourmet Light* version of the classic Hollandaise is a great favorite in my kitchen, because it is much less fattening (34 calories per tablespoon compared to 80 calories for the traditional recipe), tastes lighter, holds better than the traditional sauce, and may even be gently reheated. It is wonderful on eggs, poultry, fish, and vegetables, and with the addition of a bit of mustard, terrific with lamb as well. Note the range of uses with a slight variation in ingredients.

Regardless of the method you choose, direct heat or blender, remember Hollandaise and its cousin Béarnaise were never meant to be served hot, just warmed. Should you accidentally heat the sauce beyond 140 degrees, causing it to separate or break, put a teaspoon of acid (lemon for Hollandaise, vinegar for Béarnaise) in a food processor or blender and slowly dribble in the sauce. It will form the emulsion again.

Hollandaise Sauce
DIRECT-HEAT METHOD

❖

I prefer this method for it makes a thicker sauce more quickly. Choose a 1-quart heavy-bottomed saucepan; enamel over cast iron, lined copper, or anodized aluminum all are excellent pans.

> 4 tablespoons lemon juice
> ³/₄ cup chicken stock or canned broth
> 5 large egg yolks (whites may be frozen for another
>   use)
> 2 tablespoons butter, melted
> ¹/₄ teaspoon salt (optional)
> dash of cayenne pepper (optional)

1. In a small pan, combine the lemon juice and stock. Boil until reduced to ³/₄ cup. Cool slightly.
2. Beat the egg yolks with a whisk until foamy in the heavy-bottomed saucepan. Place on low heat and dribble in the chicken stock, whisking vigorously until the sauce thickens, about 2–3 minutes. Remove the saucepan from heat and whisk in the melted butter. Season with salt and cayenne, if desired. The sauce will thicken more on standing.

Yield: 1 cup
Calories per tablespoon: 34
Protein per tablespoon: 1g

Fat per tablespoon: 3g
Carbohydrates per tablespoon: 1g
Sodium per tablespoon: 5mg

Hollandaise Sauce
BLENDER OR FOOD PROCESSOR METHOD

❖

5 large egg yolks
5 tablespoons lemon juice
¾ cup chicken stock or canned broth
2 tablespoons butter, melted
½ teaspoon salt (optional)
dash of cayenne pepper (optional)

1. Place egg yolks and 1 tablespoon of the lemon juice in the bowl of the food processor or in the blender. Process 45 seconds.
2. Meanwhile, boil the remaining lemon juice and stock until reduced to ⅔ cup.
3. With the machine on high, dribble in broth and lemon juice.
4. Pour sauce into a heavy-bottomed 1-quart saucepan and whisk over low heat until sauce thickens, about 2–3 minutes. Whisk in the butter. Season with salt and cayenne pepper, if desired. The sauce will thicken more on standing.

Yield: 1 cup
Calories per tablespoon: 34
Protein per tablespoon: 1g

Fat per tablespoon: 3g
Carbohydrates per tablespoon: 1g
Sodium per tablespoon: 5mg

Hollandaise Variations

❖

1. Maltaise Sauce is a classic accompaniment for asparagus. Using the Hollandaise recipe, substitute orange juice for the lemon juice, adding 1 teaspoon lemon juice and a bit of grated orange rind to the finished sauce. (Or refer to the recipe for Asparagus Maltaise, page 233.)
2. A fabulous sauce for fish, cauliflower, asparagus, and broccoli, a classic Mousseline Sauce is made by folding 1/4 cup heavy cream, which has already been whipped, into a finished Hollandaise. If you have an immersion blender, you can whip skim milk and fold it into our thin version of Hollandaise for a cloudlike sauce just this side of heaven.

❖ **THINKING THIN TIP** ❖

If you tire of lemon juice on vegetables, try the juice of an orange next time.

Béarnaise Sauce
DIRECT-HEAT METHOD

❖

Béarnaise is the classic sauce for grilled steaks and roasted tenderloins. It is equally good with grilled fish, chicken, and vegetables, too.

> 2 tablespoons red wine vinegar
> 1 tablespoon finely minced shallot
> 1 tablespoon fresh tarragon or 1 teaspoon dried tarragon
> 4 large egg yolks
> 4 tablespoons chicken stock or broth
> 1–2 tablespoons butter, melted
> ¼ teaspoon salt (optional)
> freshly ground pepper to taste

1. In a 1-quart heavy-bottomed saucepan, combine the vinegar, shallot, and tarragon. Boil until reduced by half.
2. Put the egg yolks in a heavy-bottomed 1-quart saucepan and whisk until foamy over medium heat.
3. Dribble the reduced vinegar-shallot mixture into the egg yolks, whisking over low heat until foamy and slightly thickened. Remove from heat.
4. Heat the chicken stock until almost boiling.
5. Dribble chicken stock into egg-vinegar mixture over low heat. Whisk it until thickened. Whisk in butter. Season with salt and pepper. The sauce will thicken more on standing.

Yield: 1 cup
Calories per tablespoon: 21
Protein per tablespoon: 1g

Fat per tablespoon: 2g
Carbohydrates per tablespoon: 0
Sodium per tablespoon: 0

Béarnaise Sauce
FOOD PROCESSOR OR BLENDER METHOD

❖

2 tablespoons red wine vinegar
1 tablespoon finely minced shallot
1 tablespoon fresh tarragon or 1 teaspoon dried
  tarragon
4 large egg yolks
4 tablespoons chicken stock or canned chicken broth
1–2 tablespoons butter, melted
¼ teaspoon salt (optional)
freshly ground pepper to taste

1. In a small saucepan, boil until reduced by half the vinegar, shallot, and tarragon.
2. Meanwhile, process the egg yolks in the blender or food processor until foamy.
3. Dribble the vinegar-tarragon mixture into the egg yolks, with the machine on high.
4. While the machine processes the yolks and vinegar, heat the chicken stock in the now-empty pan just to the boiling point.
5. Dribble the stock into the yolks while the machine is running.
6. Pour the sauce into the empty stock pan and whisk over medium-low heat until the sauce thickens. Whisk in butter. Adjust seasoning with salt and pepper. Sauce will be frothy and light, it will thicken on standing.

Yield: 1¼ cups
Calories per tablespoon: 21
Protein per tablespoon: 1g

Fat per tablespoon: 2g
Carbohydrates per tablespoon: 0
Sodium per tablespoon: 0

Béarnaise Variations

❖

1. Add 1 tablespoon tomato paste to the finished Béarnaise to make Sauce Robert. This is an excellent sauce with meats.
2. Horseradish Béarnaise is delicious as a spread for cold roast beef. Add 2 teaspoons prepared horseradish to the finished Béarnaise.

Mayonnaise I
HEAT METHOD

❖

Probably the most used sauce in America, mayonnaise is readily available on supermarket shelves in regular and low-calorie renditions. Once you try either of these recipes, I doubt you'll often opt for the store-bought version. Either will keep in the refrigerator for a little more than a week and may be frozen. This first version is the thinner of the two and must be cooked for a couple of minutes to thicken; the second, using more oil, is necessarily weightier but needs no cooking. I prefer a light oil when making mayonnaise; a nearly tasteless vegetable oil such as corn oil produces a light-tasting sauce, but many prefer the stronger taste of an olive oil.

> 4 large egg yolks
> 1/4 teaspoon salt
> 1 tablespoon lemon juice
> 1/2 teaspoon prepared mustard
> 1/2 cup oil of your choice
> 1/2 cup chicken broth, boiling hot
> dash cayenne pepper

1. Place egg yolks and salt in a food processor or blender and process until yolks are pale yellow, about 1 minute.
2. Add lemon juice and mustard and process 30 seconds more.
3. Using only a few drops at a time to start, dribble in the oil. The success of your sauce depends on adding this very slowly.
4. Dribble in the hot broth in a slightly thicker stream. Transfer the sauce to a 1-quart heavy-bottomed saucepan.
5. Whisk the sauce constantly on medium-high heat until it thickens, about 2 minutes.
6. Use sauce as is or vary the flavor with one of the additions (see below). Sauce may be served hot or cold.

Yield: Approximately 1 ¼ cups
Calories per tablespoon: 61
Protein per tablespoon: 1g

Fat per tablespoon: 7g
Carbohydrates per tablespoon: 0
Sodium per tablespoon: 30mg

Mayonnaise II

❖

4 large egg yolks
¼ teaspoon salt
1 tablespoon lemon juice
½ teaspoon prepared mustard
¾ cup oil
¼ cup chicken broth, boiling hot, reduced to 2
*   tablespoons*
dash cayenne pepper

1. Make the sauce as described for Mayonnaise I, steps 1—4. The sauce will not have to be cooked.

Yield: Approximately 1 ¼ cups
Calories per tablespoon: 85
Protein per tablespoon: 1g

Fat per tablespoon: 9g
Carbohydrates per tablespoon: 0
Sodium per tablespoon: 30mg

Mayonnaise Variations

❖

To 1 ¼ cups mayonnaise add any of the following:

2 tablespoons chopped fresh dill for use with fish salads.

2 tablespoons chopped fresh basil for use with tomatoes (or use 1 teaspoon dried basil).

1 tablespoon chopped dill pickles, 1 tablespoon capers, 1 tablespoon fresh tarragon (or 1 teaspoon dried), and 1 tablespoon chopped chives for a Gribiche Sauce for steamed or poached fish.

1 tablespoon horseradish and 1 tablespoon minced fresh parsley for use with cold roast beef.

3 tablespoons tomato paste, 3 tablespoons minced green pepper, and 1 teaspoon snipped chives for use with hamburgers or as a dip for raw vegetables.

Flour-Based Sauces

Flour-based sauces, what Mother called white sauce and the French term Béchamel (made with milk) or Velouté (made with milk and stock), have fallen out of favor with the advent of nouvelle cuisine. Instead of being thickened with flour, sauces are now thickened with reduced cream, mounds of butter, or by reducing naturally gelatinous homemade stocks to a syrupy stage and then enriching them with butter. Naturally, with the exception of the reduced stock, none of these are appropriate for reduced-calorie cooking. Therefore for the rare, but nonetheless real occasion when a dish would benefit from a "cream" sauce, here is a recipe for *Gourmet Light* Velouté, with less than half the calories of a traditional Velouté, as well as a reduced-calorie Cheese Sauce.

Cheese Sauce

❖

Again, cheese sauces have fallen from de rigueur to déclassé, but to enliven a pallid cauliflower I offer the following. The sauce may be made ahead and reheated.

> ½ cup chicken stock
> ½ cup milk
> 1½ tablespoons cornstarch or arrowroot dissolved in
>   2 tablespoons of stock
> 1 tablespoon butter, at room temperature
> freshly ground pepper to taste
> freshly grated nutmeg
> a few shakes paprika
> 1 tablespoon sherry
> ½ to ¾ cup grated cheese such as cheddar (about
>   1⅛ to 2 ounces)

1. In a saucepan, heat the stock and milk until small bubbles appear at the edge of the pan.
2. Gradually whisk in the cornstarch over a low heat. Cook, stirring, for 1 minute. Whisk in the butter.
3. Add the pepper, nutmeg, paprika, and sherry. Stir in the cheese.
4. Cook over low heat, stirring constantly until smooth and thick, about 5 minutes.

Yield: Approximately 1¼ cups
Calories per tablespoon: 22
Protein per tablespoon: 1g

Fat per tablespoon: 1.5g
Carbohydrates per tablespoon: 1g
Sodium per tablespoon: 24mg

Velouté Sauce

❖

2 cups stock, use whatever will complement the dish:
fish, beef, or chicken
1 tablespoon grated onion
2 teaspoons cornstarch or arrowroot dissolved in
2 tablespoons milk or half-and-half
1 1/2 tablespoons butter
1/4 teaspoon salt
a dash of white pepper to taste
a few gratings fresh nutmeg

1. Combine the stock and onion in a saucepan and bring to a boil.
2. Reduce the heat to medium, whisk in the cornstarch or arrow-root, and cook, stirring, about 5 minutes or until the sauce is smooth and thick.
3. Cut the butter into 3 pieces, whisk each in after the previous one melts. Taste and season with salt, pepper, and a bit of nutmeg.

Yield: Approximately 2 cups
Calories per tablespoon: 8
Protein per tablespoon: trace

Fat per tablespoon: .5g
Carbohydrates per tablespoon: .5g
Sodium per tablespoon: 20mg

Herb-Based Sauces

Fresh herbs combined with stock, a hint of oil, and nuts or cheese make wonderful sauces for pasta, salads, and poached chicken or fish. They are a snap to make with the aid of a food processor and keep up to a week when refrigerated.

Lemon Parsley Sauce

Try this sauce smeared on thick, fresh tomato slices, then broil just until heated through or brush it on grilling chicken or fish. Thin it with a few tablespoons broth and serve it as a delightfully different dip for crudités. Toss it with pasta, add a few cooked shrimp, cool to room temperature, and serve as a hot-weather meal.

> ½ cup fresh parsley, snipped
> ½ cup fresh watercress, snipped
> 3 tablespoons dried bread crumbs
> ½ teaspoon prepared mustard
> juice of half a lemon
> 1 tablespoon oil
> 1 egg yolk
> 1 tablespoon chicken broth or consomme
> freshly ground pepper to taste
> 1 teaspoon sugar

1. Combine all the ingredients in a food processor or blender. Use as described above.

Yield: ⅔ cup

Calories per tablespoon: 22

Protein per tablespoon: 0

Fat per tablespoon: 2g

Carbohydrates per tablespoon: 1g

Sodium per tablespoon: 10mg

Basil-Walnut Sauce

❖

This Basil-Walnut Sauce is reminiscent of the ever-popular pesto minus most of the oil and with the added sparkle of balsamic vinegar. It has one-fourth the calories of a traditional pesto sauce. Its uses go far beyond a simple and delicious toss with pastas (a wonderful hot-weather dinner). Brush it on grilling chicken or fish the last few minutes of cooking, dab it on sun-warmed tomatoes, or stir it into a cool bowl of fresh Tomato Soup (page 74).

½ cup fresh parsley, snipped and loosely packed
½ cup fresh basil, snipped and loosely packed
1 tablespoon extra-virgin olive oil
1 tablespoon balsamic or malt vinegar
2 tablespoons grated Parmesan cheese
1 teaspoon sugar
2 tablespoons chicken broth, more if a thinner sauce
*   is desired*
1 clove garlic, minced
3 tablespoons finely chopped walnuts
freshly ground pepper to taste

1. Combine and process all the ingredients in a food processor or blender. Use as described above.

Yield: ¾ cup
Calories per tablespoon: 30
Protein per tablespoon: 1g

Fat per tablespoon: 3g
Carbohydrates per tablespoon: 1g
Sodium per tablespoon: 10mg

Acid-Based Sauces

The most popular sauces in today's au courant restaurants are those made by emulsifying (blending) large amounts of butter in small amounts of acid, such as lemon juice or wine. Since no magician's wand can render 8 tablespoons of butter calorie-free, *Gourmet Light* cooking will forgo any attempt to produce a beurre blanc. However, here are two acid-based sauces, one based on wine and another on lemon, which will fend off the boredom associated with reduced-calorie cooking.

Lemon Butter Sauce

When you've eaten all the dry green beans you can, try this. Simple and delicious.

> 1 1/2 tablespoons butter
> 2–3 tablespoons freshly squeezed lemon juice
> 1/2 teaspoon salt
> freshly ground pepper to taste
> 1 clove garlic, minced
> 1 teaspoon minced fresh parsley
> 1/2 teaspoon minced shallot or scallion

1. Combine all the ingredients in a small skillet or saucepan and heat until butter melts. Pour over cooked, drained vegetables.

Yield: 4 servings
Calories: 44
Protein: 1g

Fat: 4g
Carbohydrates: 1g
Sodium: 270mg

Wine Sauce

❖

A very good, hearty sauce that belies its modest ingredients and ease of preparation. Serve this with beef, such as the Paupiette on page 128. This will keep a week in the refrigerator or up to six months without flavor loss in the freezer.

> 2 teaspoons oil or noncaloric cooking spray
> 2 large carrots, scrubbed and chopped
> 2 medium onions, chopped
> 2 cups beef stock or broth
> 1/2 teaspoon meat glaze (see page 15) or 1/8
>   teaspoon commercial meat extract
> 1 cup red wine such as a Burgundy
> 2 or 3 sprigs fresh parsley
> 1/2 teaspoon salt
> freshly ground black pepper to taste

1. Heat the oil in a medium skillet. Add the carrots and onions and saute, covered, until lightly browned, about 5 minutes. When browned, reduce heat to medium low and continue cooking, covered, about 8 minutes, or until vegetables are soft.
2. Add the stock, meat glaze, wine, parsley, salt, and pepper, and simmer, covered, for 1 hour.
3. Remove cover, turn heat to high, and boil until the sauce is reduced to about 1 1/4 cups (about 10 minutes).
4. Puree the sauce in a food processor or blender.

Note: If sauce is too thin, thicken it by stirring in a slurry made by dissolving 1 teaspoon potato starch, arrowroot, or cornstarch in a tablespoon of wine. Sauce may be strained if you prefer a smooth texture.

Yield: Approximately 1 ½ cups
Calories per tablespoon: 14
Protein per tablespoon: 0

Fat per tablespoon: 0
Carbohydrates per tablespoon: 2g
Sodium per tablespoon: 52mg

❖   **DISCOLORED SAUCES**   ❖

Although aluminum is one of the best, meaning fastest conductors of heat, an unlined aluminum pot may discolor a sauce if there is acid present, such as tomato, wine, vinegar, or lemon juice. The discoloration is caused by a reaction of the acid with the stain. Unlined aluminum pans become stained when washed with a high-alkali cleanser or are used for cooking high-alkali foods such as potatoes. The acid in the sauce removes some of that stain, transferring it to the sauce, causing a grayish tint that is unappetizing but fortunately, not a health hazard.

Tomato Sauce

❖

Tomato-based sauces are used extensively in *Gourmet Light* cooking, for they score on flavor not matched by their calorie tally. Although many will opt to purchase tomato puree to make the sauce recipes called for in this book, here is a homemade version for those with gardens and/or the inclination to prepare their own.

> 2 pounds tomatoes, roughly chopped or 44 ounces canned tomatoes (2 large cans)
> 1 small onion, chopped
> 1 clove garlic, minced
> 1 tablespoon tomato paste
> 2 cups chicken stock (1 cup if using canned tomatoes)
> 4 leaves fresh basil, snipped, or 1 teaspoon dried basil
> 2/3 teaspoon sugar
> 1/2 teaspoon salt if using fresh tomatoes (omit if using canned)

1. Combine all the ingredients in a medium-size saucepan and boil, uncovered, until reduced by half.
2. Puree the mixture in a food processor or blender, and strain to remove the seeds and skins if desired.

Yield: Approximately 3 cups
Calories per cup: 96
Protein per cup: 4g

Fat per cup: 1g
Carbohydrates per cup: 21g
Sodium per cup: 380mg

Crème Blanc

❖

This simple mixture of cottage cheese and yogurt is to this book what butter, sour cream, and heavy cream are to others. It is a flavor enhancer, while contributing to good nutrition as well. Cookbook readers will note its similarity to fromage blanc. It will keep in the refrigerator for up to one week, and its flavor and texture will improve after being made.

> 4 ounces low-fat cottage cheese
> 4 tablespoons plain low-fat yogurt
> 2 tablespoons milk

1. Combine the ingredients in a food processor or blender, and mix until perfectly smooth. The sauce will thicken after being chilled about 6 hours.

Note: Two teaspoons of cornstarch (20 calories) added to this mixture will prevent it from separating during high heat cooking. You may then disregard my notes to cook crème blanc over low heat.

Yield: Approximately 1 cup
Calories per tablespoon: 11
Protein per tablespoon: 2g

Fat per tablespoon: 0
Carbohydrates per tablespoon: 1g
Sodium per tablespoon: 40mg

Chapter 3

SAVORY LITTLE SOMETHINGS

Savory Little Somethings

❖

By any name—smorgasbord, *tapas*, antipasto, *zakuska,* or hors d'oeuvres—appetizers are often pound packers. A 2-inch square of cheddar cheese, a mere ¼-inch thick (about ½ ounce), atop a cracker is an astounding 75 calories. Typical cocktail fare is generally high in fat, such as cheese, or fried in fat, such as chips, so that a few bites can really wreak havoc with the day's total calorie intake. Just 10 potato chips will bulk you up with 114 calories; an ounce of peanuts contains 160, and a tablespoon of cream cheese dip for a little celery stick has at least 50 calories.

In a cookbook dedicated to slimming meals, the emphasis on appetizers is understandably minimal; the chief ingredients are on the slender side, with vegetables and seafood predominating. But even on elaborate occasions, two or three offerings at most are sufficient. An array of appetizers makes for a very nice party or a fine dinner, but both are not needed on the same evening. If you offer your guests the sort of trim but tempting foods found here, they'll still be able to appreciate and enjoy your dinner.

There is a new trend evident at even the toniest restaurants. Customers are ordering lighter meals, often eschewing an entree in favor of, say, a side order of asparagus, followed by a salad of grilled duck breast. Saving money is not the object, banking calories is.

Most of the nibbles that follow are small tasty bites. Some, such as the Chèvre-Stuffed Artichokes, would make a lovely first course if nestled on a tangle of mixed greens dressed with a light mustard vinaigrette. Others would do well in the light supper or lunch slot, such as the Fresh Mozzarella and Tomato Pizza.

Presentation is particularly important when serving appetizers.

The mind must feast while the stomach yet waits. Mushroom caps on a white cloth napkin on a dark tray, crudités arranged attractively in baskets, chicken and pork skewers circled in spoke fashion with a tomato rose at the center—this attention to detail is key. Cooking without garnishing, no matter how simple, is like dressing in polka dots and stripes.

Chèvre-Stuffed Artichokes

❖

This recipe may be prepared with either frozen artichoke hearts or fresh baby artichokes, an easy size for cocktail fare. For larger servings, suitable for a salad, prepare the bottoms from fresh artichokes. The larger cheese-stuffed artichoke bottoms make a delicious salad or appetizer when placed in a tangle of greens and dressed with a mustardy *Gourmet Light* vinaigrette. The recipe may be made through Step 6 as much as a day before serving.

For Artichokes

1 *package frozen artichoke hearts, thawed, or 6 baby*
    artichokes or 4 large artichokes
4 *tablespoons lemon juice*
4 *tablepoons flour*
1/2 *cup cold water*

For Marinade

4 *tablespoons chicken broth*
2 *tablespoons red wine vinegar*
1 *tablespoon lemon juice*
1 *tablespoon oil*
a few sprigs fresh thyme or 1/4 teaspoon dried thyme
freshly ground black pepper to taste

For Stuffing

2 ounces chèvre (goat cheese), such as Montrachet,
    or a spiced cream cheese
2 tablespoons milk
1 tablespoon butter
½ clove garlic, minced
1 tablespoon dried bread crumbs

To prepare the artichoke bottoms

1. Lay an artichoke on its side and slice off the top third with a stainless-steel knife. With scissors cut the spiny tips off the leaves. Cut away the tough outer leaves with the knife as if peeling an orange. You'll now have an inner core of pale green leaves. Slice this off, leaving the bottom. Trim it to remove tough green fibers. As you finish each one, cut into thirds, and drop the pieces into a bowl of water with 2 tablespoons of the lemon juice added to help keep the artichoke from turning brown.

   To prepare baby artichokes, follow the preceding instructions until you get to the inner core of pale leaves. Cut the artichoke in half the long way, and scrape away the fuzzy center.

To cook

1. Make a paste with about 4 tablespoons flour in a half cup of cold water. Stir this into a quart of water with the 2 remaining table- spoons lemon juice. Bring to a simmer, stirring occasionally. Add the artichoke bottoms and simmer until tender, about 10 minutes for the larger bottoms and 6 minutes for the baby ones. Drain, and when cool enough to handle, scrape away the fuzzy center.
2. Marinate the bottoms or thawed artichoke hearts in the chicken broth, vinegar, lemon juice, oil, thyme, and pepper at least 4 hours or overnight.
3. Preheat oven to 350 degrees. Drain and discard the marinade.
4. Mix the goat cheese with the milk until smooth and creamy. Fill a pastry bag with the mixture or spoon the mixture on the artichoke hearts or bottoms.

5. Spray a baking sheet with cooking spray. Arrange filled hearts on it.
6. Melt the butter in an 8-inch skillet. When foamy, cook the garlic over medium-low heat 1 minute. Add the bread crumbs and stir until lightly browned.
7. Divide the bread crumb mixture over the cheese. Bake 10 minutes in the preheated 350-degree oven until heated through.

Yield: 12 artichoke hearts
Calories per heart: 46
Protein per heart: 1g

Fat per heart: 4g
Carbohydrates per heart: 1g
Sodium per heart: 20mg

❖ CHÈVRE ❖

Goat cheeses, collectively known as chèvres, have long been popular in Europe. In America they have recently become the darling of the upbeat food world and the star in many a recipe. Creatively turned out in various guises from stuffing for pasta to souffles, the import and local manufacture of these distinctive handmade cheeses have grown greatly.

The flavor of chèvre is best described as a clear, tangy, and fresh, not the sort of cheese to eat by itself, but in combination with other flavors. Banon (wrapped in chestnut or grape leaves) is the mildest; Crotin de Chazignol is the sharpest; and Bucheron and Montrachet perhaps the best known.

Beef with Broccoli

❖

These tasty roll ups are a snap to fix, particularly if you have some reduced-calorie mayonnaise (page 26) on hand or a bit of leftover Béarnaise (24) or Hollandaise (21). Make these as much as 8 hours ahead and chill. Cover the dish with plastic wrap until serving time. Delicatessen roast beef is very good for this recipe.

> *⅓ to ½ head broccoli, about ¾ pound*
> *5 thinly sliced pieces roast beef, about ⅓ pound*
> *3 tablespoons Béarnaise, Hollandaise, or mayonnaise*
> *a few shakes salt*
> *4 tablespoons extra sauce for dipping*

1. Discard the leaves from the broccoli. Peel the stalks with a vegetable peeler. Cut each spear into thin strips.
2. Bring a 2-quart saucepan ¾ full of water to a boil. Add the broccoli, cover, remove from heat, and let it rest 7 minutes. Drain.
3. Cut the flowerets from the stalks, cut the stalks into 1 ½-inch long, very thin pieces.
4. Trim any visible fat from the meat. Cut each slice in half the long way.
5. Place the meat on a counter so its long side is parallel to the counter's edge. Spread the 3 tablespoons sauce over the meat. Place a broccoli floweret perpendicular to the meat on the far left side of the meat strip so the broccoli stem rests on the meat and the bud shows over the top. Place 2 thin stalk pieces on either side of the floweret stem. Season with salt. Roll up tightly so stem and stalk don't show and broccoli bud does.

6. Arrange the rolls in spoke fashion on a platter, with extra sauce in a scalloped lemon half in the center.

VARIATION: Add a bit of horseradish to the Hollandaise or mayonnaise for a bit more bite.

Yield: 10 rolls
Calories per roll: 51
Protein per roll: 6g

Fat per roll: 2g
Carbohydrates per roll: 2g
Sodium per roll: 70mg

Peeling the tough outer skin from the broccoli stalk before cooking the broccoli will make the whole stalk more tender to eat.

Clam and Sausage Appetizers

❖

These clam and sausage-stuffed shells make a delicious hot cocktail nibble. The recipe may be prepared through Step 9 early in the day, and cooked at the last minute. The appetizers reheat nicely when covered with foil.

> ½ small onion, chopped
> 1 clove garlic, minced
> ½ cup chicken broth
> ¾ cup dry white wine
> 12 hard-shell (littleneck) clams (about 2 pounds), well scrubbed
> 2 teaspoons cornstarch
> 3 ounces fully cooked sausage such as kielbasa
> 3 tablespoons dried bread crumbs
> 1 tablespoon minced fresh parsley

1. "Saute" the onion and garlic in the chicken broth in a covered 2-quart saucepan until the vegetables are limp and almost transparent.
2. Add the wine (reserving 1 tablespoon for Step 3) and clams, cover pan, and steam over high heat until clams open, about 8 minutes.
3. Dissolve the cornstarch in the reserved tablespoon of wine.
4. Skin the sausage and chop it.
5. Lift opened clams from the broth with a slotted spoon. Line a sieve with a piece of cheesecloth or a heavy paper towel wrung out in water, and pour the broth through the sieve.
6. Pour 6 tablespoons strained broth back into the now-empty saucepan. Add dissolved cornstarch and cook, whisking, over medium heat until thickened. Set aside.
7. Pull clams from their shells, discard one half of shell. Chop clams roughly.

8. Combine chopped clams, sausage, and thickened broth.

9. Spoon mixture into shells. Sprinkle ½ teaspoon bread crumbs on each stuffed shell.

10. Clams may now be baked in a 425-degree oven until bubbly and browned (about 12–14 minutes) or held, chilled, for baking later in the day. Broil briefly if the crumbs don't brown in the oven. Garnish the stuffed, baked clams with parsley.

Yield: 14
Calories in each: 59
Protein in each: 5g

Fat in each: 3g
Carbohydrates in each: 4g
Sodium in each: 120mg

Chicken and Pork Skewers

❖

This tasty combination of chicken and pork is for those who like it hot. If you prefer a milder flavor, reduce or omit the chili paste with garlic. Marinate the chicken and pork as much as two days before preparing. Soaking the wooden skewers 45 minutes before grilling will keep them from scorching.

1 whole chicken breast, boned and skinned
5 ounces boneless pork from chops or tenderloin, fat trimmed
6 tablespoons soy sauce
1 tablespoon sesame oil, available at Chinese or specialty food shops
2 tablespoons chicken broth
1 scallion (white part only), chopped
a 1-inch piece of ginger root, peeled and minced
2 teaspoons chili paste with garlic, available at Chinese or specialty food shops

1. Put the pork in the freezer for 2 hours, place the chicken in the freezer about 10 minutes.
2. Slice the chicken in long, thin strips, slanting the knife slightly. Cut the pork so the strips are wide as well as long by placing what was the bone end flat on the cutting surface and slicing down.
3. Place the chicken and pork in a plastic or a glass bowl with the soy sauce, sesame oil, chicken broth, scallion, and ginger root. Marinate in refrigerator 2–4 hours.
4. Drain poultry and meat, reserving marinade. Thread the chicken and pork alternately on skewers. You may refrigerate assembled skewers up to 12 hours before cooking.
5. Mix the marinade with the chili paste. Grill or broil chicken skewers, brushing with chili paste marinade, 12–16 minutes or until done. The meat and poultry should be juicy, not overdone.

Note: Sodium-reduced soy sauce is available in many markets for those wishing to restrict the amount of sodium.

Yield: 15 skewers
Calories per skewer: 49
Protein per skewer: 5g

Fat per skewer: 3g
Carbohydrates per skewer: 0g
Sodium per skewer: 270mg

❖ **THINKING THIN TIP** ❖

A good way to become aware of calorie counts in foods you commonly eat is to keep a diary of *everything* you consume for a few days, then tally the calories with the help of a calorie listing.

Crudités and Skinny Dips

❖

Raw vegetables cut into bite-size pieces (crudités) have been a popular nibble for years. Obviously, they're just right for *Gourmet Light* cooking too, if the accompanying dip is on the slender side.

When choosing vegetables for a crudité basket, keep color and texture in mind. Mushrooms, a soft vegetable, need the crunch of a celery stick, for example, and radishes can be offset with cherry tomatoes. Choose any vegetable that can be eaten raw. Happily, most vegetables can be prepared in advance and held as long as two days in ice water, which keeps them crisp. Those that resemble a flower bud, such as cauliflower and broccoli, are great timesavers, requiring no more preparation than the snap of a stalk.

Because most baskets are too deep for the vegetables to look attractive in, a false bottom will create the illusion of bounty. Layer crumpled-up wax paper in the bottom, and cover with a cloth napkin. Position the dip, in a bowl or one made from a vegetable, in the center and arrange prepared vegetables around it.

Another pretty presentation is to choose a rectangular tray. Arrange the vegetables in "ribbons" that run diagonally, a mirror image on either end of the tray, with small bowls of different dips (also on the diagonal) in the center.

Sauce Verte

❖

A fresh herb dip, also nice on sun-warmed, ripe tomatoes.

> ½ cup crème blanc (page 37) or 2 ounces cottage
> cheese and 2½ ounces plain yogurt
> 2 tablespoons farmers cheese
> 1 tablespoon cream cheese or Neufchâtel cheese
> 5 fresh basil leaves, snipped, or ½ teaspoon dried
> basil
> 1 tablespoon minced fresh parsley
> 1 clove garlic, minced
> a few shakes salt
> freshly ground pepper to taste

1. Combine all the ingredients in a food processor or blender and mix
   well.

Yield: ½ cup
Calories per tablespoon: 23
Protein per tablespoon: 2g

Fat per tablespoon: 1g
Carbohydrates per tablespoon: 1g
Sodium per tablespoon: 70mg

Sun Spread

❖

This mix of dried fruits and nuts in a "cream" base is a delicious spread on crackers, as well as a good dip for raw vegetables. Its light, clean taste is a pleasant change.

2 tablespoons cottage cheese
3 tablespoons farmers cheese
1 tablespoon cream cheese
2 dried apricots, minced and soaked 20 minutes in
    1 tablespoon sherry
1 tablespoon sherry
1 tablespoon golden raisins
1 teaspoon chutney
1 tablespoon walnuts, roughly chopped

1. Combine the cottage, farmer, and cream cheeses in a food processor or blender until smooth.
2. Stir in the apricots and sherry, golden raisins, chutney, and walnuts. Refrigerate up to a day before serving.

Yield: ⅔ cup
Calories per tablespoon: 27
Protein per tablespoon: 2g

Fat per tablespoon: 2g
Carbohydrates per tablespoon: 2g
Sodium per tablespoon: 40mg

Roquefort Skinny Dip

If any of this is left over, it will make a romaine lettuce salad a great partner.

>   2 ounces Roquefort or blue cheese
>   ½ cup crème blanc (page 37) or 2 ounces cottage
>   cheese and 2½ ounces plain yogurt
>   2 tablespoons farmers cheese
>   ¼ teaspoon paprika
>   ½ teaspoon sugar
>   freshly ground pepper to taste

1. Combine all the ingredients in a food processor or blender and mix well.

Yield: 1 cup
Calories per tablespoon: 21
Protein per tablespoon: 2g

Fat per tablespoon: 1g
Carbohydrates per tablespoon: 1g
Sodium per tablespoon 80mg

Duxelle Melba

A delicious way to use up aging mushrooms, these cocktail toasts may be made when the spirit strikes and then frozen.

>   1 tablespoon butter, melted
>   4 slices thin-sliced white bread
>   6 ounces mushrooms

2 tablespoons shallots, minced
2 tablespoons chicken broth
1 ounce semisoft mild cheese, such as Havarti or
    Muenster, grated
1 tablespoon minced fresh parsley
1 tablespoon pine nuts or almonds, chopped
⅛ teaspoon salt
freshly ground black pepper to taste

1. Preheat the oven to 325 degrees while melting butter in an 8-inch skillet. Spray a baking sheet with cooking spray.
2. Place the bread slices in a stack and slice twice on the diagonal, making 16 triangles. Arrange on the baking sheet.
3. Dab each *croustade* (bread triangle) with melted butter on one side. Bake 12 minutes or until slightly crisp, in the preheated oven.
4. Wipe the mushrooms clean and mince them by hand or in a food processor. Scrape onto a kitchen towel, gather into a ball, twist ends of towel, and squeeze the mushrooms over the sink, extracting as much water as you can.
5. "Saute" the shallots in the chicken broth in the now-empty skillet. When liquid is evaporated and shallots are softened, spray the skillet with cooking spray, add the mushrooms, and cook at medium-low heat, gradually increasing the heat, about 5 minutes.
6. Remove mushrooms from heat, stir in the grated cheese, parsley, and pine nuts making a duxelle. Season with salt, pepper, and nutmeg.
7. Divide *duxelle* over the *croustades*, being certain to cover the bread points or they will burn. The hors d'oeuvres may be broiled now until browned, about 2–3 minutes or baked at 325 degrees until browned, about 12 minutes. You also may freeze them, uncooked, for future use.

Yield: 16
Calories in each: 30
Protein in each: 1g

Fat in each: 2g
Carbohydrates in each: 3g
Sodium in each: 50mg

Mushrooms à la Grecque

❖

The phrase "à la Grecque" means to blanch vegetables (though only mushrooms have been used here) in a pickling brine of oil, wine, and herbs (a court bouillon) and then to macerate and finally serve them in the cooking liquid. It's a pleasing change from crudités and needs no further dressing. Serve the mushrooms at room temperature or only slightly chilled for best flavor. Mushrooms and vegetables prepared this way will keep up to 4 days chilled.

8 ounces mushrooms, caps and stems or just caps (as you please)
1 cup water
1 cup chicken broth
1/2 cup dry white wine
1/2 teaspoon salt
2 tablespoons oil
1 tablespoon balsamic or red wine vinegar
juice of half a lemon
1 teaspoon fresh tarragon leaves or 1/2 teaspoon dried tarragon
1 tablespoon minced fresh parsley
1 clove garlic, sliced in 3 pieces
a few sprigs fresh thyme or 1/4 teaspoon dried thyme
1/4 teaspoon oregano

1. Wipe the mushrooms clean with a towel and set aside for use in Step 3.
2. In a nonaluminum saucepan, combine the water, broth, wine, salt, oil, vinegar, and lemon juice to make a court bouillon. Make a bouquet garni of the tarragon, parsley, garlic, thyme, and oregano by placing the herbs on a double-thick 3-inch square of cheesecloth. Roll the cloth in jelly-roll fashion, bring the ends

together, and tie in a knot. Add this herb bundle to the liquid and bring to a boil for 1 minute.

3. Add the cleaned mushrooms, boil 3 minutes. Lift vegetables with a slotted spoon to a nonmetal bowl or glass jar.

4. Boil the court bouillon over high heat until only 1 cup remains. Remove and discard bouquet garni. Pour liquid over mushrooms, and chill 2–4 hours or up to 4 days. Serve at room temperature, or slightly chilled.

Yield: 8 servings
Calories per serving: 44
Protein per serving: 1g

Fat per serving: 3g
Carbohydrates per serving: 3g
Sodium per serving: 140mg

❖   **GARLIC**   ❖

Romans fed garlic to their slaves to make them strong, and to their warriors to make them brave, and then forbade anyone having just eaten it to enter the temple of the Goddess of Nature. Perhaps the Romans didn't know that if the garlic had been simmered, long and slow, it wouldn't have been so offensive. Pureed garlic on French bread and Chicken with 40 Cloves of Garlic are popular dishes with many, the pungency of the bulb subdued thanks to long, slow cooking.

To mince garlic, cut the clove (one of the tissue paper—like wrapped crescents in the bulb) in half the long way. There's no need to peel it. Cut off the tiny brown nub at the tip. Place the garlic, flat side down, on the cutting surface, position the flat side of the knife over the clove, and smash down (carefully, on the broad side of the knife) with the heel of your hand. The garlic skin will lift off easily and the clove may be minced. Sprinkling the garlic with a little salt may help soften it to speed mincing. Lemon juice will help remove the garlic scent from your fingers.

Mussels
in Remoulade Sauce

❖

Although mussels have long been popular in Europe, until recently they've been disregarded here. Now in greater demand, mussels are being cultivated, bringing a cleaner bivalve to the market. That means less scrubbing for the cook! Poach the mussels and make the sauce the day before, assemble them as much as two hours before serving this cold hors d'oeuvre.

1   *pound mussels, about 15–20*
3   *tablespoons cornmeal*
2   *cups dry white wine*
1   *whole clove garlic*
1   *tablespoon minced fresh parsley*
1   *bay leaf*

The Sauce

1   *egg*
1   *egg yolk*
5   *drops lemon juice*
⅛   *teaspoon salt*
⅓   *cup corn oil*
⅓   *cup reserved, strained mussel broth, boiling hot*
½   *teaspoon Dijon-style mustard*
½   *teaspoon capers*
a pinch cayenne pepper
½   *tablespoon minced fresh parlsey*
sprig of parsley for garnish (optional)

To Prepare the Shellfish

1. Discard any mussels that don't close when you poke the inside of the shell hinge with a sharp knife. Cut away the beards. Cover the mussels with water, add the cornmeal, and let the mixture sit at least 30 minutes. The cornmeal is supposedly washed through the shellfish to carry out sand and grit.
2. Rinse the mussels thoroughly under running water.
3. Combine the wine, garlic, parsley, and bay leaf in a non-aluminum saucepan, cover, and bring to a boil. Add the mussels, cover, and boil until shells open, about 5 minutes.
4. Lift cooked mussels with a slotted spoon to a bowl. Chill the mussels. Discard the bay leaf from the broth.
5. Line a strainer with a double thickness of cheesecloth or a heavy paper towel wrung out in water. Pour mussel cooking broth through strainer. Let liquid rest 5 minutes, then pour through again, discarding the sediment that sinks to the bottom of the pan. Set aside while preparing sauce.

To Prepare the Sauce

1. Put the whole egg, yolk, lemon juice, and salt in a food processor and blend 20 seconds.
2. Dribble in the oil in a very fine, steady stream, almost drop by drop, while machine runs.
3. Meanwhile, heat strained mussel broth in a 1-quart nonalumimun saucepan. When boiling, dribble into the egg-oil mixture while machine runs.
4. Pour sauce into the now-empty saucepan and whisk until thickened over low heat, about 1 minute.
5. Remove from heat and stir in mustard, capers, cayenne, and parsley. Taste and adjust seasoning, add more lemon juice if sauce is too bland. You will have about 3/4 cup of sauce.

To Serve

1. Remove one half of mussel shell, discard. Free mussel from the

other half, but leave in the shell, and arrange on a platter in a spoke fashion. Place a dab of sauce on each and garnish with a tiny sprig of parsley if desired.

VARIATION: Mussels may be served warm or cold, removed from the shell and tossed with the *remoulade* sauce, then mounded on a lettuce cup. Garnish with lemon slices dipped in parsley.

Yield: 20 mussels
Calories in each: 25
Protein in each: 2g

Fat in each: 4g
Carbohydrates in each: 1g
Sodium in each: 40mg

Curried Clam Fingers

This curried clam appetizer is a moist, spicy mouthful that can be offered wrapped in lettuce leaves or more simply, mounded on baking shells. If you don't have a Chinese steamer, you may fashion one by positioning a cake rack on 4 ramekins set in a deep electric skillet. These finger rolls may be done through Step 6 up to 4 hours ahead.

6 ounces mushrooms, chopped
1 1/2 teaspoons curry powder
8 ounces canned clams, minced (about 1 1/2 cups)
2 small ribs celery, minced
1 tablespoon minced fresh parsley
3 tablespoons grated Parmesan or Romano cheese
a few drops hot pepper sauce
4–6 drops lemon juice
1 large head iceberg lettuce, outer leaves not
    removed
chutney (optional)

1. Spray an 8-inch skillet with cooking spray and "saute" the mushrooms until limp.
2. Sprinkle curry powder over mushrooms, cook over medium heat another 30 seconds.
3. Remove from heat, combine mushrooms with clams, celery, parsley, grated cheese, pepper sauce, and lemon juice. Set aside.
4. Bring 1 quart of water to a boil.
5. Core the lettuce. Remove the outer leaves without tearing. Cut away and discard the white "spine" at the base of the lettuce leaf. Cut the leaves in half lengthwise if they are very large. Dip 16–18 leaves, one at a time, into the hot water (it doesn't have to remain boiling). Immerse 2 seconds or just until wilted. Drain on a towel.
6. Place a tablespoon and a half of the clam filling on the base of each leaf. Roll tightly, tucking in the sides as you go. Place the rolls, seam side down, on a bamboo steamer. Rolls may be refrigerated at this point.
7. Put approximately 1½ cups water in a wok. Bring to a boil. Place Chinese bamboo steamer over boiling water, and steam lettuce fingers about 4 minutes. Serve with chutney as a dipping sauce if desired.

Yield: 16-18
Calories in each: 32
Protein in each: 4g

Fat in each: 1g
Carbohydrates in each: 2g
Sodium in each: 20mg

Sole and Crab Peppers

❖

These morsels may be made ahead and reheated, but for best flavor make them through Step 5, cooking just before serving. This recipe makes use of the seafood flakes (usually 35 percent crab-65 percent whitefish) now widely available. Or use 5 ounces uncooked shrimp or the real McCoy, of course. The sauce may be made ahead and reheated or omitted altogether if black bean or oyster sauce is unavailable.

4   ounces sole or other whitefish fillets
1   scallion, minced
4   water chestnuts, fresh or canned, chopped
a pinch cayenne pepper
1/2 teaspoon red wine vinegar or rice wine vinegar
1   egg white
1   teaspoon cornstarch
5   ounces crabmeat or seafood flakes
2   medium red or green peppers
1   teaspoon oil
1/2 cup chicken broth

The Sauce

1   tablespoon cornstarch
1/2 cup chicken broth
1   tablespoon black bean or oyster sauce (available at
    Oriental or specialty food shops)
1   teaspoon sesame oil

1. Put the fish in a food processor or through a meat grinder and process to a paste. Scrape into a bowl.
2. Add the scallion, water chestnuts, cayenne, vinegar, egg white, and cornstarch. Mix well.

3. Dice the crabmeat. Stir into the fish mixture.
4. Wash the peppers, cut in half, discard seeds, and cut each half in four pieces. (Don't wash the inside of the pepper or the filling won't adhere.)
5. Pack a heaping teaspoon of filling on each pepper.
6. Film a 12-inch skillet with the oil. Place filled peppers in skillet, pepper side down. Saute at high heat until peppers are just browned, add chicken broth, cover, and steam 3–4 minutes. Serve hot with black bean sauce dabbed on top or as a dip.

To Make the Sauce

1. Dissolve the cornstarch in the broth. Add black bean sauce and sesame oil. Stir over medium heat until thickened. Sauce may be reheated.

Yield: 15-16
Calories without sauce: 26
Protein without sauce: 3g

Fat without sauce: 1g
Carbohydrates without sauce: 2g
Sodium without sauce: 30mg

❖ **THINKING THIN TIP** ❖

Take a cooking course if you're not yet comfortable in the kitchen. Even if a reduced-calorie cooking course isn't offered in your area, learning your way around a kitchen will help you prepare fine reduced-calorie meals.

Seviche

❖

Seviche is the Latin American cousin of Japan's sashimi. Unlike sashimi, which is strictly raw, seviche is prepared by marinating the fish several hours in lemon juice. This firms the flesh, turning it opaque; in essence, cooking it. Like sashimi, the freshness of the fish is imperative. However, once it's marinated, seviche will keep for 2–3 days. Seviche makes a nice luncheon dish or first course as well as an appetizer. To give it a bit more body, do as a Peruvian friend of mine does; add a boiled, cubed sweet potato.

> 1 1/2 pounds scallops or delicate white-fleshed fish,
>   such as sole, cut into bite-size pieces
> 1 cup lemon juice
> 1 tablespoon finely chopped Bermuda or Spanish
>   onion
> 1/4 green pepper, finely chopped
> 1/2 red pepper, finely chopped
> 1/2 blanched, skinned, and seeded tomato, cubed
> 1/3 cup lime juice (about 2 limes)
> 2 tablespoons orange juice, freshly squeezed
>   preferred
> 3 tablespoons lemon juice
> freshly ground pepper to taste
> minced fresh parsley
> lettuce

1. Marinate the seafood in the lemon juice in a nonmetallic container overnight.
2. Drain seafood, discarding marinade. Rinse with water.
3. Combine the onion, green pepper, red pepper, tomato, citrus juices, and fish. If desired, add the remaining halves of tomato and green pepper, also chopped. Season with pepper to taste. Garnish with a bit of parsley.

4. To serve, line individual plates or a platter with lettuce, mound mixture on top.

Yield: 10 appetizer servings   Fat: 1g
Calories: 94   Carbohydrates: 5g
Protein: 16g   Sodium: 190mg

Yield: 6 first course servings   Fat: 2g
Calories: 157   Carbohydrates: 8g
Protein: 27g   Sodium: 310mg

Shrimp-Stuffed Mushrooms

❖

Stuffed mushroom caps are far from innovative, but their versatility and easy preparation make them enduringly popular. For variety, try filling the blanched caps with the red or yellow pepper puree (pages 72 or 261), or a *duxelle* (page 52) or chèvre mixed with a bit of milk. These may be made and assembled through Step 5, heating at the last moment.

> 7–8 ounces mushrooms, chosen for broad caps
> juice of 1/2 lemon or 2 tablespoons lemon juice
> 1 tablespoon butter
> 1 small rib celery, minced
> 2 ounces salad shrimp, chopped
> additional few drops lemon juice
> a few sprigs fresh thyme or 1/4 teaspoon dried thyme
> 1/8 teaspoon salt
> freshly ground pepper to taste
> 2 tablespoons dried bread crumbs

1. Wipe the mushrooms with a paper towel to remove dirt. Remove and mince the stems.

2. Bring a 2-quart saucepan half full of water with the lemon juice to a boil. Immerse cleaned mushroom caps and boil 2 minutes or just until softened. Drain on a towel, rounded-side up.
3. Meanwhile, melt the butter in an 8-inch skillet over medium heat. When foamy, add the minced mushroom stems and celery and cook, covered, 2–3 minutes, stirring often.
4. Add the shrimp, lemon juice, thyme, salt, pepper, and bread crumbs. Turn heat to high, cook 30 seconds more, uncovered.
5. Remove shrimp mixture from heat. Place a heaping teaspoon on each mushroom cap. Place stuffed mushrooms on a baking sheet.
6. Broil until bubbly, 6–8 minutes.

Yield: 12 to 14 caps   **Fat in each: 1g**
Calories in each: 22   **Carbohydrates in each: 1g**
Protein in each: 2g   **Sodium in each: 30mg**

❖ OIL-DRIED BASIL ❖

It's no wonder certain varieties of basil are used to manufacture perfume, for culinary basil has a sweet aroma matched by no other herb. Yet when dried, that special fragrance and flavor are greatly diminished. Before cold weather turns your verdant green basil crop into a blackened skeleton of its former self, try this simple curing technique. While nothing matches the fragrance of fresh, I think this comes close to its flavor.

Rinse and spin dry the basil leaves. Dishwasher sterilize a crock, such as that stone-ground mustard comes in. Lay basil leaves about 2 deep in the crock. Sprinkle lightly with salt, drizzle with oil, and repeat. Push the leaves down with a spoon handle, and continue to salt and oil the layers. Cover tightly and refrigerate. To use, pat or rinse the leaves free of oil and salt, mince and enjoy. The oil-cured leaves will keep under refrigeration until next year's new, bright growth is ready. Note: Remove leaves with very clean utensils only.

Fresh Mozzarella
and Tomato Pizza

❖

This quick recipe makes a nice lunch as well as a cocktail snack. It's a little messy to eat, so make this a casual offering. Assemble no more than an hour before serving or the tortilla will get soggy. Fresh mozzarella, the kind sold in brine and available at some specialty food stores, makes a delicious change from the supermarket variety.

>   1 flour tortilla (sold refrigerated in the supermarket
>   dairy section)
>   1 large, fully ripe tomato, thinly sliced, slices cut in
>   half
>   1½ slices (3 ounces) mozzarella cheese, cut into
>   strips
>   4 or 5 fresh basil leaves, snipped, or ½ teaspoon
>   dried basil
>   1 teaspoon extra-virgin olive oil
>   ⅛ teaspoon salt and freshly ground pepper to taste

1. Preheat oven to 475 degrees. Place the tortilla on a baking sheet. Arrange the tomato slices, overlapping them spoke fashion, on the tortilla.
2. Cover the tomato with the cheese strips.
3. Sprinkle basil over cheese, dribble on oil, then season with salt and pepper.
4. Bake in a 475-degree oven about 6 minutes until cheese is melted. Then broil until lightly browned, about 3 minutes more. Cool slightly before cutting into quarters with a pizza cutter.

Yield: 4 servings
Calories: 95
Protein: 6g

Fat: 5g
Carbohydrates: 7g
Sodium: 170mg

Chapter 4

THE SOUP
BOWL

The Soup Bowl

❖

Of soup and love, the first is best.
—Spanish Proverb

Soup—what diversity in a single bowl! From the elegance of a sparkly clear consomme to an unpretentious potato soup, from a trendy blueberry bisque to a plain old clam chowder, soups come in a fashion for every taste and occasion. Whether you're looking for a meal in a bowl or just a tasty starter, even a dessert, soup fills the bill.

Many cooks today are rediscovering the natural goodness of homemade soups. Perhaps the food processor is partly responsible for the newfound popularity, maybe it's because most soups freeze so well—a boon for today's busy cook. Maybe it's just the down-home appeal of a good bowl of soup. Regardless, soups are a natural in *Gourmet Light* cooking, for a deliciously satisfying first course can be enjoyed for less than 100 calories, or a nutritionally balanced meal consumed for under 300 calories. Naturally, you won't find heavy cream soups here, but you will find their updated, lightened versions and more. Some of the soups are skinny by nature such as Gazpacho and Two Mushroom Consomme; others have been run through the calorie reducer such as the Spinach and Oyster Bisque. Some are a snap to fix, others require a lengthier kitchen commitment.

Bouillabaisse of Scallops

❖

This soup perfumes the air. Serve it with the Fire and Ice Salad, page 102, for a fine, light cold-weather meal, or serve it chilled in summer.

> 2 leeks, white part only, thinly sliced
> 1 medium onion, thinly sliced
> 4–5 tablespoons chicken broth or bottled clam juice
> 4 large tomatoes or 2 cups canned tomatoes
> 2 cloves garlic, minced
> 4 cups fish stock or 3½ 8-ounce bottles clam juice
>   mixed with 3 ounces vermouth and 1 ounce
>   water
> 2 tablespoons orange zest
> 2–3 tablespoons orange juice, freshly squeezed
>   preferred
> 6–7 fresh basil leaves, snipped, or 1 teaspoon dried
>   basil
> a pinch of saffron
> 1 bay leaf
> ¼ teaspoon thyme
> ½ teaspoon fennel seeds
> 1 pound scallops or white fish fillets, cut into chunks
> 2 tablespoons minced fresh parsley
> a bowl of freshly grated Parmesan

1. "Saute" the leeks and onion in a 10-inch skillet with the broth. Cover the pan while cooking, adding more liquid if necessary.
2. To peel and seed the tomatoes, bring a 2½-quart saucepan ¾ full of water to a boil. Core the tomatoes, and cut a cross in each one's bottom. Immerse the tomatoes in boiling water for 15 seconds or until the skins loosen. Drain, cool under running water, and peel off the skins. Cut the tomatoes in quarters and squeeze over a

strainer to remove seeds. Press the seeds with the back of a wooden spoon to extract the juice. Reserve the juice.

3. When the leeks and onion are limp, add the garlic, tomatoes, reserved juice, stock, orange zest, orange juice, basil, and saffron. Tie the bay leaf, thyme, and fennel in a cheesecloth bag (a bouquet garni) and add to the skillet. Simmer, covered, for 30–40 minutes.

4. Add the scallops, raise heat to medium, and cook covered, until they are opaque, about 4–5 minutes.

5. Remove the bouquet garni, stir in the parsley, and taste for seasoning. Ladle the finished soup into warmed bowls and pass grated Parmesan cheese at the table.

Yield: 3-4 servings
Calories per serving: 235
Protein per serving: 31g

Fat per serving: 3g
Carbohydrates per serving: 20g
Sodium per serving: 360mg

Broccoli-Cheddar Soup

❖

This hearty soup would make a Grilled Pork and Veal Croquette, page 142, a good companion. Double the recipe and freeze half for an easy meal at a later date. Serve the soup hot or just slightly chilled.

1 bunch broccoli
½ cup chicken broth
½ cup milk
1 tablespoon cornstarch dissolved in 2 tablespoons chicken broth
1 tablespoon butter

¾ cup (2 oz.) grated cheddar cheese, lightly packed
1 tablespoon sherry
½ teaspoon salt
freshly ground pepper to taste
freshly grated nutmeg to taste
a few shakes paprika
additional chicken broth, optional

1. Separate the broccoli into flowerets and stalks. Peel the stalks with a knife or vegetable peeler. Dice the stalks, chop the flowerets. Bring a 2½-quart saucepan ¾ full of water to a boil, immerse broccoli, and boil, uncovered, until tender but crisp, about 8 minutes. Drain and set aside.
2. Meanwhile, heat the broth with the milk until bubbles appear at the edge of the pan.
3. Remove the pan from the heat and whisk in the dissolved cornstarch. Return to low heat and cook, whisking, about 1 minute.
4. Whisk in the butter, cheese, sherry, salt, pepper, nutmeg, and paprika.
5. Cook over low heat until well blended, about 2 minutes.
6. Combine broccoli with cheese mixture in a food processor or in batches in a blender. Taste for seasoning; overseason if serving chilled. Thin with additional chicken broth if soup is too thick.

Yield: 4–5 cups
Calories per cup: 160
Protein per cup: 11g

Fat per cup: 8g
Carbohydrates per cup: 15g
Sodium per cup: 540mg

❖   **BOUQUET GARNI**   ❖

To make a bouquet garni, cut a piece of cheesecloth about 6 inches by 4 inches. Place the herbs called for, generally thyme, garlic (no need to peel), fresh parsley stems, and peppercorns (crushed, please) in the center. Roll the cloth in jellyroll fashion, then bring the ends together and knot. The flavors suffuse the soup, stew, or broth, but the herbs can be easily removed before serving.

Cauliflower "Cream" with Yellow Pepper Swirl

❖

"Cauliflower is nothing but a cabbage with a college education."
—Mark Twain

In a class ahead of its cousin the cabbage or not, cauliflower is a calorie counter's dream, supplying only 28 calories a cup and a good supply of vitamin C. Here, it's pureed in a soup to be served hot or cold and garnished with a swirl of Yellow Pepper and Basil Puree, an economical way to serve the delicious but rather dear yellow peppers now coming to market. The puree also makes a delightful dip for vegetables at cocktail time. You may substitute red peppers for the yellow.

3   small leeks, white part only
1   tablespoon olive oil, extra-virgin recommended
3   cups blanched cauliflower (about ½ head)
2   cups milk
1   small potato, peeled and diced
¾   teaspoon salt
freshly ground pepper to taste
freshly grated nutmeg

For the Garnish

2   yellow peppers
1   cup loosely packed snipped fresh basil leaves or 2
      tablespoons dried basil
4   tablespoons Parmesan or Romano cheese, grated
1   tablespoon olive oil

To Prepare the Soup

1. Slice the leeks and rinse thoroughly. Place the leeks in a 1-quart

saucepan with the oil and enough water to half cover. Cover the pan, turn heat to high. When a boil is reached, reduce the heat so the liquid simmers. Uncover after 10 minutes and continue to cook until the leeks are soft, about 5 minutes more. Drain and reserve liquid.

2. Meanwhile, core the cauliflower and blanch the head in boiling water for about 5 minutes. Drain and chop it. Combine the cauliflower with the milk, potato, salt, pepper, and leeks in a 2-quart saucepan.

3. Cover the pan, bring to a boil, and reduce heat to a simmer. Simmer for 20 minutes.

4. Puree the mixture in a food processor or in batches in a blender. Thin if desired with the reserved liquid from Step 1, or milk. Add nutmeg and taste for seasoning adjustment. Overseason if serving the soup cold. Serve with a tablespoon of the yellow pepper puree swirled in.

To Prepare the Yellow Pepper Puree

1. Cut the peppers in half, flatten them with the heel of your hand, and place peppers on a baking sheet, skin side up, under a hot broiler. Broil until the peppers are completely blackened and charred, which can take as long as 10 minutes. Remove peppers to a plastic or paper bag and chill until cool enough to handle.

2. Peel the loosened skin from the peppers and discard. Chop the peppers and puree them in a food processor, blender, or food mill. See the illustrations on page 260.

3. Add the basil, cheese, and olive oil to the peppers. The puree will be thick and chunky. It will keep up to one week chilled, or it may be frozen.

Yield of soup: **4 cups**
Calories per cup: **137**
Protein per cup: **9g**

Fat per cup: **4g**
Carbohydrates per cup: **19g**
Sodium per cup: **480mg**

Yield of garnish: **1 cup**
Calories per tablespoon: **18**
Protein per tablespoon: **1g**

Fat per tablespoon: **1g**
Carbohydrates per tablespoon: **1g**
Sodium per tablespoon: **11mg**

Chilled Tomato Soup
with Tarragon Ice

❖

This is one of my favorite summertime soups because of its delightful combination of flavors and colors. There's no need to buy perfect tomatoes for this recipe, the "seconds" or bruised tomatoes offered at many farm stands are ideal. The soup freezes well, too, making it possible to enjoy the flavor of summer in the dead of February. The tarragon ice is fashioned after a basil sorbet served at the famed Four Seasons Restaurant in New York City, which like many other restaurants today offers a health-conscious menu.

For the Soup

3 pounds ripe tomatoes, cored
8–10 fresh basil leaves, snipped, or 1 teaspoon
    dried basil
2 medium onions, sliced
2 cloves garlic, minced
1–2 teaspoons sugar
1 tablespoon fresh tarragon, snipped, or 1 teaspoon
    dried tarragon
3/4 teaspoon salt
freshly ground pepper to taste
1/2–3/4 cup chicken broth, if needed

For the Tarragon Ice

1 small, ripe avocado
juice of 1/2 a lemon
2 tablespoons finely minced fresh tarragon leaves or
    1 tablespoon dried tarragon leaves
1 cup water

2 tablespoons sugar
pinch of salt

To Prepare the Soup

1. Quarter the tomatoes. Put them in a large saucepan with the basil, onions, garlic, sugar, tarragon, salt, and pepper. Turn heat to medium high, cover, and simmer until tomatoes are completely soft and pulpy, about 20 minutes. Stir occasionally.
2. Uncover the pan, lower the heat to medium-low, and cook about 30 minutes or until reduced by ⅓.
3. In batches, process soup in a food processor, blender, or food mill. Strain if desired to remove the seeds and skins. Chill and serve the soup garnished with a dollop of tarragon ice. Thin with chicken broth if needed.

To Prepare the Tarragon Ice

1. Peel and pit the avocado. Puree it in a food processor or blender with the lemon juice.
2. In a saucepan, simmer the tarragon leaves in the water for 20 minutes. Remove from the heat, add sugar and salt, and stir until dissolved.
3. Add tarragon water to the avocado in a food processor. Blend.
4. Place in an ice cream freezer and follow manufacturer's instructions to freeze. Soften before serving. It's best used within 24 hours.

Yield of soup: 4 cups
Calories per cup: 95
Protein per cup: 4g

Fat per cup: 1g
Carbohydrates per cup: 20g
Sodium per cup: 410mg

Yield of ice: ¾ cup
Calories per tablespoon: 20
Protein per tablespoon: 0

Fat per tablespoon: 1g
Carbohydrates per tablespoon: 3g
Sodium per tablespoon: 9mg

Chinese Egg Drop Soup

❖

A filling, very good lunch. Even if you haven't shopped for a week, you're likely to have the ingredients.

> 1 1/2 cups chicken broth
> 1 egg
> 1 tablespoon soy sauce, or less, to taste
> 1 tablespoon minced chives

1. Bring the broth to a boil in a small saucepan.
2. In a bowl, beat the egg and soy sauce with a fork. Stir into the boiling broth, creating a small whirlpool. Continue stirring until the egg cooks, about 45 seconds.
3. Garnish the soup with chives and serve. Slices of bean curd, peas, and cooked chicken may be added for variety.

Note: Sodium-reduced soy sauce is available in many markets for those wishing to restrict the amount of sodium.

Yield: 1 good serving
Calories: 125
Protein: 9g

Fat: 6g
Carbohydrates: 8g
Sodium: 640mg

❖   **THINKING THIN TIP**   ❖

If making a chicken stock you'll use immediately, skin the chicken before making the stock. It will save time when you degrease the pan. To slip skin from the wings and backs, put them in a roasting pan, cover with aluminum foil, and bake 15 minutes in a 500-degree oven.

"Cream" of Lettuce Soup

❖

This cream soup owes its richness more to the vegetable itself than cream, making it as healthful as it is calorie conservative. Make it in quantity when garden lettuce is in season and freeze for a taste of summer in the chill of winter. This soup is good hot or cold and may be made as much as 24 hours in advance.

> 1 head lettuce, preferably romaine (about ¾ pound)
> 2½ quarts water
> 1 can (13¾ ounces) chicken broth
> ¾ cup fresh or frozen peas
> 2 scallions, roughly chopped
> 1 tablespoon minced fresh parsley
> ½ teaspoon salt
> freshly ground pepper to taste
> ½ cup milk
> 4 tablespoons crème blanc, page 37 (optional)

1. Wash and core the lettuce, and tear the leaves in half. Bring the water to a boil. Add the lettuce leaves and boil, uncovered, for 3–4 minutes or until wilted and somewhat softened.
2. Drain the lettuce and place it in a food processor or blender in small batches, with the broth, peas, scallions, parsley, salt, and pepper. Process the mixture and leave it slightly coarse.
3. Pour the mixture into a saucepan, add milk, and simmer 15–20 minutes.
4. Before serving add a dollop of crème blanc to each serving.

Note: Overseason if serving the soup cold.

Yield: 4 cups
Calories per cup: 73
Protein per cup: 6g

Fat per cup: 1g
Carbohydrates per cup: 12g
Sodium per cup: 380mg

"Cream" of Mushroom Soup

❖

Use this recipe as an example of how to rewrite old favorites in the *Gourmet Light* way. To update, add a half ounce of sherry-soaked cepes or chanterelles at Step 8.

1 quart chicken broth plus an additional ½ cup
1 small onion, minced
1 tablespoon butter
3 tablespoons flour, instant blending recommended
12 ounces mushrooms, wiped clean
juice of half a lemon or 1 tablespoon lemon juice
2 egg yolks
½ cup milk
1 tablespoon sherry
¼ teaspoon salt
freshly ground pepper to taste
freshly ground nutmeg

1. Bring ¼ cup broth to a boil in a 10-inch skillet. "Saute" the onion at high heat until it becomes limp and transparent.
2. Meanwhile, bring 1 cup of broth to a boil in a 2½-quart saucepan.
3. When the onion is limp and the broth almost evaporated, reduce the heat to medium. Add the butter. When it's melted and foamy, stir in the flour. Stir with a wooden spoon for 1 minute over low heat.
4. Remove the skillet from the heat. Whisk in the hot broth. Whisk in an additional cup of cold broth. Transfer the ingredients to the now-empty saucepan. Add the remaining 2 cups broth.
5. Remove stems from the mushrooms. Mince the stems and slice caps. Add the stems to broth-onion mixture. Simmer, covered, for 20 minutes.

6. Place the caps in now-empty skillet, add lemon juice, and remaining ¼ cup broth, and "saute" at high heat until mushrooms are soft and liquid is evaporated. Set aside.
7. Strain the stems and onions from the broth-onion mixture. Press the vegetables with the back of a wooden spoon to extract their juices.
8. Beat the egg yolks with milk in a small bowl. Drizzle ½ cup strained hot soup base into yolks while beating with a fork. Slowly pour yolks into remaining soup base, and whisk over low heat until thickened, about 4 minutes.
9. Add mushroom caps to the soup. Add the sherry, season with salt, pepper, and nutmeg.

Note: Do not boil soup once the egg yolks have been added.

Yield: Approximately 4 cups
Calories per cup: 150
Protein per cup: 7g

Fat per cup: 6g
Carbohydrates per cup: 17g
Sodium per cup: 190mg

❖ **NUTMEG** ❖

Recipes in this book frequently specify using freshly grated nutmeg, for it is considerably more flavorful than the ground variety. Whole nutmegs—the pit of a West Indian peachlike fruit—are available at some supermarkets and specialty food shops. Mace, a similar but stronger taste than nutmeg, is the outside sheathing that covers the nutmeg. It is sold already ground. Nutmeg grinders, (similar to small pepper mills) are available as are small, inexpensive graters that often have a hinged top to store the nutmeg.

Gazpacho

❖

This zesty bowl of garden goodies, which is really improved the second day, is naturally low in calories. A friend gave me this version of the Spanish classic. Here it is with a bit less oil. For a special treat, serve with the tarragon ice on page 74.

1¾ pounds ripe tomatoes
1 medium onion, chopped
1 cucumber, peeled, seeded, and chopped
1 green pepper, seeded and chopped
1 red pepper, seeded and chopped (optional)
1 clove garlic, minced
24 ounces tomato juice
1 tablespoon extra-virgin olive oil
4 tablespoons red wine vinegar
1 teaspoon salt
a few drops hot pepper sauce
2 tablespoons chopped chives (from scallion tops)
oven-dried croutons, optional

1. Core the tomatoes and cut a cross in each one's bottom. Immerse tomatoes in boiling water for 15 seconds. Cool them under running water and strip the skins. Quarter the tomatoes. Squeeze the tomatoes in a strainer supported over a bowl to remove the seeds. Press the seeds with the back of a spoon to extract the juice. Discard the seeds.
2. In a food processor or blender, combine half of the seeded tomatoes, all the juice from the same, the onion, half of the cucumber, green pepper, red pepper, all the garlic, and half the tomato juice. Process until somewhat smooth.
3. Stir in the remaining tomato juice, oil, vinegar, salt, pepper sauce, the remaining tomato, cucumber, peppers, and all the chives.

Chill at least 2 hours; also chill the soup bowls. Serve with oven-dried croutons if desired.

Oven-Dried Croutons

1. Dice 4 slices of bread. Place on a cookie sheet in a 325-degree oven for 15 minutes, and stir the cubes occasionally. To brown slightly, spray a frying pan with cooking spray and "saute" oven-dried cubes over medium heat until lightly browned.

Yield: 6 cups
Calories per cup: 90
Protein per cup: 3g

Fat per cup: 3g
Carbohydrates per cup: 15g
Sodium per cup: 610mg

Potato and Sorrel Soup

❖

This soup is very good served cold with a simple chicken salad for a tempting hot-weather meal. If sorrel is unavailable, substitute fresh spinach seasoned with a few drops of lemon juice.

2 large or 4 small leeks
4 cups chicken broth
3 potatoes, about 1 pound (Idaho or all-purpose
*   white), peeled*
1/2 teaspoon salt
freshly ground pepper to taste
freshly grated nutmeg
4 or 5 leaves sorrel, or spinach seasoned with lemon
*   juice*

1. Discard the green ends from the leeks. Slice the white part and rinse it thoroughly.
2. Place the sliced leeks in a 2½-quart saucepan with enough chicken broth to half cover, cover the pan, and boil gently for 8 minutes or until leeks are softened.
3. Dice the potatoes. Add them to the leeks with the remaining chicken broth, salt, and pepper. Simmer, covered, for 30–35 minutes.
4. Rub potato-leek mixture through a sieve into a bowl or puree in a food processor or blender. Scoop what won't go through the sieve into the soup.
5. Season with nutmeg. Stack sorrel or spinach leaves, roll tightly in jellyroll fashion, and slice thinly crosswise (known as *chiffonade*). (See drawing on page 201.) Add the leaves to the hot soup until wilted. If serving the soup cold, allow at least 4 hours chilling time and overseason slightly as chilling weakens the flavors.

Yield: 5 cups
Calories per cup: 75
Protein per cup: 3g

Fat per cup: trace
Carbohydrates per cup: 16g
Sodium per cup: 230mg

Curried Zucchini Soup

Omit the curry if it's a spice you'd rather live without. This recipe makes good use of baseball bat–size zucchini, but remove the seeds first. Because the soup freezes well, you might like to double the recipe.

> 2 large onions, diced
> 1 quart plus 6 tablespoons chicken broth

1 clove garlic, minced
3–4 pounds zucchini, diced
1 cup cooked rice
1 tablespoon curry powder
8–10 fresh basil leaves, snipped, or 1 teaspoon
    dried basil
5–6 fresh sage leaves, snipped, or 1/2 teaspoon dried
    sage
1 teaspoon fresh thyme leaves or 1/2 teaspoon dried
    thyme
1 teaspoon salt (less if using canned broth)
freshly ground pepper to taste
1/2 cup grated cheddar cheese
1 cup milk

1. "Saute" the onions in a 10-inch skillet in the 6 tablespoons of chicken broth until they're limp. Add the garlic and cook 1 minute more.
2. In a 4-quart or larger saucepan, combine the onions, garlic, zucchini, remaining broth, rice, spices, and herbs. Cover and simmer at least 1 hour or as long as two.
3. Puree the zucchini-onion mixture in a food processor or food mill in batches. Strain the soup if desired.
4. Stir in the grated cheese and milk. Heat to blend.

Yield: Approximately 6 cups
Calories per cup: 155
Protein per cup: 9g

Fat per cup: 3g
Carbohydrates per cup: 24g
Sodium per cup: 580mg

Gingered Carrot Soup

❖

The ginger root in this refreshing chilled summer soup lends peppery zip. Make this a day or two before serving if desired.

4 large carrots, scrubbed and grated
1 medium onion, diced
3 cups chicken broth
1/2 teaspoon salt
lots of freshly ground pepper to taste
1 1/2 teaspoon sugar if using carrots sold in cello bags,
     less for those with greens attached
a 1-inch x 1/2-inch piece of fresh ginger root, peeled
     and minced
1 slice white bread, stale or lightly toasted
freshly ground nutmeg
6 tablespoons crème blanc, page 37
a bit more grated ginger root

1. In a 2 1/2-quart saucepan, combine the carrots, onion, broth, salt, pepper, sugar, and ginger root. Cover, turn the heat to high, and reduce it to medium once it begins to boil. Uncover, simmer 40 minutes or until about 3/4 to 1 cup liquid remains.
2. Puree the soup in a food processor or in a blender in batches. Crumble bread in your hand, add it to the soup, and process until smooth.
3. Add nutmeg, taste for additional salt, sugar, or pepper. Overseason if serving chilled. Top each serving with a dollop of crème blanc mixed with a little more ginger root.

Yield: 4 cups
Calories per cup: 80
Protein per cup: 4g

Fat per cup: trace
Carbohydrates per cup: 16g
Sodium per cup: 380mg

Spinach and Oyster Bisque

❖

Traditionally, a bisque is a puree of shellfish finished with cream. Today, bisque has come to mean almost anything the recipe writer wants it to be, as long as it's a creamy puree of something. Here's a *Gourmet Light* bisque that's based on shellfish, cheats on cream, and is enhanced with spinach, making it an emerald-hued soup rich in vitamin A and potassium.

> 6 ounces shucked oysters, liquor reserved
> 3 tablespoons cornstarch
> 1 1/2 cups milk
> 1 10-ounce package fresh spinach, stems removed
> 1/2 teaspoon salt
> a few drops pepper sauce
> freshly grated nutmeg

1. Mix the reserved oyster liquor with the cornstarch to dissolve.
2. Chop the oysters in a food processor or meat grinder.
3. Simmer the ground oysters in milk for 8 minutes, stirring often.
4. Meanwhile, wash the spinach. Place it in a 2 1/2-quart saucepan with the water that clings to the leaves. Cover, turn heat to high, and cook until just wilted, about 45 seconds. Drain, and chop finely, or place it in a food processor to puree.
5. Add the spinach to the oyster-milk base. Stir dissolved cornstarch into the oyster-spinach base. Cook the mixture over low heat, stirring until thickened, about 4 minutes. If a smoother texture is desired, puree it in a food processor.
6. Season the bisque with salt, pepper sauce, and nutmeg. Serve with unsalted crackers.

Yield: 4 cups
Calories per cup: 110
Protein per cup: 10g

Fat per cup: 1g
Carbohydrates per cup: 15g
Sodium per cup: 420mg

Two Mushroom Consomme

If consomme brings to mind images of Victorian ladies presiding over sherry parties, this version holds a surprise for you. It is updated with cepes, which are dried mushrooms imported from France. Their earthy scent perfumes this light soup. Although this is easily made with store-bought consomme, you might enjoy the satisfaction and rich flavor of making your own.

5 cups degreased homemade beef stock or 3 cans (10½ ounces) beef consomme
2 egg whites and the eggshells
8 ounces mushrooms, wiped clean with a cloth
3 tablespoons beef broth
2 tablespoons lemon juice
½ ounce cepes (available at specialty food stores), soaked in sherry or water to cover
⅓ cup Madeira or sherry
2 tablespoons finely minced chives

To Clarify Homemade Stock

1. Beat 1 cup cold stock with the egg whites and eggshells (yes, shells!) in a large bowl. Meanwhile, bring remaining stock to a boil.
2. Gradually pour the hot stock into the egg whites, beating all the while. Pour the whites and stock back into the saucepan and set over moderate heat. As the stock regains a simmer, stir with a spoon. As soon as the simmer is regained, stop stirring.
3. Turn the heat to low. Move the pan very gently partially off the heat, the liquid must not bubble or move too much. Let it rest for 15–20 minutes.
4. Line a colander with a double layer of cheesecloth that has been wrung out in water. Gently ladle stock-egg mixture through the

cheesecloth. Discard the shells and whites. The resulting soup should be crystal clear.

For Canned Consomme or to Finish Soup

1. Slice the mushrooms. "Saute" them in a little broth and lemon juice in an 8-inch skillet.
2. Drain the cepes, mince them, and discard the wine or strain it through a double-thick, wrung-out piece of cheesecloth before adding it to soup. Add cepes to mushrooms and heat through.
3. Combine clarified stock (or canned consomme diluted according to directions) with the mushrooms, Madeira, and chives. Serve hot in small cups.

Yield: 6 servings
Calories per serving: 45
Protein per serving: 2g

Fat per serving: trace
Carbohydrates per serving: 9g
Sodium per serving: 20mg

❖ **THINKING THIN TIP** ❖

There are times when it might be better to eat a little of something fattening than a lot of something skinny.

❖

Chapter 5

SALADS AND THEIR DRESSINGS

❖

Salads

❖

Salads have risen to new heights, both in popularity and design in recent years. Where once a few leaves of iceberg, chopped cucumber, and minced onion would suffice as a side dish, one now finds a range of rare goodies artfully presented as main-course meals. Radicchio, lamb's lettuce, and baked chèvre cheese are but a few of the new salad items popular today. To support the demand, fancy greengrocers are popping up like mushrooms from coast to coast, offering an enormous selection of fresh produce from near and—thanks to modern transportation—far.

This chapter focuses on salads as a side course. The majority of the main-dish salads are found in the chapter of the predominant ingredient. For example a Sole, Scallop, and Pea Pod Salad is found in the seafood chapter, and a Sesame Chicken Salad is found in the poultry chapter.

The Greens

❖

A simple tossed salad is so much more interesting with two or three greens. Why limit yourself to one when there's such a big garden of salad things to choose from, everything from arugula to watercress. While iceberg is probably the most popular salad green, it is also probably one of the dullest. It has its place, keeping the bread from getting soggy in a tuna salad sandwich, but it is far outclassed by other, less well known varieties. Three other types of lettuces to consider are:

Cos or romaine—large, almost rectangular leaves, dark green at the tip, paler green at the base. This is the lettuce of choice for Caesar salad, it is also excellent torn into small pieces for a tossed green salad.

Butterhead—The lettuces of this group offer soft, velvety leaves that unfortunately bruise and rust quickly. This perishable type includes Boston, a medium-size, light green head, and Bibb, a smaller, more compact head. Limestone lettuce is another Butterhead variety. For longer storage life, rinse, dry, and chill these lettuces as soon after purchase as possible. These soft-leafed lettuces are excellent for simple salads composed of mixed greens, or even alone, tossed with a vinaigrette and possibly a scattering of freshly made croutons.

Leaf lettuces—The lettuces in this group grow as clumps of leaves rather than as heads. It is quite a hardy lot, ranging from red leaf (mostly green turning to red at the tip) to salad bowl, a tangle of curly, narrow leaves. Leaf lettuces are best in combination with other greens.

Less well known, but fun to experiment with, are beet, dande- lion, and mustard greens; even nasturtium leaves lend a salad distinction. And there's watercress with its peppery crunch, chicory, endive, and . . . of course spinach. Radicchio, a red "green," and lamb's lettuce are specialty items you'll find on trendy restaurant menus or in chic produce markets. With such a wealth of greens, most of which are available year round, it seems sad to reach for the old standby every time.

Select greens with an eye for color and texture. An excellent combination is a salad of Bibb, red leaf, and watercress, the softness of the Bibb offset by the crunch of the watercress, and the red leaf adding vibrant color.

While my personal bias leans toward a salad of mixed greens graced only by a sprinkling of freshly made croutons or a bit of grated cheese, many enjoy other additions. Any vegetable in its prime that can be eaten raw is a candidate. Again, keep color, texture, and flavor in harmony.

There is no written rule that demands a tomato in every salad. When they are out of season, which sadly is most of the year, get color from other sources. Roasted, julienned red peppers (see page 260) are delicious, a bit of grated red cabbage or carrot will do the trick, as will a few leaves of red leaf lettuce. Put nothing in the salad that is tasteless, such as a winter tomato. For a change of pace, "saute" mushroom slices before adding them. I find the flavor enhanced when they're cooked.

Purchase greens that look perky, without yellow or rust spots, and if possible with most of the outer leaves intact, because these contain more nutrients than the delicate centers. Generally, the greener the leaf, the greater the source of vitamins A, C, and E as well as iron and calcium. A quarter of an average-size head contains a meager 15 calories.

Salad greens retain their nutrients best when held at near-freezing temperatures in high humidity. Head lettuce will keep in the vegetable crisper of the refrigerator for 3–4 days; some varieties will last even longer. Leaf lettuces are more perishable and keep best if rinsed, spun dry, and stored in a loose plastic bag with a few paper towels on every other layer to absorb moisture, a leading cause of rust and bad spots. Lacking a lettuce spinner, wash the lettuce, shake off excess moisture, lay leaves in a single layer on an old thick bath towel, roll loosely, and refrigerate. The lettuce will keep this way about 24 hours. Washing, drying, and chilling any lettuce about 4–5 hours before serving will make for a beautifully crisp salad. For those special occasions, don't forget to chill the plates too.

Don't store lettuce near apples, melons, or avocados because the ethylene gas these fruits give off acts as a ripening agent, maturing the lettuce before its time and turning it brown.

The Salad Syndrome or The Invisible Calorie

❖

It's become common knowledge that the culprit is the butter not the potato, but the fats in salads remain invisible to many—that is, until they show up on the waistline. "All I ever have for lunch is a salad, and I still gain weight!" is a common lament. The demon is the salad dressing. Most dressings are very high in fat, contributing 150 to 200 calories in just 2 tablespoons to an otherwise skinny bowl of greens. *Gourmet Light* dressings are based mostly on stocks or consomme, and contribute far fewer calories than commercial preparations. The recipes that follow are dressings for mixed-green salads, beyond that are recipes for specialty salads.

Vinaigrettes

Vinaigrette, a classic combination of oil and vinegar with or without additional seasonings, is the true French dressing. Following are several variations on the simple vinaigrette theme, all prepared the *Gourmet Light* way. (For more on skinny dressings, see the Primer, page 6.) First, these tips:

1. If you don't make your own naturally thick chicken or beef stock, use commercially prepared consomme or canned chicken broth. The former, because of its added gelatin, will give the best results.
2. When using homemade stock, double the amount called for in the recipe and boil it until reduced by half. This double-strength stock will give your dressings body. Don't reduce commercial broths though, for they will be too salty.
3. If you do not use canned consomme, you will need to add salt to taste.
4. If possible prepare the dressing at least 2 hours before serving, to let the flavors marry.
5. A dressing made with homemade stock or store-bought consomme will jell in the refrigerator. Remove it an hour before serving or heat briefly to liquefy.

Other Dressings

Vinaigrettes do not all salads make, of course; occasionally, we yearn for something cool and creamy. Either of the *Gourmet-Light* mayonnaises (page 26 and 27) take kindly to herb, cheese, or mustard additions. In the event that time is tight, a half-and-half mixture of plain yogurt and store-bought mayonnaise will save you 340 calories over straight mayonnaise. To use a homemade mayonnaise as a salad dressing, simply add flavorings and thin it with a bit of chicken broth. Roquefort Skinny Dip and the Sauce Verte, both in the appetizer chapter, are also excellent for salad dressings—again, thinned with a bit of broth.

Herbed French Vinaigrette

❖

A true French dressing is not the mayonnaise/ketchup variety commonly called "French," but an emulsion of oil and vinegar. Here is a skinny version.

> 5 tablespoons double strength homemade beef or
>   chicken stock or canned consomme
> 2 tablespoons red wine vinegar
> 1 teaspoon sugar
> ½ teaspoon Dijon-style mustard
> 1 tablespoon extra-virgin olive oil
> 1 clove garlic, minced
> 2 teaspoons chives, minced
> 1 teaspoon paprika

1. Combine all the ingredients in a jar, shake well, check for seasoning, and refrigerate.

Yield: ⅔ cup
Calories per tablespoon: 16
Protein per tablespoon: trace

Fat per tablespoon: 1g
Carbohydrates per tablespoon: 1g
Sodium per tablespoon: 4mg

❖   **THINKING THIN TIP**   ❖

Because *Gourmet Light* cooking uses so little oil, buy the best. Extra-virgin olive oil is the first pressing of the olives and the most flavorful. Virgin quality is the next, and so on until the final pressings, which rely on hot water poured over the pits to coax the final droplets of oil.

Lemon Vinaigrette

❖

Easy on your time and waistline.

> 5 tablespoons double-strength homemade beef or
>   chicken stock or canned consomme
> 1 tablespoon extra-virgin olive oil
> 1 tablespoon lemon juice
> 1 tablespoon red wine vinegar
> 1 teaspoon sugar
> freshly ground pepper to taste
> 1 teaspoon minced fresh parsley (optional)

1. Combine all the ingredients in a jar, shake well, check for seasoning, and refrigerate.

Yield: ½ cup
Calories per tablespoon: 20
Protein per tablespoon: trace

Fat per tablespoon: 2g
Carbohydrates per tablespoon: 1g
Sodium per tablespoon: 2mg

❖ **VINEGARS** ❖

Once used as a medicine or as a drink when heavily diluted with water and often used as a preservative with salt, vinegars are the slightly aging darling of the growing gourmet food industry. Where most kitchen cabinets once stored pretty much your basic cider variety, many shelves are now crowded with enough labels and flavors to rival a modest wine cellar. Indeed, some vinegars carry a higher price tag than jug wines! Some vinegars, such as balsamic, are even aged like spirits in oak barrels. The added cost is offset by the wonderful flavor they impart.

Balsamic-Walnut Oil Vinaigrette

❖

Balsamic vinegar, a malt vinegar aged in wooden casks, and walnut oil have become buzz words in culinary circles. Both are available at specialty food stores. Here they are combined to create a delicious dressing for mixed greens.

> *double-strength homemade beef or chicken stock or*
> *   canned consomme*
> *walnut oil (refrigerate after opening)*
> *balsamic vinegar*
> *1 tablespoon water*
> *¹/₂ teaspoon prepared mustard*
> *¹/₂ teaspoon sugar*
> *freshly ground pepper to taste*

1. In a 1-cup glass measure, pour in the consomme until the liquid reaches the ¹/₄-cup mark. Add walnut oil until the liquid measures ¹/₃ cup. Add the balsamic vinegar until the liquid measures ¹/₂ cup. Add water, mustard, sugar, and pepper. Shake well, check for seasoning, and refrigerate.

Yield: ¹/₂ cup
Calories per tablespoon: 18
Protein per tablespoon: trace

Fat per tablespoon: 2g
Carbohydrates per tablespoon: 1g
Sodium per tablespoon: 3mg

Caesar Salad Dressing

❖

Make this salad with romaine lettuce, freshly grated Parmesan or Romano cheese, and if you like, a handful of freshly made croutons. Arrange the lettuce leaves in spoke fashion around the plate, sprinkle cheese and croutons on top, and drizzle with the following dressing. To eat, pick up the leaves in your fingers, using them as scoops to hold the croutons and cheese. Delicious!

2 cups water
1 egg
5 tablespoons double-strength homemade beef or
        chicken stock or canned consomme
juice of ½ lemon
1 tablespoon extra-virgin olive oil
6 or 7 drops Worcestershire sauce
a few drops hot pepper sauce to taste
1 clove garlic, minced
freshly ground black pepper to taste
2 tablespoons freshly grated Parmesan cheese

1. The egg will need to be coddled. Bring 2 cups water to a boil. Add the egg, cover, and boil for 1 minute. Drain and cool under running water.
2. Crack the coddled egg open into a jar. Combine all the remaining ingredients, except the cheese. Sprinkle cheese over the salad greens, then drizzle with dressing.

Note: For instructions on making croutons see page 81.

Yield: ⅔ cup
Calories per tablespoon: 30
Protein per tablespoon: 2g

Fat per tablespoon: 2g
Carbohydrates per tablespoon: 1g
Sodium per tablespoon: 17mg

Sesame Seed Dressing

❖

This dressing is the perfect partner for a spinach salad with shredded hard-cooked egg and sliced "sauteed" mushrooms.

2 tablespoons sesame seeds
4 tablespoons double-strength homemade beef or chicken stock or canned consomme
2 teaspoons sesame oil, available at specialty food shops
2 tablespoons lemon juice
1 teaspoon sugar
freshly ground pepper to taste

1. Spray a baking sheet with cooking spray. Sprinkle sesame seeds over sheet. Turn oven to 350 degrees, put baking sheet in oven, and remove 10 minutes later.
2. Combine sesame seeds in a jar with all the other ingredients. Shake well, check for seasoning, and refrigerate.

Yield: ½ cup
Calories per tablespoon: 26
Protein per tablespoon: trace

Fat per tablespoon: 2g
Carbohydrates per tablespoon: 1g
Sodium per tablespoon: 1mg

Fresh Herb Vinaigrette

This is the dressing of choice for herb gardeners looking for ways to preserve summer's fragrant gifts, for it freezes nicely. Delicious on vine-ripened tomatoes (which have twice the vitamin C of hothouse winter tomatoes) or cold fish salads tossed with leftover corn cut from the cob.

> 1 cup loosely packed fresh basil leaves
> ½ cup loosely packed fresh tarragon leaves
> 2 tablespoons homemade chicken or beef stock or
>   canned consomme
> 1 tablespoon raspberry or red wine vinegar
> 1 tablespoon safflower oil
> 1 scant teaspoon sugar
> freshly ground pepper to taste

1. Put the herbs in a bowl or measuring cup and snip repeatedly with scissors until they're reduced to about half the original volume.
2. Combine the herbs in a food processor or blender with the remaining ingredients. Blend until herbs are mostly minced and sauce is a lovely pale green. Check for seasoning. May be frozen.

Yield: ¾ cup
Calories per tablespoon: 14
Protein per tablespoon: trace

Fat per tablespoon: 1g
Carbohydrates per tablespoon: 1g
Sodium per tablespoon: 2mg

Japanese Dressing
for Snow Peas

❖

Yet another alternative to a mayonnaise dressing is tofu, a soybean product. The following recipe is excellent tossed with blanched snow peas or broccoli.

4 ounces tofu
5 tablespoons double-strength homemade chicken
    stock or canned consomme
1 tablespoon sesame oil
1 tablespoon walnut oil
2 tablespoons rice wine vinegar, available at Oriental
    or specialty food stores
1 teaspoon soy sauce
1 quarter-size piece of fresh ginger, peeled and
    minced

1. Combine all the ingredients in a food processor or blender and blend. Chill.

Yield: 1 cup
Calories per tablespoon: 21
Protein per tablespoon: trace

Fat per tablespoon: 2g
Carbohydrates per tablespoon: trace
Sodium per tablespoon: 12mg

Beyond Simple Tossed . . .

❖

No matter how innovative and imaginative your mix of greens, there are times when you yearn for something different. Perhaps a Fire and Ice Salad or the pleasant bite of Counter Slaw, or maybe the cool creaminess of a Dilled Zucchini and Carrot Salad. Whatever your pleasure, scan these offerings for that which tempts you. These are side dishes, lunches, or light dinners; heavier offerings are found in the seafood and poultry chapters.

Fire and Ice Salad

❖

This salad gets its name from the flame of the brandy and the chill of the greens. Often when a recipe indicates flaming it is purely for effect; here, igniting the liquor renders it mellow. A wonderful salad for chilly nights.

The Salad

1 pound fresh spinach, stems and backbones
     removed
1 hard-cooked egg
4 or 5 black olives, pitted and chopped
4 ounces mushrooms, cleaned and sliced

The Dressing

2 strips bacon
1/2 can canned consomme or double-strength
     homemade chicken or beef stock

3 tablespoons malt or balsamic vinegar
1 tablespoon lemon juice
2 teaspoons sugar
½ to 1 teaspoon Worcestershire sauce
1 teaspoon oil
2 tablespoons brandy or bourbon

To Prepare the Salad

1. Wash and spin dry the spinach. Tear it into bite-size pieces in a large bowl.
2. Sieve the hard-cooked egg over the greens. Add the olives and mushrooms (cooked or uncooked as you like). Set aside while preparing the dressing.

To Prepare the Dressing

1. Fry the bacon strips in a small skillet. When crisp, remove and drain on paper towels. Reserve 2 tablespoons fat and discard the rest.
2. In the now-empty skillet, combine the consomme, vinegar, lemon juice, sugar, Worcestershire sauce, oil, and reserved 2 tablespoons fat. Bring to a boil.
3. Meanwhile, heat the liquor in a small pot with a long handle and a spout. When bubbles appear at the edge of the pot ignite the liquor by tipping it into the flame of a gas stove, or light it with a match. Pour the liquor into the hot dressing.
4. When the flames die out, boil just 20 seconds longer. Remove from the heat and toss with the chilled greens.

Yield: 4 servings
Calories per serving: 163
Protein per serving: 7g

Fat per serving: 11g
Carbohydrates per serving: 9g
Sodium per serving: 308mg

Dilled Zucchini
and Carrot Salad

❖

This salad may be made early in the day and placed on lettuce at serving time. Plump out the offering with cooked salad shrimp and a bit of minced green pepper if you like.

1/2 cup Reduced-Calorie Mayonnaise, page 26
2 tablespoons freshly minced dill or 1 tablespoon
    dried dill weed
1 tablespoon plain yogurt
1 · medium zucchini
3 carrots, scrubbed
1 teaspoon salt
freshly ground pepper to taste
lettuce to line individual bowls or serving plate

1. Combine the mayonnaise, dill, and yogurt in a bowl. Stir to combine.
2. Grate the zucchini and carrots by hand or with the julienning disk of a food processor. Place them in a bowl.
3. Season the vegetables with salt and pepper. Stir to combine. Add the dilled mayonnaise, and mix. Chill until serving time.

Yield: 4 servings
Calories per serving: 170
Protein per serving: 4g

Fat per serving: 14g
Carbohydrates per serving: 8g
Sodium per serving: 623mg

Wilted Cucumber Salad

❖

If soft-leafed lettuce dressed with vinaigrette is the national salad of France, a wilted cucumber salad is the fingerprint of Germany. Here's a reduced-calorie version that's as good the second day as the first.

    1 cucumber
    2 teaspoons salt
    2 tablespoons canned consomme
    1 tablespoon red wine vinegar
    1 teaspoon honey or sugar
    1 teaspoon oil
    freshly ground pepper to taste

1. Peel the cucumber and seed by slicing it in half the long way and removing the seed core with a teaspoon. Slice the cucumber very thinly by hand or in a food processor, and place it in a sieve or colander. Sprinkle salt over it and let it drain 20–30 minutes over a bowl or in sink. This removes excess water from the vegetable.
2. Rinse the cucumber repeatedly. Taste it to be sure the salt is removed. Press cucumber to help remove water. Drain it on an absorbent towel.
3. In a small saucepan, combine the consomme, vinegar, honey, and oil. Reduce the liquid over high heat until 2 tablespoons are left. Pour it over the drained cucumber, season with pepper, and chill until serving time.

Yield: 2 servings
Calories per serving: 58
Protein per serving: 1g

Fat per serving: 2g
Carbohydrates per serving: 9g
Sodium per serving: 12mg

Counter Slaw

❖

Cynthia Young, a fine Nantucket cook, gave me this recipe some years ago when we honeymooned at her Polpis guest house. It's quick, easy, and delicious, just the thing to take on a picnic to Great Point—or your favorite summer afternoon getaway spot. Coleslaw prepared with mayonnaise-type dressings contains as many as 225 calories in a ³/₄-cup serving; this counter slaw lets you save room for dessert. Add grated carrots, raisins, or a bit of onion for variety.

1 small green pepper, grated
6 cups loosely packed, shredded cabbage (about ¹/₂ small head)
¹/₃ cup chicken broth
2 tablespoons light oil, such as safflower
2 tablespoons sugar
2 tablespoons red wine vinegar
1 teaspoon caraway seeds
¹/₂ teaspoon salt
freshly ground pepper to taste

1. In a medium-size bowl, combine the green pepper with the cabbage.
2. In a 1-quart nonaluminum saucepan, combine the broth, oil, sugar, vinegar, and caraway seeds. Cook over high heat until the sugar is dissolved, about 1 minute.
3. Toss hot dressing with the vegetables. Season to taste with salt and pepper. Cover the slaw with plastic wrap and leave it at room temperature for 4 hours. Chill until serving time.

Yield: 6 servings
Calories per serving: 73
Protein per serving: trace

Fat per serving: 5g
Carbohydrates per serving: 7g
Sodium per serving: 186mg

Pear and Gouda Salad
with Pine Nuts

❖

A halved pear broiled until a cloak of Gouda cheese bubbles and browns, resting on a lightly dressed bed of curly salad bowl lettuce, makes a dish of pasta tossed with Basil-Walnut Sauce (page 32) a wonderful dinner partner. You can have it on the table in less time than it will take to drive to McDonald's.

> 1 pear, any variety, slightly underripe is fine, peeled
>   if desired
> 2 tablespoons (1 ounce) Gouda cheese, grated
> 2 tablespoons pine nuts
> ¼ head salad bowl or other leaf lettuce
> 4 tablespoons Herbed French Vinaigrette, page (95)

1. Preheat the broiler. Cut the pear in half the long way, and remove its core and woody fiber leading to the stem. Sprinkle it with lemon juice if holding more than 20 minutes before broiling. Slice a sliver from the curved side of the pear so it will sit evenly. Place on a baking sheet.
2. Divide the grated cheese over the pear halves. Broil about 8 minutes, or until the pear is softened and cheese is bubbly and browned.
3. Meanwhile, toast the pine nuts by putting them in an 8-inch skillet over high heat. Shake the pan constantly for about 1 minute until nuts turn golden brown. Remove from skillet.
4. Wash, rinse, and dry the lettuce. Divide on two plates. Center each broiled pear half on lettuce. Drizzle 2 tablespoons dressing on each salad, and sprinkle pine nuts over.

Yield: 2 servings
Calories per serving: 183
Protein per serving: 5g

Fat per serving: 11g
Carbohydrates per serving: 16g
Sodium per serving: 126mg

Bibb, Tuna, and Green Bean Salad

❖

One of my favorite lunchtime or light dinner salads.

$^{1}/_{2}$ pound green beans
1 small head Bibb lettuce
2 slices thin-sliced bread
1 teaspoon butter
1 6 $^{1}/_{2}$-ounce can water-packed tuna, drained
4 tablespoons Balsamic-Walnut Oil Vinaigrette (page 97) or other reduced-calorie vinaigrette dressing

1. Prepare the beans for cooking by aligning several at a time and cutting off their tips. Turn the beans around, align again, and slice ends again. Continue until all are "tipped and tailed."
2. Bring a 2 $^{1}/_{2}$-quart saucepan $^{3}/_{4}$ full of water to a boil. Add the beans and boil 4 minutes or until softened but still crisp. Drain and cool under running water. Pat dry.
3. Core and wash the lettuce. Spin dry the leaves or dry them on an absorbent towel. Chill until serving time.
4. With one slice bread atop the other, dice it into tiny cubes. Spray a baking sheet with cooking spray. Place the bread on the baking sheet and bake in a 325-degree oven for about 10 minutes.
5. Melt the butter in an 8-inch skillet. Saute bread cubes over medium heat until toasty. Remove from heat.
6. Remove chilled, washed lettuce from the refrigerator. Tear it into bite-size pieces and arrange it on individual plates or in a bowl. Arrange the beans, flake the tuna over, and sprinkle the salad with croutons. Dribble on the dressing.

Yield: 2 servings
Calories per serving: 250
Protein per serving: 29g

Fat per serving: 8g
Carbohydrates per serving: 16g
Sodium per serving: 115mg

Apple-Artichoke Salad
with Hollandaise

❖

The ingredients are reminiscent of a Waldorf salad, but the light Hollandaise adds a different dimension. You may expand the salad to a main-dish meal by grilling and dicing a swordfish steak, toss it with the celery and so on, and serve at room temperature or only slightly chilled. Make this salad early in the day so flavors may meld before serving time.

4   artichokes
2   tablespoons lemon juice
¼   cup flour
1   quart water, plus a little more
2   celery ribs, diced
1   apple, Red Delicious recommended, diced
1   ounce walnuts, roughly chopped
½   cup Hollandaise, page 21, or mayonnaise, page
     26
¼   teaspoon salt
freshly ground pepper to taste

1. With a stainless-steel knife, cut off the stem and upper third of each artichoke. Using scissors, remove the sharp tips of the leaves. Cut around the artichoke with a sharp knife as if paring an apple, removing the tough outer leaves. When you get to the soft inner core, slice it off. Be sure all dark green skin is removed from the bottom of the artichoke. Drop each artichoke bottom into water with the lemon juice added.
2. Make a paste of about ¼ cup flour with enough water to moisten. Bring a quart of water to a boil, stir in the flour paste, and bring to a boil in a nonaluminum saucepan. Add the artichokes and simmer for 10 minutes or until easily pierced with a fork. Remove the

artichokes from the cooking liquid with a slotted spoon and drain until cool.

3. With a grapefruit spoon, remove each artichoke's fuzzy center and discard. Set artichokes aside while preparing remaining salad.
4. In a bowl, toss together the celery, apple, walnuts, and Hollandaise (which may be cold). Season with salt and pepper. Add swordfish here if desired.
5. Line individual plates with a lettuce leaf. Place an artichoke bottom on lettuce. Fill to overflowing with celery-walnut mixture.

Yield: 4 servings
Calories per serving: 180
Protein per serving: 6g

Fat per serving: 8g
Carbohydrates per serving: 21g
Sodium per serving: 178mg

Confetti Rice Salad

Carbohydrates, the bugaboo of the diet world for years, are no longer a dirty word. The calorie conscious, particularly those who exercise regularly, need complex carbohydrates for energy; otherwise, the body will break down proteins for fuel, proteins better used to build and maintain tissues. Sadly, most carbohydrates taste better when lathered with fats: the butter on the bread, the sour cream on the potato, the dressing on the salad. Here's a cool salad, great for picnicking because it's ultimately portable, which makes the most of the carbohydrates and the least of the fat. A few smoked shrimp would make a wonderful addition.

2 *medium tomatoes*
2 *medium green peppers*
1 *medium red pepper*
3 *cups cooked rice*

2 tablespoons minced fresh parsley
10 fresh basil leaves, snipped, or 1 teaspoon dried
   basil
½ teaspoon salt
freshly ground pepper to taste
3 tablespoons oil, safflower or corn oil recommended
1 tablespoon plus 2 teaspoons rice wine vinegar,
   available at specialty food stores or Oriental
   markets

1. Dice the tomatoes. Seed and dice the peppers.
2. Place the vegetables in a bowl with the rice, parsley, basil, salt, and pepper. Sprinkle all with oil and vinegar.
3. Spray a 1-quart mold or 6 1-cup ramekins with cooking spray. Fill each ramekin ¾ full with rice mixture, press salad down with a glass or any utensil slightly smaller than the diameter of the ramekin. Cover with plastic wrap and chill at least 3 hours. (Note: For a decorative design, fashion a "flower" from a thin carrot slice and a "stem" from a parsley stem on the bottom of each ramekin.)
4. To unmold, run a flexible-bladed metal spatula between the salad and the mold. Invert a plate on mold, flip over, and lift mold off.

Yield: 6 servings
Calories per serving: 187
Protein per serving: 3g

Fat per serving: 7g
Carbohydrates per serving: 28g
Sodium per serving: 183mg

Pasta Salad
with Basil-Walnut Sauce

❖

I could eat this salad, which is best at room temperature, nearly every day and not tire of it. The sauce is reminiscent of pesto, but it's much lighter. Delicious with garden-ripe tomatoes and a simple tossed salad, or flesh the meal out with a Chicken Breast Paillard.

12 ounces egg noodles, fresh if possible
¾ cup Basil-Walnut Sauce, page 32
¼ teaspoon salt
freshly ground pepper to taste
freshly grated Parmesan cheese

1. Cook the noodles according to package directions. Drain.
2. Toss noodles with the Basil-Walnut Sauce, salt, and pepper. Serve at room temperature or warm. Top with Parmesan cheese.

Yield: 4 servings
Calories per serving: 436
Protein per serving: 14g

Fat per serving: 13g
Carbohydrates per serving: 67g
Sodium per serving: 168mg

❖ **THINKING THIN TIP** ❖

Carbohydrates, which used to be taboo for any weight-loss program, are now recognized as a necessary and vital part of any diet plan. To avoid them is to court fatigue, irritability, and failure for any prolonged weight reduction.

Pea Pod and
Water Chestnut Salad with
Sherry Ginger Dressing

❖

Make the dressing, blanch the pea pods, and grate the water chestnuts early in the day, then assemble this salad at the last minute.

> $1/2$ pound pea pods, strings removed
> 5 tablespoons double-strength homemade beef or chicken stock or canned consomme
> 1 tablespoon vegetable oil
> 2 tablespoons sherry wine vinegar, available at specialty food shops
> 1 tablespoon soy sauce
> 1 teaspoon sesame oil, available at Oriental or specialty food shops
> 1 teaspoon peeled and minced fresh ginger
> 1 scant teaspoon sugar
> 4–6 radicchio lettuce leaves or soft-leafed lettuce such as Bibb
> 2 fresh mandarin oranges, peeled and sectioned, or 1 7-ounce can mandarin oranges packed in light syrup, drained
> 8 or 9 fresh water chestnuts, peeled and blanched, or 4 ounces canned chestnuts

1. Bring a $2\,1/2$-quart saucepan $3/4$ full of water to a boil. Immerse pea pods, remove from heat, and let peas sit 4 minutes. Drain and rinse the peas under cold running water until they're no longer warm. Drain peas on absorbent towels.

2. Combine the consomme, oil, vinegar, soy sauce, sesame oil, ginger, and sugar in a jar. Shake well to combine.
3. In a small bowl, combine half the dressing with the cooked pea pods. Let the mixture rest at least 15 minutes or up to several hours at room temperature or in the refrigerator.
4. Arrange the lettuce on individual plates or a serving platter. Arrange the pea pods and orange sections alternately in a circle on the lettuce.
5. Grate the water chestnuts in a Mouli grater or food processor. Arrange in the center of the pea pods and oranges. Dribble the salad with the remaining dressing.

Yield: 4 servings
Calories per serving: 130
Protein per serving: 4g

Fat per serving: 5g
Carbohydrates per serving: 19g
Sodium per serving: 142mg

Chapter 6
MEATS

Meats

❖

America produces more meat than any other country, and we eat almost all of it. Beef is still the national favorite; it's estimated every man, woman, and child will consume 120 pounds in a single year. While there are those who will view this as eating our way to the grave, others will claim it as evidence Americans are among the best-fed people in the world. Is eating meat a dietary liability or insurance of good nutrition? And what is its place in a reduced-calorie format?

Those on the pro side of the meat question will have us know that, ounce for ounce, meat is nutrient dense. Quite simply, it supplies outstanding nutritive value. It is an excellent source of high-quality protein and essential minerals such as iron, phosphorus, and copper while contributing vitamins, too. Those on the con side point to meats, particularly red meats, as major contributors of saturated fats, which have been linked to high cholesterol levels and heart disease. And because most meat is high in fat, as a rule it is a caloric pill of no little consequence.

Does that imply one should eschew meat for tofu? Give up taste for health? After all, *Gourmet Light* professes to be a "waist not—want not" style of eating, and for many, eating red meats is one of the pleasures of the table. Others enjoy a juicy pork chop or succulent veal cutlet, and with 4 billion pounds of hamburger consumed in 1982, it's not only children who hanker for America's signature food. Whether you're interested in reducing your intake of saturated fats, calories, or both, limiting—not eliminating—the amount of fatty meats in your diet may be the answer. Selection is also key.

Disavowing Spartanism, which meat to choose when the carnivorous hunger strikes? Must one feel guilty savoring a fork-tender rib eye? No, moderation is the simple answer. And if meat is an important part of your diet, perhaps a look at sample calorie counts of each type will help when selecting a type of meat.

Veal, of course, is the leanest of the meats, because the 3-month or younger calf has developed little fat. A 4-ounce portion is roughly 176 calories. Lamb, marketed at about 6 months, has a hefty fat cover, but that can be removed before cooking. A 4-ounce serving contains about 298 calories; less when all the fat is removed. Pork weighs in at about 340 calories for a 4-ounce serving, although that is based on data from the early 1960s, and a leaner animal is now being bred. And finally, all America's favorite, beef ranges from 342 calories in a moderately fatty 4-ounce portion to a surprisingly low 163 calories in lean flank steak.

In moderation, any of these meats are perfectly permissible for the calorie conscious. But while 4 ounces of beef—about 340 calories—is within most people's limits, 6–7 ounces may not be. And you may be eating more than you think. Take careful note of package weights before cooking and determine just how much a 3½- or 4-ounce serving truly is. Or perhaps get in the habit of weighing portions for a while to train the eye to recognize how much (or little) the recommended portion size amounts to. "But it's good for me!" comes the lament. "What's wrong with a little extra meat?" For children, who need protein to grow, nothing; for the adult it may mean added pounds.

Just how much protein do we really need? And will it really make us strong? Here's a look at some protein myths and realities.

The Protein Pedestal

❖

Of the three food classifications of protein, carbohydrates, and fats, protein has long been ballyhooed to all too often mythical proportions.

MYTH 1: To be healthy we need to eat lots of protein.

Nutritionists recommend that protein constitute the smallest percentage of the daily diet. It's been estimated that most Americans eat 2 to 3 times the amount of protein they need. And more is not necessarily better. Excess protein is burned for calories, stored as fat, or simply excreted.

The recommended daily allowance of protein is 42 grams for a 120-pound person and up to 73 grams for a 200-pound person. If in a typical day you eat something like this—a glass of 2 percent low-fat milk (4 grams protein), a ham sandwich on white bread (14 grams), and a 4½-ounce hamburger (30 grams)—you've received 48 grams of protein, to say nothing of protein also eaten in the course of the day in other forms, from vegetables to the flour in desserts.

MYTH 2: Protein isn't fattening.

In truth, protein supplies the same amount of calories per gram (4) as carbohydrates. And excess protein turns to the same kind of body fat as excess carbohydrates or fats.

MYTH 3: Protein increases athletic performance.

There are no magic potions for increasing athletic prowess. Protein alone will make no one a better athlete, or even increase one's stamina. The proverbial balanced diet (with protein on the low end) will allow us to perform at our individual best. Foods don't make for athletic performance, skill and training do. But without proper nutrition we can't live up to our potential. Good nutrition is but one rung on the ladder.

For all these reasons—from a high concentration of saturated fats to bulging calorie counts—this chapter is necessarily lean. Those wishing to curb calories will do well to incorporate a larger percentage of fish and poultry in their diet. But when meat and only meat will do, by all means enjoy. Veal, selected cuts of beef and lamb, and even a lean pork tenderloin or cutlet are within the bounds of the calorie-conscious diner. Unfortunately, the leanest meats are often the toughest, and the tastiest cuts are the fattest. But even lean meats can be coaxed into tenderness if the cook understands a bit about the science of tender meat. The following factors apply mostly to beef. Tenderness for veal, pork, and lamb are discussed in the recipes for those meats.

The Science of Tender Meat

---❖---

The tenderness of meat is the cumulative effect of these factors:

1. *Connective tissue*

There are two kinds of connective tissue in the muscles: collagen, which melts into gelatin quickly in the presence of heat, and elastin, which stubbornly refuses to melt unless subjected to long, slow cooking and even then may remain unchanged. If there is a great deal of either collagen or elastin in the meat, it is likely to be tough. Connective tissue is not to be confused with the streamlets of fat that run through the muscles; this marbling is an indication of tender meat.

2. *Where the cut is from*

As a general rule, the less exercised a muscle is the more tender it will be. Choosing any cut that lies on either side of the backbone (the loin) will be the most tender, and, of course, the most fatty.

3. *Aging*

When beef is aged, enzymes in the meat naturally soften the connective tissue creating literally fork-tender meats. Aged meats are more costly because of the refrigeration and warehouse space involved. Home aging of meats is possible for good cuts of meat that are at least 4 pounds in weight, when they're covered with a protective flap of fat.

4. *Grade of the cut*

Meat is graded by government inspectors prior to sale. The carcass is inspected for conformation, quality, and finish—gibberish to you and me but the meat of the matter for the inspector before it is labeled prime, choice, or good. There are actually 5 lesser grades but not for retail sale. While prime meat is regarded as the best, the quality of choice meats is also excellent and because of reduced marbling, may be slightly less fatty.

A naturally tender steak, then, has a lot of marbling, has little connective tissue, was cut from the loin, and was hopefully aged at least a week or more. It can be either of prime or choice quality. Meat that is not naturally tender can be made so by attention to the cooking technique used.

Moist vs. Dry Heat Cooking

Virtually all the recipes you've ever read for meat fall under one of but two categories, moist or dry heat cooking. Moist heat (stewing, braising, etc.) breaks down the collagen if the meat is allowed to cook at low temperatures for a long time. Naturally, a piece of meat may not be cooked rare if it is a tough cut, it will need to cook beyond the 120 internal degrees of pink meat. Not even meat tenderizers can transform a tough cut into fork-tender steak.

It is my experience that meat tenderizers promise more than they can deliver, much as a sparkling wine is not, after all, a fine champagne. Tenderizers for the most part are made from papain, an enzyme found in papayas. This enzyme, which incidentally is injected into humans to dissolve calcium deposits on the spine, does soften tissue. However, it has some drawbacks. It is only effective on the meat's surface, unless the meat is punctured, making little escape tunnels for the juices. Further, the tenderizing activity is slow unless the meat is quite warm—reaching its peak at 176 degrees—so it may actually do nothing at all on refrigerator cold meat.

Marinating meat is another popular method for tenderizing tough cuts. Its effectiveness remains a moot point. While some cooks claim soaking meat in an acid (wine or vinegar) solution with oils and seasonings will tenderize it, there are scientific studies that both contradict and confirm the practice. It is an indisputable fact that marinating meats in an acid will result in some loss of minerals.

It seems wise then to choose the cooking method that best complements the meat. Dry heat cooking (sauteing, grilling, broiling, and roasting) is suitable for cuts that are naturally tender. These meats may be cooked rare. You can broil, pan-fry, or grill tender meat (not at too high a heat, which can destroy some of the protein) for a quick, delicious, and somewhat fattening meal. For beef lovers who wish to curb both calories and cholesterol, a bit of finagling is called for, because the cut of choice for them is a leaner, thus a tougher cut. Top round, eye of the round, flank steak, and lean sirloin steaks are lower in fat. Of the tender cuts, filet mignon (tenderloin) is the better choice.

For those who relish a moist, juicy, rare beefsteak, the Roasted Tenderloin of Beef may be the answer. For others, there are Beef Paupiettes with Sausage and Zucchini, Braised Beef with Pineapple and Papaya, and more. This section is thin, however, because of the generally high calorie count of most meats.

Beef

Despite a slightly tarnished reputation because of a bit of bad press, I'll bet the hamburger is still one of America's favorite foods. From Monday's meat loaf to Saturday's prime rib, beef has been the backbone of the American diet. But unless you've been orbiting in space for the last decade or so you also know that it is high in saturated fat, which has been fingered as a contributor to heart disease, and it is high in calories. Nutritionists have warned against indulging in too much fatty meat, which has sent the American Beef Council scrambling to remind the public that beef . . . indeed, is good food. With 3½ ounces of beef round supplying more than ½ the daily requirement of protein, more than ¼ the phosphorus, ⅙ the iron, and ¼ of the niacin for a 120-pound woman for only 261 calories, one wonders, what's the fuss? The *rest* of the story, of course, is the high concentration of saturated fats, which, if you're prone to high cholesterol levels, are health threatening. But one needn't give up fatty meats altogether. With proper cooking techniques and wise selection, moderate amounts of beef can be enjoyed.

From a caloric and a quality viewpoint, there is beef and there is beef. Unfortunately, the tastiest beef is the most fattening, the leaner the beef, the tougher and the more tasteless. Following the guidelines given above about tender meat, select and cook lean meats so as to maximize their tenderness and flavor.

Braised Beef
with Pineapple and Papaya

❖

Call it boeuf en daube, boeuf à la mode, estouffade de boeuf, braised beef, or pot roast, the technique is all the same. A tough and often fatty cut of meat is browned, liquid and vegetables are added for flavoring, and the whole is simmered until tender. It's the sort of robust meal that justifies the existence of cold weather. But because it is often made with relatively fatty cuts that drip their fat into the sauce rather than into a broiler pan to be discarded, it should not be a common meal for the calorie concerned. This *Gourmet Light* version, made with a leaner cut than the more traditional chuck, uses the natural tenderizing effects of two tropical fruits, pineapple and papaya. Both contain papain, a common ingredient in commercial meat tenderizers. Long ago, natives of tropical islands found that meat was more tender if wrapped in papaya leaves and slow roasted. Papaya leaves might be hard to come by, but most markets carry the fruit. And if need be, canned pineapple, rather than fresh, may be used. Both not only add flavor but serve as a natural tenderizer, helping to dissolve the connective tissues in the meat as it cooks. Start this recipe about 3 ½ hours before dinner, or make it in advance and reheat.

4 pounds top or bottom round beef roast
2 medium onions, chopped
1 clove garlic, mashed
2 cups beef broth
½-liter bottle dry red wine such as a Burgundy
2 cups fresh or canned pineapple, chunked
1 green pepper, seeded and chopped
1 bay leaf
a few sprigs fresh thyme or ½ teaspoon dried thyme
½ teaspoon salt
freshly ground pepper to taste
4 large carrots, cut into bite-size pieces
8 small or 4 large potatoes, peeled and halved or
    quartered
1 papaya, peeled, seeded, and sliced
2 tablespoons cornstarch

1. Spray a Dutch oven or other deep-sided heavy-bottomed skillet with cooking spray. Brown the meat at high heat on all sides and remove to a plate.
2. "Saute" the onions and garlic over medium heat in the Dutch oven in ¼ cup beef broth, covering the pot until the vegetables are soft and transparent.
3. Add the beef, wine, and remaining beef broth.
4. Add the pineapple, green pepper, herbs, salt, and pepper. Cover the pot, leaving a sliver exposed so there will be some evaporation, and simmer for 2 hours and 35 minutes. Add the carrots, potatoes, and papaya and cook until tender, about 25 minutes more. Remove the meat from the pot. Moisten the cornstarch with a few tablespoons of cooking liquid, stir it into the remaining cooking liquid over medium heat, and stir until thickened.
5. To serve: Cut meat into serving-size chunks, serve with the vegetables and sauce.

Yield: 8 generous servings
Calories per serving: 460
Protein per serving: 48g

Fat per serving: 14g
Carbohydrates per serving: 34g
Sodium per serving: 366mg

Flank Steak
in Gingered Beer Sauce

❖

Flank steak, a strip of muscle that lies on either side of the loin, is the leanest of all beef cuts, with about 163 calories in a 4-ounce serving. Because the muscle fibers are coarse and there is little fat, it is most often cooked with moist heat, though occasionally it is broiled or grilled as a steak. With its long, thin configuration, which is ideal for stuffing, flank steak makes an attractive presentation. Here it is rolled around a fruit stuffing and slow cooked in a fragrant sauce of gingered beer. The meat may be readied for cooking early in the day.

The Stuffing

5 dried apricots
2 tablespoons rum or hot water
1 small onion, minced
2 tablespoons beef broth
3 small apples, peeled, cored, and chopped
2 teaspoons minced ginger root
1/4 teaspoon salt
freshly ground pepper to taste
dash ground cinnamon

The Meat

1 3/4 pounds flank steak
Dijon-style mustard
1 onion, chopped
2 celery ribs, chopped
1 carrot, chopped

¹/₂ teaspoon salt
freshly ground pepper to taste
a 12-ounce bottle dark beer
1 ¹/₂ cups beef broth
3 tablespoons tomato paste
3 or 4 allspice berries or ¹/₄ teaspoon ground allspice
1 bay leaf
1 tablespoon fresh thyme leaves or ¹/₂ teaspoon
  dried thyme
2 unpeeled garlic cloves, halved
1 cinnamon stick
a quarter-size piece of fresh ginger root, peeled

To Prepare the Stuffing

1. Plump the apricots in the rum or hot water for at least 30 minutes or as long as 12 hours.
2. "Saute" the onion in the broth in a 10-inch skillet over medium heat until limp and the broth is evaporated.
3. Drain the apricot liquid into the onion skillet. Chop and add the apricots. Add the apples and ginger. Season with salt, pepper, and cinnamon. Cover and cook over medium-low heat for 4 minutes or until the fruits are soft. Remove from the heat and cool while preparing the pot vegetables and meat.

To Prepare the Meat

1. Place the meat between two sheets of wax paper and pound it with a cleaver until somewhat thinner and enlarged. Dip a pastry brush into a pot of mustard and brush it over the inside of meat. Set aside.
2. Spoon the stuffing (from Step 3) onto the meat, completely covering the surface; reserve any extra. Starting at the small end, roll the meat up in jellyroll fashion. Tie tightly with butcher's twine.

Gather what stuffing falls out and reserve with other stuffing.

3. Spray the skillet used for stuffing (no need to wash) with cooking spray. Add the onion, celery, and carrot, cover, and cook at high heat until the vegetables are lightly browned. Scrape them into a 5-quart Dutch oven or electric Crockpot.

4. Pat the meat dry. Spray the skillet with cooking spray. Sear the meat over high or medium-high heat, turning frequently. If the meat seems to be sticking, dribble in a bit of vegetable oil. When browned, remove to the Dutch oven. Season with salt and pepper.

5. Deglaze the skillet with 1/4 of the beer, stirring with a wooden spoon over medium heat. Pour the deglazing juices, remaining beer, and broth onto the meat. Stir in the tomato paste. Add any extra stuffing.

6. Preheat oven to 350 degrees. Cut a piece of cheesecloth to make a bouquet garni of the allspice, bay leaf, thyme, and garlic. Enclose the herbs and knot the cheesecloth. Add to the Dutch oven.

7. Add the cinnamon and ginger to the pot. Cover and bake at 350 degrees for 1/2 hour. Reduce the heat to 300 degrees and cook an additional 2 hours. Flip the meat 2 or 3 times, spooning hot juices over. To cook in an electric Crockpot, simmer for 2 1/2 hours. Don't let liquid boil. Check for evaporation, adding more broth if necessary.

To Serve

1. Remove the meat from the pot. Cut and discard strings. Let the meat rest, covered with a towel, while preparing the sauce.

2. Remove the bouquet garni, cinnamon, and ginger from the pot. Pour the sauce through a coarse strainer (or put through a food processor and then strain), pushing the vegetables with the back of a wooden spoon. Discard the pulp in the strainer, taste the sauce, and adjust seasoning. If it's too thin, boil until somewhat reduced. If there's not enough sauce, add broth or red wine, heat, and stir until it reaches the desired thickness.

3. Slice the meat in ½-inch slices, arrange in a circle on platter. Pour the sauce over and around the meat. Garnish the center of the platter with lightly buttered peas or glazed carrots or turnips.

Yield: 6 servings
Calories per serving: 267
Protein per serving: 30g

Fat per serving: 8g
Carbohydrates per serving: 19g
Sodium per serving: 375mg

❖ GINGER ❖

Ginger root is the up-and-coming spice of the 80's. It is being used in sauces, blanched and julienned like orange rinds as a garnish for poultry dishes, and used in everything from salad dressings to ice creams. Oriental cooking has long known the wonders of this root of an orchidlike plant. Of course, in powdered form ginger has been used in baked goods literally for centuries. Our grandmothers used it in pickles and chutneys, and it is a component of curry powder. To use fresh ginger root, peel the outer skin and small knobs with a knife, exposing the pale yellow woody flesh. Cut off as much as you need and mince it finely. The remaining ginger root may be stored at room temperature in an airtight container (how long will depend on the age of the root when you buy it) or immersed in oil or sherry and kept refrigerated for up to 6 months. The ginger-spiked oil or sherry is delicious anywhere ginger is welcome: eggs, fish, poultry, carrots, squash, sweet potatoes, or your favorite way.

Beef Paupiettes with Sausage and Zucchini

❖

Make the stuffing for these rolls a day in advance if you like, and assemble about an hour or so before cooking. The ground veal helps to reduce the caloric tally of the rolls while the sausage lends it zip.

1 pound thinly sliced beef; use bottom or top round
    or use minute or thin-sliced sandwich steaks
prepared horseradish
2 small zucchini
2 teaspoons salt
4 ounces ground veal
4 ounces bulk-type sausage
1/2 teaspoon fresh thyme leaves or 1/4 teaspoon dried
    thyme
2 tablespoons grated mozzarella cheese
Béarnaise Sauce (page 24) or Wine Sauce (page 34)

To Prepare the Beef

1. If using bottom or top round steak, partially freeze the meat, then slice it as thinly as possible. Place the meat between pieces of wax paper and pound it with a cleaver until thin.
2. Dip a pastry brush into the horseradish jar and spread it thinly on the meat. Set aside while preparing the stuffing.

To Prepare the Stuffing

1. Grate the zucchini into a sieve held over a bowl. Sprinkle with salt and let rest for 20 minutes. The salt removes excess moisture.
2. Remove the sausage casing. Crumble the veal and sausage into an 8-inch skillet, cook gently, stirring from time to time, over me-

dium heat until the sausage and veal are cooked through, about 7 minutes.

3. While the sausage cooks, rinse the zucchini thoroughly, then squeeze it hard to remove excess moisture. Taste to be sure salt is completely removed.

4. Add zucchini, thyme, and mozzarella to the sausage-veal mixture the last minute of cooking. Stir to combine. Remove from heat.

To Assemble the Rolls

1. Divide the sausage-zucchini mixture over the meat, don't overfill. Loosely roll up the beef, enclosing the stuffing. Tie with butcher's twine as you would a package, or secure the flaps with toothpicks (this does make cooking more difficult).

2. Spray a large skillet with cooking spray, place over high heat, and "saute" the rolls, reducing heat to medium once they've browned. Cover the pan and shake it occasionally to cook the meat evenly. The paupiettes will cook in about 12 minutes. Remove paupiettes from the pan. Snip and discard strings. Serve the rolls with Béarnaise Sauce, or Wine Sauce. They may also be grilled or broiled.

Yield: 6 servings   Fat per serving: 20g
Calories per serving: 280   Carbohydrates per serving: 2g
Protein per serving: 23g   Sodium per serving: 236 mg

Roasted Tenderloin
of Beef

❖

I've always felt that a tenderloin epitomized the best of beef. Fewer cuts are more tender, easier to carve, or serve. But tenderloin can lack flavor, for as meats go, it is fairly lean, particularly if well trimmed before cooking. Hence the tradition of wrapping a tenderloin steak in a slice of bacon before grilling, or serving the meat with a rich sauce such as Béarnaise.

To accentuate the tenderness, our *Gourmet Light* version calls for home aging (a process you may omit). For the ultimate in juicy perfection the meat is then slow roasted in a salt crust, which, rather amazingly, doesn't penetrate the roast. This makes an excellent party meal served with Reduced-Calorie Béarnaise Sauce, which holds better than the traditional sauce, for everything may be done ahead. For an even more festive treatment, butterfly the meat and stuff it, after aging, with langoustine (available frozen), crab, or lobster. Retie the roast and proceed as directed.

Tenderloins freeze well so take advantage of an occasional sale. A typical tenderloin weighs 5 1/2 pounds to about 8 pounds, before trimming. Allow about three-quarters of a pound per person of untrimmed weight for the generous servings you plan for when entertaining. A 7-pound tenderloin will weigh about 5 pounds after trimming, theoretically feeding 10 people with a generous half pound. However, I've never found this to be true. In my experience a 7-pound tenderloin (before trimming) will feed 6–8 with seconds for some. Ask the butcher to trim and tie the roast, reserving the fat if you wish to age it at home.

Prime meat has already enjoyed a lengthy aging, but choice meat often has not. For truly fork-tender meat, follow this procedure 3 days before your dinner party.

Remove the store wrappings from the meat weighing at least 4 pounds, trim any fat that remains. Place the meat on a cake rack over a baking sheet. Lay the reserved fat on the meat, covering it as much as possible. Crease a piece of aluminum foil large enough to cover the meat down the center. Position the tent of foil over the meat loosely, do not wrap tightly. Air must circulate. Refrigerate for 3 days, turning the meat and repositioning the fat once a day. During this time, the enzymes that are naturally present in the meat break down the fibers of the muscles, causing them to relax. In the process, the meat softens. You'll notice that any surface not covered by fat will darken and harden. To prepare the meat for cooking, untie the butcher's twine. Carefully pare away all the hardened flesh. Retie the roast, it is now ready for roasting.

> *a whole tenderloin, about 7 pounds before trimming,*
> *   tied and trimmed*
> *1   clove garlic, mashed or pressed*
> *10 cups kosher salt*
> *2 1/2 cups water*
> *Béarnaise Sauce (page 24)*

1. Preheat oven to 400 degrees. Pat the meat dry with paper towels. Rub the garlic over the meat.
2. In a large bowl, moisten the salt with the water bit by bit, stirring to form a paste. Because kosher salt has no additives to keep it free flowing, it is very susceptible to moisture and may or may not need the entire amount of water specified here. Add only as much (or more) as needed to form a thick paste.
3. Put half the salt paste in a roasting pan just large enough to hold the meat. Put the meat on top, add remaining salt paste, and pack tightly around the roast with your hands.
4. Place on the lowest shelf in a 400-degree oven and roast for 1 hour or until an instant-reading meat thermometer registers 120 degrees for rare or 135 degrees for medium rare. Begin temperature testing after 40 minutes to be on the safe side. The temperature of the meat at the time of roasting, the shape of the meat, and the density of the salt paste can all affect the actual roasting time; what worked last time may not work next time.

5. Remove the pan from the oven when the meat is the desired temperature. Let the meat sit for 10 minutes, and remove salt crust. Slice the meat before serving it, because the outside will be gray rather than brown since it was not seared. Serve with Béarnaise Sauce.

Yield: 8 servings
Calories per serving: 425
Protein per serving: 73g

Fat per serving: 14g
Carbohydrates per serving: trace
Sodium per serving: cannot be
calculated

Beef Stroganoff

❖

Here's an exercise in transforming a classic recipe into one for the *Gourmet Light* files. The meat is browned in cooking spray rather than fat and the sour cream is replaced by crème blanc. There's another change. Because I enjoy meat rare, I've chosen to pan-fry a solid piece of beef, rather than cook bite-size pieces, which inevitably become overdone. The meat is then given the briefest of simmers in the sauce. The sauce may be made ahead and reheated just before serving time.

 2 medium green peppers, seeded and thinly sliced
 4 tablespoons beef broth
 2 tablespoons tomato paste
 1 tablespoon plus 1 teaspoon Worcestershire sauce
 2 teaspoons prepared mustard
 1 teaspoon prepared horseradish
 ½ teaspoon salt
 1 cup crème blanc, made without milk, page 37
 6 ounces mushrooms, sliced

1 ¼ pounds sirloin strip steak
½ cup dry red wine
1 clove garlic, minced

1. "Saute" the peppers in the broth in an 8-inch skillet over medium heat until just softened. Scrape them into a bowl when done.
2. While the peppers cook, stir the tomato paste, Worcestershire, mustard, horseradish, and salt into the crème blanc. Set aside.
3. Spray now-empty skillet (no need to wash) with cooking spray. Add the sliced mushrooms, cook over high heat, reducing to low, until mushrooms are lightly browned. Add to peppers in the bowl, cover, and keep warm in a 150-degree oven.
4. Pat beef dry. Spray pan again and heat it on high heat. When it is very hot, add meat. Sear at high heat 1 minute, reduce heat to medium, cook 2 minutes more. Turn meat over, cook another 2 to 3 minutes or until it has reached the desired degree of doneness.
5. Remove meat from pan and keep warm. Add wine and garlic to the pan. Cook on high heat until wine is reduced by half to about ¼ cup. Remove from heat, add mushrooms and peppers, stir, and cool about 2 minutes. If the wine is too hot the crème blanc will curdle.
6. Add the flavored crème blanc, stirring. Add meat, simmer at very low heat just 4 to 5 minutes. The crème blanc must not boil. Serve on a heated platter on a mound of egg noodles if desired.

Yield: 4 servings
Calories per serving: 510
Protein per serving: 29g

Fat per serving: 38g
Carbohydrates per serving: 12g
Sodium per serving: 467mg

Veal Roast with Sun-Dried Tomatoes Roasted in Salt

❖

Lean meats such as veal are often dry meats, so it behooves the cook to look for ways to enhance the natural moisture of such foods. Cooking in salt seals in the juices while amazingly not contributing to the sodium content of the food. In fact, I find I often have to salt the roast at the table. Uncharacteristically, oil has been used in the stuffing. The meat is so lean as to benefit by this touch of fat, but it may be omitted if you prefer to cook the onions in broth.

1 ounce (about 5) sun-dried tomatoes, salt-cured not
    oil-cured type if possible, available at specialty
    food stores
boiling water
1 small onion, chopped
1 clove garlic, minced
1 tablespoon extra-virgin olive oil
4 ounces mushrooms, sliced
1/4 cup cooked rice (substitute dried bread crumbs if
    you have no cooked rice)
1 teaspoon fresh tarragon leaves or 1/2 teaspoon
    dried tarragon
6–8 fresh basil leaves or 1 teaspoon dried basil
1 teaspoon raspberry or other fruit-flavored vinegar
2 slices bacon, fried, drained, and crumbled
1/4 cup minced fresh parsley
freshly ground pepper to taste
a veal shoulder roast, boned, about 2 pounds
5 cups kosher salt
3/4 to 1 cup water

1. Cover the tomatoes with the boiling water. Steep for 15 minutes. Drain and cut the tomatoes into thin strips.
2. Cook the onion and garlic in olive oil in a Teflon-coated pan over medium-low heat, covered, until softened.
3. Remove the onion and garlic to a small bowl. Do not wipe the pan. Add the mushrooms, cover and cook over high heat, lowering heat if needed. Remove the cover and stir mushrooms from time to time. Uncover the mushrooms when browned, add tomatoes, stir and cook 30 seconds. Scrape into the bowl with the onion and garlic.
4. Stir the rice, tarragon, basil, vinegar, bacon, parsley, and pepper into the bowl. Set one-half cup of stuffing aside for final step.
5. Preheat oven to 450 degrees. Open the meat if it has been tied. Some veal roasts that come in netting are actually two pieces of meat. Simply spread the stuffing over one layer, top with the second layer, and tie with butcher's twine for a roast. If needed, cut a cavity into the roast for the stuffing. Wipe the meat dry.
6. Place the salt in a bowl. Add only as much water as you need, bit by bit, to make a paste.
7. Place ⅓ of the salt paste in a 9-inch by 5-inch by 3-inch loaf pan. Place the dried roast on top. Cover with the remaining salt paste, packing it down with your hand. Be sure meat is completely encased by salt paste. Place the pan in the bottom third of the 450-degree oven. Reduce heat to 350 degrees after 30 minutes and cook an additional 45 minutes or until an internal meat thermometer registers 165 degrees. Let meat rest for 5 minutes. Crack the salt crust open and discard. Lift the meat to an ovenproof platter. Pat the remaining stuffing (from Step 4) over the roast and broil 5 minutes or until lightly browned on top. Remove strings and slice thinly.

Yield: 6 servings

Calories per serving: 380

Protein per serving: 32g

Fat per serving: 24g

Carbohydrates per serving: 8g

Sodium per serving: 597mg

Veal Chops
with Red Pepper Butter

❖

Really watching calories for a few days? How about a veal chop for lunch? Too much, too fattening? Would you believe these succulent chops slathered with red pepper butter actually have fewer calories than a tuna on white bread? More costly perhaps, but would you rather pay with your pocketbook or your waistline? Besides the calorie count, an added payoff is the feeling of satisfaction after such a pampered lunch that will last till dinnertime. Because the red pepper butter keeps in the freezer indefinitely, make it in quantity—even frozen, it is sliceable. It flames a simple green vegetable, chicken, or fish fillet with flavor and color.

For the Red Pepper Butter

5 medium red peppers
4 tablespoons minced fresh parsley
1 clove garlic, minced
1/2 teaspoon salt
freshly ground pepper to taste
1 teaspoon fresh lemon juice
2 tablespoons butter

For the Meat

4 loin or shoulder (sometimes called arm) veal chops
1/4 teaspoon salt
freshly ground pepper to taste

To Prepare the Red Pepper Butter

1. Halve the peppers, discard the seeds, and flatten the peppers with your hand. Place on a baking sheet and broil until blackened and charred, about 8 minutes. Turn the sheet around once or twice to

ensure even cooking. See the illustration on page 260.

2. Scrape the peppers into a plastic or paper bag, roll it closed, and chill until cool enough to handle, about 10 minutes. (The freezer makes quick work if you're in a hurry.)

3. Peel and discard the skins and chop the flesh roughly.

4. Puree the roasted peppers in a food processor with the remaining ingredients, adding the butter after the other ingredients have been pureed. Lacking a food processor, puree the peppers in a blender or food mill, add the remaining ingredients, and puree again.

5. Scoop the pepper butter onto a double thickness of wax paper. Form it into a log shape, roll and twist ends to compact. Wrap in aluminum foil. Chill. The butter may be used as is or frozen and sliced as needed. You will only need about ½ the red pepper butter for the chops.

To Prepare the Chops

1. Preheat oven to 400 degrees. Sear the chops in a Teflon-coated skillet over high heat, a little less than a minute on each side. Season with salt and pepper.

2. Tear off 4 pieces of parchment paper (17 inches by 15 inches). The paper may be used as is, with the chops wrapped as you would a sandwich. Or for a more decorative presentation, stack the four sheets and fold in half the long way. Trim the corners so you're left with four heart shapes. Place a chop on a half of each heart. Place a tablespoon of red pepper butter on each. Fold top of heart over. Starting at the rounded top, fold and pleat the paper, making a tight seal. Tuck the pointed end under the packet. Place each packet on a baking sheet. Place in the lower third of the preheated 400-degree oven for 15 minutes or until the paper puffs. Remove the baking sheet from the oven, and let each diner open the paper at the table and enjoy the heady aroma.

Yield: 4 servings
Calories per serving: 160
Protein per serving: 25g

Fat per serving: 6g
Carbohydrates per serving: 1g
Sodium per serving: 100mg

Paupiettes of Veal
with Apple-Cabbage Stuffing

❖

A paupiette is the French term for a thin piece of meat that is pounded, stuffed, rolled, and then tied. Because of their resemblance to stuffed quail they are often called "birds." Paupiettes do require a bit of advance work: The meat needs pounding, the stuffing needs doing, and the whole needs tying. However, this is about 40 minutes work that may be done early in the day or even days before, then the paupiettes frozen for a delicious weekday meal prepared at the weekend's more leisurely pace. The cabbage and apple stuffing is also delicious served as a side dish with pork or chicken dishes.

For the Stuffing

1 small onion, chopped
1 small clove garlic, minced
6 tablespoons beef or chicken broth
2 medium apples, peeled, cored, and chopped
1 cup shredded red cabbage
½ teaspoon salt
freshly ground pepper to taste
4 ounces ground veal

For the Meat

8 veal scallops (about 1 ¼ pounds)
lemon juice
¼ teaspoon salt
freshly ground pepper to taste
5 tablespoons dry sherry
5 tablespoons chicken or beef broth or veal stock
1 tablespoon butter, at room temperature
1 tablespoon minced fresh parsley

To Prepare the Stuffing

1. "Saute" the onion and garlic in 4 tablespoons of the broth over medium-high heat until they're limp and the broth is evaporated.
2. Add the apples, cabbage, and the remaining 2 tablespoons broth. Season with salt and pepper, cover, and cook over high heat 1 minute. Reduce heat to medium low, and continue to cook, covered, 10 minutes more.
3. Uncover, add the veal, and stir over high heat until the meat loses its pinkness, about 3 to 4 minutes, or until moisture evaporates. Remove from heat.

To Prepare the Meat

1. Pound the veal scallops between sheets of wax paper until very thin. Sprinkle with lemon juice, salt, and pepper.
2. Place 2 tablespoons stuffing in the middle of the veal slice, enclose like an envelope. (Reserve remaining stuffing.) Tie the bundle with butcher's twine as if tying a package. Repeat with remaining veal. Bundles may now be refrigerated up to 8 hours before cooking or frozen until ready to cook.

To Cook the Paupiettes

1. Spray a 10-inch or 12-inch skillet with cooking spray. Saute the bundles, turning frequently. When browned, add the sherry and stock (veal stock would be lovely!), half cover, and cook for 6 minutes. Remove the paupiettes to a serving platter with a slotted spoon, raise heat to high, and boil until juices are reduced to $1/3$ cup. While the sauce is reducing, cut and discard the strings from meat.
2. Swirl the butter into the sauce over medium-low heat, and pour over the meat. Reheat the remaining apple-cabbage mixture and serve on the side. Sprinkle parsley over the veal. Serve 2 per person.

Yield: 4 servings
Calories per serving: 170
Protein per serving: 18g

Fat per serving: 7g
Carbohydrates per serving: 9g
Sodium per serving: 115mg

Veal Scallops with
Prosciutto and Mozzarella

❖

When a normally skinny veal scallop is dipped in egg, bread crumbs, and flour and bathed in fat, its calorie index jumps about 150 points higher. Here is an attempt to capture the flavor of breaded, sauteed veal without the excess calories.

> 2 pounds veal scallops, pounded thin
> lemon juice
> ½ teaspoon salt
> freshly ground pepper to taste
> 8 paper-thin slices prosciutto
> 4 ounces part-skim mozzarella cheese, grated or torn
> 1 egg white
> 1 tablespoon milk
> ½ cup plus 2 tablespoons dried bread crumbs
> 1 tablespoon vegetable oil
> 1 tablespoon butter
> ¼ cup beef or chicken broth
> 2 tablespoons Madeira or dry sherry
> 8 very thin lemon slices

1. Sprinkle the meat with lemon juice and season lightly with salt and pepper. Lay a piece of prosciutto on each veal scallop and divide the cheese over. Roll the scallop like a jellyroll.
2. Beat together the egg white and milk. Pour into a saucer.
3. Spread the bread crumbs on a sheet of wax paper. Roll the veal first in the milk, then in the bread crumbs. Chill for 20 minutes if possible to set the crumbs.
4. Heat the oil and butter in a 10-inch or 12-inch skillet until bubbly. Add the veal scallops, saute over medium-high heat a few at a time so they don't touch, until nicely browned, about 3–4 min-

utes. Return all meat to the skillet, turn heat to medium low, cover, and cook the rolls another 5–7 minutes, turning often. You may need to add a bit of oil or cooking spray. Remove the veal to a heated serving platter.

5. Add the broth to the skillet, boil until it's reduced to 2 tablespoons, add Madeira, and reduce the liquid to a syrupy glaze. Pour it over the veal and garnish with lemon slices.

Yield: 8 servings
Calories per serving: 275
Protein per serving: 30g

Fat per serving: 14g
Carbohydrates per serving: 3g
Sodium per serving: 333mg

Pork Cutlet in Cider Cream Sauce

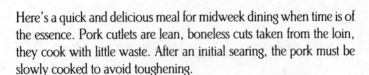

Here's a quick and delicious meal for midweek dining when time is of the essence. Pork cutlets are lean, boneless cuts taken from the loin, they cook with little waste. After an initial searing, the pork must be slowly cooked to avoid toughening.

> 2 teaspoons butter
> 1 teaspoon vegetable oil
> 1 to 1¼ pounds boneless pork cutlets
> ¾ cup cider (hard or nonalcoholic sparkling cider recommended)
> 4 small apples, peeled, cored, and thinly sliced
> ¼ teaspoon salt
> freshly ground pepper to taste
> 2 teaspoons (or to taste) stone-ground mustard (the kind made with horseradish is excellent)
> ½ cup crème blanc (page 37), made without milk

1. In a 10-inch Teflon-coated skillet, melt the butter and oil until foamy over high heat. Alternately, spray any 10-inch heavy-bottomed skillet with cooking spray, then add the butter and oil. Pat the cutlets dry. Sear the cutlets for about 1 minute on each side or until well browned.
2. Reduce the heat, add the cider and apples, season with salt and pepper, and half cover the pan. Stirring the apples occasionally, simmer for 8 minutes, or until the pork is cooked through and the apples are tender but not mushy.
3. Remove the cutlets from the pan to a serving plate, cover with a towel to keep them warm. Boil pan juices, if necessary, to reduce to ¼ cup. Cool about 1 minute, cider that's too hot will curdle the crème blanc.
4. Stir the mustard into the crème blanc. Whisk this mixture into the cider. Pour the sauce and apples over the pork cutlets.

Yield: 4 servings
Calories per serving: 472
Protein per serving: 22g

Fat per serving: 32g
Carbohydrates per serving: 24g
Sodium per serving: 513mg

Pork and Veal Croquettes with Lemon Caper Sauce

❖

Traditionally, a croquette is ground meat, poultry, or what have you bound by a white sauce and deep-fat-fried—two no-no's in *Gourmet Light* cooking. Here we temper the high-calorie ground pork with lean veal and zucchini, add cooked rice, and lightly bread the croquettes by dipping them in milk and egg white rather than the traditional whole egg. The croquettes may then be sauteed in a Teflon-coated pan, or baked. The sauce may be made ahead and gently reheated at serving time.

For the Croquettes

8 ounces ground veal

6 ounces ground pork

1 small zucchini, grated

1 onion, chopped

5–6 fresh sage leaves, snipped, or ½ teaspoon dried
sage

1 cup cooked rice

2 teaspoons capers (optional)

½ teaspoon salt

freshly ground pepper to taste

1 egg white

2 tablespoons milk

¼ cup dried bread crumbs

For the Sauce

2 tablespoons lemon juice (about ½ a fresh lemon)

¾ cup chicken broth

1 teaspoon cornstarch

2 tablespoons milk

1 teaspoon capers

2 tablespoons chicken broth

1 tablespoon butter, at room temperature

To Prepare the Croquettes

1. Combine first 9 ingredients in a bowl; mix well.
2. Beat together the egg white and milk and pour them into a saucer.
3. Spread the bread crumbs on a piece of wax paper.
4. With your hands form the meat mixture (Step 1) into "logs," each about 2 inches wide by 4 inches long.
5. Roll the meat mixture in the egg and milk, then in the bread crumbs. If sauteing the croquettes, chill for 20 minutes if time allows to set the crumbs. Spray a 10-inch nonstick skillet with cooking spray. When the pan is hot, add the croquettes, and saute, covered, over medium-high heat. Turn the croquettes of-

ten, until they are cooked through, about 10-12 minutes.

6. If you have decided to bake the croquettes, bake them in a preheated 400-degree oven. Turn them after 15 minutes in the oven to brown them evenly; they will cook in 25 to 30 minutes.

To Prepare the Sauce

1. Reduce the lemon juice to a glaze in a heavy-bottomed 1-quart saucepan over high heat.

2. Add the broth and bring to a boil.

3. Dissolve the cornstarch in the milk. Remove the boiling broth from heat and whisk in the dissolved cornstarch. Return the pan to medium-high heat and bring back to a slow boil, whisking all the while.

4. Whisk in the capers, additional broth (more or less to desired consistency), and butter. Sauce may be reheated.

Yield: 9 croquettes

Calories in each: 116

Protein in each: 12g

Fat in each: 4g

Carbohydrates in each: 8g

Sodium in each: 251mg

Yield of Sauce: ¾ cup

Calories per tablespoon: 13

Protein per serving: trace

Fat per tablespoon: 1g

Carbohydrates per tablespoon: 1g

Sodium per tablespoon: 3mg

❖ **UNOPENED FLOWER BUDS** ❖

Two spices in your kitchen are actually unopened flower buds: cloves, from a kind of evergreen tree, and capers, from a Mediterranean shrub. Capers are priced by their size, the smaller the more costly. They are most frequently preserved in vinegar, occasionally in salt. Used in salads, sauces, and as a garnish for egg dishes they lend a distinction totally their own. They will keep in the refrigerator for up to one year. Cloves are dried flower buds; they come powdered or whole. Add a few to a bouquet garni destined for a tomato dish for a pleasant, peppery sweet taste.

Roasted Pork Tenderloin
with Curried Fall Fruit Compote

❖

Pork has always been considered a fatty meat, but with better breeding today's animal is less fatty than in previous years. The tenderloin,
a long thin strip of meat taken from the unexercised backbone area, is
among the leanest of the cuts. Pork tenderloins range from 2 inches to
3 inches thick tapering down to a mere flap of meat. If you're only
able to buy the thinner tenderloin, purchase two and tie them together
with one thin tail abutting the thick body of the other. This way you'll
have a "log" of meat of uniform thickness. This recipe may be prepared early in the day and roasted just before serving. Serve it with the
Curried Fall Fruit Compote for a delicious dinner worthy of a festive
occasion.

> *Dijon-style mustard*
> *1 3/4 pounds pork tenderloin*
> *1/2 teaspoon salt*
> *1 clove garlic, minced*
> *1/4 cup unseasoned dried bread crumbs*
> *freshly ground pepper to taste*
> *4 to 5 fresh sage leaves, snipped, or 3/4 teaspoon*
> *dried sage*

1. Preheat oven to 450 degrees. Brush the mustard over the meat
   with a pastry brush. Sprinkle half the salt over the meat.
2. Spray an 8-inch skillet with cooking spray, add the garlic, and
   cook over medium heat about 30 seconds. Add the bread crumbs
   and sage. Cook, stirring until the crumbs begin to brown. Season
   with remaining salt and pepper.
3. Put half the crumbs in a roasting dish just large enough to hold the
   meat. Put the roast on top, pat remaining crumbs around and on
   top of roast.

4. Place roast in the bottom third of the preheated 450-degree oven for 10 minutes. Then reduce heat to 325 degrees and roast for an additional 50 minutes. Check meat's internal temperature after it has roasted 45 minutes. It is done when internal temperature registers 160 to 165 degrees. Let the tenderloin rest 5-10 minutes before slicing. Serve with Curried Fall Fruit Compote.

Curried Fall Fruit Compote

> ½ small onion, chopped
> 4 tablespoons beef or chicken broth
> 1 teaspoon curry powder
> ½ teaspoon ground cumin
> 1 pear, peeled, cored, and chopped
> 1 Granny Smith apple, peeled, cored, and chopped
> 1 Red Delicious apple, peeled, cored, and chopped
> 2 dried apricots, soaked 20 minutes in 2 tablespoons apricot or other fruit-flavored brandy
> 4 tablespoons golden raisins

1. "Saute" the onion in 2 tablespoons of the broth until limp. Sprinkle on the curry powder and cumin. Cook over medium-high heat, stirring, about 15 seconds.
2. Add the remaining ingredients, including the brandy, cover, and cook over low heat 20 minutes or until flavors are blended. Serve with pork dishes. Leftovers are easily reheated in a bit of broth or cider.

Yield of meat with compote:
    4 servings
Calories per serving: 275
Protein per serving: 32g

Fat per serving: 15g
Carbohydrates per serving: 2g
Sodium per serving: 360mg

Yield of Compote: 4 servings
Calories per serving: 120
Protein per serving: 1g

Fat per serving: trace
Carbohydrates per serving: 29g
Sodium per serving: 7mg

Mock Tenderloin

❖

This is one of my favorite ways to enjoy lamb, pink and succulent with a texture and taste much like that of a fine beef tenderloin. A lamb leg is completely stripped of fat, the muscles separated, marinated, cut into noisettes, and then grilled. Serve this with the Mustard Hollandaise (page 174). Alternately, the muscles may be left whole and roasted in a 450-degree oven for 15 minutes for rare meat.

> ½ leg of lamb, the shank half (about 3½ pounds total)
> 4 tablespoons red wine vinegar
> 4 tablespoons red wine
> 2 tablespoons vegetable oil
> 2 tablespoons minced fresh parsley
> 1 clove garlic, minced
> a few drops hot pepper sauce
> Dijon-style mustard
> ⅛ teaspoon salt
> freshly ground pepper to taste
> Mustard Hollandaise

1. Have the lamb boned or do it yourself. Lay the meat flat on the counter top with what was the skin side facing up. Trim and discard all the fat and gristle from the meat.
2. Cut off and freeze for another use the thin flap of meat that you'll find on one side. Pull the meat with your hands; you'll notice natural "breaks" in the muscles. Separate the muscles by pulling the white veil of connective tissues. You'll need a knife in only a few places. You'll have three separate muscles. Fold the thin ends of each muscle toward the middle and tuck underneath. Cut each muscle into rounds (noisettes), about 1½-inches thick. Each noisette will be about 3 inches across and look like a slice of beef

tenderloin. Reserve and freeze any untidy chunks of meat with the flap and use for a curry or kebabs.

3. Combine the vinegar, wine, oil, parsley, garlic, and hot pepper sauce in a jar and shake to combine. Put the meat and marinade in a leak-proof plastic bag and refrigerate, turning occasionally, for about 12 hours.

4. Pat the meat dry, brush with the mustard, season with salt and pepper, and grill until done to your liking. Or "saute" in a non-stick skillet, or broil. Serve with Mustard Hollandaise.

Note: If you sear the meat on both sides, then remove it from the fire and let it rest 20 minutes before finishing the cooking, the noisettes will be even juicier.

Yield: 4 servings
Calories per serving: 325
Protein per serving: 41g

Fat per serving: 17g
Carbohydrates per serving: 2g
Sodium per serving: 170mg

HOW TO CUT LAMB NOISETTES

1. Lay the boned lamb on the counter. Trim and discard the fat and gristle from the meat.

2. Turn the lamb over so what was the fat side is now facing down. Remove the thin triangular flap of meat. It may be saved for another use.

3. The meat will pull apart into three segments that are held together by a white, gossamer tissue and some gristle. Use your fingers and a small knife to separate the meat into three muscles.

4. Fold the thin ends of each muscle toward the middle and tuck underneath.

5. Slice each muscle into noisettes about 1½-inches thick.

6. The finished noisettes will be about 3 inches across and look like a slice of beef tenderloin.

Chapter 7

POULTRY
AND
GAME

Chicken

❖

Back when Grandma simmered a pot of baked beans on the wood stove all day long and whipped up a mess of biscuits, mile high and puffy as you please, chicken was Sunday fare, a to-do worthy of company. Today, thanks to scientific advancements in the breeding and feeding of the barnyard birds, chicken has become a standard rather than a luxury. Because the birds now come to market in a matter of weeks, rather than months, the reduced production costs translate into reduced consumer prices, making chicken not only one of our more economical but also nutritionally bountiful buys, as well. Just 4 ounces of white meat, without skin, supplies about half an adult's protein needs for less than 150 calories. But half a cup of skinned, boned chicken is hardly something to feast on, and certainly no culinary inspiration. This chapter offers more tempting treatments for chicken as well as some for turkey, duck, and quail.

Chicken, like meat, must be inspected for wholesomeness, but there's no law stating it must be graded—a letter classification (A or B) based on the bird's physical appearance. Chickens wearing a Grade A shield do so because the processor has paid USDA inspectors to grade the product, a cost that the producer, and ultimately the consumer, must pay for. And it's not likely you'll spot a Grade B shield boldly displayed on a chicken breast—who wants the world to know your product is second best? This is not to say that nongraded birds are necessarily of poor quality, only that they've not been graded. You can be assured they'll be less expensive, and in some cases, just as good.

Here are some tips when purchasing chicken:

1. The bird should be fresh, not previously frozen.

Each time a chicken is thawed it loses some of its juices. If you suspect your market is selling previously frozen birds, or ones that have unintentionally frozen when shipped on ice, snap a leg bone after roasting. It will appear reddish-black if the bird was once frozen.

2. Match the cooking technique to the bird's size.

Roasters, over 3 pounds—roast or fricassee
Fryer, 2–3 pounds—saute, roast, or fricassee
Broiler, 1 ½ to 2 ½ pounds—grill or roast

Chickens range from broiler/fryers (smallest) to roasters (largest), which is not to say a fryer couldn't be broiled or a broiler roasted. However, the long, slow cooking such as that required for a Coq au Vin might render a small bird mushy and grilling a cut-up roaster might take far too long, burning the skin before it was ever done at the bone. Adapt the recipe to the bird, remembering (logically) that large birds do best with long, slow cooking, while small birds are better suited to shorter cooking methods. Old, tough birds—fowl—need long, slow cooking in a liquid to make them tender.

3. Look for a plump bird, with a good covering of fat.

The plumper the bird, the more tender the meat. While buying only Grade A chickens pretty much ensures the best, buying plump ungraded chickens will get you to the same place for a few pennies less per pound.

4. Skin color is not an indication of flavor.

Some chicken producers routinely monitor the birds' skin pigment by taking blood samples from a few chickens. Those to be marketed in the Northeast, where yellow-skinned chickens are preferred, may have their feed bolstered by marigold petals, a completely natural substance that yellows the skin color but does not affect the flavor.

The very methods responsible for the relative inexpensiveness of chicken are held responsible by some cooks for production of a bland, flavorless bird. Free-range chickens, available at some specialty markets, are brought up "the old-fashioned way," pecking away in the barnyard. These same cooks feel the increased exercise and natural feed supplements make for a better-flavored bird. If you can find a supplier of free-range chickens, you can test the theory yourself . . . but because the old-fashioned method is more dear, be prepared to pay more.

Like fish, chicken is very perishable. It is best to freeze it if not using it within 24 hours of purchase. If you choose to rinse the chicken before cooking and it is to be browned, pat it thoroughly dry or it will more likely stew than saute.

A frozen chicken, or any other poultry, is best thawed under refrigeration, well wrapped, to inhibit water loss. This can take anywhere from 1–3 days, depending on the size of the bird.

Boning Chicken Breasts

❖

Chicken breasts are a favorite in *Gourmet Light* cooking for they make a tidy serving and neatly solve the "just one more bite" temptation. A typical chicken breast weighs 3 ounces, supplies a mere 125 calories (150 with the skin) and supplies 20 grams of protein—about half the daily requirement for most women. It's wonderfully versatile, nutrient dense, skinny, and economical, too—don't be caught without a supply in the freezer.

Although chicken breasts are readily available boned and skinned, you may wish to do the work yourself. Not only is it more economical but the bones are almost indispensable for enriching store-bought chicken broth or making your own. As you bone the breasts, toss the bones into a plastic bag in the freezer. You may add to and use from your stash as needed.

You may use any sharp knife for boning chicken breasts, you don't need a special boning knife. Place the breast on the work surface, skin side up. If whole, flatten with the heel of your hand and split by cutting through or just to one side of the breastbone. With the breastbone to the right and the rib cage section to the left, slice against the breastbone and scrape down the bones, pulling back the meat with your fingers. Always angle the knife toward the bones. Don't worry about making gorgeous, clean cuts. The meat is very gelatinous and will "glue" together as it cooks, and the bit of meat left on the bones will only serve to enrich your stock. When the meat is scraped free of the bones, cut loose at the shoulder end. This is called a supreme. Turn the supreme so the skin side is down. Notice the small strip of meat, called the filet mignon, with the white tendon running its length. By the way, if the filet became detached in cutting, don't despair, just stick it back on! Grasp the end of the tendon in your finger tips and pull it free by scraping the meat away with the tip of a small, sharp knife. Although this is a pesky task and may be omitted, the tendon, if left, tends to pull the breast out of shape as it doesn't shrink with the cooking meat. The breasts may now be skinned or not as you please. To skin, simply lift the skin in your finger tips, cutting loose where needed. With your finger tips check to be sure the supreme is free of any remaining cartilage. Trim away yellow fat. Freeze the breasts or use within 24 hours.

❖ BUTTER AND OIL ❖

Frequently in this book you'll notice small amounts of both butter and oil are called for in the sauteing of foods. Using both combines the benefits of each—the flavor of butter (which burns at a low temperature) with the higher smoking point of oil, allowing for rapid browning with good butter flavor.

Chicken Paillards

❖

A paillard is the culinary term for a piece of beef, chicken, or veal that is cooked without fat. Although this can be accomplished in a good heavy nonstick skillet, it is best suited for grills, either the indoor models with their wonderfully effective fans or a more typical outdoor version. What follows are basic instructions for preparing chicken paillards and some suggestions for varying the routine. You'll soon devise some wonderful alternatives that reflect your own tastes for this simplest and skinniest of meals. Technically, a chicken paillard is the breast boned and skinned. Should you choose to leave the skin on, add 60 calories a serving.

For the Paillards

4 boneless chicken breasts
juice of half a lemon
1/8 teaspoon salt
freshly ground pepper to taste

1. Skin the chicken breasts or not as you desire. Place the chicken between sheets of wax paper and pound to an even thickness, not to make thin.
2. Heat a grill or skillet with grill ridges. Place the chicken perpendicular to the grill rungs. After the chicken has seared, turn 1/4 turn (90 degrees) to make customary grill marks. Season with a few drops lemon juice. Turn over after 3 minutes. Repeat above procedure to make grilling pattern. Season with salt, pepper, and lemon juice, continue to cook until chicken is firm when poked with your finger in several places, about 6–7 minutes. Because the grill's heat and the thickness of chicken will vary, watch it closely. Chicken may be cooked in anywhere from 4–8 minutes.

Yield: 4 servings
Calories per serving: 115
Protein per serving: 23g

Fat per serving: 1g
Carbohydrates per serving: trace
Sodium per serving: 130mg

Mustard Paillards

Dip a pastry brush in stone-ground mustard and lavish over uncooked chicken. Spread on additional mustard if desired during cooking. This is also delicious with some of the sweet mustards on the market, such as Russian or champagne mustard. (The nutritional content is not available.)

Basil-Walnut Paillards

When fresh basil is in season, make several batches of the wonderfully delicious Basil-Walnut Sauce on page 32. It is an all-purpose flavor booster with a tiny caloric price tag. Brush 2 tablespoons on each chicken paillard before and as it cooks and serve with sauteed cherry tomatoes.

Yield: 4 servings
Calories per serving: 175
Protein per serving: 25g

Fat per serving: 7g
Carbohydrates per serving: 2g
Sodium per serving: 150mg

Red Pepper Butter Paillards

When red peppers are plentiful in early spring and fall, make the Red Pepper Butter on page 136 in quantity and freeze it. Sliced right from the freezer it cloaks a simple chicken paillard with a scarlet robe at once subtle yet piquant. Add a slice after the chicken has cooked on one side, and another when the chicken is done, just before serving, covering briefly while still on the grill to melt the butter.

Yield: 4 servings
Calories per serving: 155
Protein per serving: 24g

Fat per serving: 4g
Carbohydrates per serving: 5g
Sodium per serving: 30mg

Sesame Chicken Salad

❖

This chicken salad is Chinese in spirit with its soy marinade, Japanese in soul with its yolk-enhanced grilling technique, and very much "today" with its lightness, attention to color, and emphasis on vegetables. It is served warm, not chilled.

6 tablespoons soy sauce
2 tablespoons rice wine vinegar, available at Oriental or specialty food shops
1 scallion, minced
a quarter-size piece of fresh ginger root, peeled and diced
1 teaspoon sesame oil, available at Oriental or specialty food shops
4 boneless, skinless chicken breasts
1 egg yolk
3 tablespoons chicken broth
1 scant teaspoon sugar
1 carrot, cut into narrow strips about 3 inches long
1 small zucchini, cut like the carrot
1 small summer squash, cut like the carrot
red leaf lettuce
2 tablespoons sesame seeds, toasted

1. Combine the soy sauce, vinegar, scallion, ginger, and sesame oil in a bowl. Pour the mixture into a leakproof plastic bag or shallow baking dish, add the chicken, and marinate overnight or at least 4 hours in the refrigerator.
2. Drain the chicken, reserving marinade. Mix 4 tablespoons marinade with the egg yolk, set aside.
3. Mix the remaining soy marinade with the chicken broth and sugar. Set aside.

4. Bring a 2½-quart saucepan three quarters full of water to a boil. Add the carrots, 30 seconds later add the zucchini, and 30 seconds later add the squash. Time 1 minute more, drain and cool under running water. Toss the vegetables with half the soy-broth-sugar mixture from Step 3. Set aside while preparing chicken.
5. Grill chicken 3 minutes on each side, basting frequently with the yolk-enriched marinade. When the chicken is cooked (firm when poked with a finger), remove and slice in thin strips on the diagonal.
6. Line a serving platter with the lettuce. Drizzle with the remaining dressing from Step 3. Place dressing-tossed vegetables on lettuce and chicken strips arranged in a V-shaped column down the center. Sprinkle with toasted sesame seeds.

Note: To toast sesame seeds, place them in a skillet over high heat until they pop, shaking constantly. Sodium-reduced soy sauce is available in many markets for those wishing to restrict the amount of sodium.

Yield: 4 servings
Calories per serving: 195
Protein per serving: 26g

Fat per serving: 6g
Carbohydrates per serving: 9g
Sodium per serving: 900mg

❖   **THINKING THIN TIP**   ❖

Portion control is vital to weight control. Invest in a small food scale and use it until you can pretty well judge what a 4-ounce portion looks like.

Breast of Chicken Salad

❖

Minimum cooking with minimum effort, but the dish is pretty, appealing, and no insult to your new bathing suit. It is served warm. Or, if you wish, serve it chilled by preparing the chicken and the sauce a few hours ahead, refrigerating them, and assembling the dish just before serving.

> 4 chicken breasts (no need to skin or bone)
> 2 scallions
> a 3-inch chunk of ginger root, peeled and sliced
> 1 cup chicken broth
> 4 egg yolks
> 1/2 teaspoon salt
> 1 tablespoon lemon juice
> 1 teaspoon prepared Dijon-style mustard
> freshly ground pepper to taste
> 1/2 teaspoon sugar
> 3/4 cup safflower or other vegetable oil
> 1/4 cup reduced cooking juices from chicken
> 1 head soft-leafed lettuce such as red leaf or Bibb
> small bunch red or green seedless grapes
> 1/2 a ripe cantaloupe

To Prepare the Chicken

1. Place the chicken breasts, skin side down, in a skillet just large enough to hold them.
2. In a food processor, combine the scallions, ginger, and broth. Pour the mixture over the chicken and add just enough cold water to cover. Cover the pan and turn heat to high. When a boil is reached, immediately reduce to a simmer for 15 minutes.
3. Remove the chicken from pan, cool under running water. Turn the heat to high under cooking liquid and boil until reduced to

about 1/4 cup. Strain if there are large pieces of scallion or ginger visible.
4. Discard the chicken skin, lift the meat from bones in one piece, and set chicken aside while preparing the sauce.

To Prepare the Sauce

1. Combine the egg yolks and salt in a food processor or blender. Process for 1 minute.
2. Add the lemon juice, mustard, pepper, and sugar. Process 30 seconds more.
3. A few drops at a time, dribble in the oil. After 1/4 cup has been incorporated, the oil may be added in a thin stream instead of drops.
4. Dribble in the hot reduced chicken-cooking juices from Step 3. The sauce will thicken on standing.
5. Place a bed of lettuce on each plate. Cut the chicken on the diagonal in thin strips. Arrange the strips in spoke fashion on the lettuce. Place a small cluster of grapes in the center, and two half-moons of cantaloupe at either side. Drizzle the sauce over chicken and pass the remaining sauce at the table.

Yield: 4 servings
Calories per serving: 460
Protein per serving: 27g

Fat per serving: 32g
Carbohydrates per serving: 17g
Sodium per serving: 280mg

Chicken Saute with Cepes

❖

This recipe is ideal for today's overscheduled cook who's bored with routine meals. In just 15 minutes you can turn out a moist chicken breast with a sauce perked by raspberry vinegar and cepes. Serve it with Pea and Leek Puree (page 253) and a simple rice studded with a handful of golden raisins.

> ¾ cup chicken broth
> 1 ounce dried cepes (or porcini), available at
>   specialty food shops
> ½ teaspoon kosher salt
> 4 boneless chicken breasts, with skin
> 3 tablespoons raspberry or red wine vinegar
> 1 clove garlic, minced
> 12 mushrooms, sliced
> 1 tablespoon plus 1 teaspoon butter
> 1 tablespoon minced fresh parsley (optional)

1. Bring the broth to a boil. Break the cepes up in your fingers, add them to the hot broth, cover, and steep 20 minutes. Set aside.
2. Sprinkle a 10-inch nonstick skillet with the salt. Place on high heat. When hot, add the chicken, skin side down. Cover and saute 3 minutes, reducing heat if needed to avoid burning. Turn the chicken, cover, and continue to saute 3 minutes more, again reducing heat if needed. When chicken is firm to the touch, place it on a serving platter in a 150-degree oven while completing the sauce.
3. Remove the skillet from heat. Deglaze it with vinegar. Return the skillet to heat when sizzling stops, boil until the vinegar is reduced to a film on the bottom of skillet.
4. Wet a coffee filter (or a piece of cheesecloth or heavy paper towel), and suspend it in a wide-mouthed jar or measuring cup.

Pour the mushroom-broth liquid through, removing cepes with a slotted spoon.

5. Pour the strained mushroom liquid into the vinegar skillet. Add garlic, mushrooms, and cepes. Boil until the liquid is reduced to about 1/3 cup.

6. Reduce heat to medium-low. Whisk in the butter, pour sauce over chicken, and sprinkle with parsley if desired.

Yield: 4 servings
Calories per serving: 250
Protein per serving: 24g

Fat per serving: 14g
Carbohydrates per serving: 9g
Sodium per serving: 340mg

Chicken Fricassee
with Leeks and Carrots

❖

This economical meal makes the most of some rather simple ingredients. Boned chicken thighs (you may use the whole leg for larger servings) are wrapped around a filling of leeks and carrots, then browned, braised, and served up in a rich sauce that promises everything but high calories. True to its word, this dish pleases children and parents alike. The chicken thighs may be made ahead and kept chilled for up to 6 hours before cooking. You also may freeze them. This dish is also good reheated.

> 8 or 9 chicken thighs (about 2 1/2 pounds)
> 1/4 teaspoon salt
> freshly ground pepper to taste
> 1 cup chicken broth
> 1 cup dry red wine

1 sprig fresh tarragon or 1 teaspoon dried tarragon
1 bay leaf
1 clove garlic, speared on a toothpick
a few grindings fresh pepper
4 leeks, white part only
2 carrots, scrubbed and julienned
3 tablespoons chicken broth
1 teaspoon butter
1 teaspoon vegetable oil
1 teaspoon cornstarch
1 tablespoon chicken broth or wine
8 to 10 washed and dried fresh spinach leaves, stems
and spines removed

1. Bone the chicken thighs by slicing through the meat on the inner thigh to the bone and scraping the flesh free working from the top of the thigh down to the leg joint. When one end of the bone is free from flesh, pull bone away, and cut remaining knuckle free. Be careful not to cut through to the skin. Be sure all cartilage is removed. Reserve bones.

2. Place chicken between sheets of wax paper, flesh side up, and flatten it slightly with a cleaver or heavy flat-bottomed skillet. Season chicken with salt and pepper. Set aside.

3. Spray a 12-inch nonstick skillet with cooking spray. Add the bones, cover, and brown for 5 minutes over high heat. When browned, add broth, wine, tarragon, bay leaf, garlic, and pepper. Cover, and simmer while continuing with recipe.

4. Slice the white part of the leek on the diagonal and rinse thoroughly.

5. "Saute" the leeks and carrots in the 3 tablespoons broth over medium-high heat in a 10-inch skillet, covered, until leeks are soft, about 5 minutes, or until all the liquid is evaporated. Remove from the heat and cool slightly.

6. Place about 2 tablespoons of leeks and carrots on center of each chicken thigh, on the flesh side. Roll loosely and secure with butcher's twine as you would tie a package. Reserve any remain-

ing vegetables for the next step.

7. To brown the chicken, spray a 10-inch or 12-inch nonstick skillet with cooking spray. Heat the butter and oil in the skillet until bubbly. Brown the chicken pieces, a few at a time, so they don't touch. Remove them to the simmering broth-wine when browned. Add any remaining carrots and leeks, cover, and simmer over medium heat for about 35 minutes.

8. Remove the chicken to a heated platter. Snip and discard strings. Dissolve the cornstarch in the remaining broth. Remove and discard the bones, bay leaf, and garlic from cooking broth. Whisk in the dissolved cornstarch and stir until thickened over medium heat.

9. Make a stack of the spinach leaves. Roll them tightly. Slice them crosswise into thin strips (known as chiffonade). (See page 201.) Add the spinach to the sauce over high heat. Stir for 30 seconds or just until wilted. Pour the sauce around chicken.

Yield: 4 servings
Calories per serving: 330
Protein per serving: 38g

Fat per serving: 14g
Carbohydrates per serving: 11g
Sodium per serving: 280mg

Parchment Chicken with Tomato Vinaigrette

❖

Oven poaching a chicken breast in oodles of sweet butter is neat, simple, and fattening. Neat and simple is nice, but fattening is as welcome as the taxman. Here the French technique of oven poaching is adapted, omitting the butter and encasing the poultry in parchment paper, which seals in the natural juices of the bird and anything else you might add, such as the tangy Tomato Vinaigrette used here. Or the chicken may be oven poached in its packet and lathered with a sauce after the fact. This Tomato Vinaigrette is one with panache. The feather in its cap is a dash of vinegar—just the right touch for a moist and juicy chicken breast. Because the sauce is actually better the second day, make some ahead; it will keep under refrigeration for about a week. The Hollandaise, the Béarnaise, the Basil-Walnut Sauce, all in Chapter 2, or the Lemon Caper Sauce (page 142) also would be appropriate.

For the Chicken

1 boneless, skinless chicken breast
1/8 teaspoon salt
freshly ground pepper to taste
2 tablespoons Tomato Vinaigrette, recipe follows
2 or 3 mushrooms, sliced
parchment paper, available in specialty food shops

To Prepare the Chicken

1. Preheat oven to 425 degrees. Trim the breast of fat and gristle. Place on a square of parchment paper (see page 209 for instructions on wrapping food in parchment paper hearts if preferred). Sprinkle the chicken with salt and pepper, spoon on the Tomato Vinaigrette, and place mushrooms on top. Fold the paper around the chicken as you would for a sandwich. Place on a baking sheet in the preheated 425-degree oven. Cook for 12–15 minutes.
2. To serve, open and discard the paper and spoon juices over chicken.

Tomato Vinaigrette

A wonderfully versatile sauce, Tomato Vinaigrette may be a thick but thinning hot or cold soup, tossed with marinated chilled zucchini as a salad, and used as a braising sauce for veal chops or grilled chicken. It is best, though, made with tomatoes plump with the sun, rather than those ripened by ethylene gas.

> 1 1/2 pounds tomatoes (2–3 large), quartered
> 1 tomato, blanched, peeled, seeded, and chopped
> 2 teaspoons olive oil
> 1 tablespoon raspberry or red wine vinegar
> 4–6 fresh or oil-cured basil leaves or 1 teaspoon
>   dried basil
> 1 tablespoon minced fresh parsley
> 1 teaspoon sugar
> 1/2 teaspoon salt
> 3–4 drops hot pepper sauce

1. Quarter the tomatoes, place in a heavy-bottomed saucepan, cover, and bring to a boil over medium heat. Simmer, uncovered, 45–50 minutes or until somewhat reduced.
2. Puree the tomatoes in a food processor, blender, or food mill. Strain the tomatoes into a bowl to remove the seeds and skin.
3. Add the remaining tomato to the bowl along with the oil, vinegar, basil, parsley, sugar, salt, and pepper sauce. Stir to combine.

Yield of Chicken: 1 serving
Calories per serving: 140
Protein per serving: 25g
Fat per serving: 2g
Carbohydrates per serving: 5g
Sodium per serving: 280mg

Yield of Vinaigrette: 1 3/4 cups
Calories per tablespoon: 10
Protein per tablespoon: trace
Fat per tablespoon: trace
Carbohydrates per tablespoon: 2g
Sodium per tablespoon: 40mg

Simply Roasted Chicken

❖

Among my favorites is this recipe for roasted chicken with its simple sauce. It may be a bit more elaborate than the standard with the prebrowning of the bird and vegetables, but I think you'll find the added goodness worth the effort. A degreaser, a measuring cup with the spout coming off the bottom, is a useful gadget for defatting the pan juices. It is available at most cooking supply stores. Grapeseed oil, available at specialty food shops, is recommended because it smokes at a much higher temperature than other oils. The calorie count will be less than what is listed below if you are careful to drain away all fat.

a 3-pound chicken
1/2 teaspoon salt
freshly ground pepper to taste
1 tablespoon oil (grapeseed recommended), or other
   vegetable oil
1 carrot, diced
2 small onions, diced
a sprig fresh tarragon or 1 teaspoon dried tarragon
3/4 cup chicken broth
1/4 cup dry sherry or red or white wine
1 tablespoon butter, at room temperature

1. Dry the chicken, salt and pepper the cavity. Truss the chicken if desired, as illustrated.
2. Heat the oil in a Dutch oven. Brown the chicken on all sides, moderating the heat, because too high a temperature will cause the skin to tear. Turn the chicken with wooden spoons to avoid tearing skin.
3. Remove the browned chicken from the Dutch oven. Brown the carrot and onions in the same fat. Remove the vegetables and pat them free of fat with paper towels.

HOW TO TRUSS A CHICKEN

1. Fold a three- or four-foot length of butcher's twine in half, then lay the mid-section over the knee joints of the whole chicken.

2. "Lasso" the leg ends by pulling the twine up, then lay the twine in the hollow between the leg and the breast.

3. Flip the chicken over and cross the twine. Pull the wings snug to the body by laying the twine over them.

4. Flip the chicken back over so the breast side is up. Knot the twine and cut off the excess.

4. Preheat oven to 350 degrees.
5. Strew the vegetables over the bottom of a baking dish. You may use the same Dutch oven, wiped free of fat. Add the tarragon and broth. Place a rack on top of the vegetables and place the chicken, back side up, on the rack. Place the chicken in the preheated 350-degree oven.
6. Baste the chicken about every half hour. Turn it over so the breast side is up after 30 minutes. The 3-pound chicken will be done in 70-80 minutes (a 4-pound chicken in 75-90 minutes). It is done when the juices run clear. To test, hold the chicken vertically by upending it on a spoon held in the cavity. The first drops will be bloody, but if done the final drops will be clear. Alternately, you may prick the thigh to see if the juices run clear. Keep chicken warm, covered on a platter, while making the sauce.
7. Strain the cooking juices into a degreaser or glass measuring cup, pressing the vegetables with the back of a wooden spoon to extract the juices. Let the juices rest for 1 minute, allowing the fat to rise to the top. If using a degreaser, pour the juices into a 1-quart saucepan, or extract the fat-free juice from the bottom of the measuring cup with a bulb baster. Add the sherry and boil until reduced to $2/3$ cup. Remove from heat. Whisk in butter, pour some of the sauce over the carved chicken, and pass the remainder at the table.

Yield: 4 servings
Calories per serving: 513
Protein per serving: 54g

Fat per serving: 27g
Carbohydrates per serving: 12g
Sodium per serving: 360mg

Stir-Fried Chicken and Vegetables

❖

The signature of the world's oldest cuisine, the stir-fry, may be tailored to fit the modern principles of good nutrition perfectly. This recipe is rich in carbohydrates, while frugal with both proteins and fats. Just 10–12 ounces of meat or poultry with the bountiful use of vegetables and rice easily feeds 4. Stir-frys are also quick to cook once the chopping and slicing are accomplished, a task that can often be done as much as 5 hours in advance. This stir-fry is made spicy with hot red pepper and chili paste—both may be omitted if a milder dish is preferred. All this dish needs is a side of rice or Chinese noodles to complete the meal. The Oriental ingredients are available at specialty or Chinese food shops.

2 tablespoons soy sauce (light soy recommended)
1 tablespoon rice wine or semisweet sherry
1 tablespoon rice wine vinegar (white wine vinegar
    may be substituted)
1 teaspoon sesame oil
2 tablespoons chicken broth
2 teaspoons sugar
1 clove garlic, minced
1 stalk green onion, minced
a 1-inch piece of ginger root, peeled and minced
3/4 pound skinless, boneless breast of chicken
1 tablespoon vegetable or peanut oil
1/2 red bell pepper, sliced
1/2 green bell pepper, sliced
8 ounces fresh mushrooms, sliced
1 cup Chinese cabbage, sliced
1 carrot, blanched 5 minutes and julienned

4 ounces snow peas, strings removed
½–1 teaspoon minced hot chili pepper (optional)
½–1 teaspoon chili paste with garlic (optional)
2 teaspoons cornstarch
⅓ cup chicken broth

1. Combine the soy sauce, wine, vinegar, sesame oil, broth, sugar, garlic, onion, and ginger in a measuring cup. Mix well. Pour it into a plastic bag.
2. Cut the chicken into thin strips, marinate in the above soy mixture for 2 hours in the refrigerator or 20 minutes at room temperature.
3. Heat the oil in a wok or heavy 10-inch skillet until very hot. Lift the chicken from the soy marinade a few pieces at a time (reserving the marinade for Step 7), stir-fry in hot oil until flesh firms and becomes opaque, about 4 minutes.
4. Remove the chicken with a slotted spoon or chopsticks and drain on paper towels. Continue stir-frying until all the chicken is cooked.
5. Add the peppers and mushrooms to wok. Add a bit of chicken broth or oil if necessary. Stir-fry for 1 minute. Add the Chinese cabbage, stir-fry another minute. Add the carrots and snow peas, stir-fry about 1 minute more or until pea pods are done.
6. Stir in the chili pepper and paste if desired.
7. Moisten the cornstarch in the chicken broth, combine with the reserved marinade from Step 3. Add to the vegetables along with the cooked chicken. Stir until thickened over high heat. Serve with boiled rice or noodles.

Yield: 4 servings
Calories per serving: 205
Protein per serving: 24g

Fat per serving: 6g
Carbohydrates per serving: 14g
Sodium per serving: 360g

Poached Chicken Breast
with Mustard Hollandaise

❖

Reheating a traditional Hollandaise is a bit like space-walking: There's little room for error. You won't find yourself in orbit, though, with the *Gourmet Light* version; it may be made early in the day and reheated over low heat. Or you may choose to keep it warm in a bowl set atop an electric warming tray. Serve this Chicken Breast with Hollandaise with the Pea and Leek Puree (page 253) and some broccoli or a rice pilaf.

1 *recipe Hollandaise, page 21*
2 *tablespoons stone-ground mustard, or to taste*
1 *scallion or half a small onion, minced*
1 *sprig fresh tarragon or ½ teaspoon dried tarragon*
1 *cup water*
4 *chicken breasts, with skin and bones*
juice of half a lemon
minced fresh parsley or watercress (optional)

1. Make the *Gourmet Light* Hollandaise. Stir in the mustard and set aside.
2. In a food processor or blender combine the scallion, tarragon, and water. Blend.
3. Pour into a skillet just large enough to hold the chicken. Add chicken, skin side down. Add the lemon juice. Add water to cover. Bring to a boil, immediately reduce to a simmer. Cover and cook for 8–9 minutes or until the chicken flesh feels firm when poked with a finger.
4. Remove the chicken with a slotted spoon (cooking liquid may be reserved for making stock). Cool briefly under running water.
5. Discard the skin. Lift the chicken from bones in one piece, place

on warmed plates. Spoon Hollandaise over and garnish with the
parsley or watercress if desired.

Yield: 4 servings
Calories per serving: 255
Protein per serving: 28g

Fat per serving: 14g
Carbohydrates per serving: 4g
Sodium per serving: 170mg

Scotch Chicken

❖

Chicken, cream, and mushrooms make for a tempting trilogy often
found in French cooking. What a pity the cream brings out the calorie-conscious cringes. Fortunately, there's crème blanc, the *Gourmet
Light* replacement for overfatted dairy products. The sauce base must
be cooled a full minute as directed to avoid a curdled mess. Vary this
simple supper with the addition of some dried mushrooms such as
cepes or chanterelles.

> *2 boneless chicken breasts, skin on*
> *⅛ teaspoon salt*
> *freshly ground pepper to taste*
> *2 tablespoons Scotch*
> *½ cup chicken broth*
> *4 ounces mushrooms, sliced*
> *1 tablespoon crème blanc, page 37*
> *a few gratings fresh nutmeg*

1. Place the chicken, skin side down, in a 10-inch nonstick skillet.
   Season chicken with salt and pepper. Sear it, covered, over high
   heat 3 minutes. Turn the chicken over, reduce heat to medium,
   cover, and continue cooking another 3–4 minutes.

2. Remove the chicken from skillet to plate. Off the heat, deglaze the skillet with the Scotch. When the liquor quiets down, return to high heat, stirring constantly with a wooden spoon to loosen the particles stuck to pan bottom. Reduce the liquid until it's just a film.
3. Add the broth and mushrooms to the skillet, cover, and boil, stirring occasionally until it's reduced to about 3 tablespoons liquid.
4. Remove the skillet from heat, stir, and cool about 1 minute. Stir in crème blanc, season with nutmeg, and pour it over the chicken.

Yield: 2 servings
Calories per serving: 220
Protein per serving: 25g

Fat per serving: 10g
Carbohydrates per serving: 10g
Sodium per serving: 230mg

Herbed Chicken Breasts

❖

This recipe calls for stuffing the breast with an herbed rice mixture. Bag the proverbial two birds with one stone by doubling the stuffing portion and serving it as a side dish. All you need then to complete the meal is a salad or possibly some broccoli with Reduced-Calorie Hollandaise, which will also complement the chicken. Although this needs no sauce you might like to nap it with the Tomato Vinaigrette, page 165; the Lemon Caper Sauce, page 142, or the Reduced-Calorie Béarnaise, page 24.

½ small green pepper, diced
½ small onion, diced
4 tablespoons chicken broth
½ cup cooked white or brown rice

5–6 mushrooms, sliced
5 leaves fresh or oil-cured basil, snipped, or 1 tea-
   spoon dried basil
½ teaspoon salt
freshly ground pepper to taste
4 boneless chicken breasts with skin

1. "Saute" the green pepper and onion in 3 tablespoons broth (reserving 1 tablespoon for Step 3), covered, in an 8-inch skillet until limp.
2. Combine the pepper and onion with the rice.
3. "Saute" the mushrooms in the same skillet with the remaining tablespoon broth until limp. Add it to the rice-pepper mixture.
4. Stir basil, ¼ teaspoon salt, and pepper into the rice mixture.
5. Cut a pocket in the chicken breast by pressing down on the skin side with one hand while slicing parallel with the counter top almost, but not all the way, to the back of the breast. Open the breast (like a book) and stuff it with a tablespoon of the rice-pepper mixture. Lay the meat back over stuffing, it will "glue" together while cooking. Lift a chicken breast onto a baking dish, skin side up. Repeat with the remaining chicken breasts. Sprinkle with the remaining salt. Refrigerate, if desired, up to 6 hours, until ready to cook.
6. Roast the chicken breasts in a preheated 350-degree oven for 20 minutes. Broil about 5 minutes to brown skin.

Yield: 4 servings
Calories per serving: 215
Protein per serving: 22g

Fat per serving: 9g
Carbohydrates per serving: 9g
Sodium per serving: 430mg

Chicken Baked in a
Salt Crust

❖

Meats and poultry roasted in a crust of salt are amazingly succulent, flavorful, and juicy. The moistened salt forms a shell, locking in moisture that would otherwise evaporate. Happily, the salt doesn't penetrate the food either. For this family meal, a broiler is stuffed with rice seasoned with a garlic puree (made mild by a long simmer), trussed to keep the legs from breaking through the salt crust, then roasted. Carve the bird and serve on a platter with the natural juices retrieved from the carving board. The rice stuffing may be prepared a day ahead or early in the day, the chicken stuffed and packed in salt just before roasting. Although the bird does take 2 hours to cook, it is not lengthy to prepare for roasting and all you need to complete the meal is a green vegetable or salad.

> 1   2- or 3-pound broiler chicken
> 1   whole head garlic, cloves separated
> 2½ cups cooked rice
> 1   small tomato, diced
> 4–5 fresh or oil-cured basil leaves (see page 64) or
>   1 teaspoon dried basil
> ½   teaspoon salt
> freshly ground pepper to taste
> 10 cups kosher salt
> 1¾ cups water

1. Prepare the bird for roasting by cutting off the excess fat at the cavity opening. Cut off the wing tips at the joint, add them to your bone collection for making stock, or discard. Set aside the bird while preparing the stuffing.
2. Separate but don't peel the garlic cloves. Bring a 1-quart saucepan

¾ full of water to a boil. Boil the garlic cloves 1 minute, lift with a slotted spoon to a sieve, and cool under running water. Slip skins off. Return peeled cloves to boiling water and simmer 30 minutes. Drain, reserving 2–3 tablespoons cooking water. Puree the garlic in a food processor, adding reserved cooking water as needed, or force through a fine mesh sieve with a wooden spoon.

3. Combine the cooked rice, garlic puree, tomato, basil, salt, and pepper. Adjust seasoning if necessary.

4. Stuff the cavity of the chicken with the rice mixture, don't pack too tightly; any remaining rice may be heated in a small casserole the last 20 minutes of roasting. To truss the bird, which will keep the legs from breaking through the salt crust during baking, cut a piece of butcher's twine a yard long. Place the chicken so the cavity opening faces you. Fold the twine in half, drape midsection over drumsticks so the ends point to floor. Grasp twine 1 inch below the drumsticks on both the left and right sides, lift and twist twine so each drumstick is "lassoed" and the twine now points upward. Laying twine in the crease formed between the drumsticks and the breast, flip chicken so back is up and string is still held. Cross the twine in back, flip the chicken over again so breast side is up, and tie the string. (See illustration, page 169.) Or use any other trussing technique. Pack any stuffing that might have come loose back into cavity.

5. Preheat oven to 475 degrees.

6. Line a roasting pan big enough for the chicken with a sheet of aluminum foil which extends 10 inches over short sides.

7. Moisten the salt with some of the water, don't use all the water at once. Paste should be just wet enough to hold together when packed with your hands. Place about a third of the paste on the foil-lined roasting pan. Place the chicken on top. Pack the remaining salt all around the bird, covering any exposed spots. Pull the foil up snug to the bird, use to help pack down the salt. Place in the lower third of a preheated 475-degree oven for 2 hours.

8. To serve, peel back the foil. Break and discard the top salt crust. Lift the chicken from roasting pan by the trussing string to a cutting

board or plate, one that will trap the juices. Snip and discard string. Brush away any clinging salt. Pull and discard skin from bird. To carve, cut off legs first, cut in half at the joint. Cut off breast meat. Flip bird, remove skin, cut back in half. Scoop stuffing on to serving platter. Dribble juices from cutting board on to chicken.

Yield: 4 servings
Calories per serving: 275
Protein per serving: 28g

Fat per serving: 2g
Carbohydrates per serving: 33g
Sodium per serving: 820mg

Turkey Cutlet with Cranberried Apple Sauce

❖

Turkey cutlets—thin slices from the breast—make a quick and satisfying meal not unlike veal. If cutlets aren't available in your market, they may be cut from a whole turkey breast and the remainder of the breast may be roasted or smoked (page 182). Purchase cranberries in the fall and freeze them whole in the plastic bag for up to a year, scooping out just what you need for this sauce, which may be made ahead and reheated.

 ½ cup chicken broth
 ½ cup uncooked cranberries
 2 medium apples, McIntosh recommended, peeled, cored, and chopped
 ⅓ cup flour
 ½ teaspoon salt
 freshly ground pepper to taste

1 1/4 pounds turkey cutlets
1 teaspoon vegetable oil
1 teaspoon butter
4 tablespoons dry sherry
6 tablespoons chicken broth
1/2 cup of the cranberry-apple sauce
thin orange slices for garnish (optional)

1. In a 1-quart saucepan, combine the broth, cranberries, and apples. Bring to a boil, reduce heat, and simmer 10 minutes. Puree in a food processor, food mill, or blender. Set this cranberry-apple sauce aside.
2. Season the flour with the salt and pepper. Dredge the cutlets in the flour.
3. Spray a 12-inch nonstick skillet with cooking spray. Add the oil and butter, heat until foamy. Add the floured cutlets, sear over high heat 1 minute. Reduce heat, cook 1 minute more, turn and repeat the procedure. Meat is done when it feels firm to the touch. Remove to a heated platter while completing the sauce.
4. Deglaze the skillet with sherry, stirring over high heat with a wooden spoon to loosen the coagulated proteins. When reduced to a syrupy glaze, add the broth, reduce it until 1/4 cup remains. Stir in 1/2 cup or to taste of the cranberry-apple sauce. Remaining cranberry-apple sauce may be kept in the refrigerator for a little more than a week. Serve the sauce over turkey cutlets. Garnish the platter with orange slices if desired.

Yield: 4 servings
Calories per serving: 310
Protein per serving: 36g

Fat per serving: 12g
Carbohydrates per serving: 14g
Sodium per serving: 360mg

Chinese Tea-Smoked Turkey

❖

Tea smoking is a lovely way to impart smoked flavor to fish or poultry without a major investment of time or expensive equipment. You need a wok or any pan with a tight cover such as an electric skillet, and Chinese black tea. While the instructions are written for a boned turkey, you may use a turkey breast or even a chicken. Start the recipe a day before serving, and if using a frozen turkey or breast, 2 days before. The smoked turkey may be served simply sliced warm or at room temperature or used in other recipes such as a turkey salad. It is wonderful sliced for the buffet table accompanied with small pumpkin biscuits and pots of herbed jellies.

> 1   *4-pound boned turkey or turkey breast*
> 1   *tablespoon whole black peppercorns*
> 3   *tablespoons kosher salt*
> 2   *tablespoons Chinese black tea or contents of 4*
>   *Chinese tea bags (available at specialty food*
>   *shops)*
> 2   *tablespoons uncooked rice*
> 2   *tablespoons brown sugar*

1. Thaw the turkey if frozen and wipe it dry.
2. Combine the peppercorns and salt in a small skillet and saute over medium-high heat until the mixture is fragrant, about 2–3 minutes. Let the mixture cool and rub it into the turkey breast. Wrap the turkey in aluminum foil and refrigerate overnight.
3. Rinse the turkey breast free of peppercorn-salt mixture. Steam the breast in a steamer over 3 inches of water for 40–50 minutes. Remove the breast from steamer, let it stand at room temperature (or refrigerate overnight) until cool (about 2 to 3 hours); pat thoroughly dry. This step is important for if the meat is not cool and continues to "sweat," the moisture will prevent it from browning in the smoking step.

4. Line a wok or other deep pot that has a tight-fitting lid with a double thickness of aluminum foil. Combine the tea, rice, and sugar. Spread them over the foil. Set a rack in the pot. Place the breast on rack, skin side up. Cover and place over medium heat until the tea leaves crackle or wisps of smoke escape. Smoke the turkey for 10 minutes. Remove the lid. If the meat is not browned, cover and smoke another 5 minutes. Turkey is ready to serve or use in any turkey recipe.

Yield: 12 servings
Calories per serving: 180
Protein per serving: 17g

Fat per serving: 12g
Carbohydrates per serving: 0
Sodium per serving: 30 + mg

❖ SMOKED FOODS ❖

Smoking foods, used as a preservation technique in a time without refrigeration, has enjoyed a revival of late. Many restaurants feature smoked foods or garnish dishes with smoked tidbits. Smoked turkey breasts, hams, fishes, and shellfish are available by mail from many a modern smokehouse. Those on sodium-restricted diets should know that most smoked foods are treated heavily with salt. Some companies will supply salt-free smoked foods.

Grilled Duck Zinfandel

❖

There are a few foods that by their very presence mark a meal an occasion. Duck is one, but it does have two drawbacks: It is bony and it is fatty. This recipe compensates for both. The breast meat and legs are detached from the bird and cooked separately so the former comes to the table pink and tender while the legs, which would be too chewy if rare, are roasted to a crispy succulence. The sauce is based on a stock made from the remaining duck carcass, enriched with Zinfandel wine and a hint of light cream. It may be made the day before the event or started early and completed hours before serving. Serve both the breast and leg if the rest of the menu is small, serve only the breast (1 duck serves 2) meat if the menu is large. The breast may be grilled or roasted, the legs are roasted only.

2 whole ducks
½ teaspoon salt
freshly ground pepper to taste
2 carrots, scrubbed and diced
1 medium onion, diced
2 ribs celery, diced
1 cup Zinfandel or other red wine
2½ cups chicken broth or 1½ cans (13¾ ounces)
      chicken broth
1 quart plus 1 cup cold water
1 tablespoon fresh thyme or 1 teaspoon dried thyme
1 clove garlic, split in half, no need to peel
6–8 parsley stems
1 cup additional Zinfandel wine
2 tablespoons light cream

8 hours or up to 24 hours before dinner

1. Remove any large flaps of fat from the duck. To bone the duck: Slice off the wings and set them aside. Pull the leg from the body, slice off at the ball joint, and set it aside. Repeat with the other leg. The legs may be frozen for another use if you don't wish to use them in this recipe. Cut along the top ridge of the breastbone, freeing the breast meat by scraping down the rib cage with a knife angled toward the bones. Cut around the wishbone. Repeat on the other side. Score the skin of breast and leg, cutting through the skin but not the meat. Lightly salt and pepper the pieces. Refrigerate until 1 hour before cooking time.

2. With a cleaver or other heavy knife, chop the remaining carcass into quarters and the wings in half. Place the duck bones and wings in a heavy-bottomed skillet with a cover. Brown the bones over high heat, covered, about 25 minutes. There should be enough fat on the wings to brown the bones, but if they are sticking add a small piece of discarded fat from Step 1. When browned, remove to a stockpot or large (at least 4-quart) saucepan.

3. Without cleaning the skillet, brown the carrots, onion, and celery. Again, add a bit of fat if needed. When browned, about 10–12 minutes, remove to the stockpot.

4. Deglaze the skillet with the wine, stirring with a wooden spoon to loosen coagulated proteins. When reduced by half, add the liquid to the stockpot.

5. Add the broth, water, thyme, garlic, and parsley to the stockpot.

6. Bring to a boil, scrape any scum that rises to the surface with a slotted spoon. Reduce the heat and simmer, covered, 1 1/2 hours.

7. Strain (if a clearer sauce is desired strain through a moistened coffee filter or a piece of cheesecloth), discard bones and vegetables, and chill at least 4 hours so the fat will solidify for easy removal. (Recipe may be done 24 hours ahead to this point.)

8. As much as 8 hours before dinner but at least 1 hour before, remove the sauce base from the refrigerator and scrape off bits of floating, hardened fat. Return the sauce base to high heat and boil down to 2 cups, about 45 minutes.

9. Add remaining wine and boil down to ½ to ¾ cup, about 15–20 minutes. Be careful, the sauce evaporates very rapidly at the end and scorches easily if allowed to boil below ½ cup. Remove the sauce from heat and stir in the cream. Taste for seasoning. Sauce may be reheated, even boiled.

To Cook the Duck

1. Preheat the oven to 425 degrees or turn on the grill. If serving the legs, place them, skin side down, in a nonstick skillet over high heat. Sear until lightly browned, about 3–4 minutes on each side. Place in a roasting dish and roast 30 minutes. Cut in half at the joint to serve.
2. To grill the breasts, place them, skin side down, on the grill. When browned, flip them and brown the underside. Turn and finish cooking on the skin side. The meat is done when firm but still slightly soft. Times vary radically from grill to grill, an indoor grill may take as long as 10–14 minutes to cook the breast, while a hotter outdoor grill might take only 6–8 minutes. The meat continues to cook when removed from the grill, so undercook slightly.
3. To roast the breasts, place them skin side up, on the rack of a broiler pan. Roast 15 minutes in a 350-degree oven.

To Serve

1. The breasts may be skinned or not as you please. Slice the long way, with a knife slanted so the strips of meat are thin, ½ inch wide and the length of the breast. Film the entire plate bottom with warm Zinfandel sauce. Arrange the duck strips in a fan, with base at center of the plate. Place the leg pieces at base of the fan. Serve with wild rice. Pass extra sauce at table. The plate is pretty garnished with a bit of red—sauteed cherry tomatoes or strips of roasted red pepper tossed with pea pods.

Yield of duck breasts: 4 servings
Calories per serving: 385
Protein per serving: 25g

Fat per serving: 25g
Carbohydrates per serving: 14g
Sodium per serving: 590mg

Grilled Quail

❖

If quail are difficult to come by, try this recipe with game hens or squab. These would be delicious served on a bed of whole wheat pasta or Chinese noodles and a tossed salad.

> ⅔ cup chicken broth
> ½ cup red wine vinegar
> 2 tablespoons extra-virgin olive oil
> 1 tablespoon freshly snipped tarragon or 1 teaspoon
>   dried tarragon
> 1 clove garlic, split and minced
> freshly ground pepper to taste
> 4 quail
> ⅓ cup flour
> ½ teaspoon salt
> 1 egg yolk

1. In a glass or other nonaluminum bowl, combine the broth, vinegar, oil, tarragon, garlic, and pepper. Cut the birds in half the long way, flatten them with the heel of your hand. Marinate the birds in the herbed broth for 4–6 hours.
2. Remove the birds from the marinade. Pat dry on paper towels. Combine flour and salt in a bag. Add birds, shake.
3. Set the marinade in a 1-quart saucepan and boil over high heat until reduced to ⅔ cup. Beat the egg yolk in a cup. Dribble 2 tablespoons hot marinade into the yolk while stirring with a fork. Pour yolk-marinade mixture back into the remaining marinade, stirring vigorously with a fork, over medium heat until thickened.
4. Place the birds on a grill, brush frequently with yolk-thickened marinade. Turn often. They will cook in about 25 minutes.

Yield: 4 servings
Calories per serving: 365
Protein per serving: 27g

Fat per serving: 23g
Carbohydrates per serving: 9g
Sodium per serving: 340mg

Chapter 8

FISH AND SHELLFISH

Fish and Shellfish

❖

"Food is meant to tempt as well as nourish and everything that lives in the sea is seductive." —Jean-Paul Aron

Fish is to the calorie-conscious gourmet what polish is to wood—a gleam on the palate. Few foods are as calorie economic or as nutritionally rich. Yet, fish varies in calorie count from variety to variety. So-called fat fish (tuna, salmon, trout, and pompano) with a higher percentage of natural oils, are higher in calories than lean fish (cod, flounder, and red snapper). But a fat fish may need less fats added to it during cooking to avoid drying out. All fish is high in protein and relatively low in fat. A 3½-ounce serving of flounder supplies 30 grams of protein (¾ the daily requirement for a 120-pound woman) and 8 grams of fat for a very reasonable 202 calories. A similar-size serving of beef rump supplies somewhat less protein (24 grams) and 3 times the amount of fat (27 grams) for 347 calories. All other things being equal, substituting fish for beef 2 nights a week for 12 weeks would save 3,500 calories—the energy that when unused our body transforms into a pound of fat.

Care must be taken in the purchase and storage of fish, perhaps more so than with any other food, or the delicate flavor suffers. Today, most of us purchase fish that is already dressed, eviscerated, and scaled, with the head, fins, and tail cut off. Unfortunately, this convenience erases some of the freshness indicators, making it impossible to know if the eyes were bright, clear, and bulging; if the scales were firmly affixed; and if the internal body walls were bright in color with no bones protruding. It really isn't practical to poke fillets, either, but if you were so minded you could judge the fish's freshness by its resiliency, for your fingerprint would not make a lasting impression on a truly fresh fillet. Given the lack of physical evidence, what is a buyer to do?

Your most important clue in shopping for fresh fish is the odor of the fish. A strong smell indicates age, which in turn means poor taste. Unfortunately, fish begins to deteriorate almost as soon as it leaves the water, unlike beef which actually improves with age. This deterioration may be slowed if the fish is kept at about 30 degrees, which does not freeze the flesh but seems to stabilize it. So look for fish sold on ice. There's no way of knowing, of course, if the fish was iced aboard ship or during any processing. But again, the odor of fish cannot be masked, so if the fish you're buying smells fishy, it's time to find a new supplier. Buying from a reputable store should erase fears of purchasing something second rate. A reputable store is one supplied daily, not twice a week—don't hesitate to ask when the product came in.

With the freshest possible fish at hand, the rest is up to the consumer. Just as at market, the fish should be put in a bowl of ice (protected in a plastic bag) in the refrigerator if held more than 4 hours before cooking. Very fresh fish, just 1 or 2 days out of the water, will keep this way with very little flavor loss for 3–4 days. Remember to replenish the ice and pour off the water.

Not all parts of the country can get fresh fish, some must use frozen. Properly prepared it can be quite good. Again, there should be no odor, the package should be intact, and the edges of the fish should not be freezer burned.

In most cases, fish cooks quickly. And if it's impeccably fresh, fish needs little adornment. It is one of the few foods that truly needs only "a little lemon juice" to be enjoyable. Following are recipes for more elaborate treatments, as well as instructions for your basic broiled fillet, because even the most ardent fish fan must yearn for something a little different now and again. I urge you to substitute your local varieties of fish in these recipes. Unlike beef or poultry, products which are largely uniform from Anaheim, California, to Bangor, Maine, fish types vary from coast to coast, and in between.

Shellfish, other than shrimp, may be even more regional than fish fillets. Bivalves, such as mussels and clams, should be alive when purchased and cooked. Frozen langoustine is a somewhat credible substitution for lobster. Having been spoiled by Nantucket's November scallops, I am admittedly biased, but many feed happily on the frozen Florida bay variety.

If you've never much cared for fish but are somewhat tempted by its high-nutrition/low-calorie ratio, I urge you to give it a try with the freshest catch money will buy. Good food with little fat, what better lure is there?

Coquilles St. Jacques

❖

These may be readied several hours before serving, then broiled until warmed through. Serve with a creamy risotto and green beans with tomato nuggets for a simply delicious meal.

1 cup dry white wine or vermouth
1 tablespoon lemon juice
1 shallot, minced
1 small clove garlic, minced
1 teaspoon fresh tarragon leaves or 1/2 teaspoon
      dried tarragon
1 1/4 pounds scallops
1 tablespoon sherry
1/2 cup crème blanc, page 37, made without milk
a few gratings fresh nutmeg
1 teaspoon butter
2 tablespoons dried bread crumbs
2 teaspoons grated Parmesan cheese
1 tablespoon minced fresh parsley (optional)

1. Bring the wine, lemon juice, shallot, garlic, and tarragon to a boil in a 10-inch skillet. Reduce heat, simmer 2–3 minutes.
2. Add the scallops, cover, and simmer over low to medium heat until scallops turn an opaque milky white, about 4 minutes. Remove the scallops with a slotted spoon to ovenproof baking shells or a quiche dish.
3. Boil the wine sauce over high heat, uncovered, until reduced to ½ cup. Stir in sherry. Remove from heat, cool 1 minute, stir in crème blanc, and season with nutmeg. Pour the sauce over the scallops.
4. Melt the butter in skillet. Saute the bread crumbs until lightly toasted. Sprinkle over scallops along with grated cheese and broil until bubbly. Garnish with parsley.

Note: If the recipe has been made ahead and chilled, warm in a 350-degree oven for 10 minutes before broiling.

Yield: 4 servings
Calories per serving: 215
Protein per serving: 36g

Fat per serving: 4g
Carbohydrates per serving: 8g
Sodium per serving: 468mg

❖   **THINKING THIN TIP**   ❖

If you eat very quickly and in large bites, eat with chopsticks. It will slow you down at least until you become proficient with them.

Seafood Crepes
in Champagne Sauce

❖

The components of this dish, the crepes and fish, may be readied ahead of time, and the whole assembled as much as 2 hours before serving. Any longer though and the crepes will be sloshed with champagne, though one supposes there are worse fates. Serve with asparagus or some other aristocratic vegetable (artichoke? snow peas?). A starter of Cream of Lettuce or Gingered Carrot Soup would set the right tone.

For the Crepes

1 egg, beaten
½ cup milk
¼ cup flour
pinch salt
1 tablespoon butter

For the Seafood

1¼ pounds assorted seafood, such as ½ pound
       white fish fillets with ¾ pound shrimp, any
       combination you like, cut into bite-size pieces
1 shallot, minced
5 ounces mushrooms, sliced
1 tablespoon lemon juice
½ teaspoon salt
freshly ground pepper to taste
1 cup champagne

For the Sauce

1 tablespoon butter, softened
2 tablespoons flour, instant blending recommended

1 1/4 cups to 1 1/2 cups champagne cooking juices
     from fish
2 tablespoons light cream
1 tablespoon sherry
a few gratings fresh nutmeg
1 tablespoon minced fresh parsley

To Prepare the Crepes

1. Beat the egg and milk together, add the flour sifted with the salt, stir just to combine. Chill 2 hours.
2. Melt 1/2 teaspoon of the butter in a nonstick 8-inch skillet until foamy. Ladle just enough batter into the pan to film bottom. Pour the excess batter back into bowl after bottom sets. Cook crepe over medium-high heat until browned on one side. Flip, cook on underside just to firm, slide onto a plate and continue cooking, adding butter to skillet as necessary and placing a sheet of wax paper between the crepes as they are slid from the pan. Crepes are now ready for use or may be chilled up to 8 hours or frozen until needed. The recipe makes six 8-inch crepes.

To Prepare the Seafood
(May be done as much as 6 hours ahead)

1. Preheat oven to 350 degrees. In a nonaluminum baking dish just large enough to hold the fish, place the fish, shallots, and mushrooms. Season with lemon juice, salt, and pepper. Pour in the champagne. Cover with aluminum foil or a buttered piece of parchment paper. Place in a preheated oven for 12–15 minutes or until fish is done.
2. Lift fish with a slotted spoon to a bowl. If the dish is to be served soon, keep warm on a warming tray. Pour the cooking juices into an 8-inch skillet.
3. Mash together the butter and flour in a cup. Slowly whisk the *beurre manie* (flour and butter) into the cooking juices over medium heat, until smooth and thick. Whisk in the cream. Season with sherry and nutmeg. Taste for salt and pepper. Fold 3/4 of the

sauce into the cooked fish. This may be refrigerated up to one hour before serving.

4. Divide the fish mixture among the crepes and roll loosely. Spray a baking dish, just large enough to hold the crepes, with cooking spray. Place the crepes, seam side down, in the dish. Pour the remaining sauce over top. Broil until bubbly and browned if ingredients are still warm or heat in a preheated 350-degree oven until warmed through, about 15 to 20 minutes, and then broil to brown top. Garnish with the parsley.

Yield: 4 servings
Calories per serving: 300
Protein per serving: 36g

Fat per serving: 10g
Carbohydrates per serving: 16g
Sodium per serving: 568mg

Fillets of Sole
with Basil and Tomato

❖

You may prepare the sauce for this dish early in the day, or even 24 hours ahead, and finish the cooking in about 10 minutes on top of the stove. A few steamed mussels or clams in their shells would be a welcome addition to the sauce; add them the last 5 minutes of cooking. Complete the meal with a simple tossed salad and parsleyed rice.

6 tomatoes or 3 tomatoes plus a 10½-ounce can
  tomatoes
1 shallot, minced
1 clove garlic, minced
½ teaspoon fresh thyme or ¼ teaspoon dried thyme
1 teaspoon fresh tarragon or ½ teaspoon dried
  tarragon

1/4 teaspoon fennel seed
6–8 leaves basil or oil-cured basil or 1 teaspoon
  dried basil
1 bay leaf
1 teaspoon sugar
1 teaspoon salt (1/2 teaspoon if using canned
  tomatoes)
freshly ground pepper to taste
grated zest of 1 orange
2 tablespoons orange juice (half an orange,
  squeezed)
2 pounds sole or other firm-fleshed white fish fillets
half a lemon
6 ounces mushrooms, sliced
1 tablespoon lemon juice
1/4 cup chicken broth or bottled clam juice
1 tablespoon minced fresh parsley

1. Blanch the tomatoes by bringing a 2 1/2-quart saucepan 3/4 full of water to a boil. Immerse tomatoes, 30 seconds for very ripe ones, up to 1 minute for others. Drain and cool under running water. Spear the tomatoes on a fork, peel, and discard skins. Pull tomatoes in half. Put a strainer over a bowl. Squeeze the tomatoes over the strainer to remove seeds. Press the seeds with the back of a wooden spoon so juice drips into bowl. Discard the seeds, add squeezed tomatoes to juice. (Canned tomatoes are generally peeled; seed them as described here if desired.)
2. In a 12-inch skillet, combine the tomatoes with their juice, shallot, garlic, thyme, tarragon, fennel, basil, bay leaf, sugar, salt, pepper, zest, and orange juice. Bring to a boil. Reduce to a simmer, cover, and cook for 40–50 minutes. (On occasion you may need to add 1/4 cup red wine or chicken stock if the tomatoes boil dry.)
3. Meanwhile, prepare the fish. Place the fillets on a sheet of wax paper or aluminum foil with what was the skin side facing up. Cover with another sheet of wax paper and pound lightly with a

cleaver or flat-bottomed heavy pan. Remove the paper, sprinkle fish with a few drops lemon juice. Roll the fillets loosely with what was the skin side facing inward. Set aside or refrigerate until ready to cook. (May be held, chilled, up to 6 hours.)

4. Remove and discard the bay leaf from the simmering sauce. Puree the tomato sauce in a food processor or food mill. Strain back into the skillet. Discard dry pulp that remains in strainer. (Straining may be omitted if you prefer the sauce chunky.) Set sauce aside.

5. "Saute" the mushrooms in the lemon juice and stock in an 8-inch skillet, about 5 minutes or until softened.

6. Add the mushrooms to the simmering sauce. Refrigerate, if desired, until you're ready to complete the dish.

7. Bring the sauce back to a simmer. Lay the rolled fish fillets on top. Spoon a bit of sauce over. Cover pan. Cook 5 minutes per inch thickness of fish, about 12–15 minutes in total, at medium heat. The sauce should just simmer, not boil. Spoon the hot sauce over fish once or twice. When done, remove fish with a slotted spoon to a platter. Cover with a towel.

8. Raise heat under tomato sauce to reduce the juices the fish gave off during cooking. When reduced to about 2 cups, pour the sauce over fish, garnish with the parsley.

Yield: 6 servings
Calories per serving: 158
Protein per serving: 29g

Fat per serving: 1g
Carbohydrates per serving: 8g
Sodium per serving: 455mg

Fish Fillets
with Sauce Rouge

❖

A perfect weekday dinner, these poached fish fillets with their accompanying sauce may be done in about half an hour. With the possible exception of a single red pepper (or you may use a tomato) and a perfectly fresh fillet of fish, it's likely you'll have most of the ingredients on hand. Don't attempt this without a food processor, however, unless you leave the vegetables chunky rather than pureed into the thick, flavorful sauce as it is done here. If you're serving 2, just use half the amount of fish, the extra sauce may be refrigerated for up to 5 days.

> 1 bottle (8 ounces) clam juice
> 1 small onion, diced
> 1 medium carrot, diced
> 1 rib celery, diced
> 1 red bell pepper, seeded and diced
> 3–4 leaves spinach (use sorrel if you have it)
> 1 tablespoon minced fresh parsley
> 1½ pounds thick white-fleshed fish fillets such as
>   haddock or halibut
> ½ teaspoon salt
> freshly ground pepper to taste
> ¾ cup dry or semi-dry white wine
> 2 tablespoons crème blanc, page 37

1. Heat the clam juice in a 10-inch skillet until just bubbling. Add the onion, carrot, and celery. Bring back to a boil, reduce heat to medium, and simmer 10–12 minutes, or until the vegetables are limp and the clam juice reduced by about half.
2. Add the red pepper, simmer 5 more minutes.

3. Stack spinach or sorrel leaves. Roll tightly in jellyroll fashion. Slice, crosswise, into thin strips (known as *chiffonade*). See the drawing on page 201. Add to the vegetables with the parsley, turn heat to high, and stir until greens are wilted, about 30 seconds.
4. Place the fish fillets on the vegetables. If the fish has a thin tail, turn under to even thickness. Season with salt and pepper. Add wine, cover, and bring to a boil. Reduce the heat, barely simmer 10-12 minutes or just until fish is opaque. Remove the fish to a warmed serving platter just before it flakes easily with a fork.
5. Cover the fish with a towel to keep warm while finishing the sauce. Pour the vegetables and wine into a food processor. Puree, adding the crème blanc just before serving. Pour the sauce over fish fillets.

Note: The vegetables and wine could be pureed in a food mill as desired or left as is. Stir in crème blanc after sauce has cooled about 1 minute; if it is too hot the crème blanc will curdle.

Yield: **4 servings**
Calories per serving: **164**
Protein per serving: **34g**

Fat per serving: **trace**
Carbohydrates per serving: **8g**
Sodium per serving: **654mg**

TO CHIFFONADE

1. Stack the lettuce, or other item, to be cut, then roll it up tightly, jellyroll fashion.

2. Slice it crosswise into thin strips.

Fillets of Fish Martini

❖

Steaming fish helps to retain its fresh, clean flavor better than any other cooking technique. This quickly done dinner is easily accomplished with a Chinese steamer and wok but you may fashion a steaming arrangement with a cake rack set on custard cups inside a deep electric frying pan.

> 1 1/4 pounds fillets of fish; haddock, cod, or other
>   thick white-fleshed fish
> freshly ground pepper to taste
> 2 cups broccoli flowerets and stems
> 2 carrots, peeled and julienned
> 4–5 strips lemon peel
> 2 cups fish stock or 2 8-ounce bottles clam juice
> 1/4 cup dry white vermouth
> 3 juniper berries, crushed (optional)
> 1 tablespoon minced fresh parsley
> 2 tablespoons gin
> 2 egg yolks
> 1 teaspoon cornstarch or potato starch
> 1 tablespoon butter

1. Place the fish on the rack of a Chinese bamboo steamer. Season with pepper (add salt only if using homemade fish stock, the commercial clam juice is salty).
2. Place broccoli flowerets on one side of fish. To prepare the stems, peel the tough outer skin with a knife or vegetable peeler. Slice the peeled stem thinly on the diagonal; add to the flowerets. Arrange the carrots on the other side of the fish. Arrange the lemon strips decoratively on top of fish.
3. In the bottom of a wok or deep electric skillet, combine the fish stock (reserving 2 tablespoons for Step 7), vermouth, juniper

berries, and half the parsley. Place the bamboo steamer or rack over the wok, cover, and bring to a boil over high heat. Begin timing when the liquid boils; steam 5–6 minutes.

4. Lift the steamer or rack from wok. Boil the fish stock, uncovered, until reduced to 1 cup.

5. Meanwhile, heat the gin in a long-handled, small saucepan, preferably one with a lip, until bubbles just appear at the edge. Ignite the gin and pour it over fish (still in steamer, placed over a plate). After the flames die out, cover with a towel while completing the sauce or keep warm in a turned-off oven.

6. Beat the egg yolks in a small bowl or measuring cup with a fork. Dribble ¼ cup of the reduced fish stock into the yolks, while stirring with the fork. Whisk the yolk-fish stock mixture into the remaining fish stock in wok over very low heat. Adjusting the heat as necessary, whisk until the sauce becomes opaque and foamy.

7. Dissolve the cornstarch in the 2 tablespoons reserved fish stock. Whisk this into the yolk-fish stock mixture over medium-low heat until thickened. Whisk in butter. Garnish fish with the remaining parsley. Serve fish right from the bamboo steamer with the sauce passed at the table.

Yield: 4 servings
Calories per serving: 240
Protein per serving: 32g

Fat per serving: 6g
Carbohydrates per serving: 14g
Sodium per serving: 596mg

❖ **PARSLEY** ❖

Fresh parsley is to dried parsley flakes as Wimbledon's grass courts are to Astroturf. Fresh parsley is readily available, inexpensive, and easy to use, if you have a good knife for mincing it. Store parsley, stem ends down, in a large glass of water in the refrigerator. Make a little tepee out of a plastic bag and cover the parsley. This will help keep it fresh for a few days longer.

Broiled Fish Fillets

❖

The success of this "nonrecipe" recipe lies in the freshness of the fish, for if it is not absolutely pristine it's best to use it in another recipe where stronger flavors can carry it.

> ¾ to 1 pound white-fleshed fish fillets such as sole
> ¼ teaspoon salt
> freshly ground pepper to taste
> a few drops lemon juice
> 3 tablespoons dry white wine, more or less
> 1 teaspoon butter
> 1 small clove garlic, minced (optional)
> 2 tablespoons dried bread crumbs
> 1 tablespoon minced fresh parsley

1. Lay the fish fillet in a baking dish. Fold the thin tail under to even the thickness of the fish. Season with salt, pepper, and lemon juice. Add just enough wine to film the bottom of the pan. Place the fish under the heated broiler while preparing the bread crumbs.
2. Melt the butter in an 8-inch skillet over medium-high heat. When foamy, stir the garlic over medium heat about 30 seconds, without browning. Add the bread crumbs, stir until just lightly golden. Remove from heat and stir in the parsley.
3. When the fish has turned opaque and flakes easily with a poke of the knife tip, about 5 minutes, spread the bread crumbs over the fish. Return to broiler until crumbs are lightly browned. Serve with the cooking juices poured over the fish.

Yield: 2 servings
Calories per serving: 195
Protein per serving: 42g

Fat per serving: 2g
Carbohydrates per serving: 3g
Sodium per serving: 420mg

Fillets of Sole
with Salmon Mousse

❖

You may vary the presentation of this dish by lining a ring mold with the fish fillets and filling with the salmon mousse mixture. Unmolded and with the center filled with a fresh green vegetable, it makes a pretty party dish. Although canned salmon may be used, it is a pale substitute for fresh. Serve with Hollandaise drizzled over the fish, and Nutted Braised Celery (page 244).

> *4 fillets of sole, each about ¼ to ⅓ pound (1 pound total)*
> *½ pound fresh salmon*
> *2 tablespoons light cream*
> *½ teaspoon salt*
> *freshly ground pepper to taste*
> *1 teaspoon fresh tarragon or ½ teaspoon dried tarragon*
> *1 tablespoon minced fresh parsley*
> *2 egg whites, lightly beaten*
> *¼ cup dry white wine*
> *Hollandaise Sauce (page 21)*

1. Place the fish fillets between sheets of wax paper and flatten slightly with a cleaver or heavy flat-bottomed saucepan. Set aside. (If using a ring mold, lay the fillets, cutting as necessary, in an oiled mold with what was the skin side facing in.)
2. Steam the salmon in a rack over 3 inches of water until it flakes easily with a fork, about 5 minutes per inch thickness. Cool and pick over the salmon to remove bits of skin, gristle, and fat. Flake it into a bowl or food processor.
3. Blend in the cream, salt, pepper, tarragon, half the parsley, and egg whites. Process or beat until fairly smooth.

4. Preheat oven to 350 degrees. Place sole fillets on work surface with what was the skin side facing up. Divide the salmon mixture over the fillets, roll loosely. (Or pack into a fish-lined ring mold, and bang the mold on a kitchen counter to remove air bubbles.) Place fillets in a baking dish with wine in the bottom. (If using a ring mold, place mold in a baking dish with 1 inch water on bottom.) Bake 20 minutes for fillets, 25-30 for a ring mold. Serve with Hollandaise Sauce, and garnish with the remaining parsley.

Note: If you wish, make the Hollandaise after the fish has baked, using the juices in the bottom of the pan to replace some of the chicken broth called for in the original recipe.

Yield: 4 servings
Calories per serving: 230
Protein per serving: 35g

Fat per serving: 9g
Carbohydrates per serving: 1g
Sodium per serving: 469mg

Broiled Fish Steaks
with Basil-Walnut Sauce

❖

A perfect Monday night dinner to atone for a calorie-taxing weekend, these broiled fish steaks may be readied in less time than it takes to empty the dishwasher if you have the Basil-Walnut Sauce tucked away in the refrigerator or freezer. If you have none or if basil is out of season or unavailable, the Lemon Parsley Sauce, page 31, is also good on these fish steaks. Note that the fish does not have to be turned during broiling, since no one sees the underside anyway. This would be very nice with Fettuccine with Cepes, page 248, and a tossed salad.

> 1 1/4 pounds to 1 1/2 pounds fish steaks or fillets such
>   as cod, haddock, or halibut, about 1-inch thick
> 1/2 teaspoon salt
> freshly ground pepper to taste
> 1 tablespoon butter, at room temperature
> juice of half a lemon
> 1/4 cup dry white wine
> 1/4 cup Basil-Walnut Sauce (page 32)

1. Lay the fish in a broiling pan or roasting dish. Measure it at its thickest part. Season fish with salt and pepper and smear with butter. Squeeze a few drops lemon juice over fish. Pour the wine into pan (it should just cover the bottom, add more or less as needed). Broil 4 minutes, cover the top of fish with Basil-Walnut Sauce, and broil an additional 1–2 minutes, allowing about 5 minutes per inch thickness.

Note: For juicy fish, err on the side of undercooking.

Yield: 4 servings
Calories per serving: 190
Protein per serving: 32g

Fat per serving: 6g
Carbohydrates per serving: 2g
Sodium per serving: 382mg

Lemon-Lime Fillets
in Parchment Paper Hearts

❖

Cooking in parchment paper locks in natural juices and flavors and makes serving a snap. The paper hearts may be readied up to 3 hours ahead, but no longer or the paper will become soggy. If desired, top each of the fillets with a few scallops or shrimp. Serve with Bourbon Squash Souffle (page 280) and a salad.

> 1 lime and 1 lemon
> 2 cups water
> 2 tablespoons softened butter
> 2 tablespoons lemon juice
> 1 tablespoon lime juice
> 1 teaspoon minced ginger root
> 1 1/4 pounds white-fleshed fish fillets such as sole,
>   cod, or haddock cut into 4 serving-size pieces
> 1/4 teaspoon salt
> freshly ground pepper to taste
> 1 tablespoon minced fresh parsley

1. With a vegetable peeler, remove the rind of both the lemon and the lime, taking care to remove only the colored skin and none of the white, which tends to be bitter. Julienne the peels into strips nearly as fine as pine needles.
2. Bring the water to a boil, immerse the julienned peels, and boil 2 minutes. Drain.
3. Mash the julienned peel in with the butter, half the lemon juice, all the lime juice, and the ginger root.
4. Preheat oven to 425 degrees. Cut four parchment paper hearts, place a fish fillet on each. (You may use a double thickness of wax paper if parchment paper is unavailable.) Season the fish with salt,

COOKING IN PARCHMENT PAPER HEARTS

1. Lay the fish fillet, or other food, on half the paper heart, then fold the paper over it.

2. Pleat the paper tightly, securing the pleat with your fingertips as you move along the perimeter of the heart. Each pleat is made by making ¼-inch folds at 1½-inch intervals.

3. Continue making the pleats along the perimeter of the heart.

4. Secure the end by tucking the tip of paper under the package.

pepper, and remaining lemon juice. Divide the lemon-lime butter over it. Garnish with parsley. Fold as shown in the illustration above, pleating the edge and turning the tip under. Place on a baking sheet and bake 8 minutes in a preheated 425-degree oven. Let each diner open his/her own package and enjoy the aroma.

Yield: 4 servings
Calories per serving: 165
Protein per serving: 26g

Fat per serving: 6g
Carbohydrates per serving: 1g
Sodium per serving: 89mg

Sauteed Scallops

❖

This is an example of the "less is more" culinary school of thought, which believes food is best enhanced by simple rather than complicated cooking techniques. Its most basic tenet, "nothing but the best and the freshest," keeps the simply prepared fare from being nothing more than a bare bones offering. For this dish it is imperative the scallops be sweet and never frozen. Serve with Lemon Glazed Carrots (page 241) and Fire and Ice Salad (page 102). Ingredients may be doubled or tripled to accommodate more diners.

> ¾ to 1 pound scallops
> 2 tablespoons flour
> freshly ground pepper to taste
> 1 tablespoon butter
> 2 tablespoons dry white wine or for a sweeter touch,
>   sherry

1. Dredge the scallops in the flour, season with pepper.
2. Melt the butter in a 10-inch skillet. When foamy, add the scallops and saute over high heat, turning often, until opaque, about 5–7 minutes.
3. Add the wine to pan and stir until reduced to a syrupy glaze. Divide scallops and sauce between two baking shells and serve.

Yield: 2 servings
Calories per serving: 325
Protein per serving: 54g

Fat per serving: 9g
Carbohydrates per serving: 6g
Sodium per serving: 601mg

Grilled Shrimp
with Leeks and Fennel

❖

Grilling fish or shellfish over the feathery leaves of fennel is an old French technique. The greens protect the fish from tearing on the grilling rack while imparting a lovely, faintly sweet flavor to the flesh. If you don't have a grill, see the instructions in step 8 for broiling. This not only makes a nice meal for the calorie conscious but a delicious first course for a dinner party. Fennel bulbs are available in the fall, winter, and early spring.

> 1 to 1 1/4 pounds large, uncooked shrimp
> 1 tablespoon olive oil
> 1 tablespoon lemon juice
> 3 tablespoons fish stock, chicken broth, or clam broth
> 1 bay leaf
> freshly ground pepper to taste
> 2 red bell peppers
> 2 fennel bulbs, with stalks
> 4 leeks
> 1 cup (or less) chicken broth
> 1/2 teaspoon salt
> freshly ground pepper to taste
> 1 teaspoon oil
> 4 thin lemon slices

1. Shell and devein the shrimp. Marinate them 4 hours or overnight in the oil, lemon juice, fish stock, bay leaf, and pepper. Drain, discard bay leaf, and reserve the marinade.
2. Cut the red peppers in half and flatten them with the heel of your hand. (See illustration, page 260.) Place on a baking sheet, skin

side up, and broil, turning pan from time to time, until the skin is blackened and charred, about 8 minutes. Remove to a paper or plastic bag, roll tightly closed, and let rest until peppers are cool enough to handle.

3. Meanwhile, separate the feathery stalks from the fennel bulbs. Pare the tough, outer leaves from the fennel bulbs. Slice the bulbs on the diagonal. Rinse. Reserve the stalks.

4. Cut the leeks where the green turns to white. Discard the tops, cut white part in half the long way, and rinse.

5. Place the leeks and fennel bulb in a 10-inch skillet with enough chicken broth to half cover, season with salt, pepper, and oil. Cover and simmer 15-20 minutes or until tender. Remove cover and boil until liquid is reduced to a glaze. Set aside.

6. Meanwhile, remove peppers from the bag. Peel and discard the charred skin. Set peppers aside.

7. To grill: Place the fennel stalks directly on a hot grill. Place the shrimp on top of the stalks. Grill, turning shrimp once until cooked through, about 8 to 10 minutes. During the last 5 minutes of cooking, place peeled peppers directly on grill. Turn them after 2½ minutes. Baste shrimp and peppers occasionally with reserved marinade during cooking.

8. To broil: Place shrimp and peppers on the grid of a broiling pan. Broil, 3 inches from the coils, 2-3 minutes to a side, turning once, basting with the reserved marinade. Remove peppers if they are burning. Place fennel stalks in the bottom of broiler pan placed on a heatproof surface. Ignite the fennel stalks with a long match. *Note:* If broiling shrimp instead of grilling, it's a good idea to dry the fennel stalks, making it easier to ignite them. To dry the fennel stalks, remove the bulb for use in recipe. Cut thick stalks in half the long way. Place in a 200-degree oven on a baking sheet, turning often until dried. Place broiler grid with shrimp and peppers over burning stalks to "smoke" the food. When the flames die out, continue with recipe.

9. Divide the braised fennel from step 5 among 4 luncheon-size plates. Place the shrimp in a circle on top. Place the peppers in the

center of the circle. Place the leek halves on either side of shrimp. Garnish with lemon slices, cut in half, twisted, and placed flat side down on shrimp.

Yield: 4 servings
Calories per serving: 260
Protein per serving: 37g

Fat per serving: 6g
Carbohydrates per serving: 13g
Sodium per serving: 640mg

❖ THE NEW AMERICAN GRILL ❖

Grilling is hot. The day when barbecue meant hamburgers, steaks, and the occasional sausage is past. America's imaginative chefs are grilling everything from shrimp to squab and accompanying dishes with sauces that would leave Grandma gasping. From barbecue Hollandaise to Spicy Plum, from Burgundy Cherry to Mustard Mousse, today's concoctions make ketchup sound about as appealing as a plastic tomato. The innovations don't stop with the food and sauces, either. Where once charcoal would do, mesquite, applewood, hickory, cabernet grapevine cuttings, and cords of other woods now smoke. And all of this on equipment that makes the backyard $19.98 grill look about as current as a Model T. Gas and electric grills, covered models, water smokers, and 55-gallon tin drums are among the grill chef's options, making what was once the first and simplest of cooking techniques one where only the most sophisticated take charge. One note: While all the data is not yet in, it is suspected that browned parts of meat cooked at high temperatures by grilling, broiling, and frying may be carcinogenic.

Lobster Flamed with Drambuie

❖

This is an occasion sort of dish, the kind of dinner to commemorate a birthday, anniversary, or perhaps Christmas Eve dinner. The same proportions divided among 6 diners rather than 4 would also make a flamboyant beginning to a formal meal. Begin preparations the day before or at least early in the day as making the lobster stock requires some time. Freeze the remaining lobster glaze for up to a year for another dish. This recipe also makes an excellent sauce for pasta.

4 lobsters, about 1 1/2 pounds each
1 small rib celery, diced
2 shallots, diced
1 carrot, diced
2 cups dry white wine
2 sprigs parsley
1 clove garlic
3 tablespoons dry white wine
1 teaspoon mild paprika
4 ounces mushrooms, sliced
3 ounces pea pods, blanched 1 minute
1 leek, white part only, julienned
2 tablespoons Drambuie
6 tablespoons light cream
1 tablespoon minced fresh parsley

1. Early in the day or the day before serving, bring a lobster pot or a 10-quart saucepan ¾ full of water to a boil. Immerse the lobster, boil for 3 minutes. Turn off heat, let rest 5 minutes, drain and cool in cold water. Remove meat from shells, cut into chunks, reserve shells and legs. Chill meat.
2. Place lobster shells and legs in a nonaluminum saucepan with the celery, shallots, carrot, wine, parsley, and garlic. Add water to

cover, bring to a boil, and immediately reduce to a simmer. Simmer 2 hours.

3. Strain the lobster stock, discarding vegetables and shells. Return to high heat, boil rapidly until reduced to about 2 cups, about 35–40 minutes. Watch closely for the last 10 minutes as the glaze will quickly evaporate and burn. The lobster glaze will be very dark and salty to taste. Glaze may be refrigerated now or the recipe continued.

4. Heat ¾ cup lobster glaze with the wine and paprika in a 10-inch skillet over medium heat. Freeze the remaining glaze. Add the mushrooms, pea pods, leek, and lobster meat. Stir until warmed through, about 3 minutes.

5. Heat the Drambuie in a long-handled small saucepan, preferably with a spout. When bubbles appear at the edge of the pan, ignite the liquor and pour it on the lobster and vegetables. Stir until flames die out. Stir in cream.

6. To serve, ladle sauce and lobster onto large salad or luncheon-size plates. Garnish with the parsley. Serve with a dinner-size liner plate underneath.

Yield: 4 servings
Calories per serving: 310
Protein per serving: 48g

Fat per serving: 9g
Carbohydrates per serving: 8g
Sodium per serving: 520+ mg

Poached Salmon with Reduced-Calorie Béarnaise

Poached salmon may be offered hot or cold, unadorned or complemented by any number of sauces. You may use a bit of the cooking liquid to replace some of the chicken broth when making the Reduced-Calorie Béarnaise sauce if desired. Accompany with asparagus spears or fresh peas if in season and begin with a Pear and Gouda Salad, page 107.

For the Court Bouillon

2 quarts water
1/2 cup white wine vinegar
1 onion, sliced
3–4 sprigs fresh parlsey
1 teaspoon whole peppercorns
1 bay leaf

The Fish

2 pounds salmon roast (the midsection of the fish,
     with skin and bone intact) or 2 pounds salmon
     steaks
1 recipe Béarnaise Sauce, page 24
6–8 lemon slices (optional)
minced fresh parsley (optional)

1. Combine all the court bouillon ingredients in a 4-quart saucepan. Bring to a boil, immediately reduce to a simmer.
2. Meanwhile, wrap the fish in cheesecloth (2 layers is sufficient) or an old, thin kitchen towel. Measure the fish at its thickest part.
3. Lower the fish into the simmering court bouillon, cover, and cook 5 minutes per inch thickness. Remove fish from court bouillon and unwrap it if serving immediately. Cool first if desired.
4. Scrape off skin. Slice roast in half horizontally at the backbone and remove bones. Serve with Reduced-Calorie Béarnaise and garnish with lemon slices rimmed in minced parsley if desired.

Yield: 6–8 servings
Calories per serving: 215
Protein per serving: 17g

Fat per serving: 15g
Carbohydrates per serving: trace
Sodium per serving: 90mg

Monkfish à L'Americaine

❖

Monkfish, also known as monkey fish or lotte, is called poor man's lobster in France for its firm-fleshed texture. Here, much like mussels, it's been regarded as a junk fish and used as bait or sometimes exported to France, where it is in demand. More recently it's become available in our fish markets, and the price has risen as has interest in it. Ask your fish merchant for it if he does not now carry this mild-flavored fish. The origin of the culinary term L'Americaine is obscure. Whether it was a term attached to a seafood dish prepared with tomatoes and olive oil in commemoration of an American customer by a French restaurateur or a dish brought to America by a French chef then re-exported to France isn't known—but it is decidedly Provençal in its origin, rich in onion, garlic, parsley, and oil. You know what's been left out here.

> 4 tomatoes or a 14-ounce can of tomatoes
> 2 leeks, white part only, thinly sliced
> 3 tablespoons chicken broth
> 1/2 teaspoon salt
> freshly ground pepper to taste
> 2–3 tablespoons flour
> 1 1/2 pounds monkfish, skinned and boned or other
>   firm-fleshed whitefish, at least 2 inches thick
> 3 tablespoons Pernod
> 2/3 cup dry white wine
> 1 clove garlic, minced
> 3–4 tablespoons tomato paste
> 1 teaspoon fresh tarragon leaves or 1/2 dried tarragon
> 1 tablespoon minced fresh parsley

1. Core the tomatoes and cut a cross in each one's bottom. Bring a 2 1/2-quart saucepan 3/4 full of water to a boil. Blanch the toma-

toes 30 seconds to 1 minute, depending on ripeness. Drain and cool under running water. Spear on a fork and peel off the skins. Halve the tomatoes, extract seeds with your thumb or a spoon into a strainer held over a bowl. Dice the pulp. Press the seeds with the back of a wooden spoon to extract the juices. Discard the seeds. Add the juices to pulp. Set aside. Canned tomatoes may be used as is or seeded if desired.

2. "Saute" the leeks in the broth over medium-high heat, covered, until limp, about 5 minutes.

3. Mix the salt and pepper with the flour. Dredge the fish. Spray a 12-inch skillet with cooking spray. Place the skillet over high heat. Sear the fish for about 1 minute on each side to brown. Adjust heat as needed.

4. Add the Pernod and ignite it. When flames die out add the wine, leeks, broth, garlic, tomatoes, tomato paste, and tarragon.

5. Cover and simmer 10 minutes until the fish is cooked through, plan on about 5 minutes per inch thickness. *Note:* If monkfish fillets are over 4 inches thick, you may cut them into rounds 2-inches thick to hasten the cooking.

6. Remove the fish to a platter, cover to keep warm. If sauce is too thin, reduce it by boiling until it reaches desired consistency. Spoon over fish and garnish with the parsley.

Yield: 4 servings
Calories per serving: 200
Protein per serving: 28g

Fat per serving: 2g
Carbohydrates per serving: 17g
Sodium per serving: 510mg

Mussels in White Wine
and Saffron

❖

Mussels, long enjoyed on the continent, are coming into such favor here that we can now buy a cultivated breed. These bivalves are much cleaner than naturally occurring mussels, making light work of a once time-consuming chore. Be wary when purchasing any mussels, though. The shellfish should be kept on ice, be as fresh as possible (ask the vendor when they came in, pass over any more than two days old), and the shells should be closed. This is not a do-ahead meal, but it is very quickly cooked. The mussels may be enjoyed as a first course, light dinner, or served on a bed of pasta for heartier fare.

3–4 pounds mussels
1 shallot, minced
2 cloves garlic, minced
a few threads saffron
a few parsley stems
1 sprig thyme
1 bay leaf
1 cup white wine
1 tablespoon butter, softened
1 tablespoon flour
1/2 teaspoon turmeric (optional, for color)
2 tablespoons light cream
1 tablespoon minced fresh parsley

1. To clean the mussels: Scrub each mussel with a brush and remove the "beard" with a sharp knife. Drop them into cold water and soak 1 to 2 hours. Some cooks add a handful of cornmeal or flour on the theory that it is ingested, thus plumping and cleansing the mussels. Lift the mussels from the soaking water and rinse again.

2. In a saucepan large enough to hold the mussels, put the shallot, garlic, saffron, parsley stems, thyme, bay leaf, and wine. Add the mussels, cover, and bring to a boil, shaking the pan frequently. When the shells open, about 5 minutes, remove from heat.

3. Pour the mussels and cooking liquid into a strainer set over a bowl. Discard the bay leaf, parsley stems, and thyme sprig. Pour cooking liquid back into saucepan (but not the grit at the bottom) and boil over high heat until reduced by a third.

4. Mash the butter and flour together. Whisk it into the simmering stock in two parts over medium-low heat. Stir in turmeric and cream.

5. To prepare the mussels for serving, discard one half of each shell. Arrange the mussels on a platter neatly. Pour the sauce over mussels and garnish with the parsley.

Yield: 4 servings
Calories per serving: 195
Protein per serving: 20g

Fat per serving: 8g
Carbohydrates per serving: 12g
Sodium per serving: 390mg

❖ SAFFRON ❖

The world's most expensive spice is the dried stigma of a crocus. There are only three such threads in each flower, and they must be picked by hand. Since it takes 225,000 stigmas to make a pound of saffron, small wonder it is so costly. Saffron is the signature spice of paella, a Spanish rice dish. It is also used in breads, pilafs, and with some shellfish. It comes in powdered and dried form.

Warm Seafood Salad
with Chinese Noodles

❖

This fragrant toss of seafood and noodles is a meal all by itself. Although presented here as a warm dish, it is very good served at room temperature as well. (Do not serve it chilled, because chilling shrouds some of the flavor.) To serve at room temperature, prepare the salad in advance, tossing the seafood, vegetables and noodles with the dressing to prevent the latter from becoming gummy. Or prepare the seafood and vegetables, marinating them in the dressing for several hours but cooking the noodles at the last minute. All the Oriental ingredients listed here are available at specialty food stores. The noodles are increasingly available in produce sections of larger supermarkets.

For the Court Bouillon

2 quarts water
1/2 cup rice wine vinegar or white wine vinegar
1 onion, sliced
3–4 sprigs parsley
1/2 teaspoon salt
1 teaspoon whole peppercorns
1 bay leaf

For the Seafood Salad

1/2 pound firm-fleshed whitefish such as cod,
       haddock, or halibut
1/2 pound medium raw shrimp, shelled and deveined
1/4 pound scallops
2 stalks broccoli

For the Dressing

6 tablespoons light soy sauce
1 tablespoon sesame oil
1 tablespoon vegetable oil
*2 tablespoons rice wine, Chinese cooking wine, or
sherry*
2 teaspoons minced scallion
2 teaspoons finely minced ginger root
6 tablespoons reduced court bouillon

½ pound fresh Chinese noodles
10–12 cherry tomatoes, halved

1. Make a court bouillon by combining the water, vinegar, onion, parsley, salt, peppercorns, and bay leaf in a 4-quart saucepan. Bring to a rolling boil.
2. Wrap the fish and shellfish, individually, in double thicknesses of cheesecloth. Lower the fish into the court bouillon first, remove from heat, cover, and let it rest 30 seconds. Then add the scallops and shrimp, cover, and let them rest 5–6 minutes. Lift the fish and shellfish from the liquid and set aside to cool. Boil the court bouillon at high heat, uncovered, until reduced to about 1 cup, about 30 minutes.
3. Meanwhile, cut the stems from the broccoli flowerets. Slice the flowerets. Peel the stems and slice thinly on the diagonal. Bring a 2 quart saucepan ¾ full of water to a boil, blanch the broccoli 4 minutes, drain, and rinse under cool water.
4. Combine all the dressing ingredients in a screw-top jar and shake heartily to combine. Set aside.
5. Cook the Chinese noodles by immersing them in 2 quarts of boiling water for 2–4 minutes. Drain and rinse under cool water.
6. Heat the dressing in a wok or large skillet over high heat. Remove and discard the cheesecloth from the fish, scallops, and shrimp. Toss the seafood with the broccoli and cherry tomatoes in the warm dressing to heat through.

7. Place drained noodles in shallow, wide soup bowls (reheat if needed by dousing with a kettle of boiling water), and add the seafood salad.

Note: Noodles may be cooked as much as 30 minutes in advance, but rinse well under running water after cooking. Reheat noodles by dousing with at least 2 quarts of boiling water.

Yield: 4 servings
Calories per serving: 495
Protein per serving: 42g

Fat per serving: 9g
Carbohydrates per serving: 60g
Sodium per serving: 1910mg

Sole, Scallop, and Pea Pod Salad

❖

This salad may be prepared early in the day and served several hours later. Be sure to remove it from the refrigerator at least 30 minutes before dining as it is better closer to room temperature than chilled. Serve with crusty bread and offer a refreshing fruit sherbert for dessert.

For the Court Bouillon

1 *quart water*
2 *cups dry white wine*
1/4 *cup tarragon vinegar*
3–4 *stems parsley*
1 *bay leaf*
8 *peppercorns*
1/2 *teaspoon salt*

For the Salad

1 1/2 pounds sole
3/4 pound scallops
pieces of cheesecloth
3/4 pound pea pods, strings removed
15 walnut halves, roughly chopped

For the Dressing

4 1/2 tablespoons reduced court bouillon
3 tablespoons vegetable oil
1 tablespoon fresh lemon juice
3 tablespoons tarragon vinegar
1 tablespoon freshly chopped basil or 1/2 teaspoon
dried basil
1 garlic clove, speared on a toothpick
1/2 teaspoon salt
a few grindings fresh pepper

1. Combine all the ingredients for the court bouillon in a 3-quart nonaluminum saucepan and bring to a boil. Reduce heat and simmer for 45 minutes.
2. Wrap the fish and scallops in a double thickness of cheesecloth. Bring court bouillon back to a boil. Lower the fish and scallops into bouillon, cover, and remove from the heat. Let it rest 5 minutes. Lift the fish and scallops from liquid and rinse under cold running water to stop the cooking. Chill.
3. Put 1 cup court bouillon in a saucepan over high heat. Boil until reduced to 4 1/2 tablespoons. Set aside.
4. Bring a 2 1/2-quart saucepan 3/4 full of water to a boil. Immerse the pea pods, remove from heat, and let them sit for 4 minutes. Drain and rinse under cold running water until peas are at room temperature.
5. Combine all the dressing ingredients in a jar, shake well, and let dressing rest 1 hour. Remove the garlic just before serving.
6. The salad may be assembled as much as 4 hours before serving

but is best done no more than an hour before. Flake the fish into a serving bowl, add the scallops, pea pods, and walnut halves. Toss with enough dressing to coat lightly. Serve on lettuce cups or in hollowed navel oranges, lined with lettuce.

Yield: 6 servings
Calories per serving: 254
Protein per serving: 32g

Fat per serving: 10g
Carbohydrates per serving: 9g
Sodium per serving: less than 580mg

Swordfish with Mustard Tarragon Sauce

❖

Here's a wonderfully satisfying meal that cheats on nothing but time, going from the refrigerator to table in about 15 minutes flat. Accompany with a simple rice pilaf and a Dilled Zucchini and Carrot Salad (page 104). The Mustard Tarragon Sauce may be kept in the refrigerator up to 1 week. The fish may be broiled rather than grilled. If the fish has any odor, soak it in 3 cups water mixed with 2 tablespoons bottled or fresh lemon juice for 10 minutes. Pat it dry before grilling.

> 1 1/4 pounds swordfish or thick fish steak such as tuna
> half a fresh lemon
> 2 tablespoons mayonnaise
> 4 tablespoons plain yogurt
> 1 tablespoon plus 1 teaspoon stone-ground or
>   Dijon-style mustard
> 1 teaspoon lemon juice

> 1 tablespoon fresh tarragon, snipped, or 1 teaspoon
> dried tarragon
> ½ teaspoon capers (optional)

1. Heat a broiler or grill. When hot, cook the fish on one side for about 4 minutes. Squeeze 1 teaspoon fresh lemon juice over.
2. While the fish cooks, combine all the remaining ingredients, except the capers. Mix well.
3. Flip the fish. On a grill, cover cooked surface of fish with the sauce. Under a broiler, cook the fish 1 minute on second side before covering with the sauce. Continue to cook until the fish is no longer soft when pressed with a finger, about 4 minutes more, 8 minutes in all. Sprinkle the capers over fish the last 2 minutes of cooking.

Yield: 4 servings
Calories per serving: 245
Protein per serving: 30g

Fat per serving: 12g
Carbohydrates per serving: 2g
Sodium per serving: 120mg

❖ YOGURT ❖

Yogurt is a fermented milk product that has long been used in the Middle East but has only been used here since the 1940's. Widely regarded as a health food, it should be noted that it supplies no more nutrients than a glass of partially skimmed milk, although it does aid in digestion. Yogurt, like its roly-poly cousin, sour cream, must be cooked at low temperatures or it will curdle. Fruit-flavored yogurts are comparatively high in calories, one cup supplying about 260–300 calories.

Chapter 9

PRODUCE
PROPER

Vegetables

❖

Vegetables in this health-aware era have come into their own. Who wants the good old days when the 1941 edition of the *Fannie Farmer Cookbook* instructed Grandma to boil the green beans for 20 minutes! The vegetable is no longer an obligatory token item on the plate. Today we herald crisp but tender garden-fresh vegetables, prepared in an almost infinite variety.

Vegetables are predominantly carbohydrates, supplying us with fuel for energy. They also are sources of incomplete proteins, meaning they can't supply all the eight essential amino acids that must be gotten through foods. These amino acids—proteins—are used to build blood and other body cells. However, when whole grains, such as rice are consumed at the same meal with legumes such as dried beans, their proteins complement each other and are complete.

Most vegetables also contain fat, although in minute quantities. Some are an excellent source of vitamin A for healthy skin, teeth, and bones, and vitamin C, to aid in resisting infection. One cup of broccoli, for example, supplies three-quarters of your daily requirement of vitamin A and more than twice your vitamin C quotient. Some vegetables also supply several important minerals, particularly calcium and iron.

Making the most of these nutrients requires a bit of consumer knowledge. To that end there is a brief introduction before each of the vegetables with advice on selection, storage, and cooking methods.

Here you will find dishes suitable for both the weekday's restraint and also for the weekend's indulgences. As with all the recipes in this book, some can be accomplished with microwave speed, others require the old-fashioned investment of time. Some are truly sidekicks, others demand—and receive—the spotlight. All trade on their upbringing, nothing but the freshest and the best.

Asparagus

❖

Royalty has its privilege—Louis XIV had a gardener who provided the palace kitchen with asparagus year round. It's still a class act, though we commoners must content ourselves with a five-month season, stretching from February to June, peaking in April and May.

When purchasing asparagus, look for tightly closed heads and smooth, unwrinkled stalks. A pound of medium-size stalks holds between 16–20 spears, feeding 2–4 people depending on the menu. Asparagus's strong suit is vitamin A as well as appreciable amounts of vitamin C, potassium, and phosphorus. To protect those nutrients, store asparagus in the refrigerator crisper in a closed plastic bag or standing in an inch or so of water.

To prepare asparagus for cooking, cut or snap the stalks where the white turns to green. If the spears are more than a half inch in diameter, or if you're using white asparagus, peel to remove the stringy fibers, rendering the whole stalk edible. To peel, lay an asparagus flat on the work surface, tip facing you. Starting an inch or two beneath the tip, pull a vegetable peeler down the stalk, turning the spear after each stroke until you've peeled the circumference. Trimmings may be frozen for use in an asparagus soup.

Asparagus may be boiled or steamed. Because green vegetables tend to turn drab olive green when cooked with covers in place (see page 246 for more explanation), boiling will better retain the emerald green hue. To boil, fill a 12-inch or larger skillet ¾ full of water. Add ½ teaspoon salt. Bring to a boil. Immerse asparagus and boil for 6–8 minutes; the spears should be softened but still have some bite. Remove asparagus spears by lifting them with a slotted spoon or spatula. If you pour the water and all into a colander, they may break at the tip.

If you prefer to steam the asparagus, tie the stalks into a bundle with kitchen twine. Place an inch of water in the bottom of an asparagus steamer, stand asparagus upright, cover, and cook at high heat about 8 minutes or until somewhat softened but still crunchy. You may also fashion a steamer from any deep saucepan. Cover it with an inverted bowl or a double-boiler insert.

Asparagus looks wondrous laid upon a white linen napkin, with no more garnish than a lemon twist at the base. Pass *Gourmet Light* Hollandaise at the table, or try any of the simple variations that follow. Asparagus is so elegant a vegetable it may be served as a first course, but it also makes a first-rate casual supper alongside softly scrambled eggs.

Asparagus Mimosa

❖

The crumb topping may be prepared far in advance and gently reheated just before serving.

> 1 pound asparagus, peeled
> 1 teaspoon butter
> 2 tablespoons dried bread crumbs
> 1 hard-cooked egg yolk
> 1 tablespoon butter
> a few drops lemon juice
> 1/8 teaspoon salt
> freshly ground pepper to taste

1. Prepare the asparagus for cooking by following instructions as outlined in the introduction. While bringing the water to a boil, prepare the topping.
2. Spray an 8-inch skillet with cooking spray. Place it over medium-low heat, add the butter and when it's foamy, add the bread crumbs, stirring occasionally until lightly browned. Remove the skillet from the heat, and sieve the hard-cooked egg yolk into the

bread crumbs. Stir to combine. Scrape onto a piece of wax paper.
3. Boil or steam the asparagus, and drain it when tender but still crunchy. Lay the asparagus on a serving platter.
4. Melt the butter with the lemon juice in the now-empty skillet. Pour it over the asparagus, season with salt and pepper, and sprinkle the bread crumb mixture over the top.

Yield: 4 servings
Calories per serving: 65
Protein per serving: 3g

Fat per serving: 5g
Carbohydrates per serving: 5g
Sodium per serving: 80mg

Asparagus Maltaise

A subtle change from the ever-popular Hollandaise, Maltaise sauce is a similar emulsion spiked with orange instead of lemon juice. Serve this dish with poultry or duck. Should you have any leftover spears, serve them cold with chilled Maltaise sauce for lunch or snacks. The sauce may be prepared in advance and gently reheated over hot (only 130 degrees), not boiling water. Whisk it continuously.

1 *pound asparagus, peeled*
5 *egg yolks*
¼ *teaspoon salt, omit if using canned consomme*
¾ *cup chicken stock or canned consomme*
5 *tablespoons orange juice, freshly squeezed*
   preferred
1 *teaspoon lemon juice*
2 *tablespoons butter, melted*
salt to taste
freshly ground pepper to taste
grated zest of 1 orange

1. Prepare the asparagus for cooking and cook it by following the instructions in the introduction. While it cooks, prepare the sauce.
2. Place the egg yolks and ¼ teaspoon salt in a blender or food processor and process for 30 seconds.
3. Meanwhile, boil the stock with the orange juice and lemon juice until it's reduced to ½ cup.
4. Dribble the hot liquid into the egg yolks while the machine runs.
5. Transfer the mixture to a 1-quart heavy-bottomed saucepan over medium-low heat and whisk constantly until thickened, about 3 minutes.
6. Remove the sauce from heat and whisk in the butter.
7. Drain the hot asparagus, lay on a serving platter, and sprinkle with salt and pepper. Pour the sauce over the midsection of asparagus, garnish with orange zest.

Yield: 4 servings with
4 tablespoons of sauce
Calories per serving: 165
Protein per serving: 7g

Fat per serving: 13g
Carbohydrates per serving: 7g
Sodium per serving: 220mg

Beets

While beets are generally boiled, they are delicious baked as well. Choose medium-size smooth, firm beets for baking. Those that look shriveled or very large are apt to be too woody. The tops may be cooked like spinach, and served with a few drops of fruity vinegar. Beets are a good source of potassium, calcium, phosphorus, and magnesium and contain about 35 calories in a ½ cup.

Baked Beets

❖

1 1/4 pounds beets, stems removed
2 teaspoons butter, melted
juice of one orange
1/8 teaspoon salt
freshly ground pepper to taste
grated zest of 1 orange

1. Prick the beets in several places with a fork. Put them in a baking dish in a 350-degree oven. Bake beets until easily pierced with a fork, about an hour, maybe a little longer.
2. Peel and discard the skins. Slice the beets and place on a serving platter.
3. Combine the butter and orange juice in a 1-quart saucepan, and boil for 30 seconds. Pour the sauce over the sliced beets, season with salt and pepper, and garnish with the zest.

VARIATION: Baked or boiled beets are also delicious mashed or pureed in a food processor. Peel after cooking, mash, and add the seasonings described above.

Yield: 4 servings
Calories per serving: 95
Protein per serving: 2g

Fat per serving: 2g
Carbohydrates per serving: 18g
Sodium per serving: 150mg

❖   **THINKING THIN TIP**   ❖

Ice water is far more appealing with a slice of lemon or orange.

Broccoli

❖

Another year-round vegetable, broccoli is the health addict's dream. One large cooked stalk fulfills your vitamin C requirement by half as much again, provides half your need of vitamin A, and supplies goodly amounts of riboflavin, iron, calcium, and potassium.

When purchasing broccoli, look for unopened buds that are dark green, not yellow. The butt end of the stalk should be neither brown nor slimy. Store broccoli in a plastic bag in the refrigerator or in the vegetable crisper for not more than four days; 1 ½ to 2 pounds will serve 4.

Peeling and slicing the broccoli stalks is a wonderful way to get full value from this vegetable. Cut the stalks an inch below the buds. Separate the flower stems. Remove the leaves and if they look fresh, plan to cook them for they are rich in vitamin A. Cut the branches from the stalks and peel the stalks using a vegetable peeler or a small, sharp knife. Slice the stalks into rounds on the diagonal.

Boil or steam broccoli as you would green beans (see page

A peeled broccoli stalk is delicious to eat when it is sliced on the diagonal into thin rounds.

245), 6–8 minutes is about right for crisp broccoli. This vegetable also takes well to stir-frying, but watch that oil!

Very good hot with just a touch of butter and lemon (see the Lemon Butter Sauce, page 33), broccoli also takes well to dressing up with a cloak of Hollandaise or Cheese Sauce, both in the Primer. Don't overlook it as a cold salad tossed with a light vinaigrette.

Sesame Broccoli

❖

This recipe is a nice change from the norm. Cook the broccoli ahead and reheat in the sesame oil at serving time if desired.

> 1 1/2 pounds broccoli (1 bunch of 2 to 3 stalks)
> 1 tablespoon sesame oil, available at specialty or
>   Oriental food shops
> 2 tablespoons sesame seeds
> 1 tablespoon soy sauce

1. Prepare the broccoli for cooking. Boil or steam the broccoli, and drain it.
2. Heat the sesame oil in a skillet or wok for 15 seconds over high heat. Add the sesame seeds and the broccoli. Stir-fry until heated through. Remove from the pan to a serving dish, and pour soy sauce over.

Yield: 4-6 servings
Calories per serving: 115
Protein per serving: 7g

Fat per serving: 6g
Carbohydrates per serving: 11g
Sodium per serving: 160mg

Broccoli and Walnut Terrine

❖

An eminently portable package, this terrine makes a fine picnic lunch with, say, a side of Counter Slaw (page 106). It's also an interesting vegetable for an otherwise simple menu. It is good both hot and at room temperature. Don't be misled by the yeast in this skinny pastry, it merely lightens the dough without entailing tedious risings or kneadings. This pastry would also make any other *Gourmet Light* vegetable tarts good company and could be pressed into service for a reduced-calorie quiche. It represents a savings of more than 700 calories over a traditional flour-butter pastry dough.

For the Pastry

2 teaspoons dry granular yeast
1 1/2 tablespoons warm (105–115-degree) water
1 egg, lightly beaten
1 teaspoon olive oil
1/2 teaspoon salt
5 tablespoons each whole wheat flour and
    all-purpose flour

For the Broccoli Terrine

1 1/2 pounds (about 2 bunches) broccoli
3 eggs
2 ounces cheese (grated hard cheese such as Swiss is
    recommended)
3 ounces cottage cheese
1 onion, diced
2 sprigs fresh thyme or 1/2 teaspoon dried thyme
1 ounce (about 1/4 cup) walnuts

To Prepare the Pastry

1. Dissolve the yeast in the warm water in a small cup.
2. In a small bowl, beat together the egg, oil, and salt. When the yeast is dissolved, beat it in too.
3. In another bowl, combine the two flours. Make a well in the center and add the liquid, stirring well.
4. Flour a pastry cloth, board, or a kitchen counter. Turn the dough onto the floured surface. Knead about 15 times, adding a bit more flour if necessary. Form dough into a ball, place it in the now-empty flour bowl, and cover with plastic wrap or a kitchen towel. Let the dough rest in a warm spot about 20 minutes, or until lightened.
5. Flour the work surface again. Roll the dough out into a rectangle about 7 inches by 15 inches. The dough will be very thin. If it rips, simply patch it.
6. Spray a 9-inch by 5-inch loaf pan with cooking spray. Lay the dough gently into the pan. Set it aside while preparing the terrine filling.

To Prepare the Terrine

1. Preheat the oven to 400 degrees. Bring a 2 ½-quart saucepan ⅔ full of water to a boil. Cut the stalks from the broccoli flowerets. Roughly chop the flowerets. With either a vegetable peeler or a knife, peel the broccoli stalks. Don't discard the leaves if they look fresh. Chop the stalks. When the water boils, immerse the broccoli and leaves, cook until crisp-tender, about 4 minutes if very fresh. Drain and cool under running water.
2. While the broccoli cooks, prepare the filling. In a food processor or bowl, beat the eggs. Add the cheeses, onion, and thyme. Mix well. If using a processor, add the broccoli and process until a chunky puree is achieved. By hand, chop the broccoli quite fine, add to egg-cheese mixture, and beat with a rotary beater. Stir in the nuts in either case.
3. Pour the mixture into the prepared pan. Make it smooth. Trim and discard any pastry that drapes over the short ends of the pan.

Drape excess pastry from long sides of pan over terrine. Place in the bottom third of the oven. Bake for 15 minutes at 400 degrees, then reduce heat to 350 degrees for the last 35 minutes. The terrine is done when the filling no longer shakes; however, a knife inserted in the center will show some moisture. Run a flexible-bladed metal spatula around the rim of the pan, invert, and cool 10 minutes before slicing.

Yield: 8 servings
Calories per serving: 200
Protein per serving: 12g

Fat per serving: 9g
Carbohydrates per serving: 18g
Sodium per serving: 240mg

Carrots

When purchasing carrots, buy those that have the greens attached for the sweetest flavor. Although those sold in cellophane bags might have grown up in the same field, the green-topped ones will be much sweeter because they're probably fresher. Look to the stem end of the carrot for signs of age; if it is blackened, try another bunch. Remove the greens before storing or they will sap moisture from the carrot, causing the root to shrivel. Very fresh carrots need nothing more than a good scrubbing, older ones will be more tender if peeled.

One carrot supplies you with more than the recommended daily requirement of vitamin A. There is debate among experts about the nutritive value of cooked versus raw carrots. Some feel carrots must be cooked for the human digestive tract to fully extract all the nutrients, others disagree.

The following recipes are uncommon ways for the common carrot.

Lemon Glazed Carrots

❖

This vegetable is easily reheated.

> 1 pound carrots
> juice of one lemon
> ½ teaspoon grated ginger root
> 1 teaspoon honey
> 1 tablespoon butter
> freshly grated nutmeg
> ⅛ teaspoon salt
> freshly ground pepper to taste
> 1 tablespoon minced fresh parsley

1. Prepare the carrots for cooking by peeling if desired. Bring a 2½-quart saucepan ¾ full of water to a boil. Meanwhile, slice the carrots thinly into rounds or like matchsticks. Immerse the carrots and boil until tender, which will depend on how they are cut. Remove one every minute after five to test. When tender, drain.
2. In the carrot saucepan, combine the lemon juice, ginger, honey, and butter. Heat and stir until mixed. Add the carrots and cook over high heat, shaking the pan all the while for 1 minute.
3. Turn onto a serving platter. Season with nutmeg, salt, and pepper. Garnish with the parsley.

Yield: 4 servings
Calories per serving: 85
Protein per serving: 2g

Fat per serving: 3g
Carbohydrates per serving: 14g
Sodium per serving: 120mg

Orange-Carrot Puree

❖

Nouvelle cuisine made purees fashionable once again. This combination of carrot and orange is an example. It is very nice with lamb and excellent for parties because it easily reheats in a double boiler.

> 1 pound carrots
> juice of 2 oranges
> grated zest of 1 orange
> 1 teaspoon sugar
> 1 tablespoon butter
> 1/2 teaspoon salt
> freshly ground pepper to taste
> a few gratings fresh nutmeg

1. Scrape or peel the carrots as you desire. Roughly chop them.
2. Bring a 2 1/2-quart saucepan 3/4 full of water to a boil. Immerse the carrots, cover the pan, and boil until carrots are easily pierced with a fork, about 10 minutes.
3. Put the cooked carrots in a food processor or in a food mill and puree. Add the orange juice, zest, sugar, butter, salt, pepper, and nutmeg. Mix well.

Yield: 4-6 servings
Calories per serving: 95
Protein per serving: 2g

Fat per serving: 3g
Carbohydrates per serving: 16g
Sodium per serving: 320mg

Carrot and Squash Puree

❖

This may also be made ahead and reheated in a double boiler. Delicious with turkey or other poultry. To vary, add a few tablespoons crème blanc (page 37) with the other seasonings.

> 1 small butternut squash, peeled and chopped
> 1 pound carrots, scrubbed, peeled, and roughly
>   chopped
> 1 tablespoon butter
> 2 teaspoons dark rum
> a few gratings fresh nutmeg
> 1/4 teaspoon salt
> freshly ground pepper to taste

1. Bring a 4-quart saucepan half full of water to a boil. Add the squash, cover, and cook 8 minutes. Add the carrots, cover, and cook until both are tender, about 12 minutes more.
2. Drain and mash the vegetables either in a food mill, food processor, or by hand. Add the butter, rum, and nutmeg. Season to taste with salt and pepper.

Yield: 6-8 servings
Calories per serving: 80
Protein per serving: 2g

Fat per serving: 2g
Carbohydrates per serving: 15g
Sodium per serving: 130mg

Celery

❖

Celery is more than mere rabbit food. Cooked, it takes on a whole new personality, but with little alteration to its naturally skinny self.

One rib of this member of the parsley family (sometimes called a stalk, although technically the whole bunch is one stalk) supplies just 7 calories. It is a good source of potassium, and supplies vitamin A and C as well as fiber.

When purchasing celery, avoid stalks that appear to be pithy, woody, or have limp and yellowing leaves. It needs to be kept both cold and moist to maintain its crispy snap and to protect it from becoming a limp throwaway.

Nutted Braised Celery

❖

Try this recipe to disperse the ho-hums.

> 8 large ribs celery, strings pared
> 3/4 cup chicken stock or canned consomme
> 1/3 cup dry white wine
> freshly ground pepper to taste
> 1 teaspoon butter
> 2 tablespoons finely chopped shallots
> 1 1/2 tablespoons chopped walnuts or sliced water
>   chestnuts

1. Slice the celery thinly on the diagonal, or julienne it. Place it in a 9-inch baking dish with at least 1-inch sides (a quiche dish is appropriate).

2. Pour the stock and wine over the celery. Season with the pepper. Put the butter on top and add shallots. Cover the dish with a lid or aluminum foil, and place it in a 400-degree oven. Bake for 15 minutes, remove the cover, and stir.
3. Bake the celery, uncovered, another 20 minutes, add the walnuts, and stir. Continue to bake another 10-15 minutes, or until the liquid has been reduced to about ½ cup of semi-syrupy liquid. Serve with liquid poured over celery.

Yield: 4 servings

Calories per serving: 60

Protein per serving: 2g

Fat per serving: 3g

Carbohydrates per serving: 7g

Sodium per serving: 110mg

Green Beans

❖

Thanks to modern horticulture, the string in string beans has been permanently pulled. No longer do we have those pesky strings to contend with! And thanks to modern transportation methods, fresh green beans are available almost year-round. They are an excellent source of vitamin A and supply a fair amount of calcium, too, for their very little 31 calories a cup.

When selecting green beans, look for those that are pliant and smooth, not coarse and tough. Frequently, when harvested by mechanical means, the bean is snapped from the stem exposing the meat, leaving a spot prone to rapid decay. Avoid these beans if given a choice. One pound of beans serves 4. Store the beans in the refrigerator crisper in a plastic bag; use within three days of purchase or they will be tough.

Prepare beans a handful at a time. Align the ends and cut across. Turn beans around, realign, and cut again.

Beans may be boiled or steamed. To boil, bring 6 cups of water to a rapid boil, with or without salt. Immerse beans and boil, uncovered, about 8 minutes, sometimes more, sometimes less. Time is a variable that is dependent on your heat source, the size and maturity of beans, and so on. Count on inconsistency because what works this time may not work next. During cooking, remove a bean and bite into it or pierce it with a fork, it should be crunchy but not raw. If holding the beans for later use, as much as five hours, undercook them a bit then cool under running water.

To steam beans, prepare as above, place in a steamer over 2 inches of boiling water, cover, and cook until tender, about 8 minutes. Again, check during cooking for tenderness.

To steam or to boil? Is one superior, healthwise? Consider the facts:

Fact 1: Some B and C vitamins are water soluble, and will be lost if subjected to extended water contact. But if the vegetable is put in a large amount of rapidly boiling water, taking less time to come back to a boil and thus less time to cook, the vitamin loss is minimized. With steaming, the vitamin loss is minimized because the bean doesn't come in contact with the water at all.

Fact 2: Covered green vegetables turn drab olive green because acids, present in the vegetable, combine with heat and denature the chlorophyll. If these acids are allowed to escape in the form of steam in an uncovered pot, they simply dissipate, causing no damage. If not allowed to escape, the vegetable turns an unappetizing yellow green. If you wish to steam beans, you may somewhat circumvent this discoloration by keeping the cooking time as short as possible and uncovering the pan immediately after cooking. Or you may boil vegetables, uncovered, in *large* amounts of water—maintaining color and minimizing vitamin loss.

The Lemon Butter Sauce (page 33) is very good on either boiled or steamed beans. For a change, consider the following recipe.

Green Beans with Tomato Nuggets

❖

Prepare the beans early in the day by partially cooking them. Drain and cover them with plastic wrap. Place the beans on a counter or in the refrigerator if you're holding them for more than 2 hours. The butter sauce may also be made ahead, both elements heated and tossed together at serving time.

> 1 pound green beans
> 1 tomato, blanched, peeled, and seeded
> juice of half a lemon
> 1 small garlic clove, minced
> 1 tablespoon butter, melted
> 1/8 teaspoon salt
> freshly ground pepper to taste

1. Cook the beans according to preceding instructions. Set them aside.
2. Dice the tomato.
3. Add the lemon juice and garlic to the butter. Cook over medium heat for 30 seconds. Add the cooked beans and toss them in the pan until heated through. Add the tomato, stir just to heat through, and season with salt and pepper.

Yield: 4 servings
Calories per serving: 65
Protein per serving: 3g

Fat per serving: 3g
Carbohydrates per serving: 9g
Sodium per serving: 280mg

Mushrooms

❖

There's more to mushrooms than the bland, pale specimens commonly available. A whole new world of exotic mushrooms is coming to market, with flavors that whisper of earth and woods. Some are dried and imported such as cepes (rhymes with step), chanterelles, and morels, others are being cultivated and marketed fresh such as shitake and enoki—all are expensive but worth a pretty penny for those special occasions when you'd like to treat your guests, or yourself. The dried mushrooms are available at specialty food stores.

Although one would have to eat a lot of mushrooms to benefit from them, they are higher in minerals such as iron and copper than many other vegetables, and contain about 20 calories a cup. And few foods add such a touch of class for such little caloric expense.

Because of an already high water content and their porosity, it's better to wipe mushrooms clean rather than washing them. This is particularly true if they are coupled with a sauce that would be diluted by excess moisture.

The recipes that follow use both the readily available supermarket mushroom and the very in vogue cepe.

Fettuccine with Cepes

❖

This wonderful pasta dish makes a great first course for a dinner party or a delicious main dish for a casual supper. The sauce may be easily made ahead and reheated just before tossing with freshly cooked fettuccine.

1 ounce dried cepes, also called porcini, or other
   dried mushrooms
boiling water
4 thin strips bacon
2 tablespoons minced shallots
1 clove garlic, minced
1 1/2 cups beef stock or canned beef broth
1 cup tomato sauce (see page 36)
lots of freshly ground pepper to taste
8 ounces fresh fettuccine noodles
1 tablespoon butter, at room temperature
1 tablespoon minced fresh parsley
freshly grated Parmesan cheese

1. Cover the dried mushrooms with boiling water and soak for 20 minutes.
2. Meanwhile, fry the bacon in a 10- or 12-inch skillet. Discard the fat. Spray the skillet with cooking spray and "saute" the shallots over medium-low heat until limp. Add the garlic and cook another 30 seconds.
3. Add the beef stock and boil over high heat until reduced to 1 cup. Add the tomato sauce and boil until reduced to 1 1/2 cups.
4. Drain the mushrooms and chop them. The juice may only be used if strained twice through a piece of double-thick washed cheesecloth. Add mushrooms to sauce base. Stir to combine. Season with freshly ground pepper.
5. Cook the fettuccine noodles according to package instructions. Drain the noodles and toss with the butter. Toss the fettuccine with cepe sauce. Sprinkle minced parsley on top. Pass cheese at the table.

Yield: 4 servings
Calories per serving: 345
Protein per serving: 12g

Fat per serving: 9g
Carbohydrates per serving: 54g
Sodium per serving: 430mg

Sherried Mushrooms

❖

This recipe is very nice with beef dishes and a treat when you add half an ounce to an ounce of dried mushrooms such as cepes. Soak the dried mushrooms for 20 minutes, drain and rinse, adding them at the end of Step 2. If made ahead, reheat the dish over very low heat or the crème blanc will curdle.

> 12 ounces mushrooms
> 2 teaspoons butter
> 2 tablespoons sherry or Madeira
> 3 tablespoons crème blanc (page 37) or plain yogurt
> a few fresh gratings nutmeg
> 1/8 teaspoon salt
> freshly ground pepper to taste
> 1 tablespoon minced fresh parsley

1. Wipe the mushrooms clean and slice them, removing a sliver off the stem end if hardened.
2. Melt the butter in a 10-inch or a 12-inch skillet. When the foaming subsides, add the mushrooms and cook over medium-high heat, shaking the pan often until the mushrooms are lightly browned and all their moisture has evaporated.
3. Add the sherry, and shake the pan while the wine evaporates. Remove the pan from heat and let it cool for 2 minutes.
4. Stir in the crème blanc, and season with nutmeg, salt, and pepper. To serve, garnish with the parsley.

Yield: 4 servings
Calories per serving: 50
Protein per serving: 3g

Fat per serving: 2g
Carbohydrates per serving: 5g
Sodium per serving: 110mg

Onions

❖

Onions are as basic to the larder as shoes are to the wardrobe. While not exactly nutritional powerhouses, they do contribute lots of flavor for a minimal calorie cost.

Members of the onion family that you are likely to use include:

"Yellow" Onions: The yellow onion is the most common variety of onions. Actually brown-skinned, they are available year-round and are dried before being brought to market. They are generally sold in fishnet bags.

Spanish, Bermuda, and Red Onions: With skins ranging from yellow to red, these milder varieties of onions are often eaten raw.

Pearl Onions: These small onions with white skins are often served boiled as a vegetable side course. The slightly larger variety is called a boiling onion.

Scallions: Also called spring onions or green onions, these pencil-shaped onions are generally used raw.

Leeks: Leeks are to the French what a yellow cooking onion is to us—an all purpose flavor enhancer. In this country, however, leeks are expensive, probably a compensation for low sales volume and spoilage. This is unfortunate because leeks are more subtle than the onion. Their mild flavor is prized for soups, stews, and vegetable side courses. They look like overgrown scallions.

Shallots: Looking like pearl onions, but with brown skins, shallots taste like a cross between garlic and onion. They are much used in French cooking.

Chives: A variety of onion in which the top rather than the bulb is used, chives look like thick grass. If chives are unavailable, use the minced green of scallions.

Dry onions (the all-purpose cooking onions, Spanish, Bermuda, and red onions, pearl onions, and shallots) should be stored in a cool, dry place where they are fine until they sprout (about 3 to 4 weeks). Never store onions near potatoes, because they will sprout quickly because of the moisture the potato gives off. Leeks and scallions will keep up to 3 weeks if closed in a plastic bag in the refrigerator.

Scotch Onions

❖

This deliciously simple vegetable goes very well with roasted poultry or a beef dish. It may be made as much as a day ahead and gently reheated.

> 1 pound pearl or small white boiling onions
> 1 cup homemade chicken broth or canned
> ½ cup water
> ½ teaspoon salt
> freshly ground pepper to taste
> 2 teaspoons butter
> 2 tablespoons Scotch
> 1 tablespoon minced fresh parsley (optional)

1. Slice the ends from the onions and put a cross in the root end to prevent them from exploding.
2. Cover the onions with water in a 2½-quart heavy-bottomed saucepan and bring to a boil. Boil onions for 2 minutes, drain, and cool under running water. Slip and discard skins from the onions.
3. Return onions to the saucepan with the broth, water, salt, pepper, and butter. Cover, boil gently until the liquid is almost absorbed and the onions are tender. Onions that are 1½ inch in diameter will be done in about 12 minutes. If the onions are easily pierced with a fork before the liquid is absorbed, lift them from the pot

with a slotted spoon and boil liquid at high heat uncovered until only 2–3 tablespoons remain. Alternately, add more broth or water and extend cooking time if needed.
4. Remove the cover from the pan. Add Scotch with heat turned high. Boil uncovered until a semi-syrupy liquid remains. To serve, dribble a spoonful of sauce over onions. Sprinkle with the parsley if desired.

Yield: 4 servings

Calories per serving: 70

Protein per serving: 2g

Fat per serving: 2g

Carbohydrates per serving: 11g

Sodium per serving: 280mg

Pea and Leek Puree

❖

Leeks are very low in calories and are a good source of potassium and a fair source of vitamin C. Here they are perfectly paired with peas for a do-ahead dinner party dish worthy of the most sophisticated occasion.

Although "fresh" is today's culinary password, here I feel frozen peas will pass the test. Frozen peas, however, are higher in sodium than fresh peas; the sodium content for this recipe is for fresh peas.

> 1 bunch leeks (about 3 stalks)
> 3/4 cup homemade or canned chicken broth
> 1 cup fresh or frozen peas
> 1/3 cup homemade or canned chicken broth
> 1 teaspoon butter
> 1 teaspoon freshly snipped tarragon leaves or 1/2
>   teaspoon dried tarragon
> 1/4 teaspoon salt
> lots of freshly ground black pepper to taste

1. Cut and discard the green stalks from the leeks. Slice the white of leek in half the long way, then dice. Rinse very thoroughly in a colander.
2. Put the leeks and the broth in a 1-quart saucepan. Cover and cook over high heat until tender, about 20 minutes. When the liquid is evaporated and the leeks are limp, empty into a food processor.
3. Put the peas and the broth into the now-empty saucepan. Cover and cook for 2 minutes at high heat (a little longer for fresh peas). Empty into the food processor, unevaporated liquid and all.
4. Add the butter, tarragon, salt, and pepper. Puree. The vegetable is ready to eat or may be reheated in a double boiler before serving time.

Note: Without a food processor, you may puree the vegetables in a food mill, or in batches by hand, but you will have some difficulty pureeing it in a blender.

Yield: 4 servings
Calories per serving: 60
Protein per serving: 3g

Fat per serving: 1g
Carbohydrates per serving: 9g
Sodium per serving: 140mg

Leek Quiche with a Cornmeal Sage Crepe Crust

❖

The quiche, a luncheon favorite for the last decade or so, has been responsible for a lot of spread. A typical pastry crust for one pie tallies up a whopping 1,000 calories, and that's just the bottom of things, Add to that a heavy dose of cream, bacon, and cheese, and one little slice of quiche weighs in at about 350 calories, with a very high percentage of fat. This leek quiche, with its crepe crust and milk instead of cream, is considerably lighter and very delicious. Although the quiche may be made ahead and reheated, you'd do better to make the crepe crust and the filling beforehand, then assemble at the last minute and bake. The crepe could be prepared 24 hours in advance, the filling, 4–5 hours.

For the Crepe Crust

3 *tablespoons all-purpose flour*
3 *tablespoons yellow cornmeal*
1/2 *teaspoon salt*
4 or 5 *leaves fresh sage, snipped, or* 1/2 *teaspoon dried sage*
1 *egg*
1 *egg white*
4 *tablespoons milk*
3 *tablespoons chicken stock or canned consomme*

For the Quiche

1 *pound sliced white of leek (about 3 1/2 cups from 2 or 3 bunches)*
1/2 *cup chicken stock or canned consomme*
3 *eggs*
1 1/2 *cups milk*
freshly grated nutmeg
1/2 *teaspoon salt*
freshly ground pepper to taste
1/2 *teaspoon Dijon-style mustard*
2 *ounces Swiss cheese, grated*

To Prepare the Crepe

1. Preheat the oven to 325 degrees. Spray a 12-inch round pizza pan (or a rectangular 11-inch by 14-inch shallow baking sheet) that has 1/2-inch sides with cooking spray.

2. Sift the flour, cornmeal, and salt together in a small bowl. Mix in the sage.

3. Beat the egg, egg white, milk, and stock together in a measuring cup. Pour into the flour mixture and stir to combine.

4. Pour into the prepared pizza pan (just cover the bottom, you may not use all the batter) and bake in the oven for 15–18 minutes. Remove the pan from oven and prick a fork into any bubbles that have risen. Set the crepe aside while preparing the filling. Adjust oven temperature to 375 degrees.

For the Quiche

1. Wash the sliced leeks well. Place them in a 12-inch skillet with the stock, cover, and simmer until tender, 15–20 minutes. Remove from heat and set aside.

2. In a bowl or food processor, mix together the eggs, milk, nutmeg, salt and pepper.

3. Spray a 9½-inch quiche pan with cooking spray. Lay the crepe in it. Trim any excess pastry.

4. With a pastry brush, spread the mustard over the crepe.

5. Spread cooked leeks over bottom, cover leeks with grated cheese, and pour filling over. Set in the lower third of the hot oven and bake until puffed and golden, 30 to 35 minutes. Let the quiche rest for 10 minutes before slicing.

Yield: 6 servings
Calories per serving: 170
Protein per serving: 12g

Fat per serving: 7g
Carbohydrates per serving: 15g
Sodium per serving: 473mg

❖ **THINKING THIN TIP** ❖

Make dinner an occasion by setting the table and eating by candlelight.

Potatoes

❖

Shopping for a plain old potato poses a surprisingly large amount of choices. There are many varieties, from round white to long russet, from new potatoes to old (mature). There are waxy spuds and mealy ones, some sold loose and others in bags. What's a body to do? Short of memorizing every variety and its particular use, let this be a simple guide. Purchase new potatoes, those that look like they're suffering from bad sunburn with chafed and peeling skin, for salads, boiling, and steaming. New potatoes are less likely to break in tossing because their high-moisture/low-starch ratio means they absorb less of the cooking liquid. Happily, new potatoes will absorb less of the dressing, too. Choose the old (mature) potatoes for mashing and baking. Their low-moisture content make for fluffier mashed and baked potatoes.

Purchase only as many potatoes as you can use within 2 weeks, and don't store them in the refrigerator, if possible. Excessive cold converts the potato's starch to sugar, affecting the flavor. Store potatoes in a cool, dark spot. At room temperature they should keep 2–3 weeks. If kept in the light, green spots develop that give the tuber a bitter taste.

As has been widely reported, a plain baked potato has about the same number of calories as a banana. I can't speak for everyone, but while I would certainly eat a banana out of hand, I'd have to be awfully hungry to eat a plain baked potato. Yet nutritionally and economically the humble potato is an excellent buy. It's high in energy-sustaining carbohydrates, yet low in fat. With a good amount of iron and potassium, some calcium, phosphorus, and vitamins B1, C, and niacin, it seems sensible to enjoy potatoes. The trick is to enhance the flavor without inflating the calorie count. The following recipe is such an attempt.

Red Bliss Potato Salad

❖

Red Bliss potatoes are sometimes simply called red-skinned potatoes. This salad is quick to prepare because the potatoes don't need to be peeled. It is very good with a simple grilled fish or the Parchment Chicken with Tomato Vinaigrette on page 165.

> 1 pound Red Bliss potatoes
> 3 tablespoons sherry vinegar or red wine vinegar
> 1 teaspoon sugar
> 5 tablespoons plain yogurt
> 4 tablespoons mayonnaise
> 2 tablespoons freshly chopped dill
> 1/2 teaspoon Dijon-style mustard
> 1/2 teaspoon salt
> freshly ground pepper to taste
> 1/2 teaspoon capers, drained

1. Cover the potatoes with water by a generous inch and boil them until easily pierced with a fork, about 25 minutes. Drain, cool under running water, and let potatoes rest 10–15 minutes before slicing.
2. Pour the vinegar over sliced potatoes, and sprinkle with sugar. Set aside while mixing sauce.
3. Combine yogurt, mayonnaise, dill, mustard, salt, and pepper in a bowl. Mix. Toss the sauce gently with potatoes. Taste for seasoning adjustment. Serve just slightly chilled with capers sprinkled over.

Yield: 6 servings
Calories per serving: 125
Protein per serving: 2g

Fat per serving: 8g
Carbohydrates per serving: 12g
Sodium per serving: 260mg

Red Peppers

❖

About a dozen years ago, French chefs began experimenting with roasting red peppers, turning them into wonderful sauces or delicious salads, or combining them with herbs such as basil to create subtle but distinctive compound butters. Today it's almost impossible to open any cooking magazine without seeing at least one recipe using roasted red peppers.

Roasting a pepper, red or green, is actually to broil it, then allow it to cool in a tightly closed bag. The steam loosens the charred skin, which then pulls off as easily as old paint—if you've broiled it sufficiently but not overdone it. The broiling process cooks the flesh, turning it yet a deeper scarlet. It has a mild, sweet taste quite unsurpassed by other vegetables. It may then be marinated and served at room temperature as a salad; sauteed with any combination of vegetables; or pureed with herbs, oils, and a touch of vinegar or, if this were not a waist-conscious book, cream. As a sauce it is delicious over other vegetables such as green beans, broccoli, and the like, or over fish or even poultry. It is wonderful on spinach fettuccine as a fine first course or a casual dinner.

A red pepper is nothing more than a green pepper allowed to mature and ripen on the vine. Yet because most peppers are harvested when green, red peppers are somewhat scarce and often expensive. Although you can sometimes ripen a green pepper that has begun to blush by putting it with a cut apple in a paper bag for a day or two, it is likely to decay before becoming scarlet. When they are available, take advantage of their high vitamin A and C content by making up the following puree and freezing it.

TO ROAST PEPPERS

1. Place a seeded, halved pepper, skin side up, on a flat surface. Flatten pepper with the heel of your hand.

2. Broil pepper until it is completely blackened, cool, then peel away the charred skin and discard.

TO JULIENNE PEPPERS

A roasted or raw pepper is often sliced into julienned strips for use in cooking.

Red Pepper Puree
with Prosciutto

❖

This delicious sauce may be made ahead and reheated at serving time. When used as a sauce for vegetables, the prosciutto may be omitted.

4 large red bell peppers
1 tablespoon extra-virgin olive oil
2 tablespoons minced fresh parsley
8–10 fresh basil leaves, snipped, or 1 teaspoon
   dried basil
1 clove garlic, minced
2 ounces prosciutto, cut into thin strips
1/2 teaspoon salt
freshly ground pepper to taste

1. Cut the peppers in half. Remove and discard the seeds and inner membranes. Flatten a pepper with the heel of your hand and place it, skin side up, on a baking sheet. Repeat. Broil the peppers until they're completely blackened and charred. The skin will not peel off easily unless it's burned, so don't be shy about doing so. Don't let the peppers dry out, however. Remove the burned peppers to a plastic or paper bag, roll the bag tightly closed, and place it in the freezer until the peppers are cool enough to handle, about 10 minutes.
2. With your fingers, peel and discard the loosened skin from the peppers. Rinse the flesh under running water.
3. Roughly chop the peppers and combine them with the oil, parsley, basil, and garlic in a food processor. Puree. If using a food mill or blender, puree the vegetables first, then combine it with the other ingredients.
4. Spray an 8-inch skillet with cooking spray. "Saute" the pro-

sciutto over high heat, just to heat through.

5. Stir the meat into the red pepper puree, add salt and pepper, and taste for seasoning adjustment.

Yield with prosciutto: 6 servings
Calories per serving: 95
Protein per serving: 3g

Fat per serving: 6g
Carbohydrates per serving: 8g
Sodium per serving: 370mg

Yield without prosciutto: 6 servings
Calories per serving: 60
Protein per serving: 1g

Fat per serving: 3g
Carbohydrates per serving: 8g
Sodium per serving: 190mg

Pasta with Prosciutto and Red Pepper Puree

Use the above recipe to coat 12 ounces fresh linguine. Cook and drain noodles according to package instructions. Toss with 1 table-spoon butter and the puree. Delicious as a side dish with lamb or as a first course for a dinner party. Remember to heat the plates when serving pasta. Pass grated cheese at the table if desired. Serves 4–6.

Green Beans with Red Pepper Puree

Use the above puree, without the prosciutto, to sauce 1 pound cooked green beans tossed with 1 tablespoon butter. Serves 6.

Marinated Roasted Peppers

❖

Roasted red peppers are also delicious when marinated in oil (tiny amounts, of course!), vinegar, and herbs and served at room temperature as a vegetable side dish. This dish is best made a day ahead.

2 red bell peppers
2 green bell peppers
1 tablespoon oil, walnut oil recommended
1 tablespoon balsamic or malt vinegar, available at specialty food stores
2 tablespoons beef stock or canned consomme
1 clove garlic, minced
8 fresh basil leaves, snipped, or 1 teaspoon dried basil
⅛ teaspoon salt
freshly ground pepper to taste
1 tablespoon minced fresh parsley

1. Cut the peppers in half. Discard the seeds and inner membranes. Place the peppers, skin side up, on a baking sheet. Broil them until they're blackened and charred. Put the peppers in a plastic or paper bag, roll bag tightly closed and chill them until cool enough to handle.
2. Peel and discard the skin. Lay the peppers in a glass or ceramic dish.
3. Combine the oil, vinegar, stock, garlic, and basil. Pour the mixture over peppers. Sprinkle the peppers with salt, pepper, and parsley just before serving.

Yield: 4 servings
Calories per serving: 70
Protein per serving: 2g

Fat per serving: 4g
Carbohydrates per serving: 9g
Sodium per serving: 80mg

Wok Saute
of Peppers and Broccoli

❖

This is a basic method for sauteing any combination of vegetables with roasted red peppers. Likely combinations are sliced Chinese celery, pea pods, zucchini, and so forth. Strips of cooked ham or prosciutto are very good, too, when served with vegetable dinners. The use of a wok cuts down on the amount of fat needed, and also allows you to push the quicker-cooking vegetables up on the rim out of heat's way. If you're using a traditional flat skillet, just add the slowest-cooking vegetable first. These vegetables may be readied for cooking ahead of time, but stir-fry them at the last moment. Their freshness will be compromised if reheated.

> 4 tablespoons chicken stock or canned consomme
> 1 small clove garlic, minced
> 1 cup broccoli flowerets sliced, and stems, peeled
>   and julienned (see page 45)
> 1 teaspoon oil, possibly more if using a skillet instead
>   of a wok
> 1 cup mushrooms, sliced
> 3 red bell peppers, roasted, peeled (see Steps 1 and
>   2, page 261), and julienned
> 1/4 teaspoon salt
> freshly ground pepper to taste
> 1 tablespoon minced fresh parsley

1. Heat the wok over high heat. Add the stock and garlic and cook, stirring constantly, for 30 seconds.
2. Add the broccoli and cook over high heat, stirring until crisp-tender, about 1 minute. Push the broccoli up onto the sides of wok (or remove from the wok and keep warm).
3. Add the oil and mushrooms. Cook, stirring over high heat, about

1 minute. Push the mushrooms up onto the sides of wok.

4. Add the red peppers. Cook over high heat, stirring constantly until heated through, about 30 seconds longer.

5. Push all the vegetables down to the bottom of wok to heat through. Season with salt and pepper. Sprinkle with parsley and serve.

Yield: 4 servings
Calories per serving: 70
Protein per serving: 3g

Fat per serving: 2g
Carbohydrates per serving: 12g
Sodium per serving: 20mg

Spinach

❖

This versatile vegetable might not have made Popeye's muscles bulge, but certainly contributed to his general well-being. A mere half-cup of cooked spinach supplies an adult with twice the daily requirement of vitamin A, half the vitamin C, and one-fifth the RDA of iron. It is also a good source of folic acid, a B vitamin. All this for just 28 calories! You might have also heard that it is rich in calcium, but because of the presence of oxalic acid, the calcium is not available to the body.

When purchasing spinach, avoid spinach with yellowing or mushy leaves. Spinach sold in bulk (that is, by the pound) requires very thorough washing to remove the inevitable sand and grit. You'll also want to strip off the stems as they are both tough and slightly bitter. After stemming, soak the leaves in a sinkful of tepid water for a few minutes. Lift the leaves from the water, drain, rinse the sand from the sink, and repeat, this time with cold water.

Spinach sold in cellophane bags is generally sand-free, but you still may wish to remove the stems and backbones and rinse the leaves in cold water, especially if serving them raw in a salad.

Stored in a plastic bag in the refrigerator, spinach will keep 4 to 5 days.

Spinach-Ricotta Tart

❖

This simply made tart is quick to put together, easy to trek to a picnic, and a treat to eat hot or at room temperature. It makes a nice lunch, light dinner, or out-of-the ordinary vegetable side dish. Alternate slices of summer squash with the tomato for a colorful change. Make as much as a day in advance, but for best results, do not freeze. Phyllo is available in the frozen food section of most supermarkets. Leftover phyllo dough will keep in the refrigerator up to 4 weeks; if refrozen it tends to get crumbly.

2 pounds fresh or frozen spinach
1 16-ounce container part-skim ricotta cheese
1 onion, diced
3 eggs
10 fresh basil leaves, snipped, or 1 teaspoon dried
     basil
1 teaspoon salt
freshly ground pepper
a few gratings nutmeg
2 sheets phyllo dough
2–3 medium tomatoes
black olive (optional)
2 tablespoons crumbled blue cheese, or grated
     Parmesan cheese

1. Wash the spinach very thoroughly. Pack it into a 2-1/2 quart saucepan with the water that clings to its leaves. Cover, and cook over high heat until the leaves are wilted, about 30 seconds to one minute. Drain in a colander, pressing the spinach with the pan bottom to extract as much water as possible. If using frozen spinach, simply thaw and squeeze to remove excess moisture.
2. Put the spinach in a food processor (or chop finely and place in a

bowl), add the cheese, onion, eggs, basil, salt, lots of pepper, and nutmeg. Mix well.

3. In a 9-inch quiche pan, crisscross the two sheets of phyllo. Pour in the spinach-cheese mixture. Trim the corners of the phyllo so just 2 inches remain, and roll the edges in to create a rim of pastry. Don't be alarmed when the dough tears, that will make it appear flaky when cooked.

4. Preheat oven to 400 degrees.

5. Slice the tomatoes. Cut each slice in half. Arrange slices to resemble a flower by overlapping them in a circle on top of the tart. Put a black olive at center if desired. Season with more pepper. Spray the edges of the pastry with cooking spray.

6. Bake the tart in the lower third of the preheated oven. Sprinkle the cheese over the top after 25 minutes. Cook about 15 minutes more. The tart is done when the center no longer shakes when wiggled, and a knife inserted slightly off center comes out cleanly. Let the tart rest 10 minutes before slicing.

Yield: 6-8 servings
Calories per serving: 245
Protein per serving: 19g

Fat per serving: 11g
Carbohydrates per serving: 19g
Sodium per serving: 640mg

❖   **THINKING THIN TIP**   ❖

You can enjoy cheese, just choose those made from milk instead of cream.

Summer Squash

❖

Soft-shelled summer squash (though many varieties are available year round) is a good supplier of vitamins A and C with a virtually free calorie count—about 15 calories in a half cup. And—joy of joys!—they taste good, too.

A rundown on the most popular varieties:

Zucchini and cocozelle: both pale green, best harvested about 5 inches long and 2–3 inches in diameter.

Yellow crookneck and straightneck: pale yellow that deepens as the squash reaches maturity, sometimes has bumpy skin. Best harvested when about 6 inches in length and 3–4 inches in diameter.

Scallop, pattypan, or cymling: dish-shaped squash with a scalloped edge, pale green changing to white as the vegetable matures. Best 3–4 inches across.

Purchase summer squash when the skin is soft enough not to need peeling. Refrigerate it for up to a week. If you garden or have ever been the dubious recipient of those baseball bat-sized zucchini, don't give it to your kids for batting practice. Peeled and seeded, just as you would a cucumber, it makes a fine soup (page 82). You also may prepare it as outlined here with the addition of a little chopped onion and a sprinkling of dried bread crumbs, then freeze it. Bake it in a 350-degree oven until heated through.

Zucchini Saute

❖

This recipe works well with any of the summer squash. While it may be readied for cooking in advance, saute it just before serving. Don't be put off by the amount of salt (it's washed out).

> 3 small zucchini
> 2 teaspoons salt
> 1 tablespoon butter
> 1 whole clove garlic, peeled
> a few gratings fresh nutmeg
> lots of freshly ground pepper to taste

1. Cut the ends from the zucchini and grate either by hand or in a food processor. Place the squash in a sieve and toss with the salt. Let the vegetable rest at least 20 minutes. The salt draws excess moisture from the vegetable.
2. Rinse the salted zucchini very thoroughly under running water, tossing and squeezing the vegetable in your fingers to rinse out the salt. Squeeze the zucchini against the sieve to remove the water. Taste to be sure the salt is removed.
3. Melt the butter in a 10-inch skillet over medium-high heat. Spear the garlic clove on a toothpick and add it to the butter. When butter is foamy, add the squeezed zucchini and saute, stirring constantly until just heated through, about 2 minutes. Season with nutmeg and pepper. Remove the garlic.

Yield: 4 servings
Calories per serving: 50
Protein per serving: 2g

Fat per serving: 3g
Carbohydrates per serving: 4g
Sodium per serving: 130mg

Zucchini Boats
with Eggplant Caviar

❖

Make the eggplant caviar for this dish a day or two before serving, and prepare and assemble the boats early in the day. Bake or reheat at dinnertime. Or pile the eggplant caviar into hollowed, salted, and drained tomatoes for cool dining on sun-sweltering days. Leftover eggplant caviar can have another life as an hors d'oeuvre mounded on cucumber slices, stuffed in blanched mushroom caps for broiling, or spread on *croustades* and sprinkled with cheese.

For the Eggplant Caviar

1   *medium eggplant, a little over a pound*
1   *tomato, blanched, peeled, seeded, and chopped*
1   *clove garlic, minced*
1   *tablespoon red wine or raspberry vinegar*
1   *tablespoon extra-virgin olive oil*
1   *tablespoon minced fresh parsley*
2   *tablespoons pine nuts (or blanched almonds)*
a few drops hot pepper sauce
½ teaspoon salt
freshly ground pepper to taste

For the Zucchini Boats

3   *small zucchini or 1 overgrown one*
½ teaspoon salt
2   *tablespoons grated cheese such as Swiss, or dried
      bread crumbs*

To Prepare the Eggplant Caviar

1. Preheat oven to 400 degrees. Cut off the ends of the eggplant and pierce it in several places with a fork. Bake eggplant until soft, about 30 minutes. Cool slightly.
2. Skin the eggplant, cut it into quarters, and scoop out seeds. Put the pulp in a food processor or blender.
3. Add the tomato, garlic, vinegar, oil, parsley, pine nuts, pepper sauce, salt, and pepper. Blend but leave the mixture chunky. Taste for seasoning.
4. Refrigerate the eggplant caviar at least 2 hours to marry flavors. May be frozen without flavor loss up to 2 months.

For the Zucchini Boats

1. Cut the zucchini in half the long way. Scoop out a hollow with a teaspoon. Repeat. Seed and cut each half in thirds if using 1 overgrown squash.
2. Bring a 2½-quart saucepan half full of water to a boil. Add the halved zucchini and blanch 3 minutes (10 minutes if using a very large one). Drain.
3. Preheat oven to 350 degrees. Place the zucchini boats in an oven-tempered serving dish just large enough to hold them. Season with salt. Mound 3 tablespoons of eggplant caviar into each small half, or divide the mixture to fill the larger zucchini boats. Sprinkle with cheese or bread crumbs. Bake in the 350-degree oven about 30 minutes or until bubbly and cheese is browned.

Note: Boats may be held for several hours, even a day, before cooking.

Yield: 6 servings
Calories per serving: 90
Protein per serving: 4g

Fat per serving: 5g
Carbohydrates per serving: 8g
Sodium per serving: 420mg

Ratatouille

❖

Ratatouille is a medley of eggplant, zucchini, onions, peppers, and tomatoes heady with the perfume of sweet basil. It takes a bit of time to prepare, but is best made a day ahead. It also freezes well. Make it when summer's produce is at its peak and serve beside a cold poached salmon or a simple roasted chicken. All by itself it makes for a most satisfying lunch.

1 small eggplant, about ½ pound
3 teaspoons extra-virgin olive oil
1 medium zucchini
4 tablespoons chicken stock or canned consomme
2 green peppers, diced
2 medium onions, about 1¾ cups, diced
1 clove garlic, minced
1 pound tomatoes, blanched, peeled, and seeded
10 fresh basil leaves, snipped, or 1 teaspoon dried
   basil
1 teaspoon salt
freshly ground pepper to taste
1 tablespoon minced fresh parsley

1. Cut the ends from the eggplant and slice it into rounds ½-inch thick. Stack the slices and cut the rounds into 6 or 8 wedges.
2. With cooking spray, spray a skillet large enough to hold the egg-plant in one layer. Add 2 teaspoons of the oil and turn the heat to high. When hot, add the eggplant and cook over high heat until tender and lightly browned, about 8 minutes. Lower heat if egg-plant starts to burn. Shake pan vigorously by the handle during cooking to keep the eggplant from sticking, and to turn it. Remove to a casserole.
3. While the eggplant cooks, cut the ends from the zucchini, slice it

into rounds, stack the slices, and cut them into wedges.

4. Spray the skillet again, add the rest of the oil, along with the zucchini, and cook over high heat until lightly browned. Shake the pan often during cooking. Remove zucchini to the casserole with the eggplant.

5. Add the stock to the now-empty skillet, add the peppers, onions, and garlic, cover the skillet, and cook over medium-low heat until the vegetables are limp. If there is visible liquid after cooking, raise the heat to high to evaporate. Add these to the eggplant mixture.

6. Bring a 2½-quart saucepan half full of water to a boil. Core the tomatoes and make a cross in each one's bottom. Immerse in the boiling water until the skins loosen, about 40 seconds. Cool under running water. Skin the tomatoes. Holding a tomato over a strainer within a bowl, squeeze the seeds from each one. Chop the pulp and add it to the eggplant-onion mixture. Hold the strainer over the casserole. Press the seeds with a wooden spoon to extract the juice. Discard the seeds.

7. Snip the basil over the eggplant-tomato mixture. Season with salt and lots of freshly ground pepper. Toss to mix well. Sprinkle parsley over.

8. Casserole may be baked, covered, at 350 degrees for about 35 minutes or until heated through, or cooked over low heat, covered, on top of the stove. Be careful the vegetables don't burn on the bottom! Serve warm, at room temperature, or cold.

Yield: 6 servings
Calories per serving: 65
Protein per serving: 2g

Fat per serving: 3g
Carbohydrates per serving: 7g
Sodium per serving: 370mg

Tomatoes

❖

The only good tomato is a local tomato. It doesn't matter where "local" is—though New Jerseyites will disagree—it only matters that the tomato be allowed to ripen on the vine to develop peak flavor. Don't be misled by the "vine-ripened" label. Vine ripened does mean the fruit was picked at maturity, but possibly while still green. The reddening is accomplished by spraying the shipment with ethylene gas. Other vine-ripened tomatoes are picked when just pink. These need no booster of ethylene gas, but they do need, in my opinion, Mother Nature to raise them right. Only the sun can impart the sweet, rich flavor of a truly vine-ripened tomato, the sort you buy at a local farmstand.

Another tomato you may have seen is the greenhouse or hydroponic tomato. This is grown in water and is amazingly good, though quite expensive.

Although tomatoes, or a not so reasonable facsimile, can be purchased all year long, the season for most local tomatoes is from May to September, depending on your location. "Seconds," bruised or misshapen tomatoes, are perfect for many uses at about half the price of the perfect specimens.

An uncooked tomato supplies a little over half an adult's daily need of vitamin C, for a meager 35 calories.

The recipes that follow are for those sun-dappled months when local tomatoes abound.

Cheese Frosted Tomatoes

❖

Select small- to medium-size local tomatoes for this quick vegetable dish. To cook on a covered grill, place them on a sheet of aluminum foil. Tomatoes may be prepared for cooking hours before baking.

6 ripe tomatoes
1/4 teaspoon salt
freshly ground pepper to taste
2 tablespoons olive oil
6 teaspoons Basil-Walnut Sauce, page 32, or 15 leaves fresh basil, snipped, or 3 teaspoons dried basil
6 tablespoons grated cheese, such as Jarlsberg

1. Core the tomatoes and make a cross on each one's bottom. Bring a 4-quart saucepan half full of water to a boil. Immerse the tomatoes for 30 seconds, or just long enough to loosen the skins. Remove them, cool under running water, and peel off the skins.
2. With a melon baller, make a well where the core was. Place the tomatoes in a baking dish.
3. Preheat oven to 325 degrees. Season tomatoes with salt and pepper. Drizzle with oil. Place a teaspoon of Basil-Walnut Sauce or the basil in each tomato well. Divide the cheese over the top and bake in a 325-degree oven for 20 minutes. If desired, broil until the cheese is lightly browned.

Yield: 6 servings
Calories per serving: 90
Protein per serving: 2g

Fat per serving: 7g
Carbohydrates per serving: 5g
Sodium per serving: 110mg

Tomato and Chèvre Tart

❖

Tomatoes and cheese, a standard coupling of age-proven compatabil-
ity, are updated here with the introduction of chèvre. The production
of chèvre, essentially a cottage industry, has caught on in this country,
although most chèvre is imported. Although the import of chèvre has
increased as much as 137 percent in the last 2 years, it still accounts
for less than 1 percent of all cheese consumed in America. For your
pleasure, here's a tart that travels well and, like most vegetable tarts, is
as tempting at room temperature as it is hot from the oven.

> 3 pounds tomatoes
> 3 tablespoons homemade or canned chicken broth
> 2 medium onions, chopped (preferably mild)
> 1 clove garlic, minced
> 8–10 fresh basil leaves, snipped, or 1 teaspoon
>   dried basil
> 1/8 teaspoon fennel seed
> 1 teaspoon sugar
> 1/2 teaspoon salt
> freshly ground pepper to taste
> 3 eggs
> 1/2 cup crème blanc (page 37) or sour cream
>   substitute
> a few gratings fresh nutmeg
> 2 ounces chèvre cheese, such as Montrachet or
>   Banon (if a milder taste is preferred)
> 2 sheets phyllo dough

1. Bring a 4-quart saucepan ¾ full of water to a boil. Blanch the
tomatoes, peel the skins, and seed the tomatoes into a strainer supported over a bowl. Press the seeds with a spoon to extract the juices,

discard seeds. Chop the tomatoes roughly and set aside with reserved juices.

2. Put the broth in a 10-inch skillet over high heat. Add the onion, cover, and cook over medium-high heat until limp, about 6–8 minutes. Add the garlic the last few minutes of cooking.

3. Add the reserved juice, tomatoes, basil, fennel seed, sugar, salt, and pepper. Cook over medium-low heat, stirring occasionally, for 5 minutes. If there is more than ¼ cup liquid left, raise the heat to high to evaporate. Set the mixture aside.

4. In a bowl or a food processor, beat together the eggs, crème blanc, and nutmeg. Set it aside.

5. Crisscross the 2 sheets of phyllo in a 9-inch removable-bottom tart ring or in a 9-inch quiche pan. Trim the overhanging pastry with scissors to 1 ½ inches.

6. Preheat oven to 350 degrees. Pour the tomato-onion mixture into the pan. Pour the egg mixture over. Crumble the chèvre on top. Roll and crumple the pastry edges in to create a rim. Don't worry if the pastry tears. Spray the pastry edge with cooking spray to help it brown. Place in the bottom third of the preheated 350-degree oven and bake 45 minutes or until the center no longer wiggles when shaken. Let it rest 10 minutes before slicing.

Note: Never spray cooking spray into the oven; an explosive fire could result.

Yield: 6 servings
Calories per serving: 155
Protein per serving: 10g

Fat per serving: 6g
Carbohydrates per serving: 16g
Sodium per serving: 330mg

Winter Squash

❖

Hard-shelled squash, commonly called winter squash, is available much of the year. Some varieties such as Acorn and Buttercup are marketed throughout the year.

Squash was indigenous to the New World and unknown in Europe until explorers returned home with the new vegetable. When North American Indians introduced the English settlers to "askoota-squash," meaning eaten raw, the Europeans shortened the name to squash and proceeded to cook it. Cooking is still the norm.

The common varieties include:

Acorn: ribbed dark-green skin.

Buttercup: dark green with stripes of gray; blossom end is turban shaped.

Butternut: smooth buff-colored skin with a bulbous end.

Hubbard: warty skin with maybe blue-gray, green, or an orange tint.

Turban: two-toned with the top knot blue-gray, and the remainder an orange with stripes.

Spaghetti squash: a recently popular hard-shelled squash. It is a gourd of Oriental origin that is becoming increasingly available. When cooked, its bland but pleasantly crunchy strands resemble thin spaghetti, but with far fewer calories.

Most varieties of winter squash provide a tasty source of vitamin A, along with significant amounts of riboflavin and iron. They supply from approximately 35 to 70 calories a half-cup.

Winter squashes are long-keeping vegetables. They do best in a cool, dry, well-ventilated spot where they will keep one to four weeks.

Spaghetti Squash Primavera

❖

Spaghetti squash may be tossed with just a hint of butter and seasoned with salt and pepper, or you can gussy it up, as it is here. It is delicious with either the Basil-Walnut Sauce (page 32), or the Lemon Parsley Sauce (page 31). Though it may be baked, boiled, or steamed, I find baking the simplest.

This casserole will satisfy some appetites as a complete meal, though others may want a little something else. It may be assembled early in the day or at the last minute.

> 1 2-pound spaghetti squash
> 1 tablespoon butter, at room temperature
> 2 ounces grated Italian cheese, Fontina
>   recommended
> 1/2 bunch broccoli flowerets, sliced
> 1 cup shelled fresh peas (about 1 pound in the pod)
> 1 small zucchini, julienned
> 3 ounces cooked ham, cut into strips
> 3/4 cup sliced mushrooms
> 1 teaspoon salt
> freshly ground pepper to taste
> 2 ounces bacon, about 4 slices, fried and drained
> butter

1. Cut the squash in half the short way. Place it, cut side down, in a baking dish just large enough to hold it, with 1 inch of water.
2. Bake at 350 degrees until the shell is easily pierced with a fork and the flesh shreds when pulled with a fork, about 45 minutes. Cool, scoop out, and discard the seeds. Pull the strands from the squash into a bowl. Discard the tough skin. Toss the squash strands with the butter and the cheese.
3. While the squash is baking, prepare the vegetables. Bring a 2½-

quart saucepan ¾ full of water to a boil. Add the broccoli, boil 1
minute, add the peas, cook 1 minute more, add the zucchini, and
cook 30 seconds more. Drain and cool all the vegetables under
running water. Set vegetables aside.

4. Spray an 8-inch skillet with cooking spray, add the ham strips,
and stir-fry them until they're lightly browned. Remove strips
from the pan to a paper towel.

5. In the same pan, spraying again if necessary, stir-fry the mushrooms until lightly browned.

6. In a large bowl, combine the cooked spaghetti squash, the
drained, blanched vegetables, the mushrooms, and the ham. Season with salt and pepper and toss well to combine. Spoon into a
casserole. Crumble bacon on top. Casserole is ready to eat, or set
aside. Reheat, covered, in a 350-degree oven for 30–35 minutes with a small dab of butter on top. Uncover the last 10 minutes of cooking.

Yield: 4-6 servings
Calories per serving: 185
Protein per serving: 11g

Fat per serving: 10g
Carbohydrates per serving: 13g
Sodium per serving: 490mg

Bourbon Squash Souffle

❖

A puffy presentation of pureed butternut squash combined with bourbon and a hint of maple syrup, this souffle is just the thing when you
want a vegetable dish of distinction. Everything except beating the egg
whites may be readied far in advance of the actual cooking, making
this an easy to make dinner party dish. If you prefer, you can make the
souffle in its entirety and freeze it, uncooked. Turn the freezer to its

coldest setting. Cover the souffle with aluminum foil or plastic wrap and freeze solidly. If the souffle was frozen in a freezer-to-oven dish, bake it frozen, and double the cooking time. In a more fragile dish, thaw for 30 minutes, then bake, again doubling cooking time. Some of the dramatic puff is sacrificed in this method, but it is convenient.

> 1 medium butternut squash, about 1 1/4 pounds
> 2 tablespoons bourbon
> 3 tablespoons maple syrup
> 1/2 teaspoon salt
> freshly ground pepper to taste
> a few gratings nutmeg
> 3 tablespoons cornstarch
> 1 1/2 cups milk
> 2 egg yolks, lightly beaten
> 1 tablespoon grated Parmesan cheese or dried bread
>   crumbs
> 4 egg whites
> a pinch cream of tartar

1. Preheat the oven to 400 degrees. Peel the squash, chop into eighths, and discard the seeds. Bring a 2 1/2-quart saucepan 2/3 full of water to a boil, immerse the squash, and cook it until tender, about 20 minutes. Drain.
2. Mash the squash with the bourbon, maple syrup, salt, pepper, and nutmeg. Set the mixture aside.
3. Dissolve the cornstarch in the milk. Set it over medium-high heat and whisk until thickened, about 3 minutes. Set aside.
4. In a food processor or a bowl with a hand-held mixer, beat the egg yolks into the squash puree. Beat in the thickened milk. Set aside or refrigerate.
5. Spray a 1-quart souffle dish or other straight-sided baking dish (preferably with a 6-inch diameter) with cooking spray. Sprinkle in cheese or bread crumbs. Shake the dish to evenly distribute. Make a collar for the dish by folding a length of aluminum foil, long enough to encircle the dish with a 2-inch overlap, into thirds.

Spray the nonseamed side of the foil with cooking spray, or butter it heavily. Wrap this collar seam side out, tightly around the dish, secure it with a straight pin or paper clip.

6. When you're ready to complete this souffle, beat the egg whites until foamy. Add the cream of tartar. Beat until soft peaks form. Scoop the egg whites on top of the squash mixture. Fold them in gently. Ladle (pouring can deflate the whites) the souffle mixture into the souffle dish.

7. Put 1 inch water in an 8-inch square baking dish. Put the souffle dish in the baking dish on top of the stove. Turn heat to high, simmer for 5 minutes. Baking pan and all, slide souffle into the bottom third of a preheated oven. Check the souffle after 35 minutes, if the top is browning too fast, cover loosely with foil. Cook 15 to 25 minutes more. Souffle is done when a skewer inserted slightly off center comes out dry. Remove collar and serve immediately.

Yield: 6 servings
Calories per serving: 105
Protein per serving: 6g

Fat per serving: 2g
Carbohydrates per serving: 16g
Sodium per serving: 250mg

Chapter 10

SWEETS AND TREATS

Sweets and Treats

❖

Because the premise of *Gourmet Light* rests on fine foods skillfully prepared, there is no room for ersatz, make-do ingredients. This restriction (but certainly no limitation) excludes the use of sacharrin or other artificial sweeteners. Thus most of the desserts here capitalize on the naturally occurring sugars (fructose) in fruits and/or rely on reduced amounts of cane sugar. Most desserts are based, in some combination, on sugar, flour, and fat, either butter and/or cream. These key ingredients are among the most caloric of all foods, while contributing few nutrients. Sugar, white or brown, contains about 873 calories a cup. White sugar is virtually nutrient empty while 3 1/2 ounces of brown sugar supplies almost as much potassium as does a banana and a small amount of calcium—but at a terrific calorie toll. The second key ingredient in sweets is cream at 838 calories a cup. And flour is another 800 calories a cup, to say nothing of butter at 1,600 calories a cup, an important component of the dessert cart, however in hidden form. The body tallies these calories more accurately than the bank does your checks—not a one is ever forgotten or overlooked. This small collection of dessert recipes, in keeping the *Gourmet Light* theme, limits the use of sugar, fats, and flours. But by its mere existence this section acknowledges that one cannot live by fish and green beans alone, nor even the ideal dessert of unadorned fresh fruit. It is hoped, particularly if weight loss rather than maintenance is your goal, that portion sizes are closely watched.

Berries and Almond Cream

❖

Fresh strawberries, blueberries, or raspberries smothered in cream—
sweet heaven that can be yours given the *Gourmet Light* touch. This
custard sauce, with the texture of heavy cream and the fragrance of
vanilla or almond, is wonderful over fresh, ripe fruits or as a dipping
sauce for a fruit fondue. It is also delightful spooned over slices of
Almond Angel Cake, page 309. If you prefer a thicker custard sauce,
try Crème Anglaise, on page 286.

For the Almond Cream

1 1/2 cups milk
2 eggs
3 tablespoons sugar
a few drops almond extract or 1/2 teaspoon pure
*   vanilla extract*

For the Berries

3 to 4 cups fresh strawberries or other berries,
*   stemmed and rinsed*
1 tablespoon sugar

1. Scald the milk in a 1-quart saucepan. Set aside.
2. Meanwhile, beat the eggs and sugar together in the top part of a
   double boiler with a hand-held electric mixer until the eggs thicken
   and turn very pale in color, about 2 to 3 minutes.
3. Put 1 inch of water into the bottom part of the double boiler, set
   over high heat until it comes to a simmer. Put eggs in top part of
   double boiler over hot water, adjusting heat as necessary to keep
   water just simmering. Beat the eggs until the mixture doubles in
   volume and feels tepid to the touch. Beat in scalded milk, pour
   into a heavy-bottomed 2 1/2-quart saucepan, and stir constantly
   with a wooden spoon over medium heat until the custard sauce

thickens slightly. Insert a thermometer at the side of the pan if you wish. Stir constantly over medium heat until the thermometer registers 175. The custard sauce should not exceed 175 degrees. Without a thermometer, cook the custard sauce, stirring constantly, until it coats a metal spoon lightly and sauce is thickened, about 8 minutes.

4. Strain into a bowl, stir in extract, and chill or serve warm.
5. Clean the berries; cut strawberries in half if desired. Toss with sugar. Divide berries among serving dishes, spoon almond cream over.

Note: Some French chefs like to toss fresh strawberries with just a touch of black pepper on the premise that it heightens their flavor.

Yield: 4 servings
Calories per serving: 175
Protein per serving: 7g

Fat per serving: 4g
Carbohydrates per serving: 142g
Sodium per serving: 80mg

Burgundy Poached Pears with Crème Anglaise

For this variation on a classic dessert, poached pears perched atop a puddle of custard sauce are gently broiled until lightly browned. The components of the dish may be readied a day before, then assembled up to 4 hours before serving. The poaching liquid may be frozen and reused over and over again.

    4 pears, peeled, halved, and cored
    2 tablespoons lemon juice

For the Poaching Liquid

1 liter burgundy wine
½ cup sugar
1 vanilla bean
juice of half a lemon
a cinnamon stick
3 whole cloves

For the Crème Anglaise

4 egg yolks
3 tablespoons sugar
¼ teaspoon salt
1 cup milk, scalded
1 teaspoon vanilla extract

To Prepare the Pears

1. As you peel the pears, slip them into a bowl with the lemon juice to keep them from turning brown.
2. Bring the poaching ingredients to a boil in a 4-quart saucepan. Reduce to a simmer, immerse the pears, cover, and poach until a skewer easily pierces the fruit. Turn the pears during cooking as they will not be completely covered. Do not cook until mushy. The cooking time will depend entirely on the ripeness of the fruit, anywhere from 10-25 minutes or even longer.
3. Drain the pears when tender on a rack over a sheet of wax paper (to collect drippings). Freeze liquid for future poachings (you may leave the spices in the wine).

To Prepare the Crème Anglaise

1. In a heavy 2½-quart saucepan, beat together the egg yolks, sugar, and salt. Do not ribbon the mixture.
2. Slowly add the scalded milk, whisking all the while.
3. Insert a thermometer at the side of the pan if you like. Stirring with a wooden spoon over medium heat, notice the changes that oc-

cur. At 140 degrees, steam rises from the custard. At 155 degrees, the foam starts getting lighter, and at 165 degrees, the surface is smooth and the custard is ready. You may heat the custard to 180 degrees, but not higher, or the yolks will curdle. Without a thermometer, stir the custard over medium heat until it is thick enough to coat a metal spoon, about 3–4 minutes.

4. Strain the custard into a bowl, stir in vanilla extract.

To Finish the Dessert

1. Preheat broiler. Spread the custard sauce on an ovenproof serving dish such as a quiche dish, or on 4 ovenproof serving dishes such as baking shells.
2. Place a poached pear half, flat side down, on a cutting surface. Cut into 5–6 segments, but leave stem end uncut so the pear becomes "fanned." Repeat with remaining pears. Place the pear fan on the custard sauce and broil until heated through.

Note: A few drops of red food coloring added to the poaching liquid will heighten the color of the poached pears.

Yield: 4 servings
Calories per serving: 220 +
Protein per serving: 6g

Fat per serving: 6g
Carbohydrates per serving: 38g
Sodium per serving: 180mg

MAKING A PEAR FAN

Place a poached pear half, flat side down, on a flat surface. Cut it into five or six segments, leaving them attached at the stem end.

Candied Oranges with Melba Sauce

❖

The simplicity of this classic dessert I find very appealing—juicy seedless oranges enhanced with a sugar syrup and drizzled with ruby red raspberry sauce. It may be prepared a day in advance.

8 small navel oranges
¾ cup sugar
1½ cups water
juice of ½ lemon
2 kiwis
2 tablespoons orange-flavored liqueur such as Triple
*   Sec or Grand Marnier*
a 10-ounce package frozen raspberries, thawed

1. With a vegetable peeler, remove the rind (colored part only, no white) from 2 of the oranges. Julienne the rind and set aside.
2. In a heavy 2½-quart saucepan, dissolve the sugar in ½ cup of the water over very low heat. The solution must not boil until the sugar is thoroughly dissolved or it will crystallize. Do not stir the sugar as it dissolves, but swirl the pan by its handle.
3. When all the sugar is dissolved add the remaining cup of water, the lemon juice, and julienned orange peel. Bring to a boil for 30 seconds, lower the heat so solution simmers. Cover and simmer 1 hour.
4. Meanwhile, peel the oranges over a bowl to catch the juices. Peel the kiwis. Slice both the oranges and kiwis thinly horizontally. Reshape the oranges into their original form, interspersing the kiwi slices between the orange slices. Hold together with toothpicks. Pile into a deep glass bowl and chill until serving time.
5. Remove the sugar syrup from heat. Stir in the orange-flavored liqueur. Pour it over the oranges.

6. Place the berries in a food processor or blender and puree. Force the puree through a strainer. Discard the seeds. Stir in orange juice from peeling the oranges in Step 4. Drizzle half of the sauce over oranges, pass remaining sauce at the table.

Note: The oranges may be sauced with the sugar syrup and held at room temperature up to 6 hours before serving.

Yield: 8 servings	Fat per serving: trace
Calories per serving: 195	Carbohydrates per serving: 48g
Protein per serving: 2g	Sodium per serving: trace

Grand Marnier Mousse

This cool, cloudlike mousse literally melts in the mouth. It needs at least 2 hours chilling time to set before serving, yet it should be served within 24 hours as the egg whites break down with time.

> 1   envelope unflavored gelatin
> 1/4 cup cold water
> 1/2 cup sugar
> 1/2 cup cold water
> 4   eggs
> 1/4 teaspoon salt
> 2/3 cup freshly squeezed orange juice
> zest of 1 orange
> 3   tablespoons orange-flavored liqueur such as Grand
>   Marnier or Triple Sec
> 2   tablespoons rum
> 2   tablespoons sugar

1. Soften the gelatin in the ¼ cup water in a glass measuring cup for about 2 minutes. Place the cup in a small saucepan ⅓ full of water and warm over medium heat stirring occasionally until gelatin is dissolved and clear, about 3 minutes. Set aside.

2. Meanwhile, combine the sugar with ½ cup water in a 1-quart saucepan. Dissolve the sugar over very low heat, swirling the pan by the handle. Do not stir with a spoon. When the solution is clear, turn the heat to high and boil 1 minute. Do not let sugar syrup begin to brown. Set it aside.

3. Separate the eggs. Break the egg yolks into the top part of a double boiler, the whites into a glass, ceramic, or copper bowl. Set the bottom of the double boiler with 1 inch of water over high heat. Insert the top half of double boiler. Beat the yolks over the simmering water until thickened and very pale in color, about 2 minutes. Regulating heat so the water just simmers, continue beating while dribbling in the hot sugar syrup from Step 2. Beat until the mixture doubles in volume, thickens, and feels warm to the touch, about 6–8 minutes. Remove from heat and continue beating until mixture ribbons (falls from beaters in a wide band that lies on top of the mass for a moment before sinking in).

4. Stir the dissolved gelatin, salt, orange juice, zest, orange liqueur, and rum into the yolks.

5. Wash the beaters thoroughly and beat the egg whites until stiff. Gradually beat in the sugar.

6. Fold the whites into gelatin-yolk mixture.

7. Pour the mousse into individual glasses or a 6-cup mold sprayed with cooking spray and chill at least 2 hours to set. Unmold if desired.

Yield: 8 servings
Calories per serving: 140
Protein per serving: 4g

Fat per serving: 3g
Carbohydrates per serving: 21g
Sodium per serving: 100mg

Crepes Suzette

❖

Crepes Suzette were invented by the Franco-American cook Henri Charpentier. Quite by accident the butter sauce he was preparing caught on fire, with results that thousands of cooks have since plagiarized. Here is my reduced-calorie version. The crepes and sauce may be readied early in the day, then assembled and flamed before serving to appreciative guests.

For the Crepes

1 egg
1 egg yolk
¾ cup milk
6 tablespoons flour
pinch salt
1 tablespoon butter

For the Sauce

1½ tablespoons butter
2 tablespoons sugar
2 tablespoons orange marmalade
1 tablespoon each orange and lemon zest
juice and pulp of 3 fresh oranges (reserve 2
     tablespoons for dissolving cornstarch)
2 teaspoons cornstarch
1 tablespoon orange-flavored liqueur such as Grand
     Marnier, Curaçao, or Triple Sec
1 tablespoon kirsch (or use 2 tablespoons orange
     liqueur)

To Prepare the Crepes

(May be done as much as 1 day in advance.)

1. Beat the egg, egg yolk, and milk together, add the flour sifted with the salt, and stir just to combine. Chill 2 hours.
2. Melt ½ teaspoon of the butter in a nonstick 8-inch skillet until foamy. Ladle just enough batter into the pan to film bottom. Pour excess batter back into bowl when bottom sets. Cook a crepe over medium-high heat until browned on one side. Flip, cook on underside just to firm (this will be the inside, unseen part), and slide onto a plate. Continue cooking, adding butter as necessary and placing a sheet of wax paper between the crepes. Crepes may now be used or chilled up to 12 hours or frozen until needed. The recipe makes ten to twelve 12-inch crepes.

To Prepare the Sauce

1. Combine butter, sugar, marmalade, orange and lemon zest, and juice and pulp of oranges in a 1-quart saucepan over medium heat until heated through.
2. Dissolve the cornstarch in the reserved juice. Stir into the hot orange sauce and stir over medium heat until thickened, about 4 minutes.

To Assemble the Crepes and Serve

1. Fold the crepes in triangle shapes with the unbrowned side facing in, by folding first in halves and then into quarters. Arrange on a flameproof serving dish that has sides such as a quiche dish or a chafing dish. Overlap the crepes by ½ inch. If preparing early in the day, cover with aluminum foil. Before serving sprinkle very lightly with water and heat in a 350-degree oven for about 15 minutes, covered, until warmed through.
2. Pour the warmed sauce over the heated crepes. Keep them warm in the oven or over hot water in a chafing dish while preparing the liqueur for flaming.
3. Heat the liqueurs in a long-handled butter warmer, one with a lip

is preferred. When bubbles appear at the pan's edge, remove from the heat. Place dish of warmed crepes on the table. Ignite liqueur with a fireplace match or other long taper. Pour the flaming liqueur over the crepes. Use a spoon to lift sauce as it flames. Serve when flames die out.

Yield: 6 servings	Fat per serving: 7g
Calories per serving: 160	Carbohydrates per serving: 22g
Protein per serving: 5g	Sodium per serving: 50mg

❖ FLAMING ❖

Recipes frequently call for igniting liquor, sometimes for effect, sometimes to mellow the sharp alcohol taste. For success with flaming liquors, remember the following tips.
• the liquor must be heated just to the point where small bubbles appear at the edge of the pan
• if it boils longer than about 10—20 seconds, add more liquor
• add a pinch of sugar to ensure long burning
• select a long-handled, small pot, preferably with a spout, to heat the liquor. Butter warmers are ideal.

Cheesecake with Orange Zest

❖

This cheesecake with its light, refreshing hint of orange makes a pleasant finish to a meal. To reduce the calories even further, make it without the graham cracker crust.

For the Crust

3½ ounces (about 8 2½-inch by 5-inch) graham crackers
2 tablespoons orange juice

For the Cheesecake

1 pound cottage cheese
1 pound part-skim ricotta cheese
½ cup sugar
1 tablespoon flour
1 teaspoon vanilla extract
grated zest of 1 orange
½ teaspoon salt
2 egg yolks
1 egg
2 tablespoons sliced almonds

1. Preheat oven to 350 degrees. Pulverize the graham crackers in a food processor or blender. Moisten the crumbs with orange juice and press into the bottom of a 9½-inch pie or quiche dish "buttered" with cooking spray. Place in the preheated 350-degree oven for 12 minutes.
2. Beat together or puree in a food processor all the remaining ingredients except the almonds.
3. Pour into the graham cracker crust. Sprinkle almonds on top. Bake for 1 hour at 350 degrees. Reduce the heat to 300 degrees and bake an additional 20 or 25 minutes or until the middle is firm when wiggled. Cool and chill 2 hours.

Yield: 8 servings
Calories per serving: 275
Protein per serving: 17g
Fat per serving: 10g
Carbohydrates per serving: 29g
Sodium per serving: 540mg

Port Wine Sorbet

❖

A cool finish, perfect for a warm summer meal, this port wine sorbet is ideal with melon. To serve, fill a fluted champagne glass two-thirds full of melon balls that have been marinated in a bit of port wine and top with a scoop of this sorbet. A tiny dollop would also make a refreshing intermezzo for a formal meal. An ice cream maker is necessary to produce the needed texture. The ginger is available at specialty markets and some general food stores.

⅓ cup sugar
½ cup port wine
1 teaspoon minced crystallized ginger
1 cantaloupe
juice of 1 lemon
seedless red grapes, optional

1. Combine the sugar, wine, and ginger in a small saucepan over very low heat. Swirl handle until the sugar dissolves. Raise heat to high and boil 5 minutes, without stirring, remove from heat, and chill until cool to the touch.
2. Cut the cantaloupe in half and discard the seeds. Cut off and discard the rind. Puree the flesh in a food processor or food mill.
3. Combine the puree in the cream can of an ice cream maker with the chilled wine syrup and the lemon juice. Process according to manufacturer's instructions, then harden in the freezer.
4. Serve garnished with red grapes, if desired.

Yield: 4 servings
Calories per serving: 139
Protein per serving: 1g

Fat per serving: trace
Carbohydrates per serving: 124g
Sodium per serving: 16mg

Fruit Fondue

❖

This is more of an idea than an actual recipe, because proportions and ingredients are strictly up to the cook and the pantry. Assemble a variety of fruits. Cut them into bite-size pieces. Arrange them around a pot or chafing dish of raspberry dipping sauce. Include if you like a batch of Almond Cream (page 285) and squares of Almond Angel Cake (page 309). Diners can dip the fruits and cake into either the almond cream or the raspberry. If you prefer you may film the bottom of a small saucer with 2–3 tablespoons of raspberry sauce, place a skewer of fruit over the sauce, and drizzle almond cream on top—a light and pretty summertime dessert.

For the Raspberry Dipping Sauce

1 10-ounce package frozen raspberries or
   strawberries, thawed
1 tablespoon cornstarch
1 tablespoon orange-flavored liqueur such as Grand
   Marnier or Triple Sec
1 tablespoon kirsch (optional)

1. Puree the berries in a food processor or blender. Strain and discard the seeds.
2. Dissolve the cornstarch in the liqueurs.
3. Stir the dissolved cornstarch in the raspberry puree over medium-high heat in a 1-quart saucepan until slightly thickened. Serve hot or chilled.

Yield: Approximately 1 cup
Calories per tablespoon: 22
Protein per tablespoon: trace

Fat per tablespoon: trace
Carbohydrates per tablespoon: 5g
Sodium per tablespoon: trace

Hot Apple Tart

❖

Personally, I find any recipe that calls for a half cup of something from some other recipe immediately unappealing. After all, gearing up for one recipe doesn't mean I'm willing to make another. But I urge you to make an exception in this case, or you'll miss perhaps the best dessert in this modest collection. This thin apple tart, with its crust of phyllo and icing of Almond Cream (page 285) is best served hot. All components may be readied up to 4 hours in advance, then assembled and baked just prior to serving time. Poached pears may be used in addition to or to replace the apples. Leftovers may be gently reheated in a 300-degree oven for 10 minutes.

       1/2 ounce sliced or slivered almonds
       2 tablespoons dried bread crumbs
       1 tablespoon sugar
       dash cinammon
       2 sheets phyllo dough
       2 tablespoons butter, melted
       1 apple, Granny Smith or Yellow Delicious
          recommended
       1 tablespoon brown sugar
       4 tablespoons Almond Cream (page 285)

1. Spray a 7 1/2-inch removable-bottom tart ring with cooking spray. You may use a slightly larger pan, but results won't be as pleasing.
2. In a food processor or blender, combine the almonds, bread crumbs, sugar, and cinnamon. Pulverize until they're fine crumbs. Set aside.
3. Lay a sheet of phyllo into the tart ring, vertically, overlapping it in the middle as you would a sheet of tissue paper in a box. Butter sparingly with a pastry brush dipped in the melted butter. Sprinkle with half the nut-crumb mixture.

4. Now lay another sheet in the pan, horizontally, also overlapping in the center. Butter very lightly and sprinkle with the remaining crumbs.
5. Fold the overhang inside the rim of the pan.
6. Slice the apple in half the long way, then into quarters. Core it. Slice the quarters very thinly. Arrange the apple slices over the tart ring in circles, with pieces of the apple resting on the phyllo dough rim. Brush all with the remaining butter. Sprinkle brown sugar over the apples. Set aside, if you wish.
7. When you're ready to complete the tart, preheat the oven to 425 degrees.
8. Place the tart in the lower third of a preheated oven for 20 minutes or until the apples are softened.
9. Spread almond cream over the apple tart and broil for 4–5 minutes until the almond cream is bubbly and golden. Let the tart rest 5 minutes and serve warm. It also can be held up to 1 hour on a serving tray.

Yield: 4 servings
Calories per serving: 145
Protein per serving: 3g

Fat per serving: 9g
Carbohydrates per serving: 17g
Sodium per serving: 20mg

❖   **THINKING THIN TIP**   ❖

If you're trying to wean yourself from cream and/or sugar in coffee, try adding a 3-inch piece of vanilla bean or a cinnamon stick to the grounds when you make it. The added flavor will help.

Mimosa Sherbet

❖

Celebrate your success with this champagne-based sherbet. While it may be made without an ice cream freezer simply by hardening in a conventional freezer, it will have a smoother texture if processed in an ice cream freezer.

1 scant cup sugar
⅞ cup water
juice of 1 orange
1 cup Brut champagne
1 tablespoon orange-flavored liqueur such as Triple
      Sec or Grand Marnier
2 egg whites
mint leaves (optional)

1. Combine sugar and water in a 2½-quart saucepan. Swirl the pan by the handle over very low heat until the sugar is dissolved. Do not stir. When the solution is perfectly clear and sugar is dissolved, raise heat to high and boil without stirring for 7 minutes.
2. Remove the sugar water from heat, pour it into a bowl, and place in the freezer for 15 minutes.
3. Remove from freezer, stir in orange juice, champagne, and orange liqueur.
4. Beat egg whites until stiff, fold into champagne mixture. Freeze in an ice cream freezer according to manufacturer's instructions. Sherbet will be soft after processing. Ripen in freezer to harden. Garnish with a mint leaf if available.

Yield: 6 servings
Calories per serving: 180
Protein per serving: 1g

Fat per serving: 0
Carbohydrates per serving: 37g
Sodium per serving: 20mg

Mango Mousse

❖

This is a very light, refreshing dessert. Because its color is so pale you might like to garnish the serving dish or individual servings with a few slices of fresh, colorful fruit, more mango or perhaps oranges. Use only very ripe fruit for this mold.

1 ripe mango, peeled and pitted
1 envelope unflavored gelatin
1 tablespoon cold water
juice of 2 limes
2 egg whites
a tiny pinch salt
¼ teaspoon cream of tartar
⅓ cup sugar or 4 tablespoons fructose

1. Peel and puree the mango in a food processor or blender.
2. Soften the gelatin in the cold water until it's spongy.
3. Heat the lime juice in a 1-quart saucepan. When steaming, stir in the gelatin, stir until dissolved, about 1–2 minutes, over medium-low heat.
4. Stir the dissolved gelatin into the fruit puree.
5. Beat the egg whites and salt until foamy. Add the cream of tartar and continue beating until soft peaks form. Gradually add the sugar while beating until stiff.
6. Gently fold the whites into the puree-gelatin mixture.
7. Spray a 2-cup mold with cooking spray. Spoon mousse into mold, tap on kitchen counter to knock out air bubbles, and chill for 4 hours. Unmold and garnish with fresh fruits before serving if desired.

Yield: 4 servings
Calories per serving: 115
Protein per serving: 4g

Fat per serving: trace
Carbohydrates per serving: 26g
Sodium per serving: 70mg

Mocha Parfait Pie

❖

Here's a do-ahead confection for mocha fanciers. If you prefer, make the flavor predominantly coffee by omitting the cocoa powder and substituting Tia Maria for the crème de cacao.

For the Crust

2 cups corn flakes
1 tablespoon butter, melted
2 teaspoons sugar

For the Pie

1 5⅓-ounce can evaporated milk
1 envelope unflavored gelatin
1 tablespoon water
¾ cup milk
1 tablespoon instant coffee powder
1 egg, separated
⅓ cup sugar
1 tablespoon unsweetened cocoa powder
1 tablespoon crème de cacao
2 tablespoons sliced almonds

To Prepare the Crust

1. Preheat oven to 350 degrees. Combine all the crust ingredients in a food processor or blender and combine until the corn flakes are crushed. Pour into an ungreased 8-inch pie pan and press onto bottom and sides with the help of a wooden spoon. Place in the bottom third of a preheated 350-degree oven for 5 minutes or until slightly crisped. Remove and chill.

To Prepare the Pie

1. About 2 hours before making the dessert, pour the evaporated milk into an ice cube tray and place in freezer.
2. Soften the gelatin in the cold water until spongy, about 2 minutes.
3. Heat the milk and coffee powder until steaming, add the softened gelatin, and stir over medium heat until dissolved. Set aside.
4. Beat the egg yolk. Slowly dribble it into the hot milk, and whisk over medium-low heat until mixture thickens. Remove from the heat and cool in the refrigerator until mixture is at room temperature.
5. Beat the egg white until soft peaks form. Gradually beat in the sugar and cocoa powder.
6. Fold the beaten egg white into the milk-yolk mixture, stir in the crème de cacao.
7. Beat the icy evaporated milk until it looks like softly whipped cream.
8. Fold the whipped evaporated milk into the mocha mixture. Gently pour into prepared crust, sprinkle almonds on top, and chill at least 2 hours.

Yield: 6–8 servings
Calories per serving: 185
Protein per serving: 7g

Fat per serving: 7g
Carbohydrates per serving: 25g
Sodium per serving: 130mg

❖ **THINKING THIN TIP** ❖

There is no such thing as a forbidden food, only food that must be eaten in moderation.

Raspberry Crepes Souffle

❖

This showy dessert—a raspberry meringue folded inside a thin crepe, which is in turn doused with more raspberry—waits for no man, woman, or child. It needs to be served immediately from the oven or a slumped collection of crepes will be all you have to show for your efforts. However, the crepes and the meringue souffle mixture may be readied and assembled days in advance, frozen, and baked without thawing, making a light and lovely dessert that takes just 20 minutes from freezer to table.

For the Crepes

1 egg, beaten
½ cup milk
¼ cup flour
pinch salt
1 tablespoon sugar
1 tablespoon orange zest
1 tablespoon butter or less for frying the crepes

For the Souffle

a 10-ounce package frozen raspberries, thawed
(fresh, of course, would be wonderful)
4 egg whites
½ teaspoon cream of tartar
4 tablespoons sugar (slightly more for fresh berries)
1 teaspoon cornstarch or arrowroot
1 tablespoon orange flavored liqueur such as Grand
Marnier or Triple Sec

To Prepare the Crepes
(May be done as much as 1 day in advance.)

1. Beat the egg and milk together, add the flour (sifted with the pinch of salt) and remaining ingredients except the butter, stir just to

combine. Chill for 2 hours.

2. Melt ½ teaspoon of the butter in a nonstick 8-inch skillet until foamy. Ladle just enough batter into the pan to film bottom. Pour excess batter back into bowl after bottom has set. Cook crepe over medium-high heat until browned on one side. Flip, cook on underside just to firm (this will be the inside, unseen part of the crepe), slide onto a plate, and continue cooking, adding butter as necessary and placing a sheet of wax paper between the crepes. Crepes may now be used or chilled or frozen until needed. The recipe makes six to eight 6-inch crepes.

To Prepare the Souffle

1. Preheat oven to 350 degrees and spray an ovenproof serving dish large enough to hold 8 folded crepes with cooking spray.
2. Puree the raspberries in a food processor or blender. Strain and discard the seeds.
3. Measure ⅓ cup raspberry puree and set it aside.
4. Beat egg whites until foamy. Add cream of tartar, gradually beat in sugar, and beat until just shy of stiff peaks.
5. Fold the ⅓ cup raspberry puree into the beaten egg whites. Divide souffle mixture among the crepes, placing about 3 heaping tablespoons on the unbrowned side of each crepe. (Discard or cook separately any leftover souffle.) Fold crepe ends to middle. Place crepes seam side down, in prepared ovenproof dish. Crepes may now be frozen or they must be baked immediately. Bake unfrozen crepes souffles 12 to 15 minutes (bake frozen crepes souffles 15 to 20 minutes) or until puffed and golden. Serve with confectioner's sugar sifted over or the following sauce.
6. Combine the remaining raspberrry puree with cornstarch dissolved in the orange liqueur. Cook, whisking over medium-low heat until slightly thickened, about 2 minutes. Film serving plates with thickened raspberry puree, place puffed crepe souffle on top, or drizzle raspberry puree over the crepe souffle.

Yield: 6-8 servings
Calories per serving: 155
Protein per serving: 5g

Fat per serving: 3g
Carbohydrates per serving: 28g
Sodium per serving: 80mg

Vanilla Ice Milk

❖

This basic recipe is far better than any store-bought version you might buy. With additions this ice milk may become flavored with coffee, maple walnut, pumpkin rum, ginger, or any other concoction you might devise. It does require an ice cream maker to develop the proper texture, however.

> 4 cups low-fat milk
> 1 cup sugar
> 1 1/2 teaspoons good-quality vanilla extract
> 1/8 teaspoon salt

1. Pour the milk, sugar, vanilla, and salt directly into the cream can of the ice cream maker. Stir with a wooden spoon until sugar dissolves. Process in an ice cream maker according to manufacturer's instructions.

Yield: 12 1/2-cup servings
Calories per serving: 115
Protein per serving: 3g

Fat per serving: 2g
Carbohydrates per serving: 22g
Sodium per serving: 70mg

Coffee Ice Milk

Dissolve 4 tablespoons instant powdered coffee in the milk. Continue with the recipe.

Yield: 12 1/2-cup servings
Calories per serving: 120
Protein per serving: 4g

Fat per serving: 2g
Carbohydrates per serving: 23g
Sodium per serving: 70mg

Maple Walnut Ice Milk

Use ¾ cup sugar and ¼ cup maple syrup. Substitute 1 tablespoon maple extract for the vanilla extract. Fold in ⅓ cup nuts to the processed ice cream before hardening in freezer.

Yield: 12 ½-cup servings
Calories per serving: 140
Protein per serving: 4g

Fat per serving: 4g
Carbohydrates per serving: 22g
Sodium per serving: 70mg

Pumpkin Rum Ice Milk

Substitute 1 tablespoon rum for the vanilla extract. Add several gratings fresh nutmeg and ½ teaspoon ground cinnamon to the milk-sugar mixture. Stir in ½ cup canned or homemade unsweetened pumpkin puree to the ice milk after processing and before hardening in the freezer.

Yield: 12 ½-cup servings
Calories per serving: 150
Protein per serving: 4g

Fat per serving: 4g
Carbohydrates per serving: 23g
Sodium per serving: 70mg

Ginger Ice Milk

Simmer the milk with a 3-inch piece of peeled ginger root for 20 minutes. Discard the ginger. Cool. Stir 1 tablespoon finely minced crystallized ginger into the ice milk just before hardening in freezer.

Yield: 12 ½-cup servings
Calories per serving: 125
Protein per serving: 3g

Fat per serving: 2g
Carbohydrates per serving: 24g
Sodium per serving: 70mg

Raspberry Ice
with Cassis Sauce

❖

Tart raspberry tempered with a sweet sauce of vanilla and cassis—a
seasonless dessert thanks to the year-round availability of frozen berries. An ice cream maker is necessary to produce the fine texture. Like
most homemade ice creams and sherbets, this is best made no more
than 24 hours before serving.

> ½ cup sugar
> ½ cup water
> 2 10-ounce packages frozen raspberries (in light
>   syrup) or 1 pint fresh raspberries
> 1 teaspoon lemon juice
> 1 tablespoon crème de cassis

For the Sauce

> 3 tablespoons crème de cassis
> ½ cup vanilla ice cream, softened

To Prepare the Ice

1. Combine the sugar and water in a 1-quart saucepan over low
   heat. Swirl the pan by the handle until the sugar is dissolved. Do
   not stir. Raise heat to high, boil 5 minutes. Chill.
2. If using fresh berries add sugar, sparingly, to taste. Puree the berries in a food processor or blender. Strain and discard the seeds.
3. Combine chilled syrup with raspberry puree, lemon juice, and
   cassis. Freeze in ice cream maker according to manufacturer's
   instructions.

To Prepare the Sauce

1. Stir the crème de cassis into the softened ice cream. Serve 2 table-spoons over each serving.

Yield: 7 3-ounce servings
Calories per serving: 175
Protein per serving: 1g

Fat per serving: 1g
Carbohydrates per serving: 38g
Sodium per serving: 10mg

Almond Angel Food Cake

This quickly made cake pairs the lightness of beaten egg whites with the crunch of almonds. Baked in a ring mold, it could be served with a mound of fresh sliced fruit in the center, and the whole napped with almond cream (page 285). It would also make a nice addition to a fruit fondue tray, and is very tempting all by itself.

> *1 ounce slivered or sliced almonds*
> *1/2 cup sugar*
> *6 tablespoons cake flour*
> *1/2 cup egg whites (about 5–6)*
> *a pinch salt*
> *1/2 teaspoon cream of tartar*
> *1 teaspoon vanilla extract*
> *1/2 teaspoon almond extract*

1. Use a 4-cup ring mold, sprayed with cooking spray or buttered and floured. Preheat the oven to 300 degrees.
2. Pulverize the almonds in a food processor or blender. Do not allow them to get mushy. Set aside in a bowl.

3. Sift together the sugar and flour, mix with the almonds.
4. Beat the egg whites until foamy, add salt, and continue to beat until soft peaks form. Add the cream of tartar, and continue to beat until stiff but not dry.
5. Fold the flour-sugar-nut mixture into the egg whites along with the extracts. Do not overbeat. Spoon into the prepared ring mold and place in the bottom third of a preheated 300-degree oven. Turn heat off after 30 minutes but leave the cake in oven for another 10 minutes. Then cool, inverted on a rack for 30 minutes. Run a flexible-bladed spatula around the rim and center of the mold to release the cake. If it doesn't come free, let it cool a while longer.

Yield: 8 servings
Calories per serving: 95
Protein per serving: 3g

Fat per serving: 2g
Carbohydrates per serving: 18g
Sodium per serving: 40mg

❖   VANILLA   ❖

Vanilla beans come from a variety of orchid. When fresh, the pods are green and oddly odorless, but when dried, they become incredibly fragrant. To make your own vanilla extract, split a vanilla bean in half and make a slit along its length to expose the minute tiny beans inside. Place the beans in a 2-ounce jar (an old vanilla extract bottle is perfect), fill it with vodka, cap the jar tightly, and let it rest 1 month in a cool, dark place. The resulting extract is wonderful in many desserts. Add 2 drops to the ground coffee beans in your next pot for a delicious cup of coffee. The bean may be reused.

PART II
GOURMET
L · I · G · H · T
MENUS

Chapter 11

FESTIVE OCCASION MENUS

Festive Occasion Menus

❖

In this section are menus for those special occasions that command commemoration. From a cocktail party for fourteen to a cozy fireside dinner for four, these are meals designed to pamper your guests. Yet no one need feel guilty with every forkful. These are fresh foods prepared without excessive calories. Every effort has been made to trim the nutritional "bad guys" while enhancing the healthy; to deliver flavor unhitched to fat.

Throughout the recipes are instructions on what may be accomplished ahead of serving time. These are generally outlined in the menu introduction, then noted specifically within the recipe. Last-minute chores have been kept to a minimum.

The reader is encouraged to play with the menu suggestions as whim and availability direct, substituting here, deleting there. Although these recipes are labeled "special occasion," taken out of context, many are casual enough for family meals.

❖ A study of Masai warriors, who walk and exercise a lot each day, proved them to be in excellent physical condition. Despite a diet high in saturated fat and cholesterol, heart disease is virtually unknown in their culture. While exercise alone can't be completely credited (factors such as stress, smoking, and genetics were not taken into account), the benefits of exercise can't be overlooked either. ❖

A PATIO DINNER

Poached Swordfish with Lemon Dill Sauce

Sweet Potato Fries

Zucchini Pancakes with Tomato Relish

Nectarines and Peaches in Minted

Orange Sauce

This patio dinner for four supports the theory that a summer dinner should be as relaxed for the hostess as it is for the guests. The tomato relish will actually improve with a day's rest in the refrigerator and the mint sauce for the dessert can also be done ahead, leaving just a few tasks for the last minute.

This menu presents some unorthodox ways to treat common foods. The swordfish—most often grilled, broiled, or baked—is poached here; the zucchini shredded; the sweet potatoes oven "fried"; and the peaches and nectarines, so often eaten out of hand, are bathed in minted orange sauce. Creative—without hours in the creation.

❖ Pine nuts, also known as pignolis or Indian nuts, are costly because they must be extracted by hand from the cones of a certain tree. Buy them in small quantity and keep them in the refrigerator, as they go rancid easily. ❖

Poached Swordfish with Lemon Dill Sauce

❖

Poaching swordfish results in the same, moist, succulent fish as the more traditionally poached salmon. The cool lemon-dill sauce, which also serves as a marinade, is a pleasure on hot summer nights and simplicity itself for the cook.

> 2 tablespoons mayonnaise
> 3/4 cup plain yogurt
> 2 tablespoons minced fresh dill
> 2 tablespoons lemon juice
> 2 drops hot pepper sauce
> 1 1/2 pounds swordfish steaks or other thick-cut firm-
>   fleshed fish such as mako shark
> 2 cups dry white wine
> 1 cup water
> 4 tablespoons white wine vinegar (one flavored
>   with dill would be ideal)
> 2 bay leaves

1. Combine the mayonnaise, yogurt, dill, lemon juice, and hot pepper sauce.
2. Place fish in a plastic bag, add half the lemon-dill marinade, and marinate at least 2 hours or as long as 6 hours. Refrigerate remaining marinade to use as a sauce.
3. Remove fish from marinade. Any marinade that clings to the fish may be scraped off and added to the sauce.
4. Bring the wine, water, vinegar, and bay leaves to a boil in a 12-inch skillet. Reduce heat to a simmer. Add the fish, cover, and simmer over medium-low heat for 12 to 15 minutes, or until the flesh is firm when pressed with a finger. Remove fish from skillet; discard poaching liquid.

5. To serve, top each serving of fish with 2 tablespoons lemon-dill sauce, and pass remaining sauce at the table.

Yield: 4 servings
Calories per serving: 292
Carbohydrate per serving: 4g
Cholesterol per serving: 107mg

Dietary fiber per serving: 0g
Fat per serving: 14g
Protein per serving: 36g
Sodium per serving: 258mg

Sweet Potato "Fries"

Curry powder creates the unexpected in this simple, quick recipe.

1 pound sweet potatoes, peeled
2 tablespoons corn or other vegetable oil
curry powder to taste

1. Preheat oven to 375 degrees. Quarter the potatoes and cut into ¼-inch-thick strips (if too thin, the potatoes will burn). Spread on a baking sheet and toss with oil. Season to taste with curry powder. (I like about ½ teaspoon curry powder to a pound of potatoes, but you'll want to decide for yourself.)
2. Bake in lower third of oven for 30 minutes, stirring occasionally. Season with salt if desired.

Yield: 4 servings
Calories per serving: 132
Carbohydrate per serving: 22g
Cholesterol per serving: 0mg

Dietary fiber per serving: 1g
Fat per serving: 7g
Protein per serving: 2g
Sodium per serving: 12mg

Zucchini Pancakes
with Tomato Relish

❖

The tomato relish topping, which sets this vegetable dish apart from others, is so good you may want to double the recipe. It is based on one a friend served with slivers of pita bread one hot summer's day as a poolside snack. Best served at room temperature, it will keep two days under refrigeration. Farmstand seconds, even super-market tomatoes, do just fine here.

If you like, the zucchini pancakes may be made ahead and reheated in a microwave oven on medium-high heat for 4 minutes or warmed in a 300-degree oven for 15 minutes.

For the Tomato Relish

1   tomato, chopped
2   scallions, diced
1   small garlic clove, minced
½   jalapeño pepper, minced, or ½ to 1 teaspoon
      canned jalapeño pepper, minced
1   tablespoon extra-virgin olive oil
1½ tablespoons white wine vinegar
3–4 drops lemon juice

For the Zucchini Pancakes

4   small zucchini (about 1 pound)
1   tablespoon salt, kosher or coarse recommended
1   Golden Delicious apple
1   tablespoon cornstarch
1   tablespoon freshly grated Romano cheese
2   egg whites, beaten lightly
1   teaspoon butter
2   tablespoons corn oil

To Prepare the Tomato Relish

1. Combine all the relish ingredients and stir well. Set aside; refrigerate if holding more than 3 hours.

To Prepare the Zucchini Pancakes

1. Trim the stem end of the zucchini. Grate zucchini by hand or in a food processor. Scrape into a colander set in sink, sprinkle with the salt, and rest 20 minutes.
2. Grate the unpeeled apple with a hand-held grater and discard core.
3. Rinse the zucchini thoroughly under running water, squeezing hard to rinse out salt. Squeeze out as much moisture as possible.
4. Combine zucchini with grated apple, cornstarch, cheese, and egg whites. Mix thoroughly.
5. Coat a 12-inch nonstick skillet with cooking spray. Heat butter and 1 tablespoon oil in skillet over high heat. Spoon in the zucchini mixture, forming 4 "cakes." Reduce heat to medium-low after the underside of the cakes is browned. Turn pan often and loosen the pancakes frequently with a spatula as they cook. Adjust the heat to keep them from burning. Turn pancakes over after 10 minutes, adding the remaining tablespoon of oil. Raise heat to brown the cakes, if necessary, and continue cooking until they are nicely browned. Spoon on tomato relish at the table.

Pancakes

Yield: 4 pancakes
Calories per pancake: 132
Carbohydrate per pancake: 11g
Cholesterol per pancake: 6g

Dietary fiber per pancake: 1g
Fat per pancake: 9g
Protein per pancake: 4g
Sodium per pancake: 33mg

Relish

Yield: 12 tablespoons of relish
Calories per tablespoon: 17
Carbohydrate per tablespoon: 2g
Cholesterol per tablespoon: 0mg

Dietary fiber per tablespoon: 0g
Fat per tablespoon: 1g
Protein per tablespoon: 0g
Sodium per tablespoon: 3mg

Nectarines and Peaches in Minted Orange Sauce

❖

Nutritionists tell us nothing beats plain fruit for dessert, but how many taste buds would agree? Here's a quick recipe that makes the most of lackluster, barely ripened, supermarket fruit. You might want to double the recipe. Without the liqueur, it makes a great snack to have on hand.

2 tablespoons sugar
½ cup water
1 tablespoon snipped fresh mint
4 fruits, a combination of peaches and nectarines
2 navel oranges or 1 cup orange juice
2 tablespoons slivered almonds or macadamia nuts
fresh mint leaves for garnish (optional)
1 teaspoon orange liqueur per serving (optional)

1. Dissolve sugar in the ½ cup water in a 1-quart, uncovered saucepan over medium heat. Don't stir, but swirl the pan by the handle.
2. When sugar is dissolved, raise heat to high and boil 2 minutes or until the syrup is reduced to ¼ cup. Add mint, cover, and steep off heat for 30 minutes.
3. The mint sauce may be strained to remove the leaves (be sure to press the solids with the back of a spoon), or used as is. (The recipe may be prepared several days ahead to this point and kept chilled.)
4. Bring 2½ quarts water to a boil in a 4-quart saucepan. Add the fruits. If they are very ripe, boil just 30 seconds to loosen the skin. Unripe fruits will take longer, up to 3 or 4 minutes. Drain, peel, and slice into a glass or ceramic bowl.

5. Squeeze the oranges to extract the juice. Pour juice over fruit; add nuts. Pour the mint sauce over the fruit; stir gently to combine.
6. To serve, spoon into champagne glasses or small glass bowls. Garnish with mint leaves and a spoonful of orange liqueur, if you wish.

Yield: 4 servings
Calories per serving: 132
Carbohydrate per serving: 5g
Cholesterol per serving: 0mg

Dietary fiber per serving: 1g
Fat per serving: 3g
Protein per serving: 0g
Sodium per serving: 8mg

❖Phyllo (Greek for "leaf") dough (or Fillo) is a tissue-thin pastry made from flour and water much used in Middle Eastern cookery. It is a boon to the waist-conscious, for it is relatively low in calorie. Thaw in the refrigerator and keep the sheets covered with a damp towel when working with a single sheet. Wrap unused phyllo as airtight as possible in plastic and foil before refreezing. ❖

CHILL CHASER

"Cream" of Celery Root Soup

Pork Medallions with Cider and Apples

Barley and Mushrooms

Nutted Fall Fruit Tarts

When the scent of apples and the crinkle of leaves fill the air, we welcome hot and hearty fare. This menu makes use of some of the season's best—celery root, apples, fresh cider, and pork, a year-round meat that is particularly welcome this time of year.

Pork's fatty image has been justly deserved in the past, but new breeding and feeding techniques are now producing leaner animals, meaning less fat per serving. Boneless cutlets—be sure to trim off any visible fat—along with tenderloins are among the leaner pork cuts you can buy. There are about 198 calories in a 3-ounce serving along with healthy doses of zinc (a nutrient with an influence on growing tissues and one of the few that the typical American diet may not provide in optimal amounts) and thiamin (used in carbohydrate metabolism). Remember, health experts suggest 3-ounce servings of meat should be the norm, not just a dieting tool. With the other menu items here to satisfy appetites, this is as good as any time to make the resolution—less meat, more grains (like barley) and vegetables rich in fiber (like celery root). If you want yet another vegetable, try the Julienne of Root Vegetables (see page 395).

While this menu has been written for eight diners, you could halve the ingredients for the pork medallions and the barley to serve four or even reduce it to serve two. The soup may be frozen, so there's no need to halve it, and making anything less than eight tarts hardly seems sensible. Do take pan sizes and cooking times into account when reducing or enlarging recipes.

"Cream" of Celery Root Soup

❖

A thick, hearty soup, just right when the cold winds howl. You may freeze it for up to one month without flavor loss. Reheat it gently in a double boiler.

> 1 pound celery root, peeled and cubed
> 1½ pounds leeks, trimmed, sliced, and rinsed
>   (about 4½ cups)
> 1 small onion, chopped (about 3 tablespoons)
> 1 potato, peeled and sliced (about 1½ cups)
> 3 cups homemade chicken stock or canned broth
> 3 cups water
> 1 teaspoon salt
> 1 teaspoon arrowroot
> 1 cup plain yogurt
> 1 tablespoon minced fresh dill
> 1 teaspoon Dijon mustard
> freshly ground black pepper to taste

1. In a 4-quart saucepan combine the celery root, leeks, onion, potato, stock, water, and salt. Cover, bring to a boil, then reduce heat and simmer 25 to 30 minutes or until vegetables are tender.
2. Puree the soup in batches in a food processor or blender.
3. Stir the arrowroot into the yogurt. Stir it into the soup, then stir

in dill and mustard. Add fresh pepper and taste, correcting seasoning if necessary.

Yield: 8 1-cup servings	Dietary fiber per serving: 2g
Calories per serving: 113	Fat per serving: 2g
Carbohydrate per serving: 21g	Protein per serving: 5g
Cholesterol per serving: 4mg	Sodium per serving: 667mg

Pork Medallions with Cider and Apples

❖

Deliciously quick!

> 1 ¾ pounds boneless pork cutlets, trimmed of all fat
> ½ teaspoon salt (optional)
> freshly ground black pepper to taste
> 2˙ tablespoons corn or other vegetable oil
> 3 Granny Smith apples, peeled, cored, halved, and sliced
> 2 cups apple cider
> 1 tablespoon applejack or Calvados (optional)
> ½ teaspoon dried rosemary
> 1½ tablespoons arrowroot
> 3 tablespoons plain yogurt
> 1 tablespoon minced fresh parsley (optional)

1. Pound the meat between pieces of wax paper, flattening to about ¼-inch thickness. Salt and pepper meat if desired.
2. Heat oil in two 12-inch nonstick skillets over high heat. (Or sear meat in one pan in two batches.) Sear meat one minute,

flip, and brown other side, adjusting heat if necessary to prevent burning.

3. Add sliced apples, cider, applejack, and rosemary. Cover, reduce heat, and simmer 5 or 6 minutes.

4. Stir arrowroot into yogurt. Whisk yogurt into skillet without removing the meat. Stir over low heat until the sauce is thickened, 1 to 2 minutes. Garnish with minced parsley, if desired.

Yield: 8 servings
Calories per serving: 257
Carbohydrate per serving: 14g
Cholesterol per serving: 67mg

Dietary fiber per serving: 1g
Fat per serving: 14g
Protein per serving: 20g
Sodium per serving: 203mg

Barley and Mushrooms

❖

An all-but-forgotten grain, barley provides a welcome change from standard starches. And its strong nutritional profile makes it one well worth serving. A rich source of carbohydrates with moderate amounts of protein, it is also a significant source of cholesterol-combatting fiber—for about the same number of calories per serving as a baked potato.

The cooking instructions here are for regular barley; if you can buy quick-cooking barley, follow package directions. Any left-over lamb bones, simmered along with the barley, would add wonderful flavor. Trim away any fat, and chop the bones into 4-inch chunks with a mallet before adding them to the pot. Discard the bones before serving.

1 cup medium pearl barley
2 quarts water
1 teaspoon salt

2 tablespoons unsalted butter
12 ounces mushrooms, sliced
2 tablespoons minced fresh parsley
freshly ground black pepper to taste

1. Bring the barley, water, and salt to a boil in a covered 4-quart saucepan. Reduce heat to a gentle boil and cook, stirring occasionally, until the barley is tender and all water has evaporated. This will take about 2 hours. Stir in butter. (Barley may be made ahead and reheated either conventionally or in a microwave oven on high for 2 minutes before completing recipe.)
2. Coat a 12-inch nonstick skillet with cooking spray. "Saute" the mushrooms over high heat until lightly browned, about 5 to 6 minutes. Stir into the barley with the parsley and pepper.

Yield: 8 ½-cup servings
Calories per serving: 124
Carbohydrate per serving: 21g
Cholesterol per serving: 8mg

Dietary fiber per serving: 2g
Fat per serving: 4g
Protein per serving: 3g
Sodium per serving: 297mg

Nutted Fall Fruit Tarts

❖

You might need a double batch of these to satisfy the peanut-butter-and-jelly crowd as well as company. Comfortable on fine china or a paper plate, they make an after-school snack you'll encourage your children to eat. Minimum mess, maximum taste—who could ask for more?

3 tablespoons unsalted butter
3 pears, peeled, cored, and cubed
2 Granny Smith apples, peeled, cored, and cubed

2 tablespoons maple syrup or dark brown sugar
1 teaspoon cinnamon
a dash ground cloves
a few gratings fresh nutmeg
2 tablespoons slivered almonds
2 tablespoons applejack or Calvados (optional)
2 sheets phyllo dough (about 14 by 18 inches)
1 teaspoon cinnamon and sugar (about 7/8
    teaspoon sugar mixed with 1/8 teaspoon
    cinnamon)

1. Melt butter in a small saucepan over medium heat to clarify.
   Remove from heat, let rest 5 minutes. Spoon off the foamy top
   layer (may be used over vegetables); spoon off and set aside
   the clear, yellow, clarified butter; and discard the bottom, white,
   liquid layer. (It's easier to clarify a whole stick at a time, and
   it will keep for weeks in the refrigerator, too.)
2. Heat half the yellow clarified butter (reserving the remaining
   butter for step 5) in an 8-inch skillet over high heat. When hot
   add the cubed fruit, maple syrup or sugar, cinnamon, cloves,
   and nutmeg. Toss to combine, reduce heat to medium, and
   cover. Cook, stirring occasionally, until fruit is tender (about 3
   to 4 minutes for ripe fruit, longer for unripe).
3. Uncover and add almonds and applejack. Boil 30 seconds, then
   remove from heat to cool.
4. Preheat oven to 375 degrees. Coat an 8-cup muffin tin (each
   cup a 3-inch diameter) with cooking spray. Cut 32 4-inch
   squares from the phyllo. (If you don't mind the rest of the
   phyllo sheets being short, this is most easily done by cutting a
   4-inch-wide strip from a one-pound stack of phyllo leaves, and
   cutting the strip into 4-inch lengths. It is a bit wasteful, but time
   efficient, and the uncut leaves may be carefully rewrapped and
   frozen.)
5. Press 2 squares of phyllo into each muffin cup. Divide the fruit
   among the cups. Press 2 more squares on top of the tarts, tucking
   in the edges; don't worry that it looks messy now. Brush re-

maining clarified butter over tart tops, and sprinkle with the cinnamon-sugar.

6. Bake on the top rack of the oven for 15 minutes or until toasty brown. Remove and cool on a rack for 10 minutes before removing the tarts from the tin with a flexible-bladed spatula. The tarts may be made a day ahead or frozen. They may be reheated in the muffin tin (300 degrees for 10 minutes) or on a serving dish in a microwave oven (high power for 1 minute).

Yield: 8 tarts
Calories per tart: 118
Carbohydrate per tart: 20g
Cholesterol per tart: 8mg

Dietary fiber per tart: 2g
Fat per tart: 5g
Protein per tart: 1g
Sodium per tart: 31mg

Focus: Cholesterol

❖

Cholesterol is a fatty substance important for a variety of functions. It is a structural component of all cells and is used to make vitamin D (which aids in the absorption of calcium and phosphorus), bile acids (which help in digestion), and some hormones (which regulate many body processes). However, although it is an essential part of body chemistry, our bodies make all we need after the age of six months, so even a cholesterol-free diet poses no problem.

How the Deed Is Done

Atherosclerosis—a thickening of the artery walls caused by the accumulation of cholesterol and connective tissue—begins when cholesterol carrying lipoproteins invade the arterial wall. The damaged wall responds by growing new tissue that traps the cholesterol, resulting in a thickening called plaque. If the plaque becomes pronounced enough it can restrict the blood supply. If a coronary artery is blocked, and part of the heart doesn't get the oxygen it needs and dies, a heart attack results. If blood is restricted to the brain, a stroke results. Sometimes the artery walls respond to the plaque by ballooning. This is called an aneurysm. If a large artery is involved and bursts, it may be fatal. Plaque also can lead to the formation of blood clots.

Two Sides to the Coin

There is as yet no clear-cut proof that elevated cholesterol blood levels are a direct cause of atherosclerosis. Some studies of population groups have found a correlation between high blood cholesterol, triglyceride concentrations, and heart disease, while other studies have not. Based on the enormous amount of evidence now available, many health experts recommend limiting the fats that contribute to high cholesterol levels, while others suggest dietary changes are insignificant in preventing cardiovascular disease.

Who to believe? First of all, remember no one suggests that you absolutely will not die of a heart attack if you eat a low-fat, high-polyunsaturate diet (see *Focus: Heart Disease Risk Factors,* page 504), for, after all, other factors do come into play. But also know that in the last twenty years as Americans have increased their use of polyunsaturate fats while decreasing their intake of saturated fats, fewer deaths have been caused by heart disease, leading some to believe that waiting for incontrovertible proof may prove deadly.

What HDL and LDL Cholesterol Can Mean to You

While levels of cholesterol are of concern, how it is carried in the bloodstream is also important. Like other fats, cholesterol does not dissolve in liquid so it is transported in the blood by lipoproteins—most of it by low-density lipoproteins, known as LDL, the "bad" cholesterol, and to a lesser extent by high-density lipoproteins, HDL, the "good" cholesterol. Generally, high levels of LDL cholesterol appear to increase the risk of heart disease by keeping cholesterol in circulation, while high levels of HDL cholesterol seem protective by clearing the artery walls of cholesterol and transporting it to the liver where unneeded cholesterol is removed.

Some studies have shown moderate to vigorous physical activity may increase the HDL and lower the LDL concentrations in the blood. Genetic factors as well as diet may also influence your lipoprotein profile.

In What Foods?

Cholesterol is only found in animal foods such as meats, fish, dairy products, poultry, and cheese. Highly saturated fats (those which are solid at room temperature) may raise blood cholesterol levels, however, even if they contain no cholesterol themselves. Be wary then of labels proclaiming, "Made with pure vegetable oil," or "No Cholesterol," for the products could be made with coconut or palm oils or hydrogenated vegetable shortening, all of which are high in saturated fats and hence can raise blood cholesterol levels.

Remember too that low-fat foods are not always low-cholesterol foods. Beef liver and veal are both rather low in fat, but liver is very rich in cholesterol and veal is moderately high, too.

If It's Too High, Then What?

A blood test and your doctor will determine if your cholesterol level is dangerously high. Should you decide to control the level there are two steps to take:

First—Restrict your daily cholesterol intake to less than 300 milligrams a day.

Second—Reduce the total fat in your diet to 25 to 30 percent. Ten percent should come from polyunsaturated fats, 10 percent from monounsaturated fats, and no more than 10 percent from saturated fats. (Read *Focus: The Difference in Fats*, page 479.)

FIRST NIGHT

Saffron Consomme with Shrimp

Roast Loin of Lamb Persillade

Green Beans with Pecans

Potato and Fennel Puree

Iced Fruit Mousse

The title for this menu for four is borrowed from Boston's citywide celebration of New Year's Eve, First Night, a clamorous evening of controlled excess. What's in store here is a bit less boisterous, but with all the markings of a festive occasion worth celebrating. There are shrimp, saffron, an elegant loin of lamb, and a special potato puree, all topped off with a light but indulgent fruit dessert.

Happily, many of the cooking chores can be prepared ahead. The consomme will actually improve with a day's rest in the refrigerator. The potato and fennel puree may be made a day before serving and reheated in a double boiler or in a microwave oven. The iced fruit mousse should be made through step 2 at least a day in advance. This will leave only the meat to trim and prepare for roasting, the green beans to trim and steam, and the final whipping of the fruit mousse to be done on the day of the dinner. Like champagne, this menu offers a simple elegance, heady with flavor and long on class.

❖ According to a survey conducted by the Department of Health and Human Services, the top five contributors of fat to the typical American's diet are: **Hamburger**—7.0%; **Hot dogs, luncheon meats**—6.4%; **Whole milk**—6.0%; **Doughnuts, cakes, cookies**—6.0%; **Beef steaks, roasts**—5.5%. ❖

Saffron Consomme
with Shrimp

❖

Light, with a distinctive splash of Pernod, this soup improves with a day's aging, but add the shrimp just before serving to avoid overcooking them.

> 1 leek, white part only
> 1 carrot
> 1 celery rib
> 1 8-ounce bottle clam juice
> 1 can (13¾ ounces) chicken broth or 1¾ cup
>   homemade chicken stock
> ½ cup dry vermouth or white wine
> 2 teaspoons minced fresh parsley
> ¼ teaspoon crumbled saffron threads
> a few shakes paprika
> 1 tablespoon Madeira
> 1 teaspoon Pernod (optional)
> 1 pound medium-size raw shrimp (about 15),
>   peeled and deveined

1. Quarter the leek the long way and rinse thoroughly to remove all traces of dirt. Peel the carrot. Julienne the leek, carrot, and celery in a food processor, or shred on the coarse side of a grater.
2. Combine the vegetables with the clam juice, chicken broth, vermouth, parsley, saffron, and paprika in a 2-quart saucepan. Simmer, uncovered, at least 20 minutes or up to 1 hour. (Soup may be prepared to this point and refrigerated 24 hours ahead.)
3. Stir in Madeira, Pernod, and shrimp. Cover and simmer just until shrimp turn pink, about 1 minute. Do not allow to boil. Ladle into consomme cups.

Yield: 4 1-cup servings
Calories per serving: 82
Dietary fiber per serving: 1g
Fat per serving: 1g

Carbohydrate per serving: 6g
Cholesterol per serving: 62mg
Protein per serving: 11g
Sodium per serving: 606mg

Roast Loin of Lamb Persillade

❖

A loin of lamb makes an elegant offering. Succulent, with its own distinctive flavor, it is simple to cook, simple to serve, and subtly suggests this is no ordinary dinner. Such gracious ease must cost, of course; what you don't pay in the kitchen you will at the butcher, but it's money well spent. A loin of lamb—generally, a special order—comes from that unexercised backbone area that tends to be tender. The roast consists of the kidney chops, unsplit, but cracked for easy carving. Order not by the pound but by the number of chops you want; one per diner is certainly sufficient, with perhaps one or two extra for the meat lovers of the group. Don't try to roast fewer than four chops, but you can roast more than specified in the recipe. Be sure to have the butcher crack the bones, and trim the fat yourself as if you were wielding a scalpel.

> a lamb loin of 5 chops, about 1¾ pounds, bone
>   cracked
> ¼ teaspoon salt
> freshly ground black pepper to taste
> 1 tablespoon unsalted butter
> 1 garlic clove, minced
> 3 tablespoons dry bread crumbs
> 2 tablespoons minced fresh parsley
> 1 teaspoon finely grated lemon rind (zest)

1. Preheat the oven to 450 degrees. Trim all fat from the lamb loin. Salt and pepper the meat.
2. Melt the butter in an 8-inch nonstick skillet until foamy. Cook the garlic over medium heat, stirring with a wooden spoon until soft but not browned, about 2 minutes.
3. Add the bread crumbs and saute over medium-high heat until lightly browned, about 4 minutes. Remove from heat and stir in the parsley and lemon zest. (Crumb mixture may be prepared as much as a day in advance, but do not press it onto the meat until just before roasting.)
4. Place the loin on a rack in a roasting pan. Press the crumb mixture evenly onto the meat. Roast in the lower third of the oven for 30 to 35 minutes or until an instant-reading meat thermometer registers 135 degrees for medium-rare (145 degrees for your basic gray with a blush at the center). Rest 10 minutes, loosely covered with foil, before carving.

Yield: 4 servings, one extra chop
Calories per serving: 325
Carbohydrate per serving: 4g
Cholesterol per serving: 131mg

Dietary fiber per serving: 0g
Fat per serving: 14g
Protein per serving: 42g
Sodium per serving: 286mg

Green Beans with Pecans

❖

Green beans are a good source of Vitamin C, which aids in resisting infection, and a B vitamin that promotes good vision and healthy skin. The beans may be done through step 2 and held, covered, at room temperature for up to two hours.

> ¾ pound fresh green beans
> 1 tablespoon unsalted butter
> 1 tablespoon lemon juice

2 tablespoons chopped pecans
½ teaspoon salt
freshly ground black pepper to taste

1. "Tip and tail" the beans by lining up a handful at a time and cutting across both ends.
2. Bring 1½ cups water to a boil in a 2½-quart saucepan fitted with a steamer. Add the beans, cover, and steam 6 to 8 minutes or until beans are tender but still crisp. Drain. (Undercook beans slightly and rinse them under cold water to stop the cooking if you are not immediately continuing.)
3. Melt the butter in a 10-inch skillet until just foamy. Add the beans, lemon juice, and pecans. Season with salt and pepper. Grasp the skillet by the handle and shake the beans once or twice over high heat until beans are coated and heated through.

Yield: 4 servings
Calories per serving: 80
Carbohydrate per serving: 8g
Cholesterol per serving: 8mg

Dietary fiber per serving: 1g
Fat per serving: 6g
Protein per serving: 2g
Sodium per serving: 295mg

Potato and Fennel Puree

❖

If you're cutting back on butterfat, mashed potatoes lose a lot of appeal. Puree them with fennel, though, and a smooth, rich taste is gained, without a lot of saturated fat. The puree may be done several hours in advance and reheated in a double boiler or in a microwave oven on high power for a minute and a half.

2 medium potatoes (12 ounces), peeled and
   halved
1 pound fennel

1 tablespoon plus 1 teaspoon unsalted butter
3 tablespoons low-fat or skim milk
2 tablespoons freshly grated Parmesan cheese
½ teaspoon salt
freshly ground black pepper to taste
a few gratings fresh nutmeg

1. Place the potatoes in a 2½-quart saucepan. Cover them with water, cover the pan, and boil on high heat for 10 minutes.
2. Meanwhile, trim the root end, tough outer shell, and the feathery tops of the fennel bulbs. Mince some of the feathery top and reserve for garnish.
3. Quarter the fennel bulbs and add to the potatoes. Boil, half covered, over medium-high heat for an additional 20 minutes or until tender. Drain.
4. Puree the fennel and potatoes in a food processor or food mill with the butter, milk, cheese, salt, pepper, and nutmeg. Taste to correct seasoning. Garnish just before serving with minced fennel, if desired.

Yield: 4 ½-cup servings
Calories per serving: 228
Carbohydrates per serving: 23g
Cholesterol per serving: 35mg

Dietary fiber per serving: 1g
Fat per serving: 13g
Protein per serving: 6g
Sodium per serving: 365mg

Iced Fruit Mousse

❖

A frothy fluff of a dessert. The fruit may be frozen days or even months ahead, then whipped with the egg white and touch of honey the day of serving. Desserts such as this are a great way to take advantage of summer's sweet and fragrant fruits by freezing them for use during cold weather.

1 nectarine
½ cup orange juice, freshly squeezed preferred
1 banana, sliced
1 egg white
1 teaspoon honey
a few drops lemon juice
1 tablespoon Crème de Cassis (optional)

1. Drop the nectarine into boiling water to cover for 30 seconds or until the skin is softened. (This will take longer for unripe fruit.) Cool under running water, peel off skin, and slice fruit.
2. In a food processor or in batches in a blender, puree the orange juice, banana, and nectarine. Freeze until firm, at least 3 hours. (Fruit may be kept frozen up to 5 to 6 months.)
3. Soften the frozen fruit at room temperature for about 1 hour or until it can be roughly broken up with a knife. Combine the fruit with egg white, honey, lemon juice, and liqueur in a food processor (or in a bowl with a hand-held mixer). Beat for 2 to 3 minutes (longer for a hand-held mixer), or until frothy and doubled in volume. Iced mousse is now ready to serve or maybe kept chilled (not frozen) for up to 24 hours.

Yield: 4 ½-cup servings
Calories per serving: 63
Carbohydrate per serving: 15g
Cholesterol per serving: 0mg

Dietary fiber per serving: 1g
Fat per serving: 0g
Protein per serving: 1g
Sodium per serving: 14mg

❖ Arrowroot is much used in *The Enlightened Gourmet* because it has twice the thickening power of flour, making for a tidy calorie saving. It is made from the root of a tropical plant and is so called because it was once used to treat wounds caused by poison arrows. Arrowroot is flavorless, and for best results, should be cooked neither too long nor at too high a temperature. ❖

DINNER BY THE FIRE

Grilled Vegetable Salad

Grilled Ginger-Lime Pork Tenderloin

Potato and Leek Gratin

Red Cabbage with Chestnuts

Meringued Poached Pears

Here is a simple menu for four to enjoy by a fire in the cool of the year. Don't abandon the idea if you don't have a grill; the hot vegetable salad lends itself well to broiling and the pork tenderloin may be roasted. If you've never cooked a pork tenderloin before, you might be surprised by its tenderness and flavor. Best of all it is relatively low in fat and calories, supplying a reasonable 240 calories for a 3½-ounce portion. Pork is high in potassium (important in fluid balance), phosphorus (for bones and teeth), and iron (for building blood).

Serve the pork with a tasty grilled vegetable salad, a low-fat potato gratin, colorful and crunchy red cabbage, and meringued poached pears. These are foods to warm cool nights.

❖ The iron from greens is not as readily absorbed as the iron from animal sources. It can be enhanced, though, by eating a good source of vitamin C—oranges, strawberries, or tomatoes for example—at the same meal. ❖

Grilled Vegetable Salad

❖

A wonderful change of pace from the ubiquitous tossed salad. If you haven't time to salt the eggplant (which removes the bitterness), omit it, or substitute another vegetable such as summer squash. You will need eight 10-inch-long, thin wooden skewers.

1 small eggplant
1 tablespoon salt, kosher recommended
1 green bell pepper
1 red bell pepper
1 tomato
¼ pound mushrooms

For the Dressing

4 tablespoons olive oil
¼ cup white wine vinegar
2 scallions, minced
1 garlic clove, minced
1 shallot, minced
3–4 leaves fresh basil, snipped
1 tablespoon sesame seeds
⅛ teaspoon salt
freshly ground black pepper to taste
juice of one lemon
1 small head Boston or other soft-leafed lettuce,
      rinsed and spun dry
oil and vinegar or lemon juice (optional)

1. Soak the skewers in cold water for at least 30 minutes or as much as 2 hours before cooking.
2. Trim the ends from the eggplant. Peel eggplant and cut it into 1-inch-thick slices. Quarter the slices. Place on a double thickness

of paper towels, sprinkle both sides with the tablespoon of salt, and rest 20 minutes.

3. Meanwhile, core the peppers and cut them in eighths. Quarter the tomato. Cut mushrooms if necessary or leave whole.

4. Combine the oil, vinegar, scallions, garlic, shallot, basil, sesame seeds, salt, and pepper in a large bowl. Toss with peppers, tomatoes, and mushrooms.

5. When eggplant has rested 20 minutes, rinse it thoroughly to remove all salt. Drain. Combine with marinade and other vegetables. Cover bowl with plastic wrap and refrigerate up to 8 hours or leave on the counter, up to 1 hour while the vegetables marinate. (Or you may complete the recipe to this point a day ahead if desired.)

6. Alternate the vegetables on the skewers. Grill, turning frequently and brushing with any remaining marinade and the lemon juice, until lightly browned, about 20 minutes. To broil, place the skewers on a rack 4 inches from the coils. Turn frequently and brush with any remaining marinade and the lemon juice until lightly browned, about 10 minutes.

7. Meanwhile, line the salad plates with lettuce leaves. Dress them with a sprinkling of oil and vinegar or a few drops of lemon juice, if desired. Slide the vegetables off the skewers onto the lettuce.

Yield: 4 servings
Calories per serving: 219
Carbohydrate per serving: 15g
Cholesterol per serving: 0mg

Dietary fiber per serving: 3g
Fat per serving: 12g
Protein per serving: 4g
Sodium per serving: 99mg

Grilled Ginger-Lime
Pork Tenderloin

❖

Simple and succulent, this pork tenderloin dish may well become one of your standards. For piquant variety, try substituting citrus juices for the lime juice. If you prefer, the meat may be roasted in a 325-degree oven for about an hour.

> 1 pound pork tenderloin, trimmed of all fat
> ½ cup reduced-sodium soy sauce
> ½ cup Chinese cooking wine or dry white wine
> juice of one lime
> 1 tablespoon dark brown sugar
> 1 scallion, minced
> 3 tablespoons minced fresh ginger
> 2 small garlic cloves, minced

1. Place the tenderloin in a leakproof plastic bag or non-metallic baking dish. Combine the remaining ingredients, pour marinade over the meat, and marinate at least 4 hours in the refrigerator or overnight. Turn occasionally.
2. Remove meat from the marinade. Pat it dry so it will sear quickly. Reserve marinade. Grill the meat over a low fire for 40 minutes, turning and basting frequently with reserved marinade. Check the internal temperature after 40 minutes with an instant-reading meat thermometer. Cook until it registers 145 degrees (160 degrees if you prefer the meat without the barest blush of pink). To serve, slice in ½-inch rounds.

Yield: 4 servings
Calories per serving: 186
Carbohydrate per serving: 8g
Cholesterol per serving: 79mg

Dietary fiber per serving: 0g
Fat per serving: 4g
Protein per serving: 27g
Sodium per serving: 1145mg

Potato and Leek Gratin

❖

Potato lovers· will feel more than satisfied with this tasty dish and enjoy it all the more knowing it is low in fat. It may be completed several hours in advance and held covered and chilled until baking.

3 leeks, white part only, diced and rinsed
3 medium baking potatoes, thinly sliced
½ cup low-fat cottage cheese
⅔ cup homemade chicken stock or canned broth
1 rounded teaspoon arrowroot
½ teaspoon salt
freshly ground black pepper to taste
a few gratings fresh nutmeg
2 teaspoons chopped fresh chives
3 tablespoons dried bread crumbs
1 tablespoon unsalted butter
1 tablespoon freshly grated Parmesan cheese

1. Combine the leeks and potatoes in a 2½-quart saucepan. Add cool water to cover the vegetables by 2 inches. Cover the saucepan and place over high heat. As soon as a boil is reached, reduce the heat so the water boils gently. Boil 5 minutes, then drain the vegetables.

2. Coat a quiche pan or a 9-inch baking dish, preferably one which can go to the table, with cooking spray. Layer the potatoes and leeks in the pan. Set aside.

3. Preheat the oven to 350 degrees. In the bowl of a food processor or in a blender, combine the cottage cheese, chicken stock, and arrowroot. Process until smooth.

4. Turn the sauce into an 8-inch skillet. Place the skillet over high heat and whisk until the sauce thickens and is smooth, about 2 minutes. Reduce the heat to medium-high to prevent the sauce from boiling as the pan heats up.

5. When the sauce is thick, pour it over the potatoes and leeks in the baking dish. Season with the salt, pepper, and nutmeg.
6. Sprinkle the dish with the chives, then with the bread crumbs. Dot with the butter. Sprinkle cheese on top. The dish is ready to bake. (If you prefer, the dish may be chilled for several hours, covered with plastic wrap. Drizzle with a few tablespoons of milk if necessary and allow to come to room temperature, or increase baking time by 5 to 10 minutes.)
7. Bake the potatoes in the top third of the preheated 350-degree oven for 15 to 20 minutes. Run under the broiler if necessary to brown the top.

Yield: 4 servings
Calories per serving: 234
Carbohydrate per serving: 41g
Cholesterol per serving: 11mg

Dietary fiber per serving: 2g
Fat per serving: 4g
Protein per serving: 10g
Sodium per serving: 488mg

Red Cabbage with Chestnuts

Red cabbage is a colorful vegetable, long on spunk yet light on pound-potential. The chestnuts aren't integral, just a nice touch, so don't pass over the recipe if the nuts are nowhere to be found. This dish reheats nicely.

3 ounces chestnuts
12 ounces red cabbage, shredded (5 cups)
¾ cup homemade chicken stock or canned broth
a few drops fruity vinegar, such as raspberry vinegar
1 tablespoon brown sugar
¼ teaspoon salt
freshly ground black pepper to taste

1. Cut a cross in the flat side of each nut. Put the nuts in an 8-inch pan and cover them with water. Cover the pan and bring the nuts to a boil. Boil 1 to 2 minutes. Drain, cool under running water, and peel. Roughly chop or leave whole, as you wish.
2. Place the cabbage and the chicken stock in a 12-inch skillet. Add the vinegar, brown sugar, salt, and pepper. Cover and simmer over medium heat until tender, about 15 minutes. (Recipe may be prepared to this point several hours before serving. Refrigerate if holding more than 1 hour. Reheat in a skillet.)
3. A minute or so before serving, add the chestnuts to the cabbage to heat through.

Yield: 4 1-cup servings
Calories per serving: 78
Carbohydrate per serving: 16g
Cholesterol per serving: 0mg

Dietary fiber per serving: 3g
Fat per serving: 1g
Protein per serving: 2g
Sodium per serving: 155mg

Meringued Poached Pears

❖

Here are poached pears in a meringue disguise, stuffed with oats, nuts, raisins, and spices. Save the poaching liquid in your freezer—it will keep indefinitely—for poaching any kind of fruit. If you would like a bit of sauce, boil a cup of the poaching liquid to reduce it to ¼ cup.

The pears may be poached and stuffed up to a day in advance; the meringue may be made an hour ahead and held, covered with a plate. Frost and bake the pears just before serving. If you'd prefer, the pears may be completely baked and reheated on medium power in a microwave oven for 45 seconds.

4 pears, Bosc recommended
2 cups Burgundy wine
2 tablespoons sugar
2 cups water
juice of half a lemon
1 cinnamon stick
1 whole nutmeg
2 tablespoons oats, quick-cooking recommended,
   not instant
2 tablespoons raisins
1 tablespoon slivered almonds
½ teaspoon ground cinnamon
a dash ground cloves
4 egg whites
2 tablespoons sugar
1 teaspoon vanilla extract
1 tablespoon finely grated unsweetened chocolate

1. Peel the pears. Take a thin slice off the bottom of each pear so it sits upright. Core each pear from the bottom as if it were an apple.
2. In a 3-quart saucepan combine the wine, sugar, water, lemon juice, cinnamon, and nutmeg. Cover and bring to a boil. Add the pears, cover, and adjust heat so pears just simmer (10 minutes for very ripe pears, as long as 45 minutes for unripe pears). Pierce with a fork to check for tenderness. When tender, remove from poaching liquid, drain, and cool. (Poaching liquid may be frozen to use for poaching other fruits.)
3. Meanwhile, coat a baking sheet with cooking spray. Spread the oats on it and toast in a 350-degree oven (no need to preheat). Stir oats once or twice as they cook until lightly browned, about 10 minutes. Leave oven on if you're completing the dessert now.
4. Combine oats with raisins, almonds, and spices. Press 2 tea-spoons of this mixture into the cavity of each pear. Place upright

on the baking sheet. (Pears may be covered with plastic wrap and held at room temperature up to 2 hours or chilled up to 24 hours before continuing.)

5. Beat the egg whites until stiff, sprinkle in the sugar, and continue to beat until stiff glossy peaks form. Beat in the vanilla. (Meringue may be made an hour before baking pears. Cover bowl with a plate and leave at room temperature.)

6. Frost the pears with the meringue; the meringue need not be smooth. Bake in the lower third of a preheated 350-degree oven just until meringue browns, about 5 or 6 minutes. Divide grated chocolate over pears just before serving.

Yield: 4 servings
Calories per serving: 240
Carbohydrate per serving: 47g
Cholesterol per serving: 0mg

Dietary fiber per serving: 5g
Fat per serving: 6g
Protein per serving: 6g
Sodium per serving: 52mg

❖ Chili peppers abound with more than 200 varieties grown for market around the world. Chili peppers, native to the New World, were probably introduced to Europe by explorers who had found them easy to dry and helpful in disguising the less than well preserved food on long ocean voyages. Columbus is said to have named chili peppers by coupling the Indian word "chili" with "pepper" (he mistook them for the Asian peppercorn). The seeds and white membrane are the hottest part of a chili pepper. ❖

DINNER AT EIGHT

Gingered Beef Consomme with Crepe Pillows
Grilled Veal Loin Chops
Dilled New Potatoes
Swiss Chard with Bacon and Balsamic Vinegar
Bananas Creole

Here's a meat-and-potatoes meal for traditionalists who like "soup to nuts" but are minding their fats and calories. This chic menu, for eight lucky diners, could easily be organized and carried off in a few hours time if necessary. But it's an ideal do-ahead menu. Advance preparation could include the gingered beef consomme (up to two months in advance, kept frozen), the crepe pillows (one day ahead, kept chilled), the herb butter for the potatoes (may be frozen indefinitely), the potatoes themselves (several hours ahead if you have a microwave oven for reheating), the bacon fried and Swiss chard prepared for cooking (early in the day), the dessert rice (a full day ahead), and the bananas and final dessert assembly (two hours before your guests arrive). If you don't have a grill, instructions are given for oven roasting the veal chops. This menu, simple yet sophisticated, is one meat lovers are sure to enjoy.

Gingered Beef Consomme with Crepe Pillows

❖

Soups make a wonderful first course for they rarely require any last-minute fuss. Do keep the entire menu in mind, though, when planning a first course soup. The soup should be light—an appetite tickler, not satisfier. This jewel-bright, clear consomme with its crepe pillow is a perfect example—a just right start to a wonderfully satisfying meal. If you've neither the time nor the inclination to make and clarify your own beef stock, a canned product will do nicely. The hot oil and sesame oil are available at some supermarkets and at Oriental markets.

For the Consomme

6 cups homemade beef stock or 3 10½-ounce cans beef consomme

3 egg whites and the crushed shells (only if using homemade stock)

For the Crepe Pillows

½ cup low-fat milk or skim milk

1 egg, lightly beaten

¼ cup flour, instant blending recommended

pinch of salt

1 tablespoon corn oil

2 scallions, green part only, minced

2 teaspoons very finely minced fresh ginger

½ red bell pepper, minced

½ green bell pepper, minced

8 whole chives or strips of scallion green

For the Soup

1 cup Madeira
½ cup reduced-sodium soy sauce
a few drops hot oil
½ teaspoon (or to taste) sesame oil

To Clarify Homemade Stock

1. (Canned consomme does not need clarifying.) Beat 1 cup
   cold stock with the egg whites and shells in a large bowl.
   Meanwhile, bring the remaining stock to a boil in a 2½-quart
   saucepan.
2. Gradually pour the hot stock into the egg white mixture,
   beating constantly. Pour the whites and stock back into the
   saucepan and set over medium-high heat. Stir until the stock
   regains a simmer; stop stirring as soon as it begins to simmer.
   Reduce heat to low. Move the pan gently half off the burner.
   Cover and rest 15 to 20 minutes.
3. Set a colander into a large bowl. Line colander with a double
   layer of cheesecloth that has been wrung out in water. Gently
   ladle stock-egg mixture into the colander. Discard the shells
   and whites. The stock should now be clear and may be kept
   chilled (for 24 hours) or frozen (up to 2 months) until
   ready to serve.

To Prepare the Crepe Pillows

1. With a beater, food processor, or blender mix together until
   smooth the milk, egg, flour, salt, and oil. Refrigerate
   overnight or for 8 hours in a screw-top jar.
2. Coat an 8-inch nonstick skillet with cooking spray and heat
   over medium-high heat. Ladle 1½ tablespoons of crepe batter
   into the pan, tipping the pan in a circular motion so the
   batter spreads over the entire bottom. Cook until lightly
   browned, about 45 seconds, then flip and cook about 10
   seconds more. Remove crepe from pan. Crepes may be
   stacked between layers of wax paper and held at room

temperature up to 5 hours before serving. Continue to cook the remaining crepes, spraying pan as necessary to prevent sticking. (Makes 8 to 10 crepes.)

3. Mix together the scallion, ginger, and peppers. Set aside 3 tablespoons for the crepe pillows. Reserve the remaining scallion mixture for the soup.

4. Place 1 teaspoon of scallion mixture on the center of each crepe. Gather the edges and tie with a whole chive or scallion strip. Set aside. (Pillows may be held, covered and chilled, for up to 24 hours.)

To Prepare the Soup

1. Combine the clarified stock (or canned consomme diluted according to label instructions) with the wine, soy sauce, hot oil, sesame oil, and remaining scallion mixture in a 2½-quart saucepan. Heat until steaming, then taste and adjust seasoning if necessary. Place a crepe pillow in each consomme cup and ladle soup over it.

Yield: 8 6-ounce servings, each with 1 crepe pillow
Calories per serving: 83
Carbohydrate per serving: 8g
Cholesterol per serving: 35mg

Dietary fiber per serving: 1g
Fat per serving: 3g
Protein per serving: 5g
Sodium per serving: 695mg

Grilled Veal Loin Chops

❖

With no calorie-crutches such as sauces, mustardy bread crumbs, or herb butters, this simple recipe demands the best veal money can buy—creamy textured, with more white than pink. Because a good veal loin chop will run as much as 8 or up to even 12 ounces each, this is the meal for the meat lovers among us. Some of the weight is bone, of course, but this is still quite a hefty serving, so the rest of the meal has been kept light. If the grill is buried beneath a blanket of snow and you don't have an indoor model, instructions are given for oven roasting.

> 8 1½- to 2-inch-thick veal loin chops
> vegetable oil
> ½ teaspoon salt
> freshly ground pepper to taste

1. Trim any visible fat from the chops. Brush oil over the grill rungs or broiler rack. Season meat with salt and pepper. Grill (or broil, but watch timing) 12 minutes on each side or until an instant-reading meat thermometer placed in the center of the chop reads 140 for meat with the barest blush of pink, or 165 for a more well-done chop.
2. For oven cooking: Preheat oven to 400 degrees. Sear the chops in an ovenproof skillet, using cooking spray or a bit of safflower oil. Cook 3 to 4 minutes on one side. Flip, reduce heat to medium, and brown the other side another 3 to 4 minutes. Place the skillet in the bottom third of the oven and roast another 7 minutes for medium-rare or 10 minutes for medium.

Yield: 8 generous servings
Calories per serving: 426
Carbohydrate per serving: 0g
Cholesterol per serving: 240mg

Dietary fiber per serving: 0g
Fat per serving: 26g
Protein per serving: 45g
Sodium per serving: 359mg

Dilled New Potatoes

For variety you might like to substitute other herbs, such as mint or a mixture of parsley, rosemary, and thyme, for the dill. The herb butter may be doubled and kept chilled for a week or frozen almost indefinitely. Be sure to bring it to room temperature before using.

1 pound red bliss potatoes
4 tablespoons unsalted butter, at room temperature
4 tablespoons minced fresh dill
½ teaspoon salt
freshly ground black pepper to taste
sprigs of fresh dill for garnish (optional)

1. Cut a thin slice from the bottom of each potato so it sits upright. Using the larger side of a melon baller, scoop out a ball from the top center of each potato. Discard these trimmings.
2. Bring 3 quarts water to a boil in a 4-quart saucepan. Boil potatoes over medium-high heat, uncovered, for 25 minutes or until tender when pierced with a fork. Drain.
3. Meanwhile, in a food processor or blender, or with a fork, mix the butter, dill, salt, and pepper. Scrape herb butter onto a sheet of wax paper. Roll up herb butter in the paper into a sausage shape and twist the ends tightly in opposite directions.
4. Place the potatoes upright on a serving dish. Place slices of herb butter in the scooped-out center of the potatoes. (If potatoes are to be reheated in a microwave oven, cover them with plastic wrap and chill up to 8 hours. Repeat on medium-high heat power for 3 minutes or until steamy.) Garnish with fresh dill.

Yield: 8 servings, about 1 potato each
Calories per serving: 80
Carbohydrate per serving: 7g
Cholesterol per serving: 15mg

Dietary fiber per serving: 0g
Fat per serving: 6g
Protein per serving: 1g
Sodium per serving: 255mg

Swiss Chard with Bacon
and Balsamic Vinegar

❖

Swiss chard is a pleasing change from the more common spinach. Here's a tasty and satisfying way to serve it without butter.

> 6 ounces bacon
> 2½ to 3 pounds Swiss chard, rinsed and stems
>   removed
> 3 tablespoons safflower or corn oil
> 4 tablespoons balsamic vinegar

1. Fry the bacon in a 12-inch skillet until crisp. Remove and drain on paper towels. Drain fat from skillet and wipe clean with paper towels.
2. Stack the Swiss chard leaves, roll up jellyroll fashion, and slice crosswise into thin strips.
3. Heat the oil in the same skillet over high heat. Add the Swiss chard, tossing with two wooden spoons until wilted, about 3 to 4 minutes. Sprinkle with vinegar, crumble bacon over the top, toss again, and serve.

Yield: 8 servings
Calories per serving: 98
Carbohydrate per serving: 3g
Cholesterol per serving: 5g

Dietary fiber per serving: 0g
Fat per serving: 9g
Protein per serving: 3g
Sodium per serving: 193mg

❖ Nutmeg was such an essential ingredient in eighteenth-century European cuisine that women weren't considered well dressed unless adorned with an ornamental nutmeg grater. ❖

Bananas Creole

❖

Rice fanciers will take to this showy yet calorie-modest dessert. Prepare the rice the day before serving, and finish assembling the dessert two hours before, leaving broiling and flaming for the last minute.

1½ cups low-fat milk
1 vanilla bean or 1 teaspoon vanilla extract
a few gratings fresh nutmeg
1 cinnamon stick
½ cup converted rice
2 tablespoons honey
1 teaspoon unsalted butter
a pinch salt
1 egg, lightly beaten
the zest (grated rind) of 1 lemon
4 bananas
5 tablespoons rum
3 tablespoons brown sugar
1 tablespoon oats, quick-cooking recommended,
    not instant
3 tablespoons ground walnuts
1 tablespoon unsalted butter, melted
1 teaspoon sugar

1. Simmer the milk, vanilla bean (if you are using it), nutmeg, and cinnamon for 10 minutes in a covered 2½-quart saucepan over medium heat. Remove the vanilla bean and cinnamon stick.
2. Add the rice, honey, 2 teaspoons butter, and salt. Simmer, covered, over medium heat until the liquid is absorbed, about 35 to 40 minutes.

3. Remove from heat, beat in the egg, cover, and let rest 15 minutes. Stir in the lemon zest. If you are using vanilla extract, add it now. Set rice aside. (Rice may be prepared a day in advance and held, covered, in refrigerator.)

4. Cut the unpeeled bananas in half the long way, taking care not to tear the peels. Set the 8 banana skins aside. Slice the fruit in ½-inch-thick slices. Combine 3 tablespoons of the rum with the brown sugar. Add the banana slices and marinate for at least 10 minutes. Cover with plastic wrap if holding more than 30 minutes (they may be held up to 2 hours).

5. Half fill a 2½-quart saucepan with water. Bring to a boil. Drop the banana skins into the water, boil 1 minute, drain, and pat dry.

6. Place the skins in a 10-inch round, ovenproof serving dish as if they were the petals of a flower, tips meeting in the center, yellow side down. Divide the dessert rice among the banana peels. Arrange banana slices on rice.

7. Mix together the oats and walnuts. Sprinkle over bananas and drizzle with melted butter. (Dessert may be held, covered with plastic wrap, for up to 2 hours before finishing.)

8. Broil the dessert until the oats are lightly toasted, about 10 minutes. Rotate dish occasionally for even browning.

9. To flame: Combine the remaining 2 tablespoons rum and the teaspoon of sugar in a long-handled ½-cup pot (a butter warmer with a lip is ideal). Heat just until tiny bubbles appear at the edges, about 1 minute. Ignite and pour over bananas. *Note:* For safety's sake ignite and pour liqueur at the table.

Yield: 8 servings
Calories per serving: 204
Carbohydrate per serving: 35g
Cholesterol per serving: 37mg

Dietary fiber per serving: 1g
Fat per serving: 5g
Protein per serving: 4g
Sodium per serving: 72mg

❖ Lemons and limes are juicier if left at room temperature as are tomatoes, plums, grapefruits, and nectarines. ❖

A CANDLELIGHT CLASSIC

Oyster Basil Pan Roast

Tossed Green Salad with Shredded Radishes

Veal Medallions with Mushrooms and Marsala

Potato and Artichoke Gratin

Baked Apple Slices with Bourbon Sauce

❖ ──────────────────────── ❖

This delightfully satisfying meal for six seems perfect for cold weather and the flickering flames of candlelight and a fire. If you'd like to spread out the jobs, let this be your cooking guide: Prepare the salad greens and dressing the day before; leave the apple for the last minute so it does not turn brown. The veal medallions may also be partially prepared the day before, leaving just the sauteing of the meat and finishing the sauce. The bourbon sauce for the dessert may be mixed and frozen a day early as well, though it only takes a few minutes to prepare. The potato and artichoke gratin may be prepared two hours before dinner and held chilled, covered with plastic wrap, or baked and reheated in a microwave oven. The apple slices may be treated the same way. Although the oyster pan roast could be made a day in advance, the oysters will run the chance of getting tough when they are reheated; so if possible, prepare this dish (which is very simple) just before serving.

Oyster Basil Pan Roast

❖

This pan roast, really a soup, takes so very little time to prepare you might want to keep it in mind for a hurried weekday meal with a poppy-seed-dressed salad and a loaf of hot French bread. It may be made ahead if necessary, but reheat very gently so as not to overcook the oysters. Serve it in shallow soup bowls.

1½ shallots, minced (about 3 tablespoons)
3 celery ribs, minced
2¼ cups bottled clam broth or homemade fish stock
4 tablespoons cottage cheese
4 tablespoons plain yogurt
2 tablespoons arrowroot
12 fresh basil leaves
1½ pints shucked oysters, liquor reserved
3 tablespoons dry white wine
a few drops hot pepper sauce
a dash cayenne pepper (optional)

1. "Sauté" the shallots and celery in 1½ cups of the clam broth in a covered 12-inch skillet until limp, about 5 to 6 minutes.
2. Meanwhile, in a food processor or blender combine the cottage cheese, yogurt, and arrowroot. Set aside.
3. Stack the basil leaves, roll up jellyroll fashion, and slice thinly crosswise.
4. Add the remaining broth and oyster liquor to the shallots and celery along with the wine, basil, and oysters. Cover and simmer over medium heat, stirring occasionally, until the edges of the oysters curl, about 5 to 6 minutes.
5. Remove from heat, and cool by stirring constantly for 1 minute. When slightly cooled, stir in the cottage cheese mixture and

serve immediately. If soup is prepared in advance, reheat it gently over just simmering water in a double boiler.

Yield: 6 servings
Calories per serving: 199
Carbohydrate per serving: 22g
Cholesterol per serving: 93mg

Dietary fiber per serving: 1g
Fat per serving: 5g
Protein per serving: 19g
Sodium per serving: 828mg

Tossed Green Salad with Shredded Radishes

❖

Salads represent a real challenge for the enlightened cook. Although the basic ingredients tip the scale on the low side, the real taste pleasers, such as bacon, croutons, cheese, and oils, deliver unhealthy amounts of saturated fats and calories. A good dressing and a little innovative use of some common crunchables help make the most of salad standards.

The dressing recipe is sufficient for eight servings; save time by doubling it. If it jells in the refrigerator, warm briefly or heat in a microwave oven to liquefy.

For the Dressing:

⅔ cup canned beef consomme or homemade beef stock
½ cup ketchup
⅓ cup extra-virgin olive oil
1 tablespoon grated onion
1 garlic clove, minced
1 tablespoon Worcestershire sauce

For the Salad

*5 cups mixed greens, rinsed and torn, such as
Boston, salad bowl, and red leaf lettuce*
*1 bunch radishes (6 ounces), roots and stems
removed*
1 apple, any variety
1 cup bean sprouts

To Prepare the Dressing

1. Combine all the dressing ingredients in a screw-top jar. Shake
   well to combine. Refrigerate any unused portion or if not
   using immediately.

To Prepare the Salad

1. Toss the greens in a salad bowl. Shred the radishes in a food
   processor or with a grater. Core the apple and slice thinly.
   Toss the radishes, apple, and bean sprouts with the greens.
   Then toss with about 1 cup dressing.

Yield: 6 servings, with some
dressing left over
Calories per serving: 126
Carbohydrates per serving: 11g
Cholesterol per serving: 0mg

Dietary fiber per serving: 1g
Fat per serving: 9g
Protein per serving: 2g
Sodium per serving: 110mg

Veal Medallions with Mushrooms and Marsala

❖

This is a light yet rich dish, which you may partially prepare ahead.
It may seem odd to start with a rib chop, then remove the bone,
but there is method to this madness. The bones will transform a

canned broth (buy the type marked "double strength" but don't add water) into a fairly quick *demi-glace* and the rib chop meat is more tender than a cutlet. However, cutlets will certainly do. *Note:* If you have homemade beef stock, you will not need the carrots, chopped onion, thyme, and water, as it will be flavorful and thick enough to make a good sauce.

> 3 pounds veal rib chops (1 per diner)
> 2 10½-ounce cans beef broth, double strength, or
>   2½ cups homemade beef stock
> 2 carrots, chopped
> 1 onion, chopped
> a sprig fresh thyme or ½ teaspoon dried thyme
> 1 cup water
> ½ pound pearl onions
> 2 teaspoons arrowroot
> 2 tablespoons wine or water
> ¼ cup flour
> 1 tablespoon plus 1 teaspoon safflower oil
> 2 teaspoons unsalted butter
> 8 ounces mushrooms, sliced
> 6 tablespoons Marsala wine

1. Bone the rib chop by following the bone with the tip of a small paring knife to free the meat. Chop the bones into 4-inch lengths with a cleaver.
2. If you are using canned broth, combine it with the bones, carrots, onion, thyme, and water in a 4-quart saucepan. Cover and simmer at least 30 minutes, but preferably 1 hour or more. If you are using homemade beef stock, boil the stock with the bones, uncovered, over high heat until it has reduced to 1½ cups, about 15 to 20 minutes.
3. Meanwhile, butterfly the veal by slicing it sideways, keeping your knife parallel to the work surface, and cutting to within ½ inch of what was the bone side of the meat. Place the meat

between 2 sheets of wax paper and pound slightly. Meat may be left unpounded (adjust cooking instructions) if desired.

4. Trim the root end from the onions. Cut a small cross into the bottom of the onions so they won't explode during cooking. Bring a quart of water to a boil, add onions, and boil 3 to 4 minutes. Drain, and when cool enough to handle, slip off the skins.

5. When the broth or stock has simmered the suggested amount of time and reduced to 1 ½ cups (raise heat to boil to reduce more, or add more broth to adjust level if necessary), strain, pressing the solids with the back of wooden spoon. (Recipe may be completed to this step a day ahead.) Set near stove to have handy for step 8.

6. Dissolve the arrowroot in the wine or water. Set near stove for step 8.

7. Dredge the veal in the flour. Melt the oil and butter in a 12-inch skillet until bubbly. On high heat, saute the veal on one side for 2 minutes. Reduce heat to medium, turn veal over, add the onions and mushrooms, cover, and cook 2 minutes more. Transfer meat to a platter. Return heat to high, cover, and cook vegetables about 1 minute, stirring often, until nicely browned.

8. Add reduced broth or stock and Marsala, and boil, uncovered, for 2 minutes. Over medium-low heat, whisk in the dissolved arrowroot. Add the meat and spoon the sauce over it. Half-cover the pan and simmer 2 minutes more before serving.

Yield: 6 servings
Calories per serving: 568
Carbohydrate per serving: 11g
Cholesterol per serving: 235mg

Dietary fiber per serving: 1g
Fat per serving: 36g
Protein per serving: 44g
Sodium per serving: 295mg

❖ For trivia buffs, 75,000 crocuses (I have it on the best authority!) with their three stigmas each must be picked, and the stigmas plucked (by hand), to produce a pound of saffron. Crush the saffron in your fingertips just before adding to the cookpot. ❖

Potato and Artichoke Gratin

❖

What we have here is the prince and the pauper—the regal artichoke teamed up with the peasant potato. The butter-thirsty tuber is rendered moist without much fat, thanks mostly to the artichoke bottoms. Although you may use the more convenient frozen artichoke hearts, the fresh will pay off in royal dividends, lending an understated, yet distinctive flavor.

The gratin can be held chilled, covered with plastic wrap, for 2 hours before baking or completely baked and reheated in a microwave oven on medium power for about 8 minutes.

> 3 artichokes
> 6 tablespoons homemade chicken stock or canned broth
> 2 teaspoons lemon juice
> 3 large potatoes (1½ pounds), peeled and sliced ⅛-inch thick
> 2 tablespoons extra-virgin olive oil
> 1 clove garlic, halved lengthwise
> ½ teaspoon salt
> freshly ground black pepper to taste
> a few gratings fresh nutmeg
> 3 cups whole milk
> 3 tablespoons grated mozzarella cheese

1. Cut off the stem of one artichoke. With a stainless steel knife, pare the artichoke as if peeling an apple, removing the top 2 or 3 layers of tough, deep green leaves. Cut off the top third of the artichoke. Turn the artichoke upside down and be sure all the tough, dark green leaves are removed from the bottom. (See illustrations on pages 363–64.) Spread the leaves at the top of the artichoke apart. With a spoon, remove the fuzzy center (the choke). Repeat with other artichokes. Turn

1. To remove the tough outer leaves of an artichoke, pare it as you would an apple.

2. Cut off the top third of the artichoke.

3. To remove the inedible core of the artichoke, spread the leaves apart with your fingers. At the very center will be a cluster of small, sharply pointed leaves and under those a fuzzy core. Remove this with the tip of a teaspoon.

the artichokes bottom side up and slice crosswise in ¼-inch-thick slices.

2. Preheat the oven to 375 degrees. Coat a 10-inch skillet with cooking spray. Add the artichoke slices, the chicken stock, and lemon juice. Simmer, covered, over high heat until tender, about 10 minutes. You may need to reduce heat to medium and add more stock if it boils away before the artichokes are tender. The stock should have evaporated by the time the artichokes are done.

3. Meanwhile, put the sliced potatoes in a 2½-quart saucepan, cover with cold water, and bring to a boil, uncovered. Once a boil is reached, boil potatoes for 5 minutes, then drain.

4. Uncover the artichokes, add oil to the dry pan, and saute over high heat, stirring frequently, until lightly browned, about 3 to 4 minutes. Toss potatoes with artichokes off heat.

5. Rub a 10-inch quiche dish with the garlic halves, then coat the dish with cooking spray. Put potato and artichoke mixture in dish, smoothing the top. Season with salt, pepper, and nutmeg. Add milk and top with cheese. Bake in the upper third of the preheated 375-degree oven for 45 minutes or until potatoes are tender and most of the milk is absorbed. Broil briefly to brown top if necessary.

Yield: 6 servings
Calories per serving: 210
Carbohydrate per serving: 25g
Cholesterol per serving: 20mg

Dietary fiber per serving: 1g
Fat per serving: 9g
Protein per serving: 8g
Sodium per serving: 290mg

Baked Apple Slices with Bourbon Sauce

❖

Apples and cinnamon, pecans and maple syrup, the buttery crunch of a streusel—you'll do more than just imagine such taste treats with this warm dessert for cold weather. The apples may be prepared for baking up to 3 hours ahead and held covered with plastic wrap, or they may be baked and then reheated in a microwave oven just before serving. The bourbon sauce may be made up to a day ahead and kept frozen.

5 Granny Smith apples, peeled and cored
3 tablespoons cider
1 tablespoon bourbon
2½ tablespoons unsalted butter
4 tablespoons quick-cooking oats, not instant
4 tablespoons chopped pecans
½ teaspoon ground cinnamon

a dash of ground cloves
a dash of ground allspice

For the Bourbon Sauce

1 cup vanilla ice milk
2 teaspoons bourbon
2 teaspoons maple syrup
a few gratings fresh nutmeg

1. Slice the apples into thin slices, crosswise. Coat a 12-inch oven-proof platter or pizza pan with cooking spray. Lay the apple slices on the pan in rings, overlapping as little as possible. Sprinkle with cider and bourbon.
2. Preheat the oven to 375 degrees. Melt the butter in an 8-inch skillet over medium-high heat. When foamy add the oats and pecans, stirring until very lightly browned, 2 to 3 minutes. Stir in spices. Sprinkle this topping over apples. (Set aside, covered, for up to 3 hours if desired.)
3. Bake in the upper third of the oven for 15 minutes. Reduce temperature to 275 degrees and bake 15 more minutes. If the dessert is browning too much, cover it loosely with foil.

To Prepare the Sauce

1. Soften the ice milk in a bowl at room temperature, about 15 minutes, until slightly runny. Stir in the bourbon, maple syrup, and nutmeg. (The sauce may be made a day ahead and frozen. Soften it at room temperature for 15 minutes before serving.)
2. To serve, place a few hot apple slices on a dessert plate. Top with 2 heaping tablespoons sauce.

Yield: 6 servings
Calories per serving: 196
Carbohydrate per serving: 27g
Cholesterol per serving: 16mg

Dietary fiber per serving: 3g
Fat per serving: 9g
Protein per serving: 2g
Sodium per serving: 65mg

Chapter 12

MENUS FOR INFORMAL ENTERTAINING OR FAMILY DINNERS

Menus for Informal Entertaining or Family Dinners

❖

Looking for an out-of-the-ordinary do-ahead casserole for a weekend away? Or a quick but special meal to prepare in microwave speed? Maybe a long, leisurely lunch is in order. These, and more, are the subject of this section. Some of the menus are quick, others require a bit more commitment, and all give detailed information on advance preparation when feasible.

As always, the reader is urged to play with the menu items, to mix and match, or combine with your own favorites. If a guilt-free dessert is your hankering, there are several in this section. If you're looking for some interesting ways with vegetables for the family dinner table, you've come to the right place.

These are a collection of meals, for good friends or family, that showcase your good nutritional sense and culinary savvy.

These are a collection of meals, for good friends or family,. that showcase your good nutritional sense and culinary savvy.

❖ Persons attempting to lose weight would do best to restrict their intake of fats and proteins before restricting their carbohydrates. Carbohydrates (4 calories to the gram) are the body's most efficient source of fuel. If these are limited, the body will break down protein (4 calories to the gram), which is best used for tissue building and repair, or fats, which at 9 calories to the gram will take longer to use. ❖

REEL GOOD

Crumbed Codfish with Lemon Mustard Sauce

Spaghetti Squash Parmesan

Steamed Broccoli

Cappucino Cream

To ensure "reel-fresh" seafood, check that:

- the fish is kept on ice;
- the store receives daily deliveries;
- the fish is odor-free;
- the flesh is smooth and resilient, not slimy and mushy;
- the fish is weighed as you buy it, not prepackaged.

Once home, keep the fish in a bowl of ice in the refrigerator, just as it is kept at the market, if it won't be cooked within 8 hours. Should it have an off-odor despite all precautions, refresh it by soaking five minutes in a bowl of cool water with two tablespoons added lemon juice. Pat it dry before continuing with the recipe.

Fish in hand, these recipes, each serving four, are uncompli-cated. Note that the dessert does require three to four hours overall chilling time, so start it early in the day or even a day ahead. The lemon sauce can be prepared several hours ahead or as the fish cooks. The spaghetti squash can be prepared a day in advance or started before the fish preparation. Use the Steamed Broccoli recipe on page 452, doubled to serve four. If you miss the traditional starch, include a few breadsticks.

Focus: Fish

❖

If you love it you don't need to be convinced, but if the thought of fish brings to mind off-odors and an unpalatable mushiness, there probably isn't much fish in your diet—a food that studies published in the *New England Journal of Medicine* suggest may be instrumental in preventing heart disease.

In one study, Dutch researchers kept track of a large group of men, comparing their health records and diets over a period of 20 years. They found that those who ate as little as an ounce or more of fish a day were two and a half times less likely to die from heart disease than men who ate none at all. Men who ate 7 to 11 ounces of fish per week, that's 2 to 3 servings, had an impressive 64 percent lowered risk.

The researchers investigated other heart disease risk factors such as high blood pressure and high blood cholesterol, but the fact that the fish eaters consumed more cholesterol and fat than the non-fish eaters led them, along with other factors, to conclude that fish consumption all by itself appeared to help protect against heart disease.

Originally, it had been believed that one needed to eat large quantities of fish, particularly cold-water fatty fish—salmon, trout, and mackerel—with their beneficial fatty acids to achieve cardio-vascular benefits. But this study suggests that only 2 weekly meals of lean fish may be just what the doctor ordered.

This isn't to suggest that other steps in preventing heart dis-ease—quitting smoking, controlling high blood pressure, or cutting back on total fat—should be ignored; instead fish-eating is considered just one more measure.

How to work fish into a fish-hater's diet? *One:* Be sure the fish is pristinely fresh, absolutely without odor. *Two:* Choose light-tasting fishes such as sole, cod, and haddock rather than strong-flavored ones such as swordfish or bluefish. *Three:* Begin with recipes that use just a little fish in conjunction with other foods. *Four:* When ready to serve fish as the entree choose a recipe with a light sauce, such as Crumbed Codfish with Lemon Mustard Sauce, below, or one with a smattering of vegetable flavors, such as Halibut with Nutted Confetti, page 389. Offer them up, hot and tempting with a healthy serving of the facts; it's no fish tale.

Crumbed Codfish with Lemon Mustard Sauce

❖

There's nothing, to my way of thinking, quite so good as fish when it's fresh, or so awful as fish when it's old. If you have access to "reel" fresh seafood, you have one of the healthiest of protein foods and one of the quickest to prepare to boot. This simple recipe's greatest demand is that you stop by a reputable fish market the day you plan to serve it.

Fish does not take well to doing ahead—but this is a quick preparation requiring little more than 15 to 20 minutes. The sauce is easily whipped up while the fish bakes; if you prefer, it may be prepared several hours in advance, kept chilled, and reheated for a minute or two over low heat.

For the Lemon Mustard Sauce

1 *teaspoon arrowroot*
¾ *cup low-fat milk*
1 *egg yolk*
2 *tablespoons lemon juice*
1 *tablespoon unsalted butter, at room temperature*
½ *teaspoon dry mustard*

¼ teaspoon salt
a few drops hot pepper sauce

For the Fish

1¼ pounds codfish or other thick white-fleshed fish
½ cup low-fat milk
2 tablespoons dry bread crumbs
the grated rind (zest) of one lemon
¼ teaspoon salt
a dash cayenne pepper
1 tablespoon lemon juice
2 teaspoons safflower oil

To Prepare the Sauce

1. Dissolve the arrowroot in 2 tablespoons of the milk in a 1-quart saucepan over medium heat. Add the remaining milk, and cook, still over medium heat, stirring, until the mixture thickens, about 2 minutes.
2. With a fork, beat the egg yolk in a measuring cup. Continue beating as you slowly dribble ½ cup of hot milk into the yolk. Return the mixture to the saucepan with the remaining milk and stir over low heat, 1 minute, until thickened.
3. Whisk in lemon juice, butter, and dry mustard. Season with salt and hot pepper sauce to taste. (The sauce may be covered and kept in the refrigerator for several hours.)

To Prepare the Fish

1. Preheat the oven to 450 degrees. Soak the fish in the milk for 10 minutes. Drain and pat dry.
2. With cooking spray, coat a baking dish just big enough to hold the fish. Mix the bread crumbs and lemon zest on a piece of wax paper. Roll the fish in the crumbs, then place it in the baking dish.
3. Season the fish with salt and pepper. Sprinkle with lemon juice and safflower oil.
4. Measure the thickest part of the fish. Calculating 8 to 10

minutes per inch thickness, bake the fish in the upper third of
the oven accordingly. The fish may have to be broiled briefly
to brown the crumbs.

5. While the fish is baking, reheat the sauce (if it has been
   chilled) over low heat, stirring frequently, until warmed
   through—just a few minutes. Pour the sauce over the fish or
   pass it at the table.

Yield: 4 servings fish, with ⅓ cup
sauce each
Calories per serving: 290
Carbohydrate per serving: 10g
Cholesterol per serving: 160mg

Dietary fiber per serving: 0g
Fat per serving: 14g
Protein per serving: 32g
Sodium per serving: 475mg

Spaghetti Squash Parmesan

❖

A relative newcomer to our markets, spaghetti squash has been
known in the Orient for many years. Like other hard-skinned
squashes it keeps wonderfully well in the refrigerator, assuring a
fresh vegetable for the dinner table even if you haven't shopped for
several days.

This is a basic way to prepare the crunchy, mild-flavored
squash. For variety, top with sesame seeds, mix with minced fresh
basil, or combine with chopped tomatoes. A 3-pound squash yields
about 6 cooked cups, enough for 6 to 8 servings. The uncooked
section may be wrapped in plastic wrap and kept chilled for up to
4 days. Cooked leftovers will keep about 2 to 3 days in the
refrigerator, and may be reheated conventionally or in a microwave
oven.

½ of a 3½- to 4-pound spaghetti squash
1 tablespoon unsalted butter
1 tablespoon freshly grated Parmesan cheese

¼ teaspoon salt
freshly ground black pepper to taste

1. The squash may be microwaved, baked, or boiled. To microwave: Place the squash cut side down in a pan just large enough to hold it; add ¼ cup water. Microwave on high for 14 to 15 minutes. To bake: Place the squash cut side down in an 8-inch-square baking pan with ¼ cup water. Cook in a 350-degree oven for 45 minutes. To boil: Cut the half into quarters and boil 20 minutes in a covered pot in 4 inches of water.
2. When skin pierces easily with a fork, drain and cool. Scoop out and discard the seeds. With a fork transfer the spaghettilike strands from the shell to a casserole if preparing ahead (may be kept chilled a day in advance), or to a serving dish if serving immediately. Discard the shell.
3. Stir in the remaining ingredients. Taste to correct seasoning. The squash is ready to serve or may be kept covered and chilled for up to a day before serving. Reheat in a 350-degree oven until warmed through or in a microwave oven on medium-high power.

Yield: 4 1-cup servings
Calories per serving: 80
Carbohydrate per serving: 10g
Cholesterol per serving: 10mg

Dietary fiber per serving: 2g
Fat per serving: 4g
Protein per serving: 2g
Sodium per serving: 200mg

Cappucino Cream

If you love the flavors of coffee and cinnamon with an accent of chocolate, this cloudlike dessert is for you. Start cappucino cream 3 to 4 hours before serving, or up to a day before, as it must chill. Although

"Reel Good" is a menu for 4, this dessert makes 7 servings. You may enjoy the extras, confident they are not pound packers.

> 1 envelope unflavored gelatin
> 1/4 cup plus 2 tablespoons sugar
> 2 cups skim or low-fat milk
> 2 eggs, separated
> 1 teaspoon instant espresso coffee
> 2 teaspoons Tia Maria or other coffee-flavored liqueur
> 2 tablespoons semisweet chocolate chips, pulverized in a food processor
> 3 tablespoons finely chopped walnuts
> 7 thin cinnamon sticks for garnish (optional)
> grated unsweetened chocolate for garnish (optional)

1. Combine the gelatin and sugar in a 2 1/2-quart saucepan. Set aside.
2. Beat together the milk, egg yolks, and coffee in a 1-quart bowl until frothy. Stir into the gelatin saucepan.
3. Cook mixture over low heat for about 7 minutes, stirring constantly. It will thicken very slightly. Remove from heat and transfer back into the 1-quart bowl. Stir in liqueur and chill until the mixture mounds when dropped from a spoon, about 1 1/2 to 2 hours.
4. If the coffee mixture has jelled, beat it to make it smooth. Stir in the pulverized chocolate chips.
5. Beat egg whites until stiff, then fold into the coffee mixture. Divide the cappucino cream among 7 champagne glasses, sprinkle with nuts, and chill for 2 to 3 hours or overnight. To serve, garnish with a cinnamon stick and a dusting of grated chocolate, if you wish.

Yield: 7 servings
Calories per serving: 130
Carbohydrate per serving: 18g
Cholesterol per serving: 80mg

Dietary fiber per serving: 1g
Fat per serving: 5g
Protein per serving: 5g
Sodium per serving: 60mg

VARIATION ON A THEME

Chicken Breasts with Spinach and Feta
Braised Celery with Red Peppers
Rice à la Grecque
Grilled Bermuda Onion Slices

This menu is really just the same old tune—chicken and rice—redone to please the enlightened cook. The chicken skin with its fifty calories and nearly two grams of saturated fat (ironically, the removed fat doesn't lower the cholesterol count!) is gone. The lemon sauce is rich and zesty, but without cholesterol-heavy egg yolks and mounds of butter; the celery is braised rather than raw; and the rice has a golden glow. All the recipes are easy variations on an old familiar theme. These variations make this menu dressy enough for a get-together dinner with friends (although the recipes serve four, they could easily be doubled), or for a family treat.

If you have a willing partner in the kitchen and wish to embellish the theme a bit more, a little knife work can turn the chicken into a dazzler. Cut each cooked breast the long way into about five strips, slanting the knife slightly to create wide slices of spinach-stuffed meat. Film each dinner plate with the lemon sauce. Arrange the chicken like petals of a flower on the plate, filling the spaces with servings of the rice and the celery and red peppers. Cut the onion in half, and set the halves on either side of the plate.

To help plan your work schedule: The chicken may be stuffed and wrapped up to six hours before cooking, and the sauce prepared either as the chicken simmers or a few hours before. The rice is simply put together about one hour before dinner; plan on ten to twelve minutes cooking time for the celery, and about twenty-five minutes for the onions.

Chicken Breasts With Spinach and Feta

❖

A skinless chicken breast offers an excellent source of protein (70 percent of an adult woman's RDA) and niacin, which promotes healthy skin and nerves (95 percent). It's also a good source of phosphorus, a structural component of bones and teeth (27 percent of her RDA) and potassium, important in fluid balance (13 percent), all for a treat-allowing 173 calories (based on average of 3½ ounces per serving). Yet, steamed or broiled without the skin or added fat, pallid poultry can be most unappetizing. Here, stuffed with a tried-and-true spinach-feta combo and drizzled with a complementing lemon sauce, it is a bird of a different feather.

If you have a supply of rich homemade chicken stock, substitute it for the canned broth and eliminate the carrot, onions, celery, and parsley. Omit steps 2 and 8. The lemon sauce could be prepared several hours in advance and kept chilled, but it is quite easily done while the chicken cooks. Parchment paper is available from specialty shops and some supermarkets. Use foil if parchment is unavailable.

> 4 chicken breasts, preferably with bones, with or
>   without skin
> 3 cups homemade chicken stock or canned broth
> 1 carrot, diced
> 1 small onion, diced

1 rib celery, diced
a few sprigs parsley
5 ounces raw spinach, backbones removed
2 ounces feta cheese, crumbled
1 tablespoon pine nuts (optional)

For the Lemon Sauce

1 teaspoon arrowroot
½ cup low-fat milk
1 egg, lightly beaten
juice of ½ lemon
2 teaspoons unsalted butter, at room temperature
¼ teaspoon salt
a dash cayenne pepper

To Prepare the Chicken and Cooking Liquid

1. Bone the breasts (reserving the bones if you are using canned broth) and discard the skin. To cut a pocket in the chicken breast, lay one breast on the counter surface with what was the skin side down and with what was the tip of the breast bone pointing away from you. Place one hand on top of the breast meat while slicing from right to left, parallel to the counter, to within 1 inch of the left side. Repeat with each breast. Keep the chicken chilled while preparing the cooking liquid.

2. Break up the bones with a mallet. Combine them with the canned broth in a 2½-quart saucepan. Add the carrot, onion, celery, and parsley. Cover and simmer 30 minutes or up to 1½ hours, adding water if the liquid drops below the original level.

3. Meanwhile, prepare the stuffing: Rinse the spinach leaves and pack them into a 2-quart saucepan. Cover and cook over high heat just until wilted, about 1 minute. Drain any water. Combine the spinach with the feta in a food processor or by hand, mixing well. Turn into a bowl.

4. Toast the pine nuts by tossing them in an ungreased 8-inch

skillet over high heat, about 1 minute, until lightly browned. These burn easily, so watch carefully. Stir the pine nuts into the spinach.

5. Stuff the pockets of the chicken breasts with the spinach stuffing. Press closed with the heel of your hand.

6. Tear off 4 pieces of parchment paper, each about 17 inches by 15 inches. Stack the four sheets together. Fold in half the long way, trimming corners to make a heart shape.

7. Place a chicken breast on one half of each heart. Fold the other half of the heart over it. Starting at the rounded top, fold and pleat the paper, making a tight seal around the chicken. Twist and tuck the pointed end under the packet. (Refer to the illustrations as you do this.) Repeat with remaining chicken and parchment hearts. Set wrapped chicken aside while you complete the cooking liquid.

8. When the broth has simmered at least 30 minutes, set a colander into a medium-size bowl. Pour the chicken broth through it. Press the solids with the back of a wooden spoon, then discard. (Recipe may be prepared to this point early in the day. Refrigerate wrapped chicken and strained broth.)

To Cook the Chicken and Prepare the Sauce

1. Pour the broth into a 12-inch skillet. Add the parchment packets, cover, and simmer over medium-high heat, 8 to 10 minutes. Turn packets over after 4 to 5 minutes of cooking. Adjust the heat to prevent boiling.

2. While the chicken cooks, prepare the sauce. Begin by dissolving the arrowroot in 2 tablespoons of the chicken broth (from the skillet) in a cup.

3. In a 1-quart saucepan set over high heat, heat the milk just until tiny bubbles appear at the edge. Reduce heat to medium-high. Stir in the dissolved arrowroot and continue to stir until the mixture is thickened, about 3 or 4 minutes. Adjust heat to prevent boiling.

4. Remove the pan from the heat. Beat the egg with a fork. Add 3 to 4 tablespoons hot milk to the egg, while continuing

1. Lay the chicken breast, or other food, on half the paper heart, then fold the paper over it.

2. Pleat the paper tightly, securing the pleat with your fingertips as you move along the perimeter of the heart. Each pleat is made by making ¼-inch folds at 1½-inch intervals.

3. Continue making the pleats along the perimeter of the heart.

4. Secure the end by tucking the tip of paper under the package.

to beat with the fork. Pour the egg into the remaining milk mixture in the saucepan, beating with the fork as you pour.

5. Return the saucepan to medium-low heat. Whisk in lemon juice. Whisk until the sauce coats the back of a metal spoon, about 2 minutes more. Whisk in the butter and seasonings. Taste to correct seasoning, and cover to keep the sauce warm off the heat.

6. When the chicken has simmered 8 to 10 minutes and is firm when pressed, lift the chicken packets from the broth, draining by tipping them on end. Cut the package open and discard the paper. Place a breast on each plate and top with 3 tablespoons of sauce. (The cooking liquid may be frozen and used whenever chicken stock is called for.)

Yield: 4 servings
Calories per serving: 299
Carbohydrate per serving: 14g
Cholesterol per serving: 162mg

Dietary fiber per serving: 1g
Fat per serving: 12g
Protein per serving: 34g
Sodium per serving: 452g

Braised Celery with Red Peppers

❖

It's a rare vegetable that doesn't require a bit of salt to be tasty, but celery's naturally high sodium content puts that shaker on hold. You won't miss butter here either while you enjoy appreciable amounts of potassium and fiber. Braised celery also provides a tasty alternative to the "Broccoli, again?" glares I sometimes get at my house. For an added spark, it is tossed here with red bell peppers. The recipe may be prepared several hours ahead and reheated, covered, over low heat or in a microwave oven on high power for 1 minute.

2 red bell peppers
4 celery ribs
1½ cups homemade chicken or beef stock or
    canned broth
freshly ground black pepper to taste

1. Cut the peppers in half, lengthwise. Discard the seeds. Flatten the peppers with the heel of your hand. Place on a cookie sheet skin side up, and broil, turning the sheet once to ensure even browning, until the peppers are charred and blackened. Scrape the peppers into a plastic or paper bag, roll tightly closed, and allow to cool. Peel off the skin and slice the flesh into thin strips. Set aside.
2. Trim the celery; remove the strings. Cut each rib lengthwise into 3 to 4 thin strips. Cut the strips across into thirds.
3. Bring the broth and celery to a boil in a 10-inch skillet. Reduce heat to medium-high. Boil gently, uncovered, until the celery is almost tender and the liquid has reduced to about ¼ cup, about 7 to 8 minutes.
4. Add the pepper strips, raise heat to high, and boil until only a few tablespoons of syrupy liquid remain, 2 to 3 minutes. Season with pepper.

Yield: 4 servings
Calories per serving: 26
Carbohydrate per serving: 4g
Cholesterol per serving: 0mg

Dietary fiber per serving: 1g
Fat per serving: 0g
Protein per serving: 1g
Sodium per serving: 45mg

❖ A calorie is a unit of measure. It is the amount of energy needed to raise 1 gram of water (a little less than ⅕ teaspoon) 1 degree Centigrade. ❖

Rice à la Grecque

❖

Rice is terrific with chicken, if taste is the sole criterion, but its pale color does little to enhance the poultry. Rice à la Grecque solves the problem nicely with a confetti effect of red pepper and green peas. What's more, this is one rice dish moist enough not to require pat after pat of butter.

2 tablespoons minced onion
2¾ to 3 cups homemade chicken stock or canned broth
1 tablespoon safflower oil
1 cup brown rice
½ teaspoon salt
½ cup fresh shelled or frozen peas
¼ cup minced red bell pepper
freshly ground black pepper to taste

1. "Saute" the onion in 4 tablespoons of the chicken stock in a 10-inch skillet over medium-high heat until the onion is softened but not browned, about 4 to 5 minutes. Add a bit more broth if necessary, or raise the heat to evaporate the liquid when the onion is tender.
2. Add the oil and the rice. Raise heat to high and brown the rice, stirring constantly, about 2 minutes. Add 2½ cups of broth and the salt. Cover and simmer, stirring occasionally, until the rice is tender, about 50 minutes. Add more broth if needed to prevent the rice from sticking.
3. Cook the fresh peas in 2 cups water in a 1-quart covered saucepan for 10 minutes or until they are tender. Drain. If you are using frozen peas, cook them according to package instructions and drain.
4. Stir the peppers and peas into the rice, season with ground

pepper, and taste for seasoning adjustment. The rice may be held in a double boiler for up to 1 hour or reheated in a microwave oven on high for 2 minutes (add a bit more broth).

Yield: 4 servings	Dietary fiber per serving: 4g
Calories per serving: 225	Fat per serving: 4g
Carbohydrate per serving: 42g	Protein per serving: 5g
Cholesterol per serving: 0mg	Sodium per serving: 315mg

Grilled Bermuda Onion Slices

This simply prepared vegetable does require a grill; unfortunately a broiler won't produce the same results. If you prefer onions on the mild side, soak the slices in warm water 30 minutes before cooking, changing the water once or twice. Vidalia onions would make a delicious substitute for the Bermuda.

> 3 medium Bermuda onions (about 21 ounces),
>   peeled and cut into ½-inch thick slices
> 2 tablespoons olive oil
> 1 tablespoon homemade chicken or beef stock or
>   canned broth
> 6–8 fresh basil leaves, minced

1. Brush oil over the rungs of the grill and on one side of the onion slices. Place onions, oiled side down, on the rungs. Grill, twisting the onion slices and loosening them from the rungs with a spatula. Baste occasionally with a little of the oil and stock.
2. After 15 minutes, turn the onions over. Baste again and cook 10 minutes more or until the onions are tender. Be sure the

onions don't stick to the rungs. Sprinkle with basil and drizzle with any remaining oil 5 minutes before the onions are done.

Yield: 4 servings
Calories per serving: 95
Carbohydrate per serving: 8g
Cholesterol per serving: 0mg

Dietary fiber per serving: 1g
Fat per serving: 4g
Protein per serving: 1g
Sodium per serving: 2mg

Focus: Rice

❖

There are any number of rices available from Italian Arborio to Minnesota wild, but the basic supermarket choices are brown or white, long-grain or short-grain, converted or regular. Each type is best suited to a particular use and cooking method. Here are some guidelines:

Brown rice: All rice starts out as the seed of a cereal grass. The seeds are cleaned and the outer tough husk removed. This leaves a brown grain with much of the nutritive value in its now outermost bran layer. Brown rice takes about 50 minutes to cook, has a nutty flavor and texture, and is moist and compact. It accounts for only 1 percent of the rice purchased in this country, but is the type most used where rice is the mainstay of the diet.

White rice: This rice undergoes an additional milling process from brown rice, which removes the outer bran layer, resulting in a white or polished rice. In America this nutritionally deficient rice is sprayed with a solution of thiamin, niacin, and iron, replacing the nutrients that have been lost. Such rice is labeled "enriched."

Converted rice: This may be either white or brown. It is subjected to very high temperatures that force some of the nutrients of the bran layer back into the grain. This partial cooking results in less home-cooking time, though very little less for converted brown rice.

Long-grain, medium-grain, and short-grain: Long-grain rice cooks a bit more quickly than either medium- or short-grain rice, and maintains the shape of the individual grains after cooking. This makes a drier, fluffier rice. Medium- and short-grain rice tend to be more tender, moister, and stickier. Generally, long-grain is preferred as a vegetable side dish or for a salad dish, while the medium- and short-grains are used for puddings and molds, or any recipe that has to hold together.

Nutritionally, rice pales in comparison with a potato, as it is somewhat higher in calories and lower in some minerals and vitamin C. But it is an excellent source of carbohydrate, the "fuel" our bodies run on, and is also very easily digested.

A few quick ideas for varying the standard:

1. Cook rice in chicken broth for excellent, full-bodied flavor.
2. Add slivers of dried apricots (3 whole apricots is appropriate for a rice dish serving 4), which have been soaked ½ hour in hot water, and drained.
3. Add currants, white raisins, or other dried fruits, about ½ cup for 4 servings.
4. Add ½ cup tomato juice to the water for Italian- or Spanish-flavored recipes.
5. Add ½ cup orange juice to the cooking liquid when serving with veal.
6. Flavor with sage when serving with pork or poultry, or basil when serving with tomatoes.
7. Color with turmeric or season with saffron for a delicious dish to serve with fish.
8. Mix with other vegetables such as onions, peppers, and peas (see Rice à la Grecque, page 384).

Any of these, singly or in combination, provide a new slant on the predictable.

POUND CHASER

Halibut with Nutted Confetti
Fruited Rice
Honey-Tarragon Dressing for Mixed Greens

Fish, cooked with little fat, is not only excellent for the heart (see *Focus: Fish,* page 370) but also for the waistline. A generous six-ounce serving contributes less than two hundred calories, almost all of an adult woman's daily protein needs, all her niacin and vitamin A, and a healthy dose of some minerals all with a very conservative fifty milligrams of cholesterol (daily intake should not exceed three hundred milligrams). In "Pound Chaser," a menu for four that could be easily adapted to serve as few as two or as many as six, halibut is quickly steamed and topped with a colorful peppering of vegetables and accompanied with an equally speedy rice with apricots and crisp salad. This is a healthy and satisfying meal to prepare, not ahead, but in less than an hour. Diet food? Hardly, just good and good-for-you without superfluous calories and saturated fats. It is indeed a pound chaser.

Halibut with Nutted Confetti

❖

Nutted confetti is very descriptive of this halibut's red and green pepper topping studded with almonds. This is not an etched-in-stone type recipe but a guide for any thick (1 or more inches) white-fleshed fish. Diced tomatoes, carrots, leeks, or celery would be a nice added touch, with or without snipped fresh herbs such as thyme and basil. And while instructions here are for steaming, any number of cooking methods—baking, grilling, or broiling—would do nicely. Do the topping ahead by several hours if it seems easier, but cook the fish just before serving.

1 tablespoon olive oil
1 small red bell pepper, diced
1 small green bell pepper, diced
1 shallot, minced (about 2 tablespoons)
2 tablespoons slivered almonds
1 tablespoon lemon juice
2 cups homemade chicken stock or canned broth
    or homemade fish stock
1¼ pounds halibut
¼ teaspoon salt
thin lemon slices for garnish (optional)

To Prepare the Confetti Topping

1. Heat the oil in a 10-inch skillet until hot. Add the peppers and shallot. Cover and saute over medium heat until tender, about 10 to 12 minutes, stirring frequently. Adjust heat as necessary to prevent burning. Add a tablespoon or so of chicken broth or fish stock if the vegetables start to stick.
2. Uncover and raise heat to high. Stir in almonds and cook 1 minute or until heated through. Add lemon juice. Keep warm on a warming tray or over very low heat until the fish is

ready. (Confetti topping may be prepared several hours ahead, kept chilled, and reheated over medium heat just before serving.)

To Cook the Fish

1. Meanwhile, bring the chicken stock to a boil in a 12-inch skillet. Measure the fish to calculate cooking time (8 to 10 minutes per 1 inch of thickness). Add the fish to the stock, season with salt, and cover. Cook over high heat until the flesh is opaque. Remove the fish from the skillet with a slotted spatula, letting the stock run off.
2. Place the fish on a platter, top with the confetti topping, and garnish with lemon slices.

Yield: 4 servings
Calories per serving: 215
Carbohydrate per serving: 4g
Cholesterol per serving: 70mg

Dietary fiber per serving: 1g
Fat per serving: 8g
Protein per serving: 30g
Sodium per serving: 235mg

Fruited Rice

❖

Apricots provide the simple variation needed to give interest to an otherwise common dish. For other ideas, see *Focus: Rice* on page 386.

3 dried apricots
1 cup long-grain converted white rice
1 cup homemade chicken stock or canned broth
1½ cups water
½ teaspoon turmeric
½ teaspoon salt
1 tablespoon unsalted butter

1. Soak the apricots for 30 minutes in hot water to cover.
2. Place the rice, broth, water, turmeric, and salt in a 2½-quart saucepan. Cover and bring to a boil over high heat. Reduce heat to medium and boil gently, stirring occasionally, until the liquid is absorbed. (Converted rice takes about 15 minutes to cook.)
3. Drain apricots and cut them into thin strips. Add them to the rice 5 minutes before it is done.
4. Toss cooked rice with butter. The rice will keep warm off the heat, covered, for about 10 minutes; it is best made fresh, not reheated.

Yield: 4 servings
Calories per serving: 210
Carbohydrate per serving: 42g
Cholesterol per serving: 10mg

Dietary fiber per serving: 1g
Fat per serving: 3g
Protein per serving: 3g
Sodium per serving: 300mg

Honey-Tarragon Dressing for Mixed Greens

❖

If you've been used to low-cal store-bought dressings, salads are probably something you think you should eat, rather than enjoy eating. This smooth herb dressing might make those thinning greens a favorite again.

When choosing salad greens, remember that the darker green leaves, usually the outer ones, are richest in vitamin A (needed for healthy skin, eyesight, and bones). Select non-garden items for the salad bowl, particularly in winter, to add variety and interest. Apples are delicious, as are pears, sunflower seeds, or pine nuts (use seeds and nuts—high calorie items—sparingly). Canned kidney, shell, or garbanzo beans add important fiber, tastily, while sliced water chestnuts and bean sprouts provide different textures and olives add pizzazz. Canned pimientos add flavorful color, unlike winter's so-called tomatoes, as does a tablespoon or so of canned corn or sliced beets. Grated cheese is great, and so is a shower of grated egg white. Think color and texture contrasts, and salads might just get fun and flavorful again. Particularly nice with this salad dressing is a combination of Boston lettuce, watercress, and sliced apples. Use four cups of salad ingredients, cook's choice.

> 1 egg
> 1 tablespoon tarragon vinegar
> 1 teaspoon Dijon mustard
> 1 teaspoon honey
> 1 teaspoon dried tarragon
> ½ cup safflower oil
> ½ cup canned beef consomme or homemade beef stock

1. In a food processor or blender process the egg, vinegar, mustard, honey, and tarragon for 15 seconds. Add the oil in a very thin, steady stream while the machine runs on high power. Slowly add the consomme. The dressing will keep under refrigeration up to 5 days.
2. Toss the salad with the dressing, estimating 3 tablespoons of dressing per serving.

Yield: 4 servings salad and 1½ cups dressing
Calories per serving: 154
Carbohydrate per serving: 1g
Cholesterol per serving: 39mg

Dietary fiber per serving: 0g
Fat per serving: 16g
Protein per serving: 1g
Sodium per serving: 31mg

FLASH IN THE PAN

Pan-seared Lemon Veal
Julienne of Root Vegetables
Poppy Seed Pasta

More often than not, when there just isn't much time for preparing dinner, old standbys get pressed into service. Tried and true as such dishes may be, are they as low in calories as you might wish? Here's a quick (less than one hour) and calorie-conscious menu for two, guaranteed to ease a harried cook's schedule, as well as satisfy that "looking for something good" appetite.

For this meal and anytime when pasta is served, it's a good practice to heat the dinner plates to prevent rapid cooling. A microwave oven is excellent for this, but remember to add a glass of water to absorb energy.

There's not a lot of planning involved in this meal. Because the vegetables hold well without getting too soggy, you might start there, then boil the pasta as you cook the veal.

Pan-seared Lemon Veal

Veal has the deserved reputation of being a fairly lean meat—a good choice for those trying to limit their calories. Oddly, however, it isn't lower in cholesterol than other red meats or even roast chicken. A three-ounce serving of veal contains 84 milligrams of cholesterol (the American Heart Association recommends eating no more than 250 to 300 milligrams a day), lean beef contains 73 milligrams, roast chicken with or without the skin has 76 milligrams, and flounder has 52 milligrams. Further, a surprising 48 percent of veal's total fat is saturated, the same as beef. Is veal no nutritional bargain then? Yes and no. Overall, it has less total fat than most red meats, but do remember fish is lower in cholesterol and saturated fat.

For those times, though, when red meat and only red meat will do, here is a recipe with tight reins on the fat.

> 7 ounces veal cutlet
> flour for dredging
> ¼ teaspoon salt
> freshly ground black pepper to taste
> 2 teaspoons safflower oil
> 1 tablespoon lemon juice
> 2 tablespoons Marsala wine
> thin slices lemon for garnish (optional)

1. Dredge the veal in the flour, then season with salt and pepper. Coat a 10-inch skillet with cooking spray, then heat the oil until it is very hot. Add the veal and sear on one side, about 1 minute. Reduce the heat to medium and continue to cook an additional minute.
2. Flip veal over and turn heat to high, if necessary, to sear. Cook 2 minutes more over medium heat, adjusting heat if necessary to prevent burning.
3. With the meat still in the pan, add the lemon juice. Allow it to boil away (raising heat to high if necessary). Add Marsala and continue to boil. Remove the pan from the heat when just a teaspoon or two of liquid remains. Transfer veal to dinner plates or a serving platter and spoon pan juices over it. Garnish with lemon slices if desired.

Yield: 2 servings
Calories per serving: 220
Carbohydrate per serving: 1g
Cholesterol per serving: 100mg

Dietary fiber per serving: 0g
Fat per serving: 16g
Protein per serving: 19g
Sodium per serving: 380mg

Julienne of Root Vegetables

❖

My husband has second helpings of these. Not a bad endorsement from a guy whose idea of vegetables begins with a very well buttered potato and ends with French fries. The combined flavor of root vegetables is much better than any single one and oddly needs no butter or other fat, which most vegetables seem to crave. Of course, you could add a teaspoon or two of safflower oil or a bit of minced garlic or even other vegetables. Don't omit the parsnips, though, even if you think you don't like them. Their slightly sweet flavor and smooth texture are key to the whole concoction.

> 2 small carrots, peeled and julienned
> 2 leeks, white part only, rinsed and julienned
> 2 small purple-top turnips, peeled and julienned
> 2 parsnips, peeled and julienned
> ½ cup canned beef consomme or homemade beef stock
> freshly ground black pepper to taste
> 1 teaspoon minced fresh parsley

1. Coat a 10-inch skillet with cooking spray. Combine the carrots, leeks, turnips, and parsnips with the consomme in the skillet. Cover and bring to a boil over high heat. Stir often and reduce heat to medium after 3 minutes.
2. When vegetables are tender, about 5 to 6 minutes, transfer them to a serving platter. If necessary, uncover the pan, raise heat to high, and boil any remaining broth until only a tablespoonful remains. Pour it over the vegetables. Season with pepper and garnish with parsley.

Yield: 2 generous servings
Calories per serving: 160
Dietary fiber per serving: 8g
Fat per serving: 1g

Carbohydrates per serving: 38g
Cholesterol per serving: 0g
Protein per serving: 4g
Sodium per serving: 95mg

Poppy Seed Pasta

❖

Homemade pasta recipes can be found in the PASTA PASSIONS section of this book, but a store-bought product will save considerable time for this "Flash in the Pan" menu recipe. If available, purchased fresh rather than boxed pasta is much nicer.

> 2 ounces fresh fettucine noodles
> 2 teaspoons unsalted butter
> ¼ teaspoon salt
> freshly ground black pepper to taste
> 1 tablespoon poppy seeds
> zest (grated rind) of 1 lemon

1. Cook the noodles according to package instructions. Drain, toss with butter, salt, pepper, poppy seeds, and lemon zest. Serve onto warmed dinner plates.

Yield: 2 ½-cup servings
Calories per serving: 170
Carbohydrate per serving: 25g
Cholesterol per serving: 10mg

Dietary fiber per serving: 1g
Fat per serving: 6g
Protein per serving: 5g
Sodium per serving: 295mg

Focus: Cutting Fat

❖

Cutting down on fat means more than going easy on the butter. Here are some practical suggestions for limiting this highest calorie nutrient:

1. Trim all visible fat from meats and skin from poultry.
2. Use few processed lunch meats such as hot dogs, bologna, or salami. At the deli counter, choose lean roast beef, ham, or turkey.
3. Use mayonnaise rarely. If a sandwich is your typical lunch, choose one that doesn't need mayonnaise, or at least use it sparingly. Tuna is low in calories only when it isn't mixed with gobs of mayo.
4. Use low-calorie salad dressings at home exclusively. If any are unavailable when eating out, opt for mere droplets of oil and vinegar or lemon juice. An oil and vinegar dressing is generally better than those awful, overprocessed, chemical wonders most salad bars offer, anyway.
5. Use low-fat or skim milk exclusively. And of course no cream. Make "cream" sauces based on cottage cheese. Use plain yogurt instead of sour cream.
6. Avoid hard cheeses. Softer cheeses have a higher water content so they are generally lower in calories, but they are still hardly low-cal. And some soft cheeses, such as Triple Crèmes, are very high in fat, so use caution.
7. Don't be deceived by the ad that says cream cheese has half the calories of butter. Sure it does, but who spreads cream cheese as thinly as butter on a slice of toast?
8. Baked goods are usually high in fat and sugar. Muffins aren't better for you than doughnuts; they may not be fried but they are heavy with sugar and fat.
9. When planning menus emphasize the vegetables, fruits, and starches instead of often fatty meats. Use your energy in preparing a terrific low-fat potato dish instead of the meat course. Over time, these "understudies" will take on heightened significance if you do them justice, and you'll be less tempted by the higher fat foods.
10. Never fry. Steam, boil, braise with minimal fats, bake, grill, microwave, or roast.
11. Use cooking spray and nonstick skillets.

12. Use chicken broth instead of oil when you saute foods such as onions or mushrooms.
13. Snack on unbuttered popcorn, not chips.
14. Buy and use a degreaser whenever you make pan sauces from drippings.
15. Fresh fruit is seldom as appealing to most of us as a thick slab of chocolate cake, but if you buy the best fruits and give them an honest chance you'll be surprised how good fresh, sweet pineapple is or how satisfying a crisp, cool pear can be. Break out of the rut; splurge on exotic fruits and berries. Raspberries may be costly, but you'll pay less where it really counts.

❖ Under the all-too-familiar category of possible carcinogens must now fall the common *raw* mushroom. One study has linked cancer in mice with a diet that included raw mushrooms. This discovery has led some researchers to theorize that hydrazines—a natural substance that protects the plant from some predators—may have adverse effects on people too. Mushroom lovers are advised to cook or dry them, which destroys most of the harmful hydrazines. It hasn't yet been determined how many raw mushrooms one would have to eat to be affected. ❖

DOUBLE TAKE

Turkey Breast with Port and Mushrooms

Orzo*

Mushroom-stuffed Leek Rolls

Avocado-Pear Salad with Hot Lime Dressing

There's a double take in store for four dinner mates with this menu, for things are not what they may seem. The meat looks like veal, it cooks like veal, it tastes a lot like veal, but it costs less. Yes, it's turkey cutlets. The fluffy white starch looks like rice, it cooks much the same as rice, it has the same texture as rice, but it's somehow different. Yes, it's orzo, a rice-shaped macaroni product. (No recipe needed, just follow package instructions.) You can create interest and variety without hours in the kitchen or lots of fattening additives; all it takes is a little planning.

While the avocado, a high-fat fruit, may seem out of place in a book of thinning foods, let it be a reminder that there are a few forbidden foods in the enlightened cook's repertoire. Used sparingly, almost any food can be enjoyed.

Begin your preparation with the salad dressing and washing the greens. (If greens are washed, spun dry, put loosely in a plastic bag that is left slightly open, and refrigerated, they can successfully be washed a day ahead.) The Mushroom-stuffed Leek Rolls may be prepared early in the day; they reheat nicely. Boil the orzo while doing the turkey. Both are easy to keep hot while you assemble the salad.

Turkey Breast with Port and Mushrooms

❖

Sliced, skinless turkey breast cutlets, now available in many markets, may be used much as you would veal. Supplying about 157 calories and 70 milligrams of cholesterol in a 3½-ounce portion, they are an excellent resource for the health-conscious cook. Further, while 3½-ounce servings of some protein foods, particularly fish, strike many appetites as too meager, it seems quite satisfying here. If you can't buy cutlets, opt for the whole frozen turkey breast and slice and pound your own cutlets. The remainder may be used in a stir-fried recipe, or ground and used as you would ground beef in lasagne or spaghetti sauce. This recipe may be prepared several hours in advance and reheated if a microwave oven is available (3 minutes on medium high). Reheating in the oven or on top of the stove will toughen the turkey. This dish would be very nice garnished with a spoonful of cranberry relish.

> ½ ounce dried Tree Ears, an oriental mushroom
>   available at specialty food shops
> 2 teaspoons arrowroot
> ¾ cup Tawny Port
> 2 tablespoons safflower oil
> 12 ounces skinless turkey cutlets cut from the
>   breast
> ¼ teaspoon salt
> freshly ground black pepper to taste
> 4 ounces mushrooms, sliced
> ½ cup homemade chicken stock or canned broth

1. Soak the Tree Ears in hot water to cover for 20 minutes. Drain. Remove any tough segments, chop, and set aside.

2. Dissolve the arrowroot in 2 tablespoons of the port. Set near stove to have ready for step 6.
3. Coat a 12-inch skillet with cooking spray. Add half the oil, heat over high heat for 1 minute. Sear for 2 minutes as many cutlets as will fit in the pan without overlapping. Season with salt and pepper, adjusting heat to prevent burning. Turn cutlets over and brown. Reduce heat to medium and cook 2 minutes more. Transfer cutlets to a serving platter. Cover them with a kitchen towel and foil to keep them warm while you complete the sauce. Repeat with the remaining turkey and oil.
4. Add the Tree Ears and mushrooms to the skillet. Stir over high heat until the mushrooms are lightly browned, about 2 to 3 minutes.
5. Add the remaining port and broth to the skillet. Boil until they are reduced to a little more than a half cup, about 2 minutes.
6. Reduce heat to medium. Stir in the dissolved arrowroot. When the sauce has thickened, about 1 to 2 minutes, return the turkey to the skillet. Cover and heat through, about 2 to 3 minutes, stirring from time to time.

Yield: 4 servings
Calories per serving: 180
Carbohydrate per serving: 7g
Cholesterol per serving: 50mg

Dietary fiber per serving: 0g
Fat per serving: 8g
Protein per serving: 22g
Sodium per serving: 215g

❖ Potatoes are natural partners with other vegetables, too: potato and turnip puree, flavored with garlic; potato and leek puree, flavored with garlic and Parmesan cheese; potato and celery root, flavored with mustard; potato and beet puree, flavored with a hint of orange and orange zest; sweet potato and squash or pumpkin, flavored with curry. ❖

1. Cut three-quarters of the way through the leek, leaving the outer two or three layers intact.

2. You will now have two or three uncut outer leaves for the leek rolls.

Mushroom-stuffed Leek Rolls

❖

These slender rolls are easily prepared early in the day and heated conventionally or in a microwave oven. Buy the largest leeks available or the rolls will be pitifully tiny, and be sure to trim off the outer leaves that are stringy and tough.

> 4 very large leeks
> 2 carrots, scrubbed
> 8 ounces mushrooms
> 2 tablespoons olive oil
> 1 garlic clove, minced
> ½ cup plus 1 tablespoon homemade chicken stock
>   or canned broth
> ¼ teaspoon salt
> freshly ground black pepper to taste
> a few gratings fresh nutmeg

1. Cut through each leek where the color turns from white to green. Discard the green stalk. Trim the root end. Peel away and discard the 2 or 3 tough outer layers surrounding the white, bulb end. Make a cut running from the bulb to the tip, three-quarters of the way through the leek. Do not cut all the way through. Peel off the intact, uncut, outer leaves; there will be 2 or 3 such leaves per leek. (Refer to the illustrations as you do this.) Set these aside in a colander. Chop the remaining leek and put in the colander. When all the leeks have been prepared, rinse them thoroughly. Leave them to drain while continuing.
2. Half-fill a 2-quart saucepan with water and bring it to a boil. Blanch the whole leek leaves 1 to 2 minutes or until tender. Rinse under cool water and drain. Set aside.
3. Julienne the carrots in a food processor or shred with a grater. Set aside.

4. Mince the mushrooms in a food processor or very finely by hand. Scrape into an absorbent towel and twist the ends to form a ball. Wring out over a sink to remove excess moisture from the mushrooms. Set aside.

5. Coat a 10-inch skillet with cooking spray, then place it over high heat. Add the oil, heat it for 1 minute, then add the garlic. Cook the garlic over medium heat until tender but not browned, about 1 minute.

6. Add the chopped leeks, carrots, and ½ cup chicken stock. Cover and cook over medium-high heat until the vegetables are tender, about 3 to 4 minutes.

7. Add mushrooms and cook, stirring, over medium heat 4 to 5 minutes, or until the vegetables are tender and dry. Season with salt, pepper, and nutmeg. Remove from heat.

8. Preheat the oven to 300 degrees. To assemble the rolls, lay the leek leaves on the work surface with the whitest end facing you. Put a rounded teaspoon of the mushroom stuffing on the end closest to you and roll up loosely. Coat an oven- or microwave-proof serving dish with cooking spray. Arrange the leek rolls, seam side down, in a column in the center of the dish. Spoon the remaining filling over the center of the rolls. Sprinkle with the remaining broth. (The rolls may be completed to this point early in the day and held in the refrigerator until baked.)

9. Bake the rolls in the lower third of a preheated 300-degree oven for 10 to 15 minutes (30 minutes if chilled) or in a microwave oven on medium-high for 3 minutes.

Yield: about 8 rolls; 4 servings
Calories per serving: 105
Carbohydrate per serving: 10g
Cholesterol per serving: 0mg

Dietary fiber per serving: 1g
Fat per serving: 7g
Protein per serving: 2g
Sodium per serving: 165mg

Avocado-Pear Salad with Hot Lime Dressing

❖

A spicy-hot, citrus-cooled dressing on avocado and pear wedges creates a clean, refreshing salad. The dressing may be made a day or so ahead, but slice the avocado and pear at the last minute to keep them from turning brown.

For the Dressing

juice of 1 lime (about 1 1/2 tablespoons)
1/4 to 1/2 fresh jalapeño chili pepper, minced, or 2
*   teaspoons minced canned jalapeño chilis*
1 1/2 tablespoons lemon juice
1 tablespoon plain yogurt
1 tablespoon mayonnaise
1/8 teaspoon salt

For the Salad

2 cups torn soft-leafed salad greens, Bibb
*   recommended*
1 small, ripe avocado, peeled and pitted
1 pear, cored
1/2 small red bell pepper, minced

1. Combine all dressing ingredients in a screw-top jar. Shake vigorously and refrigerate until serving time.
2. Divide the greens among 4 salad plates. Slice the avocado and pear; divide the slices among the plates, alternating a pear slice with an avocado slice. Spoon 1 to 2 tablespoons dressing over each serving. Garnish with the pepper.

Yield: 4 servings, 1/2 cup dressing
Calories per serving: 140
Carbohydrate per serving: 13g
Cholesterol per serving: 0mg

Dietary fiber per serving: 3g
Fat per serving: 11g
Protein per serving: 2g
Sodium per serving: 110mg

PLAYIN' CAJUN

Pan-blackened Swordfish

Hoppin' John

Okra and Tomatoes

Pan-blackened fish, okra, and black-eyed peas; say it with a drawl and smell the magnolias. It also starts one thinking; for a nation of adventuresome eaters who have been drawn to foreign cuisines like moths to a flame, we've been amazingly slow to experience the culinary diversity within our own borders. Until now that is. Red, white, and blue are the current colors of choice in many a leading restaurant. Only a few years back, a translator was needed for a menu that now proudly boasts of "American specialties."

Paul Prudhomme, Cajun cooking guru, has been largely responsible for today's interest in New Orleans-style cooking and "pan-blackening." Be forewarned: It's a technique to be used only in well-ventilated kitchens or outdoors; if your kitchen is so equipped, do give it a try. It is a very quick cooking method and wonderful for thick fish steaks. My recipe is not a strictly authentic rendition; Prudhomme mixes chilies, herbs, and spices for a delightfully hot dish, and here lemon and soy create a piquant glaze. Because of the smoke, I think it's best to prepare the fish for no more than four, cooked all at one time either in a twelve-inch cast-iron skillet or simultaneously in two eight-inch skillets.

The serving size of fish in this menu for four is small, a modest quarter pound, for the black-eyed peas and rice are an excellent source of protein (see *Focus: Complete Vegetable Protein*, page 473) all by themselves. As well as contributing healthy amounts of carbohydrate, some vitamins, and minerals including iron, legumes (the catch-all term for dried beans) are an excellent source of Type II fiber, a suspected anticholesterol agent.

Another Southern "import" one rarely used to find north of the Mason-Dixon line is okra. Quick-cooking and low in calories, it adds another possibility when you're green-beaned out. It has a natural affinity for tomatoes and corn, which provides a colorful concoction.

Start the meal by soaking and cooking the black-eyed peas and rice recipe; the okra takes about fifteen minutes, the fish the same.

Pan-blackened Swordfish

❖

Due to the immense popularity of Cajun cooking, many cookbooks, scads of restaurants, and nearly every food magazine offer their version of a pan-blackened something. It's a technique particularly well suited to health-conscious cooks—just overlook the usual final butter drenching. You'll need an inexpensive, well-seasoned cast-iron skillet, which is best reserved for pan blackening only, and a very efficient kitchen fan. Disconnect any nearby smoke alarms. Choose thick (at least ¾-inch), firm-fleshed fish for this, such as halibut, swordfish, or tuna.

> 1 pound swordfish steaks
> 4 tablespoons lemon juice
> 3 tablespoons reduced-sodium soy sauce

1. Heat a 12-inch cast-iron skillet over high heat until the bottom turns a grayish color, about 8 to 10 minutes. Add the fish and sear it on one side for 1½ minutes. Flip it over and sear the other side another 1½ to 2 minutes. Poke with a finger or flake

with a fork to determine doneness; different fishes will cook at varying rates.

2. While fish cooks, mix the lemon juice and soy sauce. When the fish is done, remove the pan from the burner (leaving fish in skillet), but keep it close to the fan.

3. Pan cover in hand, add the lemon-soy to the skillet, and cover immediately. Rest until smoke subsides, about 1 minute. Uncover. If more than 2 tablespoons of sauce remain, return the skillet to high heat to boil briefly.

4. Transfer fish to plates or a serving platter. Spoon a bit of sauce over fish and serve.

Note: If you must do fish in two batches or in two skillets, add another tablespoon lemon juice and another tablespoon soy sauce.

Yield: 4 servings
Calories per serving: 150
Carbohydrate per serving: 2g
Cholesterol per serving: 60mg

Dietary fiber per serving: 0g
Fat per serving: 5g
Protein per serving: 23g
Sodium per serving: 500mg

Hoppin' John

❖

Hoppin' John, or black-eyed peas and rice, is a well-known Southern dish that everyone, regardless of region, would do well to give a try. Not only tasty and easily prepared, it ranks high on the nutritional scale as well. That's because rice and beans (or in this case black-eyed peas) together make a complete protein—as nutritionally complete a protein, in fact, as that found in meat, poultry, or fish, but without the cholesterol or saturated fats of animal foods. Unlike most bean recipes, the cook needn't start 24 hours ahead preparing this simple one, for the peas will boil up tender in just 15 minutes after a mere hour's soak. If your family isn't yet accustomed to meatless meals, but you'd like to offer up more fat-lowered menus, begin by serving big dishes of vegetable protein foods, such as this Hoppin' John, with small servings of meat, poultry, and fish. Gradually reduce the animal protein until an occasional meatless meal is as accepted as spaghetti.

¾ cup dried black-eyed peas
2 cups boiling water
½ small onion, minced (about 2 tablespoons)
¼ cup chopped celery (use mostly leaves)
2¾ cup homemade chicken stock or canned broth
½ cup long-grain white converted rice
½ teaspoon salt
1 teaspoon cumin or to taste
hot pepper sauce to taste
1 tablespoon minced fresh parsley
1 tablespoon unsalted butter

1. Cover the peas with the boiling water and let rest 1 hour. Pour off water, rinse, and drain. (Peas also can soak overnight, if you wish.)
2. Combine the onion and celery with ½ cup of the chicken stock in a 2½-quart saucepan. Cover and cook over medium-high heat until they are tender, about 3 to 4 minutes.
3. Add the peas and remaining chicken broth, cover, and bring to a boil over medium-high heat. Reduce heat to a simmer and cook until peas are tender, about 15 to 20 minutes.
4. Stir in the rice, salt, cumin, and hot pepper sauce. Cover and simmer until rice is tender, about 15 minutes.
5. Toss with parsley and butter, and serve. (Although it is better served freshly cooked, Hoppin' John can be prepared ahead and kept warm in a double boiler or reheated 2 minutes on medium-high power in a microwave oven.)

kept warm in a double boiler or reheated 2 minutes on medium-high power in a microwave oven.)

Yield: 4 servings
Calories per serving: 160
Carbohydrate per serving: 28g
Cholesterol per serving: 5mg

Dietary fiber per serving: 1g
Fat per serving: 3g
Protein per serving: 5g
Sodium per serving: 320mg

Okra and Tomatoes

❖

Okra is relatively low in calories—46 in a cooked cup—and a fair source of both vitamin A and calcium. Another plus, preparing it is quite simple, requiring nothing more than snipping off the stem end and slicing the pod into rounds. Don't overcook okra, though, or the mucilaginous quality that makes it so crucial to gumbo will leave this simple recipe a gummy mess. For that reason, it is best cooked just before serving. While fresh tomatoes and corn would definitely be tastier, canned products can be used.

> 8 ounces fresh okra, trimmed and sliced into
>   rounds (about 2 cups)
> 3 tomatoes (about 1½ pounds), cored, peeled,
>   and diced
> 1 ear corn, uncooked but scraped from the cob
> 2 tablespoons minced onion
> 1 tablespoon safflower oil
> 1 bay leaf
> ½ teaspoon salt
> hot pepper sauce to taste

1. Place all ingredients in a 2½-quart saucepan. Cover. Place on high heat. When a boil is reached, uncover, and simmer for

12 minutes, stirring occasionally. Remove bay leaf before serving.

Yield: 4 servings
Calories per serving: 90
Carbohydrate per serving: 14g
Cholesterol per serving: 0mg

Dietary fiber per serving: 2g
Fat per serving: 4g
Protein per serving: 3g
Sodium per serving: 310mg

Focus: Hidden Fat

❖

Most of us consume about 35 to 40 percent of our total calories in fat, but health experts warn fat should account for no more than 35 percent, and ideally no more than 20 percent, of our calorie intake. Short of having a dietary analysis done, it's hard to pinpoint the amount of saturated and other fats we eat. Learning to spot hidden fat, however, will save calories, and avoiding saturated fats could save your heart. Remember, a gram of fat contributes more than twice the calories of protein or carbohydrate.

It's far from being just the butter spread on toast or the oil in the frying pan—nearly everything we eat has some fat. A banana has some fat, as does a shrimp; even a carrot has some, though in tiny amounts. But these aren't the sorts of hidden fats we need to be wary of. The single largest contributor of saturated hidden fat is the very food we baby boomers were brought up to eat more of—meat. In fact, many high-protein foods are also high-fat foods. Take cheese, a delicious protein substitute for meat. With a few exceptions, cheese is a high fat item.

Below is a chart of some common fatty foods with a few lower fat items thrown in for comparison. Note, SFA stands for saturated fatty acids (given in grams); this is only a portion of the fat found in a food. In addition there are polyunsaturates and monounsaturates, but other than being contributors of calories, these fats are not a health threat. Tips on how to cut the fat in your diet are given on page 396 in *Focus: Cutting Fat*.

FOOD	CALORIES	SFA
BEEF		
3½ ounces chuck, lean and fat	409	13.89
chuck, lean only	299	7.65
bottom, lean and fat	274	6.78
bottom, lean only	224	4.01
sirloin steak, lean and fat	297	8.37
sirloin steak, lean only	219	4.11
POULTRY		
chicken, light meat, with skin	222	3.1
chicken, light meat without skin	173	1.3
egg, 1 poached	79	1.7
CHEESE		
cheddar, 1 ounce	114	0.6
cottage cheese, regular, 4 ounces	117	3.2
cottage cheese, low-fat, 4 ounces	82	0.7
cream cheese, 1 ounce	99	6.2
feta, 1 ounce	75	4.2
muenster, 1 ounce	104	5.4
ricotta, part skim, ½ cup	171	6.1
MILK		
whole, 1 cup	150	4.9
low-fat, 2 percent, 1 cup	121	2.9
skim, 1 cup	86	0.3
vanilla ice cream, 10 percent fat, 1 cup	269	8.9
SALAD DRESSINGS		
farm style, from mix, 1 tablespoon	53	0.9
French, from mix, 1 tablespoon	97	1.4
Italian, from mix, 1 tablespoon	69	1.4
Russian, 1 tablespoon	76	1.1
mayonnaise, 1 tablespoon	100	1.6

MICRO-EASE

Salmon Steaks with Green Sauce
Mapled Butternut Squash
Brown Rice with Walnuts

A microwave oven isn't required to cook this menu for four, but it does streamline one or two of the cooking tasks. Microwave ovens are particularly well-suited for cooking winter squashes. Not only are they quick, but because they require only a tiny amount of water, the squash is kept from being soggy. A microwave oven is also used here to poach the fish, but either job can be done conventionally.

At the heart of this "Micro-ease" dinner is salmon, a cold-water fish with unique kinds of fats that are more polyunsaturated than vegetable oils, meaning they may actually help to unclog the arteries. Because of its high fat content, salmon takes well to poaching. The cooking liquid in turn is quickly whirred into a green sauce, rich in taste but not in calories.

Accompanying the fish recipe are jiffy ways to enliven the flavor of butternut squash and simple brown rice.

1. Remove the skin and bones from a salmon steak with the tip of a small knife, leaving two strips of meat. Each will be a little thicker at one end than the other.

2. To re-shape the salmon steak, hold the thick end of one salmon strip against the thin end of the other salmon strip.

3. Curl the remaining thin end around the other thick end, forming a boneless, skinless steak.

Salmon Steaks
with Green Sauce

❖

This recipe makes a lovely presentation with the coral of the salmon accented by the soft green of the sauce. It may be prepared on the stove top, as well as in a microwave oven.

1 pound salmon steaks, each about ¾- to 1-inch
   thick
1 bottle (8 ounces) clam broth
⅓ cup dry white wine
1 bay leaf
1 tablespoon minced chives
1½ teaspoons arrowroot

1 tablespoon white wine or water
1 cup julienned raw spinach leaves, stems removed
1 tablespoon plain yogurt
1 tablespoon non-fat dry milk powder
1 tablespoon cottage cheese
2 teaspoons Madeira
a few drops lemon juice

1. To prepare the fish: Carefully remove the skin with the point of a paring knife. Continuing with the knife point, cut around the central bone and the sets of long, thin bones attached to it. Use your fingers to locate these delicate bones, and be sure none are left behind. You'll now have two boneless, skinless steak halves, each a little thicker at one end and tapering to a thinner tail. Place them on the counter so one thick end abuts the other half's thin end. Secure with a toothpick. Press the other thicker end snug against the now secured thicker end and press the free thin tail to the outside of both thicker ends. This will form a solid, circular salmon steak. Secure with another toothpick. Repeat with each salmon steak. (See illustrations on pages 414–415.)
2. Place a serving platter in the oven and heat it to 150 degrees.
3. To poach the salmon in a microwave oven: Combine the clam broth, wine, bay leaf, and chives in a microwave-proof dish just large enough to hold the fish. Add the salmon. Cover or use plastic wrap to hold in steam. Microwave at medium-high for 8 minutes or until the flesh is resistant when pressed. Flip once during cooking. (To cook on a stove burner: Combine ingredients in a 12-inch skillet, cover, and simmer 15 minutes, turning fish over once.)
4. Transfer the fish to the warmed platter, remove the toothpicks, and keep the fish warm in oven.

To Prepare the Sauce

1. Dissolve the arrowroot in the tablespoon of wine or water. Set near stove to have handy for step 3.

2. Remove bay leaf from the poaching liquid. Transfer liquid to a food processor. Add the spinach, yogurt, dry milk powder, cottage cheese, and Madeira. Pulse just to combine; don't puree spinach.
3. Pour sauce into a 10-inch skillet. Over medium-high heat, whisk in the arrowroot until the sauce is lightly thickened, about 2 minutes. Season to taste with lemon juice. Pour over salmon steaks and serve.

Yield: 4 servings	**Dietary fiber per serving: 1g**
Calories per serving: 270	**Fat per serving: 16g**
Carbohydrate per serving: 4g	**Protein per serving: 28g**
Cholesterol per serving: 75mg	**Sodium per serving: 340mg**

Mapled Butternut Squash

This vegetable, ultrarich in vitamin A and potassium, is a snap to prepare with the help of a microwave oven. If you prefer, try it with acorn squash, although the relative dryness of the butternut lends itself ideally to this method.

> 1 2-pound butternut squash
> 1 tablespoon unsalted butter
> 2 tablespoons maple syrup
> 2 teaspoons rum
> ½ teaspoon salt

1. Cut the squash in half at its "equator." Remove the seeds with a spoon. Place the halves, cavity side up, in a microwave-safe baking dish with ½-inch water. Divide the butter, maple syrup, rum, and salt between the halves. Cover with plastic wrap. (The

squash may be held up to one hour on the counter before cooking.)

2. Microwave at high power for 10 to 12 minutes, or until tender when pierced with a fork. To serve, cut the halves in half. (To bake, prepare as for microwave cooking, but don't cover with plastic wrap. Bake in a 350-degree oven for 45 to 50 minutes, or until tender when pierced with a fork.)

Yield: 4 servings
Calories per serving: 175
Carbohydrate per serving: 38g
Cholesterol per serving: 10mg

Dietary fiber per serving: 3g
Fat per serving: 3g
Protein per serving: 3g
Sodium per serving: 300mg

Brown Rice with Walnuts

Brown rice is the whole grain before the outer bran layer has been removed (for more on rice see *Focus: Rice*, page 386). It has nearly three times the cholesterol-binding type of fiber of white rice. Here, its nutty flavor and texture are perfectly complemented by the small addition of chopped walnuts. Because it only cooks 10 minutes faster in a microwave oven, save that appliance for the fish and squash in the menu, and cook the rice on a stove burner.

> ¾ cup long-grain brown rice
> 2¼ cups homemade chicken stock or canned broth
> ½ teaspoon salt
> 2 tablespoons chopped walnuts
> 1 tablespoon unsalted butter, at room temperature
> freshly ground black pepper to taste

1. Place the rice, broth, and salt in a 2½-quart saucepan. Cover and bring to a boil over high heat. When a boil is reached, reduce heat so the liquid simmers. Simmer 45 to 50 minutes or until the liquid is absorbed. Stir occasionally with a fork and adjust heat as needed to prevent sticking.
2. Remove rice from heat, stir in walnuts and butter, and season with pepper.

Yield: 4 servings
Calories per serving: 180
Carbohydrate per serving: 30g
Cholesterol per serving: 10mg

Dietary fiber per serving: 3g
Fat per serving: 6g
Protein per serving: 4g
Sodium per serving: 305mg

❖ It's been estimated that 200 to 600 milligrams of sodium a day is adequate for a healthy diet. A daily intake (for healthy persons) of 1100 to 3300 milligrams is considered safe. Most Americans consume 2300 to 6900 milligrams of sodium daily. To help you gauge added salt (though sodium is also found in foods and water) remember 1 teaspoon of table salt equals 2300 milligrams of sodium. ❖

Chapter 13

PASTA PASSIONS

Pasta Passions

❖

When I was growing up, we called them noodles and spaghetti—welcome food, homey food, comfortable stuff to sink your teeth into. Now the word is pasta, covering an entire array of noodles in countless shapes and fascinating flavors, with innumerable sauces, and presented in all kinds of combinations. It's still great stuff to sink your teeth into, but it needn't be predictable anymore.

If you've never made noodles, the length of these recipes may seem intimidating and the thought of buying special equipment yet another deterrent, but I urge you to reconsider with these simple arguments:

1. A hand-cranked, chrome pasta maker, which kneads, rolls, and cuts the dough into two basic shapes, is relatively inexpensive and easy to store and clean.
2. After one batch you'll be a pro at any shape pasta, from angel hair (vermicelli, very thin) to lasagne noodles (flat and broad).
3. The instructions for making noodles may seem complicated or long, but they are detailed to help you succeed. Unless you live within a block of a store that carries fresh pasta, you can probably make it faster than if you go out to pick up a package.
4. Fresh pasta is much tastier and offers more possibilities than packaged products.

Not convinced? You'd still settle for a P.B. & J. rather than make your own noodles? Get out the grated cheese, because fresh noodles are increasingly available in specialty stores and supermarkets everywhere. And every pasta recipe here, with the exception of the Seafood Raviolis with Tomato Cream Sauce, can be made with store-bought noodles.

To me, pasta dishes are among the most creative and fun to cook. Combinations and variations are seemingly endless, proportions rarely need to be exact, and many dishes are as good at room temperature as they are hot, making them perfect for casual entertaining or take-along meals. Even finicky children like noodles served up with just a little butter and without that "icky" sauce (more for the grown-ups, thank you!). And joy of all joys, nutritionists urge us to eat more complex carbohydrates and fewer fats. A plate of noodles interestingly sauced with vegetables and perhaps a smattering of shellfish, gets a clean bill of health.

A few cautionary words: Do watch the butter or oil drizzled on those noodles. Olive oil, rich in monounsaturates and recently suspected of actually helping to lower blood cholesterol levels, is a healthier choice than butter, when feasible. But for calories' sake, do be stingy with either. Always heat the plates or soup dishes that a hot pasta dish will be served in, for noodles cool off quickly. And never attack the aftermath of a noodle-making session with a sponge, or you'll have glue for your efforts. Scrape the work surface with a pastry blade or knife, then scrub with a dry brush, and finally wipe up with a damp sponge. A chrome pasta machine never needs washing. To prevent rust, simply dust off with a dry cloth.

It is always difficult to say how many people a recipe will feed, and even more difficult with noodles. So much depends on the individual's appetite and what else is offered. If you use any of these recipes out of context, for example as a side dish when it was intended as a main course, keep proportions in mind. The recipes may feed more people or fewer, depending on the rest of the meal.

Noodles are healthful, delicious, and fun. After a glance through this chapter, and maybe a sample, I hope you'll agree.

Focus: Pasta

❖

The most basic of ingredients (flour, salt, and water) combine to form an enormous variety of noodle shapes to be eaten at a range of temperatures and at nearly any course. Pasta, literally "dough," was supposed to have originated in the Orient, but records show that as early as a century before the citizens of Pompeii were feasting on noodles. Thomas Jefferson returned from Italy with a spaghetti machine, and Americans, along with many of the world's people, have been noodle fans ever since. Macaroni and cheese, and spaghetti and meatballs rank right up there with apple pie and the Statue of Liberty as all-American symbols.

Fresh pasta, though, is a bit of an unknown to many of us without Italian grandparents or big city stores. Contributing to the mystery can be the confusion over names. Even in Italy a pasta by one name in one district may go by another name in a neighboring one. But finding or making a recipe's specified pasta shape is often unnecessary, since pasta by any other name is still pasta.

Fresh pasta is best cooked within an hour of being made, though it may be dried for later use or wrapped in a plastic bag and refrigerated for up to 12 hours. Uncooked pasta may be frozen, but will be brittle and break easily. Fresh pasta doesn't expand when it is cooked as much as dried pasta, which may double.

Salt is sometimes added to the cooking water 1) on the theory it is absorbed by the pasta and 2) it ever so slightly raises the temperature of the boiling water, and the hotter the water the better the pasta. (I don't bother with salting the water.) Oil is added to prevent sticking (more important with fresh noodles) and boil-overs. Stir pasta several times when it is cooking to also help prevent it from clumping together. Use 3 quarts of water for every 8 ounces of pasta; too little water makes for sticky pasta, as does overcooking. Some have been known to test spaghetti by throwing a strand on the wall, but a more hygienic method is to pinch a noodle in half. If any white starchiness is visible at the core, boil the pasta a bit longer, but test it often.

❖ Sodium-conscious consumers should keep in mind that a product with little or no salt added is not necessarily sodium free. There are 70 different sodium compounds used in processed foods, to say nothing of the sodium naturally occurring in foods. ❖

EAST MEETS WEST

Buckwheat Pasta Salad with Spinach and Scallops
Tomato Slices with Basil and Extra-virgin Olive Oil

Buckwheat, soy, mirin, and ginger—trademarks of Oriental cuisine—ally here with tomatoes, basil, and olive oil to form a most compatible union. This is casual stuff, great for a foursome as a picnic or a light patio supper on a hot summer night. Prepare the buckwheat pasta salad early in the day, and dinner's a breeze with nothing more taxing than tomatoes to slice. Easily varied, the salad is good with sliced radishes, shrimp instead of scallops or as a complement for them, and slices of water chestnuts. A spoonful of tahini paste (available at specialty food shops and some grocery stores) would be delicious stirred in with the soy sauce and cooking wine. Serve the salad dish warm, at room temperature, or slightly chilled, but not too cold (low temperatures dull the flavors).

If you prefer not to make your own noodles, buckwheat noodles may be purchased at most Oriental and some health food stores.

❖ Cigarettes, alcohol, and medication can interfere with the body's normal vitamin requirements. Cigarette smokers may need extra vitamin C. Drinkers or those who eat lots of sugar may need more of the B vitamins, as may persons on antibiotics for long periods of time. A vitamin supplement is not necessarily in order, though; extra helpings of fruits and vegetables will do the trick. ❖

Buckwheat Pasta Salad with Spinach and Scallops

❖

When you've tired of the increasingly predictable pasta salad, give this one a try. Very Japanese in spirit with its buckwheat noodles, ginger, and soy, this dish is as good the second day as the first. It's eminently portable too—a natural candidate for the picnic basket if you choose. Pack chopsticks rather than forks, for after all, with this dish, East meets West.

Buckwheat flour—prepared from the seeds of an herb plant, not a grasslike wheat—is available at health food or specialty food shops, and some supermarkets. If there's none to be found in your area, buckwheat pancake mix, which is carried at most stores, will do just fine. (Or buy buckwheat noodles at Oriental markets or health food stores.) Because the buckwheat pasta strips need to dry at least 15 minutes but no more than 30 minutes, begin by making the noodles. While the strips dry, put together the sauce, then cut the noodles and cook them. Toss the two together and serve the salad warm, room temperature, or slightly chilled.

The Chinese cooking wine or mirin, hot oil, and sesame oil are available at Oriental food shops and specialty food shops.

For the Buckwheat Noodles
½ cup buckwheat flour or buckwheat pancake mix
½ cup all-purpose flour
1 teaspoon salt
1 egg
about 3 teaspoons water

For the Sauce

4 ounces mushrooms, sliced
1 garlic clove, minced
3 tablespoons homemade beef stock or canned
    beef broth or consomme
¾ pound scallops
juice of half a lemon
1 teaspoon arrowroot
2 tablespoons reduced-sodium soy sauce
¼ cup Chinese cooking wine or mirin
2 teaspoons minced fresh ginger
1 scallion, minced
3 cups chopped raw spinach, stems removed
¼ teaspoon or to taste hot oil

To Complete the Dish

1 tablespoon peanut oil
1 teaspoon or to taste sesame oil

To Prepare the Buckwheat Noodles

1. To make the noodles in a food processor: Pour the flours into
   the bowl of a food processor. Add the salt and egg. Process,
   adding drops of water, until the dough can be formed into a
   ball. Buckwheat flour takes more water than white flours and
   the dough is more crumbly. Pinch the dough with your
   fingertips to determine if it will hold together rather than
   allowing a ball to form in the food processor. To make by
   hand: Pour the flours and salt into a mixing bowl. Make a
   well in the center and put the egg in it. Mix together with a
   fork or your fingertips, adding drops of water, until the dough
   can be formed into a ball.
2. Pinch off half the dough and work with one half at a time.
   To knead the dough, set the smooth rollers of the pasta
   machine as far apart as possible (generally, the lowest setting,
   1, on most pasta machines). Dust the dough with flour and

feed it through the rollers. Buckwheat dough is very crumbly and will break apart in the first few rollings. Don't despair; simply fold the dough over and keep rolling, dusting with flour to prevent sticking, until a smooth strip is formed.

3. To roll out the dough: Set the machine to the second notch and feed the strip through the rollers. Repeat, advancing the notch a setting higher after each rolling so the rollers progressively come closer together and the dough gets thinner. Continue until the dough is rolled through the last setting (7).

4. Dust the pasta strip with flour on both sides and let it rest at least 15 but no more than 30 minutes while you make the sauce. Repeat the kneading and rolling steps with the remaining dough.

To Prepare the Sauce

1. Combine the mushrooms, garlic, and beef stock in a 10-inch skillet. "Saute" the mushrooms and garlic over high heat until the stock has evaporated and the mushrooms are limp, about 3 minutes.

2. Add the scallops to the skillet. Season with lemon juice and cover. Cook at high heat, stirring occasionally, until the scallops are opaque, about 3 to 4 minutes.

3. While the scallops cook, dissolve the arrowroot in the soy sauce.

4. Uncover the skillet. Stir in the soy sauce, cooking wine, ginger, and scallion. Stir over medium-high heat until the sauce thickens slightly, about 2 minutes.

5. Remove the skillet from heat. Stir in the spinach. It will wilt slightly from the heat of the sauce. Add a few drops of hot oil to taste. (Sauce may be held, off heat, covered, for up to ½ hour. If you want to hold it longer, cover and refrigerate.)

To Cut and Cook the Pasta and Complete the Dish

1. When the sauce is completed, feed a single pasta strip through the narrow cutting blades of the pasta machine. The noodles are ready to cook immediately, or they may be dried

(draped over the back of a chair or on a pasta rack to dry) as long as 2 hours. They will be brittle and may break easily if they are held longer.

2. Bring 6 to 8 quarts of water with the tablespoon of peanut oil to a boil. Set a sieve or colander into the sink. Gently drop the noodles into the water. Stir to prevent them from sticking together. Freshly made noodles will be done (no bright white center when a noodle is pinched apart) in 2 minutes; dried ones in 5 to 6 minutes. Drain the noodles in the colander.

3. Turn the drained noodles into a large bowl. Season the noodles with the sesame oil. Toss with the sauce. Taste and adjust seasoning if necessary. The salad may be served immediately or held chilled, covered with plastic wrap, up to 24 hours before serving.

Yield: 4 servings
Calories per serving: 226
Carbohydrate per serving: 31g
Cholesterol per serving: 92mg

Dietary fiber per serving: 2g
Fat per serving: 3g
Protein per serving: 20g
Sodium per serving: 5097mg

Tomato Slices with Basil and Extra-virgin Olive Oil

❖

The finest of summer salads is, I think, the simplest. Ripe-to-bursting tomatoes drizzled with best-quality olive oil and a snipping of basil requires no time and no imagination, but is unsurpassed by more elaborate concoctions. For peak flavor, the tomatoes should be at room temperature, not chilled. A bit of chèvre crumbled over the dressed tomatoes is an added treat.

2 large, very ripe tomatoes
1½ tablespoons olive oil, extra-virgin
  recommended
2–3 fresh basil leaves, snipped
⅛ teaspoon salt
freshly ground black pepper to taste

1. Core the tomatoes and slice them crosswise into ¼-inch-thick slices. Place, slightly overlapping, on individual salad plates or on a small serving platter.
2. Drizzle the tomatoes with the oil, sprinkle with basil, and season with salt and pepper. Serve within half an hour.

Yield: 4 servings
Calories per serving: 59
Carbohydrate per serving: 3g
Cholesterol per serving: 0mg

Dietary fiber per serving: 1g
Fat per serving: 5g
Protein per serving: 1g
Sodium per serving: 100mg

Focus: Osteoporosis and Calcium

❖

One quarter of American women over the age of 65 suffer from a potentially debilitating weakening of the bones. Osteoporosis, loss of bone matter, is of particular concern to women, for the rate of bone loss accelerates after menopause. Women who check off two or more of the following risk factors—compiled by the University of California, Berkeley Wellness Letter—may well be concerned about the amount of calcium in their diet, their estrogen level, and how much weight-bearing exercise they're getting. At risk are those who:

- smoke,
- exercise infrequently,
- are fair-skinned,
- are small-boned,
- have dieted frequently,
- regularly take three or more drinks,
- have been underweight most of their life.

The first noticeable signs of osteoporosis may be a decrease in height, the beginnings of a humped back, and proneness to fractures, most notably of the hip and spine.

Although the Food and Nutrition Board, a branch of the National Academy of Sciences, currently recommends consuming 800 milligrams of calcium daily (new RDAs are expected in the future), many health experts are urging women of all ages to get 1000 to even 1500 milligrams daily. The chairman of the Food and Nutrition Board believes it is as important for young women as for menopausal women to get enough calcium.

There is some debate, though, about the advisability of popping calcium supplements, which women are doing in ever-increasing numbers. Nay-sayers warn of kidney stones, lowered zinc and iron absorption, wasted calcium if the diet isn't high enough in phosphorous (since calcium can't be put into the bones except as calcium phosphate), constipation, and possible interference with the absorption of needed medicines. They would have us get all our calcium needs from food. Those in favor of calcium supplements suggest that if the mineral isn't supplied in sufficient quantity by the diet—which it frequently isn't—pills may be in order.

Women aren't the only persons who need be concerned about getting enough calcium, however. Adolescent girls, persons with high blood pressure, and persons with family histories of colon cancer might want to consider the mineral more seriously. Teenage girls, for example, frequently stop drinking milk in the perpetual pursuit of slimness. Surveys have shown that calcium intake has dropped 10 percent from the already inadequate level found during the early

1970s. Many doctors are urging women to raise calcium intake during young adulthood as an important preventive measure.

In two studies, calcium has also been shown to have a positive effect on high blood pressure. In a report from Memorial-Sloan Kettering Cancer Center, patients with a family history of colon cancer benefited from increased calcium. Though none of the patients had colon cancer, cells taken from their colons did resemble those from actual cancer victims. After two to three months of increased calcium, the subjects' colon cells returned to a more normal growth pattern.

It seems sensible then to boost the family's calcium intake at the dinner table. Below are valuable, lower-calorie dietary sources of calcium.

FOOD	SERVING SIZE	PER SERVING MILLIGRAMS
Skim milk	1 cup	302
Low-fat yogurt (plain)	1 cup	415
Cheddar cheese	1 ounce	204
Cottage cheese	½ cup	136
Parmesan cheese	1 ounce	390
Swiss cheese	1 ounce	272
Broccoli	1 cup	136
Beet greens, cooked	1 cup	198
Collard greens	1 cup	357
Bean curd	4 ounces	154
Sardines with bones	3 ounces	372
Salmon (canned with bones)	3 ounces	167

❖ Thirty-five hundred extra calories are needed to make a pound of body fat. To lose a pound of fat in a week, you need to create a calorie deficit of 500 calories a day, either by eating less, exercising more, or both. ❖

UP SCALE

Dry-fried Salmon Fillets

Red Pepper Pasta with Vegetables and Herb Vinaigrette

Three-Green Salad with Champagne-Orange Vinaigrette
and Melted Goat Cheese

Strawberry-Buttermilk Sherbet

Here's a decidedly "up scale" meal with salmon, goat cheese, and red pepper pasta that will not up your weight scale. An easy-on-the-cook, informal gathering of spring's best, this dinner for eight may be started early on the day of serving and completed in just a few hours, leaving only the salmon to dry-fry and the cheese to briefly heat at dinner time. This menu epitomizes *The Enlightened Gourmet*, for it is delicious as well as healthy. Salmon, for example, has been found to contain a particular kind of fat that can actually help reduce the amount of cholesterol in the bloodstream; pasta mixed with lots of fresh vegetables gives a strong serving of important complex carbohydrates; olive oil has recently been shown, in one study where the subjects were fed a diet with forty percent-fat content (two-thirds of it being monounsaturated like olive oil), to be *more* effective in lowering blood cholesterol than only a twenty percent-fat diet; buttermilk and goat cheese offer up a bit of bone-strengthening calcium. All in all, not a bad way to eat well and eat right.

Dry-fried Salmon Fillets

❖

One of spring's many gifts is salmon, and one of the best ways to cook it is as little as possible. This "dry-fry" (there's no butter or oil) requires a good nonstick skillet and a decent fan, but there is nowhere near the smoke of the Pan-blackened Swordfish on page 407. Be sure to buy the freshest possible salmon and keep it on ice in the refrigerator if it isn't to be cooked within a few hours.

> 2 lemons
> 1 tablespoon minced fresh parsley
> 2½ pounds salmon fillets

1. With a zester (a small tool that cuts a ridge in the lemon; its use is optional) remove strips about ½-inch apart around one lemon working from the blossom end to the tip. Reserve the strips of zest for another use or discard.

2. Slice this lemon crosswise into 8 thin slices. Poke out the seeds. Hold a lemon slice so the center is pushed out and the edges are up. Dip the center of the lemon slice in the parsley. Repeat with remaining lemon slices. Set slices aside for garnish.

3. Coat two 12-inch nonstick skillets lightly with cooking spray. (Or dry-fry the fish in two batches.) Heat the pans over high heat until a drop of water skitters on contact. Put the fish, skin side down, in the hot pans. Dry-fry the fish, frequently loosening it from the skillets with a spatula and turning the pans to ensure even heat, about 2 minutes on the skin side. Reduce the heat only if the fish starts to stick. Flip the fish over and cook at high heat for 2 minutes more on the other side. Season with the juice of the remaining lemon when the fish has about a minute left to cook.

4. Transfer the fish from the pans to a serving platter. Garnish each fillet with a parslied lemon slice. If fish is done in 2 batches,

keep the first batch warm in a preheated, then turned off, 150-degree oven, or on a warming tray.

Yield: 8 servings
Calories per serving: 171
Carbohydrate per serving: 1g
Cholesterol per serving: 50mg

Dietary fiber per serving: 0g
Fat per serving: 5g
Protein per serving: 28g
Sodium per serving: 91mg

Red Pepper Pasta with Vegetables and Herb Vinaigrette

❖

Ribbons of homemade red pepper pasta generously tossed with crisp vegetables and a garden fragrant herb sauce—what could be better? Moreover, because the dish is served at room temperature or slightly chilled, it is completely prepared ahead. As a take-along or eat-at-home recipe, this is sure to be the star of any meal. It will serve 8 as a side dish, or 5 to 6 as the main dish.

Of course, store-bought fresh or boxed fettucine egg noodles will do fine in place of the homemade. And view the vegetable list (types and proportions) with an eye toward availability.

For the Red Pepper Pasta

2   cups all-purpose flour
1   teaspoon salt
½   teaspoon dried red pepper flakes
1   tablespoon olive oil
2   eggs

a few drops water
1 tablespoon vegetable oil for the cooking water

For the Vinaigrette

½ cup snipped fresh basil
½ cup minced fresh parsley
2 tablespoons minced fresh tarragon
2 tablespoons balsamic vinegar
¼ cup olive oil, extra-virgin recommended
⅓ cup homemade beef stock or canned beef consomme
3 tablespoons freshly grated Parmesan cheese
freshly ground black pepper to taste

For the Vegetables

6 ounces fresh asparagus
2 ounces fresh pea pods from snow peas or sugar snap peas
2 ounces fresh green beans
½ package frozen artichoke hearts (thawed and sliced) or 2 fresh artichokes
4 ounces mushrooms, sliced
juice of ½ lemon (about 2 tablespoons)
1 red bell pepper, diced

To Prepare the Pasta

1. To make the pasta in a food processor: Pour the flour into the bowl of a food processor. Add the salt, red pepper flakes, olive oil, and eggs. Process, adding drops of water, until the dough can be formed into a ball. To make the pasta by hand: Pour the flour, salt, and red pepper flakes into a mixing bowl. Make a well in the center and put the oil and eggs in it. Mix together with a fork or your fingertips, adding drops of water, until the dough can be formed into a rough ball.
2. Pinch off half the dough and work with one half at a time.

To knead the dough, set the smooth rollers of the pasta machine as far apart as possible (generally, the lowest setting on most pasta machines). Dust the dough with flour and feed it through the rollers. Reroll this strip 4 or 5 more times, folding under the ragged edges. Dust the dough with flour to prevent sticking, when necessary.

3. To roll out the dough: Set the machine to the second notch and feed the strip through the rollers. Repeat, advancing the notch a setting higher after each rolling so the rollers progressively come closer together and the dough gets thinner. Roll until dough has gone through the second to last setting (6). Leave the dough on the counter as you repeat steps 2 and 3 with the remaining half of dough.

4. To cut the pasta, feed the rolled strips through the wide blades of the pasta machine. Hang to dry slightly (10 to 20 minutes) on a pasta rack or over the back of a chair in a single layer.

5. To cook the pasta: Bring 6 to 8 quarts water with the tablespoon of vegetable oil to a boil. Gently stir in the noodles, stirring from time to time to prevent them from sticking together. Place a strainer or colander in the sink. When noodles are tender and cooked through—this will take about 2 minutes for fresh ones, 4 to 5 minutes for dried (to test for doneness, pinch a noodle in half; if traces of pure white remain at the center, boil for a few seconds more)—pour the noodles into the strainer.

6. Rinse the noodles with cool water and drain them. Set aside in a large bowl while you prepare the vinaigrette and vegetables. (If you are holding noodles more than half an hour, toss them with a bit of olive oil to prevent clumping.)

To Prepare the Vinaigrette and Vegetables

1. Combine all ingredients listed under vinaigrette in the bowl of a food processor or a blender. Process until well blended. Toss with the noodles.

2. Snap off and discard the tough white end of each asparagus stalk. Peel the stalks with a vegetable peeler if they are thick. Cut the stalks into bite-size pieces. Set the asparagus aside.
3. Remove the strings from the pea pods. Add to the asparagus.
4. Line up a handful of green beans and cut off the "tips and tails." Repeat with remaining beans.
5. Fit a 2½-quart saucepan with a removable steaming basket. Add an inch of water, cover, and bring the water to a boil. Add the green beans. Cover. Re-cover, and time 1 minute. Add the asparagus and pea pods. Add the frozen artichoke hearts if you are using them. Time 4 to 5 minutes, stirring vegetables once or twice, until vegetables are tender but still crisp.
6. Lift the steaming basket from the pan, and immediately run the vegetables under cold water to stop the cooking. Allow the vegetables to drain.
7. To prepare the fresh artichoke hearts: Cut off the stem of one artichoke. With a stainless steel knife, pare the artichoke as if peeling an apple, removing the top 2 or 3 layers of tough, deep green leaves. Cut off the top third of the artichoke. Turn the artichoke upside down and be sure all the tough, dark green leaves are trimmed from the bottom. (See illustrations on pages 363–64.) Spread the leaves at the top of the artichoke apart. With a spoon, remove the fuzzy center (the choke). Slice the heart into ⅛-inch-thick slices. Repeat with the remaining artichoke.
8. Coat an 8-inch skillet with cooking spray. Heat the pan over high heat, uncovered, until a drop of water skitters on contact. Add the mushrooms, sliced fresh artichoke hearts, and lemon juice. Saute at high heat until the liquid is evaporated, about 4 minutes. Add mushrooms and artichokes to other cooked vegetables.
9. Toss the cooked vegetables and the diced red pepper with the noodles. The pasta is ready to serve or may be held, covered with plastic wrap, at room temperature up to 3 hours or refrigerated up to 24 hours before serving. If you do chill it,

allow it to come to room temperature before serving. Pass extra grated Parmesan at the table if desired.

Yield: 8 side dish servings	**Dietary fiber per serving:** 2g
Calories per serving: 256	**Fat per serving:** 11g
Carbohydrate per serving: 33g	**Protein per serving:** 9g
Cholesterol per serving: 62mg	**Sodium per serving:** 378mg

Three-Green Salad with Champagne-Orange Vinaigrette and Melted Goat Cheese

❖

This special salad with its delightfully light vinaigrette is a tangle of arugula, red leaf, and salad bowl lettuces served with a dollop of warmed, runny goat cheese.

Arugula is a perfumy, tangy green better known in southern European countries than in the United States. In peak season from May to October, it's a treat not to be missed, particularly if you enjoy the flavor of watercress. It is very high in calcium, vitamin A, and vitamin C.

One needn't buy a fine champagne for the dressing; any drinkable bottle will do. On the outside chance you'd rather cook with the remaining champagne, there is a recipe for Mimosa Sherbet in *Gourmet Light*. The walnut oil is available at specialty food stores; keep it refrigerated after opening.

Prepare the dressing and wash and dry the lettuces up to 24 hours in advance. The cheese may be crumb-coated several hours ahead, but slide it into the oven (a microwave oven won't do) just 10 to 15 minutes before serving. The cheese should still be warmed when served with the crisply cool greens.

For the Dressing

4 tablespoons walnut oil
3 tablespoons dry champagne
2 teaspoons lemon juice
1 teaspoon sugar
grated rind (zest) of an orange

For the Salad

3 ounces goat cheese, such as Montrachet or
   Bucheron
2 tablespoons dried bread crumbs
1 teaspoon walnut oil
1 bunch arugula, rinsed and spun dry
½ head red leaf lettuce, rinsed and spun dry
½ head salad bowl lettuce, rinsed and spun dry

To Prepare the Dressing

1. Combine all the dressing ingredients in a screw-top jar. Shake well to combine. The dressing may be used immediately or held up to 48 hours before using.

To Prepare the Salad

1. Preheat oven to 400 degrees. Coat the cheese in the bread crumbs. Place the cheese in a small baking dish. Drizzle with the teaspoon of walnut oil.
2. Bake the cheese until it is runny, about 10 minutes. Slide it under the broiler briefly, if needed, to brown the crumbs.
3. Meanwhile, tear the greens into a salad bowl and toss with the vinaigrette. Serve the salad onto 8 chilled salad plates, making a little well in the center of each plate.
4. Place a spoonful of cheese in the well and serve.

Yield: 8 servings
Calories per serving: 113
Carbohydrate per serving: 3g
Cholesterol per serving: 8mg

Dietary fiber per serving: 0g
Fat per serving: 10g
Protein per serving: 3g
Sodium per serving: 92mg

Strawberry-Buttermilk Sherbet

❖

Who would believe buttermilk could be the base of a most delicious, waist-conscious dessert? Yet here it is, smooth and tangy-sweet, and you need nothing more complicated than your refrigerator. Start the sherbet the day before serving to allow for adequate chilling; it will keep in the freezer about 2 to 3 days before becoming grainy. Don't worry about wasting the leftover quart of buttermilk; there are several recipes using buttermilk in this book (Whole Wheat Oatmeal Muffins, Buttermilk Salad Dressing, and more). The leftover strawberries are excellent spooned over this sherbet.

> 1¼ cups frozen strawberries with sugar
> 2 cups skimmed buttermilk
> 4 tablespoons sugar
> 2 egg whites
> 1 teaspoon vanilla extract

1. Thaw the strawberries on the counter or in a microwave oven.
2. Combine the berries with the buttermilk and sugar in a food processor or blender. Blend.
3. Pour the strawberry mixture into an 8-inch-square baking pan or other shallow container and freeze until it has the consistency of mush, about 1 to 2 hours. Chill a mixing bowl at the same time the strawberry mixture goes into the freezer.

4. Scrape the strawberry mixture into the chilled bowl. Add the egg whites and vanilla. Beat with a hand-held mixer until the sherbet is well blended and smooth.
5. Return the mixture to the shallow pan and freeze until firm, about 3 hours, stirring every so often. Sherbet is now ready to serve or may be beaten and refrozen for greater smoothness. Soften the sherbet at room temperature about 20 minutes before serving.

Note: An ice cream freezer will give a smoother product with fewer ice crystals, of course. Follow steps 1, 2, and 4, omitting the freezing and chilled bowl step. Follow manufacturer's directions for freezing in the ice cream maker.

Yield: 1 quart; 8 ½-cup servings
Calories per serving: 93
Carbohydrate per serving: 20g
Cholesterol per serving: 3g

Dietary fiber per serving: 0g
Fat per serving: 1g
Protein per serving: 3g
Sodium per serving: 78mg

❖ A study to determine the single largest contributor of salt to a teen-ager's diet found a rather surprising culprit. It wasn't the salt shaker on the table or at the stove, nor the chips or other salty snack foods kids seem to crave, but bakery products—cookies, cakes, muffins, breads, and the like—that accounted for the largest dose of sodium. ❖

COOKING TO GO

Vegetable Lasagne with Spinach Noodles and Three Cheeses

Romaine Lettuce with Garlic Vinaigrette

"Lasagne" needn't conjure up the greasy ground-meat-and-tomato-sauce version served at many a steam table. This "Cooking to Go" dinner for four offers a lightened version, chock-full of vegetables and bound with a creamy (but low-fat!) white sauce. A pasta machine is needed to make the homemade spinach noodles, but store-bought lasagne noodles would certainly pass. All in all, it's a tempting change from the ordinary that travels well and/or freezes, too.

A quick glance at the ingredient list may deter readers who feel their daily protein quota requires at least a small serving of meat, fish, or poultry. But another glance at the nutritional analysis proves otherwise. A serving of this vegetable lasagne supplies 19 grams of protein, 35 percent of an average woman's needs, a very respectable amount for a single meal. For more on meatless meals see *Focus: Complete Vegetable Protein,* on page 472.

With the lasagne, offer a simple tossed salad with a zingy garlic vinaigrette and crispy croutons prepared without fat. Hearty appetites would appreciate heated Italian bread.

Vegetable Lasagne with Spinach Noodles and Three Cheeses

❖

This is a do-ahead, non-meat meal studded with nearly every color of the garden. While instructions are given here for making your own spinach pasta (you'll need a pasta machine), 8 store-bought lasagne noodles would do just fine. Even meat lovers will find nothing wanting in this delicious vegetarian variation of an old standby. Because the dish freezes well, you might consider doubling the recipe.

If you make the single recipe of spinach pasta, there will be a very small amount left over; it's difficult to work with any less than ½ cup of flour when making noodles. Double the noodle recipe and freeze the unused portion if you prefer not to be wasteful.

For the Spinach Lasagne Noodles

½ cup all-purpose flour
1 tablespoon tightly packed, chopped, cooked, and
    squeezed dry spinach
¼ teaspoon salt
½ of a beaten egg
a few drops olive oil

For the Vegetables

2 leeks, white part only, rinsed and diced
½ cup homemade chicken stock or canned chicken
    broth
2 small carrots, shredded
½ cup chopped, cooked broccoli
⅔ cup chopped, cooked spinach
1 red bell pepper, diced
1 cup sliced mushrooms

For the Sauce

1 tablespoon unsalted butter
1 garlic clove, minced
1 tablespoon all-purpose flour
1 cup homemade chicken stock or canned chicken
   broth
1 egg yolk
1 cup low-fat cottage cheese
2 tablespoons freshly grated Parmesan cheese
freshly ground black pepper to taste
freshly grated nutmeg to taste
1 tablespoon arrowroot
1 tablespoon Madeira

To Complete the Recipe

1 tablespoon vegetable oil for the cooking water
2 ounces part-skim mozzarella cheese, grated

To Prepare the Spinach Noodles

1. To make the pasta in a food processor: Pour the flour into
   the bowl of a food processor. Add the spinach, salt, and egg.
   Process, adding the oil, until the dough can be formed into a
   ball. (It is unlikely but possible that you'll need to add a few
   drops of water to make the dough form a ball.) To make the
   pasta by hand: Pour the flour into a mixing bowl. Make a
   well in the center and put the spinach, salt, and egg in it.
   Mix together with a fork or your fingertips, adding drops of
   olive oil, until the dough can be formed into a rough ball.
2. Pinch off half the dough and work with one half at a time.
   To knead the dough, set the smooth rollers of a pasta
   machine as far apart as possible (generally, the lowest setting
   on most pasta machines). Dust the dough with flour and feed
   it through the rollers. Reroll this strip 4 or 5 times, folding
   under the ragged edges and dusting the dough with flour,
   when necessary, to prevent sticking.

3. To roll out the dough: Set the machine to the second notch and feed the strip through the rollers. Repeat, advancing the notch after each rolling so the rollers progressively come closer together and the dough gets thinner. As you roll, dust the dough with flour to prevent sticking. Finally roll the strip through the last notch to make it as thin as possible.
4. Set the strip onto a floured counter. Trim it to approximately 3½ by 11 inches. Repeat steps 2 and 3 with the remaining dough and dough trimmings. (Noodles may be made up to 2 hours ahead and held at room temperature before boiling.)
5. Bring 6 to 8 quarts of water with the tablespoon of vegetable oil to a rolling boil. Carefully drop the noodles into the boiling water. Stir gently to prevent them from sticking together. Boil 3 minutes for homemade noodles, or follow package directions for purchased noodles. Drain and cool under running water. Lay the noodles flat in a single layer on kitchen towels to drain. Pat dry. (The cooked noodles may be held at room temperature, covered with the towels, for up to 2 hours before completing the recipe.)

To Prepare the Filling

1. Combine the leeks with 4 tablespoons of the chicken stock in a 10-inch skillet. Cover, bring to a boil over high heat, and boil for 2 to 3 minutes or until tender, stirring occasionally.
2. Add the carrots, stir, cover, and cook another 2 minutes. Scrape into a bowl.
3. Stir the broccoli, spinach, and red pepper into the bowl with the carrots and leeks.
4. In the same skillet, "saute" the mushrooms over high heat in the remaining 4 tablespoons chicken broth until the mushrooms are limp and the broth has evaporated, about 4 to 5 minutes. Combine the mushrooms with the other vegetables in the bowl. Set aside. (Vegetable mixture may be made several hours ahead and held, covered, in the refrigerator.)

To Prepare the Sauce

1. In the same 10-inch skillet, heat the butter and garlic over high heat until the butter is foamy, about 1 minute. Stir in the flour, reduce heat to medium, and cook, stirring constantly, until the flour is just golden, about 1 minute.
2. Remove the skillet from the heat. Whisk in the chicken broth. Continue to whisk until smooth.
3. Return the pan to medium heat, and whisk 2 to 3 minutes or until the sauce is smooth and lightly thickened. Pour into a food processor.
4. Add the egg yolk, cottage cheese, Parmesan cheese, pepper, and nutmeg to the sauce in the food processor. Process until smooth. Meanwhile, dissolve the arrowroot in the Madeira.
5. Pour the sauce back in the skillet. Place the skillet over medium-high heat. Stir in the Madeira. Stir until thickened, about 2 to 3 minutes. Taste and adjust seasoning. (Sauce may be made several hours ahead and held, covered, in the refrigerator.)

To Assemble

1. Preheat the oven to 350 degrees. Coat an 8-inch-square baking pan with cooking spray. Film the bottom of the pan with a few tablespoons of the sauce.
2. Mix half of the sauce with the vegetables, and set the remaining sauce aside for the top. Cut the noodles in half across. Place two noodle halves in a single layer over the sauce. (The noodles should cover the bottom.) Smooth half of the vegetable and sauce mixture over the noodles. Top with a second noodle layer. Smooth the remaining vegetable mixture on top. Cover with the third noodle layer. Smooth the remaining sauce on top. Top with the grated mozzarella. (Casserole may be made ahead to this point and frozen for up to a month without flavor loss or chilled up to 8 hours before baking. Add 20 minutes to the baking time for a frozen casserole, or 5 minutes for a chilled casserole.)

3. Bake the casserole in the upper third of the oven for 35 minutes or until it is bubbly and lightly browned. If necessary, broil briefly to brown the top before serving. Let the casserole rest 5 to 10 minutes before you cut it into fourths to serve.

Yield: 4 servings
Calories per serving: 280
Carbohydrate per serving: 32g
Cholesterol per serving: 121mg

Dietary fiber per serving: 3g
Fat per serving: 10g
Protein per serving: 19g
Sodium per serving: 555mg

Romaine Lettuce with Garlic Vinaigrette

A creamy "Italian" type dressing best suited to romaine, chicory, and salad bowl lettuces, this salad is the perfect accompaniment for Vegetable Lasagne or anytime a garlicky dressing is in order.

For the Dressing

1 garlic clove, minced

1 egg

1 teaspoon Dijon mustard

2 tablespoons lemon juice

3 tablespoons freshly grated Parmesan cheese

¼ cup canned beef consomme or homemade beef stock

½ cup olive oil, extra-virgin recommended

For the Salad

2 slices bread, white or whole-wheat
½ head romaine lettuce, rinsed and dried
a few leaves salad bowl lettuce, rinsed and dried
½ cup shredded red cabbage
a few rings Bermuda onion
½ cucumber, sliced

To Prepare the Dressing

1. Place the garlic, egg, mustard, lemon juice, and cheese in the bowl of a food processor or blender. With the machine on, gradually add the consomme, then the oil. Transfer the dressing to a screw-top jar and keep chilled. It will keep up to 1 week in the refrigerator.

To Prepare the Salad

1. Cube the bread by stacking the two slices and making 5 lengthwise cuts, and then 5 crosswise cuts.
2. Spray an 8-inch nonstick skillet with cooking spray. Add the bread cubes and toss them over medium-high heat until lightly browned, about 5 to 6 minutes. Reduce heat as necessary to prevent burning. Remove the croutons from the pan and set aside. (Croutons also can be oven baked.)
3. Combine the remaining ingredients in a salad bowl. Dress with just enough garlic vinaigrette to moisten. Garnish the salad with the croutons.

Yield: 1 cup dressing; 4 salad servings
Calories per serving: 112
Carbohydrate per serving: 11g
Cholesterol per serving: 16mg
Dietary fiber per serving: 1.5g
Fat per serving: 8g
Protein per serving: 3g
Sodium per serving: 115mg

QUICK EATS

Grilled Shrimp

Angel Hair Pasta with Chèvre

Steamed Broccoli

Time constraints brought on by nightly meetings, juggled schedules, and the like don't have to mean boring, hurried meals. Here's a savvy, flavorful dinner for two (the recipes are easily doubled to serve four) to cook up in about twenty-five minutes—maybe less.

Grilled Shrimp

Buy the freshest, largest shrimp you can for this quick dinner treat. It would also make a simply delicious first course or luncheon dish. The shrimp may be broiled as well as grilled. Cooking times will differ greatly from stove to stove and grill to grill, so use suggested times as a guide only. You will need 2 10-inch bamboo skewers.

> 2 raw jumbo shrimp (about 5 to the pound),
>   unpeeled
> juice of ½ a lemon
> 1 tablespoon safflower oil
> 1 small garlic clove, minced
> 2 lemon wedges for garnish

1. Cover the skewers with water and soak them for 20 minutes.
2. Meanwhile, shell and devein the shrimp. Butterfly the shrimp with a single cut on the underside of the shrimp from tip to tail. Be careful not to cut all the way through the shrimp.
3. Combine the lemon juice, oil, and garlic.
4. Push a skewer through the center of each shrimp, working from tail to tip. Marinate the shrimp in the oil mixture at room temperature for 10 minutes or in the refrigerator, covered, for up to 6 hours.
5. Grill the shrimp over low coals, basting with the marinade and rotating often, for about 12 to 15 minutes or until shrimp are firm (but not dried out) and pink. To broil: Place the oven rack about 4 inches from the broiler. Broil the shrimp, basting frequently, about 2 minutes on each side. Serve the shrimp on the skewer with the lemon wedge on the side.

Yield: 2 servings
Calories per serving: 100
Carbohydrate per serving: 2g
Cholesterol per serving: 57mg

Dietary fiber per serving: 0g
Fat per serving: 7g
Protein per serving: 7g
Sodium per serving: 53mg

Angel Hair Pasta with Chèvre

❖

Quick, easy, and good. The angel hair noodles may be homemade or purchased. Chèvre is available from fancy produce stores. Select a young, mild chèvre such as Banon or St. Chevalier. Tiny cooked green peas would be a colorful addition.

½ pound purchased or homemade angel hair noodles or very thin pasta

3 ounces mild chèvre, at room temperature
4 tablespoons low-fat milk
1 tablespoon minced fresh parsley
1 tablespoon unsalted butter, at room temperature
¼ teaspoon salt
freshly ground black pepper to taste

1. Boil the pasta according to package instructions.
2. While the pasta cooks, prepare the sauce. Combine the chèvre, milk, and parsley in a food processor and process until smooth. Or by hand, combine the chèvre, milk, and parsley in a bowl, and mix with a fork or beater until smooth.
3. Drain the pasta. Toss with the butter, salt, and pepper. Then toss with the cheese sauce. The pasta may be held in a double boiler for 30 minutes or so, but add a few more drops of milk to keep it moist.

Yield: 2 servings
Calories per serving: 604
Carbohydrate per serving: 88g
Cholesterol per serving: 50mg

Dietary fiber per serving: 0g
Fat per serving: 17g
Protein per serving: 24g
Sodium per serving: 613mg

Steamed Broccoli

❖

Broccoli is the wonder kid of the vegetable world. High in vitamins A and C, and the minerals iron, calcium, and potassium, it also contains appreciable amounts of fiber. This member of the much-touted cruciferous vegetable family (which includes Brussels sprouts, cabbage, and cauliflower) is now believed, by some researchers, to be a cancer fighter. Broccoli is available all year 'round and is at its peak from October to May, an otherwise bleak season for the fresh produce counter. If the stems are peeled with a swivel-bladed vegetable peeler and sliced into thin rounds or sticks they're every bit as good as the flowerets. Steaming the broccoli makes the most of the water-soluble B vitamins and the heat-sensitive ascorbic acid. Generally, one 2-pound bunch serves 4.

> 1 stalk broccoli (about ½ pound)
> 1 tablespoon lemon juice
> 2 teaspoons unsalted butter, at room temperature
> ⅛ teaspoon salt
> freshly ground black pepper to taste

1. Place 1 inch of water in a 2½-quart saucepan. Fit a collapsible steaming basket in the saucepan. Cover the pan and bring it to a boil.
2. Meanwhile, separate the flowerets from the stalk. Slice the flowerets into roughly 2- to 3-inch bite-size pieces. Peel the stalk (the leaves, which are very high in vitamin A, may be added to the flowerets if you wish). Slice the stalk lengthwise into quarters. Slice the quarters in half lengthwise again. Cut the stick shapes into 2- or 3-inch lengths.
3. Place the broccoli flowerets and stems into the steamer. Cover the pan and return it to a boil. Steam 6 to 7 minutes, occasionally stirring the vegetables from the bottom to the top. The broccoli is done when a stem is tender but still crisp when pierced with a fork.
4. Lift the steamer from the saucepan and turn the broccoli into a serving bowl. Season with the lemon juice, butter, salt, and pepper, and serve. Leftover broccoli reheats nicely in a microwave oven (about 45 seconds at high power depending on the amount) with a little added water.

Yield: 2 servings
Calories per serving: 61
Carbohydrate per serving: 6g
Cholesterol per serving: 10mg

Dietary fiber per serving: 1.3g
Fat per serving: 4g
Protein per serving: 3g
Sodium per serving: 177mg

Focus: Exercise and Longevity

❖

A recent study of 17,000 Harvard College alumni proved what many exercise gurus have long touted—that vigorous exercise does indeed lengthen life, on the average about two years, or as much as if all cancer were wiped out.

The study found that men between the ages of 35 and 54 who jogged at a moderate pace only 3 hours a week or walked briskly 20 miles a week—expending at least 2000 calories by exercising in the seven days—could expect to live an additional 2½ hours for every hour they spent in vigorous exercise.

Men over the age of 50 benefited most from exercise; those who were physically fit had an almost 50 percent lower death rate than their sedentary peers.

❖ Orange juice poured over cut-up fruit for a salad will help retard loss of vitamin C. ❖

Chapter 14

DINNER IN
THE KITCHEN

Dinner in the Kitchen

❖

Much as we might like to, few of us sit down to elegantly prepared and served meals every night of the week. Indeed, in most busy households such occasions are peppered—sparsely at that—during the year, and casual, albeit predictable, meals are the norm. Not that predictability is unappealing—the success of the fast food mega-industry attests to that—unless predictability includes cooking habits that overuse saturated fats and pay little heed to other nutritional guidelines.

The meals—somehow "menu" sounds far too formal—in this "Dinner in the Kitchen" section are intended for those casual, everyday times when cooking chores get squeezed between other obligations and a bit of blessed free time. We'd like something good to eat, and we'd like to serve healthy foods too, but often there just isn't time to fuss nor the energy to bother.

These are the times to put the lower fat and calorie concepts in *The Gourmet Light Cookbook* to work for you. Don't reach for the oil, butter, or margarine when sauteing those onions; opt instead for chicken broth, a nonstick skillet, and cooking spray. Thicken the stew with arrowroot, not flour. Enrich the soup with dry milk powder or low-fat milk and a bit of arrowroot, not cream. Save the butter for the table; use cholesterol-free oils in cooking. Think legumes, whole wheat breads, and fresh vegetables instead of slabs of fatty meat or greasy fried chicken. Offer a fresh, instead of frozen, vegetable. (The freshness factor does more than a hollandaise could ever do.) Modifying your standard, everyday recipes takes more resolve than anything else. Once you've decided to cook more healthily, the doing isn't so tough. For those times when you'd like to try something new and different for family or other informal gatherings, try some of the recipes in this "Dinner in the Kitchen" section.

Here you'll find mussels or eggs as the main course, oatmeal muffins, a cornbread loaf, and whole wheat breadsticks. There are recipes using legumes like lentils, white beans, and kidney beans. Taken out of context, many of the recipes, particularly a few of the desserts, would do a more formal meal proud. As a group, these menus are meals for family and friends who join you in the kitchen.

Focus: Health Food or Junk Food?

❖

Some foods have an undeserved "good-for-you" image. Nutrition-savvy consumers have to be good label readers if they want to avoid empty-calorie foods, foods high in saturated fats, or other foods with a built-in health risk factor. Don't be duped by these innocent appearing "natural" or so-called "light" products:

Granola cereals or some others with a homey "100% natural" label: These breakfast cereals promote a health food image that is unwarranted when the calories and total fat values are weighed. A serving of a representative brand of granola cereal has a teaspoon of added fat; a serving of another "all-natural" cereal (remember there's nothing unnatural about fat or sugar) has a teaspoon and a half of added fat, while a bowl of cornflakes has an insignificant amount. And cornflakes are less fattening, ounce for ounce.

Fruit bars: These are indeed made with fruit—and lots of sugar. Supplying less than 2 percent of the RDA of vitamins, fruit bars are a weak second to the real thing. An orange, for instance, supplies more than 100 percent of the RDA for vitamin C.

Ten percent fruit juice sodas: These are indeed made with fruit juice and 90 percent sugar and water.

Croissants: This seems obvious, but one company does market a frozen croissant as "Deliciously light." It's not the company's fault, of course, that "light" has come to be associated with lower calorie, but no one can deny that it has. And at 109 calories with an added teaspoon and a half of fat per roll, a croissant cannot be considered low calorie or low in fat. (By comparison, a slice of white bread has about ⅕ teaspoon of fat.)

Cholesterol-free, lactose-free frozen desserts (ice cream substitutes): Certainly a boon for lactose intolerant people, these may not be right for cholesterol or calorie counters. Check the label for the kind of oil used in processing, and avoid those that are high in saturated fats like coconut oil. One brand supplies 345 calories in a ¾ cup serving, second only to a popular premium brand of ice cream.

❖ The hardest part about losing weight is making up your mind. The way you look has to be more important to you than how much you eat. But you can eat well and still be thin, as this book tries to show. ❖

SOME LIKE IT HOT

Shrimp and Crab Gumbo

White Rice*

Tossed Salad with Raspberry Vinaigrette

The recent culinary obsession with all things American has caused a celebration of regional cuisines like Creole and Tex-Mex. One fingerprint of Creole cookery, the gumbo, is particularly well suited to the interests of health-conscious cooks. Heavy on vegetables and light on often fatty meats, gumbos—a dish out of Africa by way of the West Indies—are highly personal renditions of a few basic ingredients: tomatoes, onions, and garlic with a little meat, poultry, or shellfish simmered with Cajun spices and served on rice. What the nutritionists term "complex carbohydrates" amounts to "good ol' eatin'" if spicy, hot foods appeal to you.

Unlike lots of slow-cooked concoctions, gumbo is a jiffy affair—about 35 minutes or so are all that are required. In fact, if it overcooks and okra has been used in it, a gummy, too heavy stew is the unhappy result.

Serve this shrimp and crab gumbo for six with simply boiled white rice (follow package instructions or your favorite recipe), crusty French bread for hearty appetites, and a tossed salad (recipe included or use your personal favorite). If hot foods (hot in seasoning that is) don't appeal to you but the other ingredients do, go easy on the Creole Spice Mix.

Focus: Low-Calorie Staples

❖

Keeping the following food items and equipment on hand will help you pare unneeded calories from your daily cooking:

Lemons: Use lemons where you might use salt (on poultry and fish), or oils (on veal or salads), or butter (on vegetables). Use the zest on pasta.

Canned consomme: Use it to replace about half the oil in your standard salad dressing.

Canned chicken and beef broth: Don't be without them for the "sauteing" of onions, garlic, and the like; for cooking mushrooms; or anytime a recipe calls for cooking, not browning, a food in a few tablespoons of butter or other fat.

Plain yogurt: Use yogurt in place of mayonnaise. Stir a teaspoon of arrowroot into ½ cup of yogurt to use in place of cream.

Mustards: Get exotic with mustard. It's a low calorie replacement for mayonnaise, and a delicious spread on grilling chicken and meats. Spread it liberally on crisp bread (the dark brown crackers; one brand is Wasa), top with a thinly sliced chicken breast, and top with another mustard-coated cracker. Wrap the sandwich tightly in foil and refrigerate up to 24 hours—the crackers will soften like bread.

Arrowroot: Use arrowroot for thickening; it has fewer than one-third of the calories of flour.

Fresh ginger in sherry: the ginger is terrific grated on grilling chicken or fish, and the sherry is excellent as a deglazing liquid after pan-sauteing of meats.

A scale: Weigh those meat portions until you can spot a 3-ounce serving.

Parchment paper: Use for steaming of chicken, fish, and vegetables without added fats.

Cooking sprays: Use them on nonstick skillets to get truly fat-free cooking without sticking.

Freshly grated Parmesan cheese: At 20 calories per tablespoon, it's a terrific way to add flavor and calcium to vegetables and salads, without adding lots of fat.

Parsley: Parsley keeps fresh in a tall glass of water in the refrigerator for several days. Use to delight the eye as well as add flavor without calories.

Vinegars: There are so many wonderful vinegars on the market, make use of them often for flavor without calories. Try a few drops on greens such as spinach instead of butter; use with a little broth to deglaze a skillet after pan-frying meat or poultry; use to enliven staid, ordinary salad dressings.

Fresh herbs: Grow a few fresh herbs; the most basic are thyme, rosemary, tarragon, and basil. All are very simple to care for and most can be brought in for the cold months. Cooking with fresh herbs rather than dried ones (particularly if a container of dried herbs never gets tossed unless it's empty) is as dramatic a difference as garden fresh vegetables are to their canned or frozen counterparts. With fresh herbs, you'll be less inclined to coax out flavor with butter and other fats.

Shrimp and Crab Gumbo

❖

Once a regional dish, gumbo has traveled north and west beyond the Mason-Dixon line to newfound popularity nationwide. A frequent ingredient of this tomato-based stew is okra, a pod-shaped vegetable available from late spring to early fall. Okra, a good source of calcium, has a mucilaginous quality when it is cut, which makes it useful for thickening soups and stews, but it can become unpleasantly slimy if overcooked. Plan accordingly and reheat leftovers as briefly as possible. Another thickener in the gumbo pot—although some purists would decry using both at once—is filé powder. An Indian invention, filé powder is made from the leaves of a sassafras tree. It is available at specialty food shops. It too can become stringy when overcooked, so it is added when the gumbo is completely cooked and has been removed from the heat.

Like most stews the ingredients and the proportions listed below are suggestions. You'll have more Creole Spice Mix than you need for this recipe because it is difficult to make in smaller batches. A teaspoon added to the cooking water of new potatoes or green beans is quite good, or you may sprinkle it on any grilled fish or meat. It keeps indefinitely in a screw-top jar in a dark, cool spot.

For the Creole Spice Mix

1 tablespoon sweet paprika
¾ teaspoon dried red pepper flakes
1 teaspoon ground black pepper
½ teaspoon dried oregano
¼ teaspoon onion powder
¼ teaspoon celery salt
1 teaspoon ground dried thyme

For the Gumbo

1 large onion, diced
1 green bell pepper, diced
1 celery rib, diced
2 garlic cloves, minced
1¾ cups homemade chicken stock or canned chicken broth
3 tomatoes, blanched, peeled, and seeded, or 2 cups canned tomatoes, seeded, with their juice
5 ounces trimmed okra, sliced
1 8-ounce bottle clam broth

2 tablespoons tomato paste

2 tablespoons snipped fresh chives

2 teaspoons or to taste Creole Spice Mix

¾ pound mussels (about a dozen), cleaned and debearded

½ pound large raw shrimp, shelled and deveined

6 ounces crab meat, fresh or frozen and thawed

1 teaspoon filé powder

1. Combine all the ingredients for the Creole Spice Mix in a screw-top jar. Cover and shake well to combine. Set aside.

2. Combine the onion, green pepper, celery, garlic, and 4 tablespoons of the chicken stock in a 4-quart or larger saucepan. Cover and bring to a boil over high heat. As soon as a boil is reached, lower the heat to medium and simmer, covered, until the vegetables are tender, about 6 to 7 minutes.

3. Stir in the tomatoes, okra, the remaining 1½ cups chicken stock, clam broth, tomato paste, chives, and 2 teaspoons Creole Spice Mix. Cover and reduce heat to medium-low so the liquid just simmers. Simmer 20 to 25 minutes, stirring occasionally.

4. Uncover the pan and add the mussels. Cover, increase heat to medium-high, and cook 1 minute. Add the shrimp and crab. Cook over medium heat just until the shrimp are pink and the mussels have opened, about 2 minutes.

5. Taste and adjust seasoning. Remove the pan from the heat and stir in the filé powder. Let the gumbo stand, covered, 2 to 3 minutes before serving it over white rice.

Yield: 6 servings
Calories per serving: 146
Carbohydrate per serving: 13g
Cholesterol per serving: 103mg

Dietary fiber per serving: 1g
Fat per serving: 2g
Protein per serving: 19g
Sodium per serving: 406mg

Tossed Salad with
Raspberry Vinaigrette

❖

For meals such as this one where the salad should complement and
cool, not overpower or take precedence, here is a very basic tossed
salad. The dressing will keep up to 4 days in the refrigerator.

For the Salad

6 cups prepared assorted greens, such as spinach,
    red leaf lettuce, Bibb lettuce, and romaine
½ bunch of watercress or arugula, if desired
1 carrot, grated
1 apple, such as Granny Smith or McIntosh, cored
    and diced

For the Dressing

1½ tablespoons olive oil
3 tablespoons safflower oil
2 tablespoons fruity vinegar such as raspberry or
    white wine vinegar
2 tablespoons canned beef consomme or
    homemade chicken stock
freshly ground black pepper to taste

1. Tear the greens into a salad bowl. Roughly chop the watercress
   or tear the arugula. Mix with the greens. Grate the carrot onto
   the greens, then toss the apple with the greens. (The salad may
   be prepared to this point up to 2 hours before serving. Keep
   chilled, covered with plastic wrap.)
2. Combine the dressing ingredients in a screw-top jar. Shake well
   and chill. Just before serving toss it with the greens.

Yield: 6 servings
Calories per serving: 89
Carbohydrate per serving: 6g
Cholesterol per serving: 0mg

Dietary fiber per serving: 1g
Fat per serving: 7g
Protein per serving: 1g
Sodium per serving: 28mg

❖ You'll more likely stick to an exercise program if you start with another person. Each can reinforce the other on those inevitable days when you simply don't want to do it. Once you get the habit of exercise and begin to see and feel the results, you'll make yourself carry on— but a little help from a friend is really useful in the beginning. ❖

SIMPLE, NOT PLAIN

Chicken Paillards with Fresh Herb Salsa

Lentils with Parsley and Scallions

Roasted Asparagus "Al Forno"

Here's a meal that is simple—in thought—but not plain in taste. Boneless, skinless chicken breasts are perked up with a fresh herb sauce that heightens but doesn't mask their flavor. Grilled, or pan sauteed, these paillards take only a few minutes to cook. Equally quick are roasted asparagus. Yes, roasted asparagus spears. A technique used by a popular Rhode Island restaurant, high temperature oven-cooking concentrates the sugars yet leaves a crisp, brilliantly green vegetable. You might try the same idea with thin sliced potatoes, or green beans (see page 484).

Rounding out this midweek supper are lentils. Unlike many of their cousins, these good-for-you legumes cook up in little more than half an hour's time—ten minutes if presoaked.

Simple needn't be synonymous with plain or predictable. This menu serving two proves otherwise.

Focus: Grilling Chicken

Come summer Saturdays, the sum of my cooking creativity seems to amount to: How shall we do the chicken on the grill this time? Like most families we harbor a few idiosyncrasies when it comes to grilled chicken. We don't like heavy, sugary barbecue sauces, we do like really moist meat, and we do like—no love—the crispy, crunchy, browned skin that the grill turns out so right. Imagine then my husband's horror when I mentioned that the chicken—the first of the season yet—would go on the grill without the health-threatening (it's high in saturated fat and calories) but delicious skin! A culinary skeptic of the "Show me" school, he found, much to his surprise, that the skinless chicken was just as good as the old way. Here are a few tips for delicious, grilled, skinless chicken:

1. Shake the skinned chicken pieces in a plastic bag with about ½ cup of bread crumbs and a couple tablespoons of flour; add salt and pepper to taste. An added teaspoon of dried rosemary, oregano, tarragon, or thyme (not all at once) is compatible with chicken.

2. Combine the following in a 1-cup measure for a basting sauce: a tablespoon or so of safflower oil, the juice of 1 lemon, ½ cup dry white wine, a crushed clove of garlic, a tablespoon of Dijon or Pommery mustard, and a shake or two of curry powder if you like. Whisk with a fork and use to baste chicken as it cooks.

3. Cook the chicken over very slow coals, or the lowest setting if you are using a gas grill. While grill temperatures will vary, I find 55 to 65 minutes for cut-up chicken to be about right.

4. Turn the chicken frequently, and twist as it cooks to ensure even cooking.

5. Partially precooking the chicken in a microwave oven before browning it on the grill makes for very tender chicken. Shake the chicken with the bread crumbs after microwaving.

6. Use mesquite or other woods for interesting flavors. I doubted mesquite offered any real flavor after various tries in restaurants until I used it myself with a covered grill. When the chips are soaked about 20 minutes (water is fine, though spirits or juices can be tried) and the cover is used throughout the cooking, mesquite does indeed impart a distinctive yet subtle flavor. Cherry, apple, and hickory woods are good, too.

Chicken Paillards with
Fresh Herb Salsa

❖

This is a quick and tasty dish for the warmer months of the year when the kitchen herb patch is in full bloom (though dried proportions are included). A chicken paillard is the breast boned, skinned, and cooked without fat. The Fresh Herb Salsa recipe can be halved, as it provides more than is needed for just these paillards. But it keeps for a little more than one week and is so versatile, you might like to have it on hand. Try a spoonful on grilled or baked white fish or stirred into hot vegetables such as green beans, or use it as a dip for crudités.

You may grill or pan saute the paillards as you wish.

For the Fresh Herb Salsa

1 red bell pepper
¼ cup chopped sweet onion, such as Vidalla or
    Bermuda
½ cup minced fresh parsley
1 tablespoon snipped fresh tarragon or ½ teaspoon
    dried tarragon
6 to 7 fresh sage leaves or ½ teaspoon dried sage
1 tablespoon snipped fresh chives
1 garlic clove, minced
dried red pepper flakes to taste
2 tablespoons olive oil, extra-virgin recommended
5 tablespoons homemade chicken stock or canned
    chicken broth
1 tablespoon balsamic vinegar
¼ cup plain low-fat yogurt

For the Chicken Paillards

2 chicken breasts, boned and skinned
2 teaspoons safflower oil for pan sauteing

To Prepare the Salsa

1. Combine all the salsa ingredients except the yogurt in the bowl of a food processor. Process until the mixture is well blended; the herbs should still be coarse, not pureed.
2. Add the yogurt and pulse the machine just to combine. Store the mixture in the refrigerator in a covered container. It will keep slightly longer than a week.

To Prepare the Chicken

1. To saute the chicken breasts: Coat an 8- to 10-inch skillet with cooking spray and place the pan over high heat. Add a film of safflower oil. When the oil is hot, add the chicken and brown. When lightly browned, about 2 minutes, reduce the heat to medium and coat the top side of each breast with a tablespoon of fresh herb salsa. Continue to cook the chicken 2 minutes more, with the pan covered. Uncover the pan, flip the breast over, and again film the pan with safflower oil. Return the heat to high, if necessary, to brown the other side. When browned, about 1 to 2 minutes, coat the top side of each breast with another tablespoon of salsa. Re-cover the pan, reduce the heat to medium, and continue to cook about 1 to 2 minutes until the paillards are firm but not hard when pressed. Transfer paillards to a serving platter.
2. To grill the chicken: place the breasts over the hot coals (or heating element). Coat the top surface of each breast with a tablespoon of herb salsa. Twist the breasts as they cook to guarantee even heat. When they are browned on one side and partially cooked, about 4 minutes, flip them over. Coat the remaining side with another tablespoon of herb salsa.

Cook, twisting the paillards from time to time, until they are firm but not hard when pressed. Serve the paillards hot from the grill with another spoonful of herb salsa, if desired.

Yield: 1 cup Fresh Herb Salsa; 2 servings chicken with 2 tablespoons each of salsa
Calories per serving: 306
Carbohydrate per serving: 3g

Cholesterol per serving: 73mg
Dietary fiber per serving: 0g
Fat per serving: 20g
Protein per serving: 27g
Sodium per serving: 67mg

Lentils with Parsley and Scallions

Unlike lots of legumes, lentils are relatively quick cooking. If soaked for about an hour, they'll cook up in a mere 10 minutes. If they are set to simmer with no presoaking, plan on 30 to 35 minutes. A staple in Middle Eastern cooking, lentils are compatible with parsley, scallions, shallots, garlic, and mint (not all together!). An excellent source of vegetable protein, lentils make a little meat or chicken go a long way. Lentils are also a good source of carbohydrates and fiber, and contribute fair amounts of potassium (aids water balance in body tissues) and phosphorus (good for bones and teeth). They're delicious too. Try the red ones if they are available; they have great color.

½ cup lentils
2 tablespoons minced fresh parsley
1 tablespoon minced scallion
1 teaspoon safflower oil
2 teaspoons unsalted butter, at room temperature
¼ teaspoon salt
lots of freshly ground black pepper to taste

1. If you wish, soak the lentils in water that covers them by 2 inches for 1 hour; drain. Place the lentils in a 2½-quart saucepan with 2 cups of fresh water. Cover and bring to a boil over high heat.
2. Reduce the heat so the liquid just simmers. Simmer the lentils until they are tender (determine by munching a few), about 10 minutes for soaked lentils, or 30 to 35 minutes for unsoaked lentils. Drain.
3. Toss the lentils with the parsley, scallions, oil, butter, and salt. Mix well to combine. Add pepper and taste for seasoning adjustment. Serve hot. Lentils may be reheated in a microwave oven at high power for 1½ minutes, if needed.

Yield: 2 generous servings
Calories per serving: 219
Carbohydrate per serving: 29g
Cholesterol per serving: 10mg

Dietary fiber per serving: 2g
Fat per serving: 7g
Protein per serving: 12g
Sodium per serving: 310mg

Roasted Asparagus "Al Forno"

❖

A fine restaurant in Providence, Rhode Island, named "Al Forno" (meaning "from the oven") runs many of its vegetables through very high heat ovens. Asparagus come out crisp yet tender and superbly flavored with very little added fat and no salt. This simple recipe is my adaptation of their unique technique.

½ pound asparagus, peeled
1 teaspoon olive oil, extra-virgin recommended
2 lemon wedges
freshly ground black pepper to taste

1. Preheat the oven to 500 degrees. Place the asparagus on a baking sheet in a single layer, not touching. Drizzle with the oil.
2. Roast the asparagus in the upper third of the oven, turning occasionally, until the spears are tender when pierced with a fork. This will take about 8 to 10 minutes, depending on the thickness of the spears.
3. Place the asparagus on a serving platter. Garnish with lemon wedges and pass a pepper mill at the table.

Yield: 2 generous servings
Calories per serving: 49
Carbohydrate per serving: 6g
Cholesterol per serving: 0mg

Dietary fiber per serving: 1g
Fat per serving: 3g
Protein per serving: 4g
Sodium per serving: 3mg

Focus: Complete Vegetable Protein

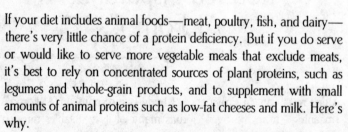

If your diet includes animal foods—meat, poultry, fish, and dairy—there's very little chance of a protein deficiency. But if you do serve or would like to serve more vegetable meals that exclude meats, it's best to rely on concentrated sources of plant proteins, such as legumes and whole-grain products, and to supplement with small amounts of animal proteins such as low-fat cheeses and milk. Here's why.

The body builds protein from units called amino acids. There are 20 such acids; the body produces 11, and 9 must come from food. If any single amino acid is missing—known as the limiting amino acid—the body can't form protein, the "building block" of life.

All animal foods, except gelatin, contain all 9 essential amino acids, making them excellent protein sources. Vegetables, however, have a limiting amino acid. (Soybeans and nuts do contain all the amino acids, but not in sufficient quantity for growth.) For the body to synthesize protein from vegetable foods then, they must be paired so all 9 amino acids are present at the same meal. An example is rice and beans (see Hoppin' John, page 408), where the limiting amino acid in the rice is compensated for by the black-eyed peas and vice versa.

Vegetable protein can also be boosted by adding a bit of animal protein. Chili's a good example; predominantly kidney beans, with a little meat, it makes for a nutritionally complete meal as does fettucine with clam sauce, or cereal and milk. We really don't need meat or other animal foods to stay healthy, but it does make good sense to heed a little nutritional science.

❖ Skipping meals is a pretty ineffective way to achieve permanent weight loss. 1) It doesn't modify the habits that contributed to the weight gain to begin with, and 2) you'll be so hungry and self-righteous about not eating that it's far easier to be tempted into snacking on high-calorie foods, like cheese and crackers or chips. ❖

OVERNIGHT SUCCESS

Veal and Artichoke Ragout

Apple, Walnut, and Roquefort Salad

Buttered Egg Noodles*

Spiced Pumpkin Rum Chiffon

Veal is considered such a luxury by most people that its presence in this "Dinner in the Kitchen" section may seem odd until the recipe is closely read. Inexpensive veal chunks and a package of frozen artichoke hearts are the prime ingredients of this do-ahead stewlike recipe. Double the Veal and Artichoke Ragout if you like; half may be frozen, providing an easy meal for a hurried day. Or cook the dish a day before serving, keeping it chilled and covered for up to twenty-four hours. Like many dishes where the flavors must mingle and marry, this is a true "overnight success."

Salads are a natural with stews. This menu, which serves four, offers a delightful salad of walnuts, apples, and Roquefort cheese. The dressing will keep under refrigeration for up to five days; toss it with the salad just before serving. Serve the ragout and salad with packaged egg noodles, though heartier appetites might enjoy another vegetable. The Roasted Green Beans (page 484), Lentils with Parsley and Scallions (page 470), or a saute of summer squash would complement the meal nicely. If dinner is not dinner without dessert, try the Spiced Rum Pumpkin Chiffon. It too is best made a day ahead, and will provide a dessert for yet another meal.

Veal and Artichoke Ragout

❖

A simple dish, low in fat but heavy on satisfaction and welcome in cool weather. For a change, serve with lentils (page 470) tossed just before serving with a diced tomato for color. Select a casserole dish that can be placed on direct heat as well as in the oven to reduce the number of cooking dishes.

> 1¼ pounds boneless veal for stew, trimmed of any fat
> 1 tablespoon safflower oil
> 1 tablespoon all-purpose flour
> ¼ teaspoon salt
> freshly ground black pepper to taste
> 3 tablespoons brandy
> 6 tablespoons dry white wine or vermouth
> 2 large or 3 medium shallots, chopped
> 1 large garlic clove, minced
> 1 teaspoon fresh thyme or ½ teaspoon dried thyme
> 4 tablespoons balsamic vinegar
> 1 tablespoon brown sugar
> 1 cup homemade chicken stock or canned chicken broth
> 1 9-ounce package frozen artichoke hearts
> 1½ teaspoons arrowroot

1. Preheat the oven to 375 degrees. Cut the veal into bite-size chunks if necessary. Pat the meat dry on paper towels.
2. Coat a 12-inch nonstick skillet with cooking spray. Add the oil and place the skillet over high heat. When it is hot, add the meat cubes so they are in a single layer and not touching. (Saute the meat in two batches if necessary.) Saute the meat over high

heat, stirring frequently with a wooden spoon, until the cubes are browned on all sides, about 4 minutes.

3. Reduce the heat to medium. Sprinkle flour, salt, and pepper over the meat and stir to combine.

4. Scrape the meat into an ovenproof 1 ½-quart casserole. Return the skillet to medium-high heat. Add the brandy. Ignite and stir with a wooden spoon for about 30 seconds to loosen particles from the skillet. Only a glaze—a very thin film on the bottom of the pan—should remain.

5. Add the wine, shallots, and garlic to the skillet, stirring frequently. Reduce the heat to medium, if necessary, to prevent burning. Cook the shallots and garlic until tender, about 1 minute.

6. Add the thyme, vinegar, and brown sugar to the shallots and garlic. Over medium heat stir to combine for 1 minute. Pour the mixture over the meat in the casserole.

7. Reserving 1 tablespoon of chicken stock, stir the remaining stock into the casserole. Cover the dish and bake it for 45 minutes in the middle of the preheated oven.

8. Remove the casserole from the oven. Stir in the artichoke hearts. Re-cover the dish and reduce the oven temperature to 300 degrees. Return the casserole to the middle of the oven for 45 more minutes.

9. When the meat is tender, dissolve the arrowroot in the reserved tablespoon of chicken stock. Transfer the meat and artichoke hearts with a slotted spoon to a serving platter or bowl. Stir the dissolved arrowroot into the casserole juices. Set the casserole over high heat (pour the juices into a skillet if your casserole would break over direct heat) and stir until the juices are lightly thickened, about 1 minute. Return the meat to the casserole dish to serve, or pour the juices over the meat on a serving platter.

Yield: 4 servings
Calories per serving: 381
Carbohydrate per serving: 18g
Cholesterol per serving: 145mg

Dietary fiber per serving: 1g
Fat per serving: 18g
Protein per serving: 30g
Sodium per serving: 325mg

Apple, Walnut, and Roquefort Salad

❖

One of my favorite salads, a double portion with a hunk of crusty bread makes a great, light dinner.

For the Dressing

2 tablespoons sesame oil, available at Oriental or specialty food markets

2 tablespoons olive oil, extra-virgin recommended

¼ cup canned beef consomme or homemade beef stock

1 tablespoon plus 1 teaspoon lemon juice

3 drops or to taste hot oil, available at Oriental or specialty food markets

2 tablespoons minced fresh chives

For the Salad

torn greens including red leaf lettuce, arugula if available, and Bibb

2 ounces crumbled Roquefort cheese, room temperature

1 ounce roughly chopped shelled walnuts

1 apple, Granny Smith or McIntosh recommended, cored and chopped

1. Combine all the dressing ingredients in a small bowl. Blend with a fork and chill. It will keep in the refrigerator for up to 5 days.
2. Toss the greens in a large bowl. Sprinkle with the cheese, walnuts, and apple. Just before serving add the dressing and toss.

Yield: 4 generous servings
Calories per serving: 248
Carbohydrate per serving: 8g
Cholesterol per serving: 14mg

Dietary fiber per serving: 2g
Fat per serving: 22g
Protein per serving: 6g
Sodium per serving: 266mg

Spiced Rum Pumpkin Chiffon

❖

This recipe is for pumpkin and spice lovers. The unorthodox dry milk powder whipped with the egg whites contributes body without the fat calories of whipped cream. This dessert may be made the day before serving; plan on at least 3 to 4 hours chilling time if it is to be served the day it's made. Although the menu is for four, this dessert serves 6 or even 8. The leftovers will keep in the refrigerator for 2 or 3 days, covered with plastic wrap.

> 2 envelopes unflavored gelatin
> ½ cup apple juice or cider
> 1 tablespoon cornstarch
> 1 cup low-fat or skim milk
> 1 tablespoon dark brown sugar
> 4 tablespoons molasses
> 2 eggs, separated
> ½ teaspoon ground cinnamon
> 1 teaspoon freshly grated fresh ginger
> freshly grated nutmeg
> ½ cup canned or fresh, mashed, cooked pumpkin
> a pinch of salt
> 1 tablespoon sugar
> 2 tablespoons instant dry milk powder
> 2 teaspoons dark rum

1. Soften the gelatin in the apple juice in a 1-quart saucepan; let stand 1 minute. Then stir over medium heat for 1 minute until the gelatin is dissolved. Set aside.
2. Dissolve the cornstarch in the milk in a 2½-quart saucepan. Stir over medium-high heat until lightly thickened, about 2 minutes. Stir in the brown sugar and molasses and remove the pan from the heat.

3. Beat the egg yolks in a small bowl until frothy. Whisk into the milk-cornstarch over medium-high heat until the mixture is thickened, about 2 to 3 minutes.
4. Remove from heat and beat in the cinnamon, ginger, nutmeg, pumpkin, and dissolved gelatin. Turn into a bowl and chill until the mixture mounds slightly when dropped from a spoon, between 1 hour and 3 hours, depending on the refrigerator.
5. Beat the egg whites with the pinch of salt until soft peaks form. Beat in the sugar and continue to beat until stiff peaks form. Beat in the milk powder and rum. Fold into the pumpkin mixture. Divide among 6 to 8 parfait glasses and chill at least 3 to 4 hours.

Yield: 6 to 8 servings
Calories per serving: 95
Carbohydrate per serving: 15g
Cholesterol per serving: 70mg

Dietary fiber per serving: 0g
Fat per serving: 2g
Protein per serving: 4g
Sodium per serving: 115mg

Focus:
The Difference in Fats
❖

"Saturated," "monounsaturated," and "polyunsaturated" are terms that refer to the chemical makeup of fats. If a fat molecule were a sports stadium and every seat was taken it would be a saturated fat, monounsaturated if a few seats were empty, and polyunsaturated if many seats were empty.

Polyunsaturated fats tend to help the body get rid of cholesterol, saturates tend to raise cholesterol, and monounsaturates are neutral.

When vegetable oils are processed to make them firm, as for some margarines, those imaginary seats in the stadium are filled with hydrogen atoms. This hydrogenation makes a more saturated fat. When buying margarines, look for those with liquid vegetable oil as the first ingredient, or buy the softest margarine available.

Let this brief chart be a guide to fats.

POLYUNSATURATES	MONOUNSATURATES	SATURATES
corn oil	almonds	butter
cottonseed oil	olive oil	lard
fish	avocados	chocolates
grapeseed oil	peanut butter	palm oil
margarine (most)	cashews	coconut oil
mayonnaise	walnuts	cheese
safflower oil	peanut oil	poultry skin
sesame oil		meat
		milk
		egg yolk

❖ Coriander is an herb that supplies both seeds and green, lacy leaves (also known as cilantro or Chinese parsley). Much used in Mexican, Indian, and Oriental cooking, its pungent taste and distinctive odor may take some getting used to. Very easy to grow in a small kitchen herb garden, coriander is a natural with tomatoes and fruits such as apples and pears. ❖

CHOPSTICKS

Chinese Steamed Chicken with Mushrooms and Broccoli

Chinese Noodles

Roasted Green Beans

Steaming foods is an excellent cooking method for the calorie-conscious, because flavors intensify and sauces are superfluous. It's also quick and requires no special equipment, though an inexpensive wok and bamboo steamer come in handy. In this quick dinner for two, boneless chicken breasts pair with mushrooms and broccoli in a typically Chinese-style duo. Half an hour—certainly no more than forty-five minutes—is all that's needed from the first chop of the knife to the first click of the chopsticks. Served with the steamed dish are fresh Chinese noodles (store-bought) and unique high-heat-roasted green beans.

If you've never eaten with chopsticks before, give it a try. My husband and I started using them several years ago when we were trying to eat more slowly. For a while, a very short while, perhaps we did eat less and linger over each mouthful longer. But you get good, very quickly. Hunger is a great incentive.

If Chinese noodles aren't available at your market, use spaghetti or substitute a simple boiled rice.

Chinese Steamed Chicken
with
Mushrooms and Broccoli

❖

Fragrant with ginger and nearly fat-free, this is a recipe you'll reach for often. A wok and bamboo steamer work best, but a similar arrangement can be fashioned by placing a cake rack on 4 inverted ramekins in a deep electric skillet that has a cover.

> 2 chicken breasts, skinned and boned
> 3 ounces mushrooms, sliced
> 1 cup broccoli flowerets
> 1 teaspoon minced fresh ginger
> 1 small garlic clove, minced
> 2 tablespoons water
> 2 tablespoons reduced-sodium soy sauce
> 2 tablespoons Chinese cooking wine or rice wine,
>   or 1 tablespoon dry wine plus 1 tablespoon dry
>   sherry
> 1 tablespoon cornstarch
> 2 teaspoons peanut oil
> ¼ teaspoon sesame oil, available at Oriental and
>   specialty food markets
> 1 recipe Chinese Noodles (see next page)

1. Slice the chicken on the bias into 1-inch-wide pieces. Set aside.
2. Combine all the remaining ingredients except the noodles in a medium-size bowl. Stir to combine as well as to dissolve the cornstarch. Add the chicken pieces to the bowl. Stir well to combine.
3. Tear off a sheet of aluminum foil about 20 inches long. Pour the chicken mixture onto the center of the foil. Spread it out so

the meat is as nearly as possible in a single layer. Roll the foil closed, keeping the package as flat as possible. (Recipe may be prepared to this point and kept chilled up to 4 hours.)

4. Bring 2 cups of water to a boil over high heat in a wok fitted with a bamboo steamer. When a boil is reached, place the foil package in the steamer. Cover and steam, adjusting heat if necessary, for 15 minutes.

5. Remove the foil package from the steamer using tongs and an oven mitt. Arrange the Chinese Noodles on a serving platter. Open the chicken package and pour the contents over the noodles.

Yield: 2 servings
Calories per serving: 245
Carbohydrate per serving: 11g
Cholesterol per serving: 68mg

Dietary fiber per serving: 1g
Fat per serving: 7g
Protein per serving: 31g
Sodium per serving: 674mg

Chinese Noodles

Look for fresh Chinese noodles in the produce section of most large supermarkets. They are delicious and easy to prepare. An opened package of noodles will keep in the refrigerator for 2 to 3 days.

> 4 ounces fresh Chinese noodles
> 1 teaspoon minced scallion
> ½ teaspoon minced fresh ginger
> 2 teaspoons peanut oil
> 1 teaspoon reduced-sodium soy sauce

1. Fill a 2½-quart saucepan three-quarters full with water. Cover and bring to a boil over high heat. When the water is boiling,

remove the cover and add the noodles. Boil, stirring occasionally, for 3 minutes.

2. Drain the noodles. (Noodles may be cooked as much as 1 hour in advance and left to drain. Reheat by dousing with 2 to 3 quarts boiling water.)

3. Return the drained noodles to the saucepan. Combine with the scallion, ginger, oil, and soy sauce. (The seasoned noodles may be held in a double boiler up to 45 minutes over low heat, or held off the heat, covered, for up to 1 hour. Reheat gently before serving.) Serve warm.

Yield: 2 servings
Calories per serving: 320
Carbohydrate per serving: 33g
Cholesterol per serving: 7mg

Dietary fiber per serving: 0g
Fat per serving: 18g
Protein per serving: 8g
Sodium per serving: 97mg

Roasted Green Beans

Borrowing again from Al Forno Restaurant in Providence, Rhode Island (see Roasted Asparagus, page 471), these green beans are remarkably well flavored.

> ½ pound fresh green beans
> 2 teaspoons olive oil, extra-virgin recommended
> fresh lemon juice to taste
> freshly ground black pepper

1. Preheat oven to 500 degrees. Prepare the beans for cooking by lining up several beans and cutting across the tips. Realign and cut across the bottom ends. Repeat until all the beans are

"tipped and tailed." Spread the beans in a single layer on a baking sheet.

2. Drizzle the beans with the oil. Roast the beans in the middle of the preheated oven, turning 2 or 3 times, until they are tender, about 5 or 6 minutes.
3. Transfer the beans to a serving dish. Season with lemon juice and pepper.

Yield: 2 generous servings
Calories per serving: 76
Carbohydrate per serving: 8g
Cholesterol per serving: 0mg

Dietary fiber per serving: 2g
Fat per serving: 5g
Protein per serving: 2g
Sodium per serving: 7mg

Focus: Natural Vitamins— Are They Better?

❖

To the body, or a scientist, a vitamin is a vitamin is a vitamin. Whether it originates in a test tube and is labeled ascorbic acid or in an orange and commonly called vitamin C, biochemically the synthetic and the natural vitamin are identical. Some "natural" vitamin products—with their implied superiority—are in fact mostly synthetic with a small amount of vitamin from a natural source added. Ascorbic acid with rose hips or B vitamins in a yeast base are predominantly manufactured nutrients, no better than a generic, synthesized vitamin, which in turn is no better or worse than a natural vitamin. The only counter to this rule is vitamin E, which is somewhat different chemically, and hence less effective when manufactured.

❖ Chilling will congeal the bit of fat in canned broth, making it easy to spoon off. ❖

PICNIC PACK

Ham and Bean Salad

Whole Wheat Oatmeal Muffins

Fresh Fruit and Cheese

As wholesome as the out-of-doors, this picnic or backyard spread for four (easily more if the salad is doubled) is little effort. The ham and bean salad only gets better after a few hours in the refrigerator, and is easily mixed together in the morning. Make the muffins then too if you like; they'll stay moist up to twenty-four hours if wrapped tightly in foil. And the dessert is a hundred-percent no-cook noneffort.

Of particular nutritional interest are the many forms of fiber offered here. Beans, oatmeal, All-Bran cereal, whole wheat flour, and fruit are all significant and taste-appealing sources. For more on fiber see *Focus: There's Fiber . . .*, on the next page.

In addition to fiber, there's also plenty of protein. Although the salad calls for only a half-pound of meat, the beans and cheeses contribute important amounts of this "building block" nutrient. For calorie and fat control, increase the proportion of beans and deemphasize the animal proteins.

There is much room for such "play" in these recipes; they are the sort where you may let your creativity run. The salad easily plays host to a variety of other ingredients; kielbasa or other sausages, grilled zucchini, bits of red onion, grated and cooked corn, and a smattering of fresh thyme or basil would all lend their individual spunk. The muffins could be altered with wheat germ, nuts, raisins, a few tablespoons of millet, molasses instead of brown sugar, or half a mashed banana substituted for a bit of the buttermilk. Cooking's a lot more fun—and the results a little uncertain—when it's spontaneous. Believe me, we've laughed (and groaned) our way through a few spontaneous creations at my house!

Focus: There's Fiber, and then, again, There's Fiber

❖

Fiber, what our grandparents called "roughage," has been the subject of considerable attention in both the popular and scientific press. Once considered important only as a sort of system "regulator," it is now widely touted as a cancer preventative, weight-loss aid, and cholesterol reducer. But just what is fiber? Does it all work the same in the body and have all the claims been justified?

Definitions first. Fiber is the blanket name given several kinds of undigestible residues from plant foods. Some labels list "crude fiber" values and others "dietary fiber." Crude fiber is the term given the residue of a food sample after the lab has treated it with a solvent. Crude fiber values are really of limited use, since they may account for as little as one-seventh of the actual total dietary fiber of a food. Dietary fiber is the term given food residues that are not broken down by enzymes and absorbed into the bloodstream—in other words, what's left in the intestine after digestion. These residues are several different kinds of compounds found in the cell walls of plants. Therefore there is fiber, and then, again, there is fiber.

Basically all the compounds of dietary fiber fall into two categories, either Type I fiber or Type II.

TYPE I: acts like a sponge, absorbing many times its weight in water. Cellulose is an example of a Type I fiber. Found in wheat bran, whole-grain breads, and cereals, this fiber may help prevent colon cancer by removing carcinogens and by reducing the level of bile acids. It also helps to relieve some digestive problems and helps prevent constipation.

TYPE II: acts chemically to reduce or prevent some substances from being absorbed into the bloodstream. Pectin is an example of a Type II fiber. Found in fruits, vegetables, nuts, brown rice, barley, and oats, this type of fiber may help to lower the level of LDL cholesterol (the bad kind) without decreasing the amount of HDL cholesterol (the good kind). It does less to keep the system "regular" than Type I, however.

The benefits of both types of dietary fiber have been shouted from the rooftops in the last year. Here is a quick glance at the suspected benefits, with the most substantiated claims first. Remember, not all the tests are conclusive, not all the facts are in . . .

- Fiber relieves constipation.
- Fiber may help prevent diverticulosis, a disorder of the large intestine.
- Fiber has been implicated in the reduction of serum cholesterol, one of the chief risk factors in heart disease.
- Fiber may be instrumental in preventing colon cancer.
- Fiber may have an effect on high blood sugar levels of diabetics.
- Fiber may help with weight-loss or maintaining ideal weight by satisfying the appetite without adding lots of calories.

Health experts theorize the average American eats between 5 and 10 grams of dietary fiber a day, but ideally should be consuming at least twice that amount. It stands to reason that if lowering cholesterol is your health goal, you should be eating more Type II fiber—the fruits, vegetables, barley, oats, and brown rice. If you have a family history of colon cancer or wish to guard against constipation, eating more wheat bran, whole-grain breads, and cereals—the Type I fiber—might be in order.

Can you eat too much fiber? If the diet is nutritionally poor to begin with, too much fiber could interfere with the body's ability to absorb zinc, iron, magnesium, and calcium, but this shouldn't be a problem if you eat a wide variety of foods. Intestinal gas is another possible adverse effect; adding fiber gradually to the diet should overcome the problem.

This chart will help you spot high-fiber foods, and help you calculate your daily intake. Nutritionists recommend eating about 25 grams of fiber daily. Remember, fruits and vegetables eaten raw and with the peel generally have more fiber.

FOOD	SERVING SIZE	GRAMS OF FIBER
All-Bran cereal	½ cup	12.6
peanuts	3 ounces	8.0
Grape Nuts cereal	½ cup	7.5
corn	1 medium ear	5.2
raspberries	½ cup	4.6
bran muffin	1 medium	4.2
apple	1 medium	4.0
pear	1 medium	4.0
potato (baked)	1 medium	3.9
broccoli (cooked)	½ cup	3.8
banana	1 medium	3.0
spaghetti	3 ounces	3.0
brown rice	½ cup	2.4
beets (cooked)	½ cup	2.1
carrot (raw)	1 medium	1.8
strawberries	½ cup	1.6
whole wheat bread	1 slice	1.3
celery (raw)	1 stalk	1.1

❖ To keep mint from taking over the herb garden, plant it pot and all. The pot will help confine the roving roots. ❖

Ham and Bean Salad

❖

Here are ham 'n' beans as you've never had them before, in a do-ahead, even-better-the-second-day salad. Ideal for the picnic basket or a hot summer evening meal, this salad is easily put together in the cooler morning hours or up to 24 hours before serving. A practical way to introduce legumes to a meat-and-potatoes family, the proportion of animal proteins may be increased or decreased to suit your tastes. If meat is omitted altogether, the salad makes an excellent side dish or entree if it is served with a complementing protein such as milk.

The beans may be soaked the night before, or quick-soaked in the morning. If you want to omit the soaking and cooking and prefer to used canned (drained and rinsed) beans such as cannellini (white kidney beans) or red kidney beans, or a mixture of the two for more color, you should omit steps 1 and 2.

1½ cups dry small white beans or white kidney beans

1 Chinese eggplant or ½ pound regular eggplant

2 teaspoons safflower oil

8 ounces ready-to-eat ham, trimmed of any fat and diced (about 1⅓ cups)

4 ounces cherry tomatoes, halved

2 ounces mild cheddar cheese, diced

¼ cup fresh minced parsley

2 scallions, minced

⅓ cup fresh lemon juice

4 tablespoons olive oil, extra-virgin recommended

2 tablespoons homemade beef stock or canned beef broth

2 teaspoons Pommery or other whole-grain mustard

1 large garlic clove, minced
½ teaspoon salt
a few drops hot pepper sauce to taste
lots of freshly ground black pepper
several lettuce leaves (including watercress or
*   arugula if desired) to line serving platter*

1. To soak beans overnight: Place the beans in a large bowl. Cover with 6 cups water. Drain and continue the recipe at step 2 in the morning or after 8 hours. To quick-soak beans: Place the beans in a 2½-quart saucepan. Cover with 6 cups water. Cover the pan and bring it to a boil over high heat and let it boil for 2 minutes. Remove the pan from the heat. Let the beans rest, covered, for 1 hour. Drain and continue.

2. Place the beans in a 2½-quart saucepan. Cover beans with about 5 cups fresh water. Cover the pan and bring the beans to a boil over high heat. When a boil is reached, reduce the heat and simmer the beans until the skins ripple and break when a few beans are held in a spoon and blown on. This will take about 30 minutes for small white beans, and as long as an hour for larger beans. Drain the beans and pour them into a large bowl.

3. While the beans simmer, prepare the eggplant. Cut the Chinese eggplant in half the long way; cut regular eggplant in ½-inch-thick slices. Chinese eggplant doesn't need salting; regular eggplant does. To salt the eggplant, liberally sprinkle the slices with kosher or regular salt on both sides and let the slices rest on paper towels for 20 minutes. Thoroughly rinse the eggplant and pat dry. To grill either kind of eggplant (if grilling is convenient): Brush eggplant with half the safflower oil. Grill one side (the flesh side of Chinese eggplant) over low coals about 5 to 6 minutes. Baste top with remaining safflower oil. Turn over and grill the other (the skin side of Chinese eggplant) for another 4 to 5 minutes or until the flesh is tender when pierced with a fork. Remove from the coals and cool a few minutes. Slice the eggplant into large bite-size pieces and add to the bowl

with the beans. To broil: Preheat the broiler. Place the eggplant slices on a baking sheet. Brush the top side with half the safflower oil. Position the sheet about 4 inches from the broiler. Broil until the eggplant is lightly browned, about 3 to 4 minutes. Turn the slices over, brush again with the remaining oil, and broil until the under side is browned, about 3 to 4 minutes, and the slices are tender when pierced with a fork. Remove and cool slightly. Quarter the slices and add to the bowl with the beans.

4. Add the ham, tomatoes, cheese, parsley, and scallions to the beans and eggplant. Stir to combine.

5. In a small bowl or jar or a measuring cup, combine the lemon juice, olive oil, beef stock, mustard, garlic, salt, hot pepper sauce, and black pepper. Mix with a fork and pour over the salad. Toss to combine.

6. The salad may be served at once or chilled (covered with plastic wrap) up to 24 hours before serving. Bring it to room temperature before serving to enhance its flavor. To serve, line a serving platter with lettuce. Mound the salad over the lettuce.

Yield: 4 entree servings
Calories per serving: 535
Carbohydrate per serving: 50g
Cholesterol per serving: 42mg

Dietary fiber per serving: 18g
Fat per serving: 25g
Protein per serving: 30g
Sodium per serving: 1287mg

Whole Wheat Oatmeal Muffins

❖

These tasty little treats are a snap to prepare and are good warm or cold. I used the All-Bran cereal with extra fiber, then worried that the NutraSweet (aspartame) in that product, which turns bitter when heated, would ruin the muffins. It didn't! We (our kids too, joy of joys!) found them quite delicious. Make them in tiny muffin cups for more calorie-conscious servings. Try the leftovers at breakfast, split and toasted under the broiler, then spread with a bit of butter and sprinkled with cinnamon sugar.

> 1 cup quick-cooking (not instant) oatmeal
> ½ cup All-Bran cereal
> 1½ cups skimmed buttermilk
> 2 tablespoons margarine at room temperature
> 2 tablespoons brown sugar
> 1 egg
> 1 cup whole wheat flour
> 1 teaspoon baking powder
> 1 teaspoon baking soda
> ⅞ teaspoon salt
> cinnamon and sugar

1. Soak the oatmeal and bran cereal in the buttermilk in a medium-size bowl for 45 minutes to 1 hour.
2. Preheat the oven to 400 degrees. In another medium-size bowl with an electric beater or in the bowl of a food processor, cream together the margarine and brown sugar. Then beat in the egg.
3. Stir in the flour, baking powder, baking soda, and salt. Stir just to combine. (Overmixing makes tough bread products.) Stir in the oat-buttermilk mixture. Stir just to combine.
4. Coat 2 6-cup medium-size muffin tins with cooking spray. Fill the cups two-thirds full of batter. Sprinkle the tops of the muffins with the cinnamon-sugar mixture.
5. Bake in the middle of the preheated oven for 15 to 20 minutes or until a toothpick inserted slightly off center in a muffin comes out clean. Serve warm, or cool and wrap in plastic wrap and then foil. Muffins will stay moist at room temperature or chilled up to 24 hours.

Yield: 12 medium-size muffins
Calories per muffin: 113
Carbohydrate per muffin: 18g
Cholesterol per muffin: 20mg

Dietary fiber per muffin: 3g
Fat per muffin: 4g
Protein per muffin: 4g
Sodium per muffin: 311mg

Fresh Fruit and Cheese

❖

This oldest of desserts is remarkably satisfying, to say nothing of nutritious and simple, but with the good news there is bad. First, on the up side of things, is the satiability factor. A dessert of fresh fruit and cheese staves off hunger. Fructose, the natural sugar in fruit, takes longer to digest than sucrose (table sugar), so it "stays with you" longer than, say, a cookie. Cheese, relatively high in fat, also takes some time to digest, because fats are metabolized more slowly than either proteins or carbohydrates.

Another advantage for the cook who has a million things to do, is the ease of preparation of this dessert. Finding a good cheese store is all there is to it. Cheeses should be cut to order or, at the very least, cut frequently. The quality of the cheeses is more important than how many varieties the store carries. Delicate cheeses should be stored away from strong ones, and customers should be free to sample.

On the down side of things, the nutrition-minded menu planner will need to plan carefully when offering a fruit and cheese dessert. Planning is necessary in order to keep the lid on fats— unfortunately often high in most cheeses. Cheeses labeled "part-skim" are indeed lower in calories, but not enormously; about 10– 20 calories an ounce less is the extent of it. Do choose cheeses made from milk, not cream, and skim milk when possible. As a rule the softer, more fluid cheeses like Brie and Camembert have a higher water content and therefore lower calorie level (and fewer important minerals like calcium) than hard cheeses like cheddar. Other lower calorie cheeses are goat cheese, lappi, Neufchâtel (this mixes easily with flavorings), Port du Salut, Sapsago, and string cheese—but remember this is not to say they are low calorie. Ranging from about 80 to 100 calories an ounce, these are foods to eat with discretion. An ounce of cheese isn't much to look at, but it is a concentrated source of calories and fats. Weigh a typical bite of cheese to shock yourself into portion control. Plan on no more than an ounce of cheese per person and perhaps one serving of fruit. (For more information on cheese, read *Focus: The Low-Down on Cheeses* on the next page.)

While there are several imitation and low-calorie cheeses on the market, for my money they can stay there; I'd never bring them home.

Fruits to serve depend, of course, on what's available. Generally speaking, tart apples such as Granny Smiths are excellent when served crisp and cold with cheeses. Pears, at room temperature for best flavor, are terrific. And no one would quibble with a handful of grapes or some sweet cherries in season. The lucky few to whom calorie is a meaningless word will welcome crackers or biscuits. English graham biscuits (a brand name is Wheatolo) are marvelous with fruit and cheese.

Cheeses (other than cottage or farmer's cheese) are best served at room temperature. But they should be kept well chilled half an hour or so before serving to discourage spoilage. Buy cheese in small quantities, as cut pieces never store as well as larger ones.

Focus: The Low-Down on Cheeses

❖

Cheeses are delicious, convenient, and come with a good-for-you reputation, but many are quite high in saturated fats and sodium. Let this little chart be your guide for cooking and snacking.

SODIUM: mg/oz	FAT: grams/oz	CALORIES/oz
LOW SODIUM: 0–99		
Farmer's, no salt added	3	40
MODERATE SODIUM: 100–199		
Swiss	8	107
Mozzarella, whole milk	6	80
Neufchâtel	7	74
Jarlsberg	7	100
Mozzarella, part-skim	5	79
Port du Salut	8	100
Ricotta, part-skim (½ cup)	10	171
MODERATELY HIGH SODIUM: 200–299		
Tilsit, whole milk	7	96
Creamed cottage cheese (½ cup)	5	120
HIGH SODIUM: 300–399		
Feta	6	75
Romano	8	110
VERY HIGH SODIUM: 400+		
Parmesan	7	111

❖ SUMMER BREEZE

Chicken and Broccoli Salad

Molded Rice Ring with Chinese Mayonnaise

Strawberries with Strawberry Cream

Not even Escoffier would want to spend time in a sweltering kitchen when cooling summer breezes beckon, yet it is pleasant to sit down to a well-cooked, appetizing, light meal when the sun sets. This menu for four, which might more appropriately be a "Dinner on the Porch" rather than a "Dinner in the Kitchen," lets you enjoy your day and still serve a refreshing and delicious dinner.

"Summer Breeze" features the common combination of rice and chicken in a little different style. Key to both is a homemade mayonnaise flavored with sesame oil and other Oriental ingredients. Once the mayonnaise is done—a quick job in either a food processor or blender—the rice ring and chicken and broccoli salads can easily be made in less than an hour's time. While the chicken salad may be served immediately, the rice needs a good three hours to chill so it will unmold nicely. Both can be made early in the day and kept refrigerated until dinner time. Dessert is a simple affair—long stemmed strawberries with a creamy dipping sauce. Plan on ten minutes for its preparation. This, too, may be whipped up in the morning, but let the strawberry cream come to room temperature for maximum flavor.

Chicken and Broccoli Salad

❖

Can chicken salad have personality? It may seem an odd thought, but in this case, it is apt. See for yourself with this do-ahead meal. Remember to remove the salad from the refrigerator about a half an hour before dinner. The hot oil and sesame oil are available at Oriental markets and specialty food shops.

> a 1-inch-long piece of ginger root, peeled and sliced
> 1 scallion, chopped
> 3 chicken breasts (with skin and bones are fine)
> 1 large stalk broccoli, about 12 ounces
> 1 red bell pepper
> ¾ cup Chinese Mayonnaise (page 500)
> ¼ teaspoon salt
> a few drops hot oil, to taste
> ¼ teaspoon sesame oil
> 1 recipe Molded Rice Ring (page 500)
> lettuce to line serving platter
> 5 to 6 cherry tomatoes, halved (optional)

1. Fill a 10- or 12-inch skillet three-quarters full of water. Add the ginger and scallion. Cover and bring to a boil over high heat. Meanwhile, if you are using a whole chicken breast, make a 4-inch-long cut through the breast along the top length of the breastbone so it will lie flat. Add the chicken breasts, skin side down, to the skillet.

2. Re-cover the pan and return the water to a boil. When a boil is reached, immediately reduce the heat so the liquid just simmers. Simmer the chicken for 10 minutes. Turn the breasts over and simmer for another 5 to 8 minutes or until the flesh is springy but not too soft when pressed. Remove the pan from the heat and let the chicken rest in the hot liquid, covered, for 5 more minutes. Then cool the chicken on a plate. (Chicken may be

microwaved if desired, but it tends to be juicier if cooked traditionally.)
3. Cut the flowerets from the broccoli stalk. (Reserve the stalk for another use.) Cut the flowerets into bite-size pieces.
4. Transfer the chicken from the cooking liquid to a plate to cool. Strain the cooking liquid into a 2½-quart saucepan. Discard the ginger and scallion. Add enough water to the cooking liquid in the saucepan to make the pan three-quarters full.
5. Cover the pan and bring the liquid to a boil over high heat. Uncover, add the broccoli, and boil until it is tender when pierced with a fork, about 5 to 6 minutes. Drain.
6. Cut the red pepper in half the long way. Remove the seeds and whitish membrane. Flatten the pepper halves with the palm of your hand. Place on a baking sheet and slide under the broiler. Broil until blackened and charred, about 5 to 6 minutes, turning the sheet occasionally to ensure even cooking. Transfer the peppers to a paper or plastic bag. Roll the bag tightly closed and put into the freezer to cool.
7. Discard the skin from the chicken. Lift the meat from the bones with your fingers. Chop the meat into fairly large bite-size pieces and put them into a large bowl. Add the drained broccoli to the bowl.
8. Remove the peppers from the freezer. Peel off and discard the blackened skin from the peppers and slice them into ¼-inch-wide strips. Add the pepper strips to the chicken and broccoli.
9. Add the mayonnaise, salt, hot oil, and sesame oil to the chicken mixture. Stir carefully to combine. Taste; adjust seasoning if necessary. (Salad may be made ahead to this point and chilled, covered, up to 12 hours before serving.)
10. Tuck lettuce leaves around the outside of the unmolded rice ring. Decorate with halved cherry tomatoes if desired. Scoop the salad into the center of the mold.

Yield: 4 servings

Calories per serving: 439

Carbohydrate per serving: 8g

Cholesterol per serving: 106mg

Dietary fiber per serving: 2g

Fat per serving: 34g

Protein per serving: 27g

Sodium per serving: 367mg

Molded Rice Ring
with Chinese Mayonnaise

❖

This is an attractive and simple way to serve a chilled rice salad. For variety, mold the rice in individual ramekins if desired. While designed to be served with the Chicken and Broccoli Salad for this "Summer Breeze" menu, the rice ring would be very nice for a picnic (keep it well chilled) or as a side dish with a simple grilled chicken breast. Make the mold early in the day or at least three hours before serving. The cooking wine, rice vinegar, sesame oil, and hot oil are available at Oriental markets and specialty food shops.

For the Rice

1 cup converted white rice
1 1/2 cups homemade chicken stock or canned
        chicken broth
1 cup water
1/4 teaspoon salt
1/4 cup fresh minced parsley
1 tablespoon slivered almonds

For the Chinese Mayonnaise

1 egg
1 tablespoon Chinese cooking wine
2 teaspoons rice vinegar or white wine vinegar or
        distilled white vinegar
1 tablespoon lemon juice
1 teaspoon Dijon mustard
2/3 cup peanut oil

1 teaspoon sesame oil
a few drops hot oil to taste

1. Combine the rice, chicken stock, water, and salt in a 2½-quart saucepan. Cover and bring it to a boil over high heat. Once a boil is reached, reduce the heat so the liquid just simmers. Cook the rice until all the liquid is absorbed, about 16 minutes.
2. While the rice cooks, make the mayonnaise. Combine the egg, cooking wine, vinegar, lemon juice, and mustard in the bowl of a food processor or in a blender. Process a few seconds to combine.
3. With the machine running, very slowly dribble in the peanut oil. Add the sesame oil and hot oil. Set the mayonnaise aside.
4. When the rice is tender, remove it from the heat, uncover, and let it cool until tepid.
5. Stir the parsley and almonds into the rice. Combine the rice with ¼ cup of the Chinese Mayonnaise, reserving the remaining mayonnaise for the Chicken and Broccoli Salad on page 498 (or chill for some other use).
6. Coat a 1-quart ring mold with cooking spray. Pack the rice into the mold. Smooth the top with a spatula. Cover the mold with plastic wrap. Refrigerate the rice at least 3 hours or as long as 12 hours before serving.
7. Run a flexible-bladed spatula around the outer and inner rims of the ring mold to free the rice. Place a serving platter upside down over the rice mold. Invert. Lift mold from the rice and garnish as described on page 499.

Yield: 4 servings
Calories per serving: 184
Carbohydrate per serving: 40g
Cholesterol per serving: 0mg

Dietary fiber per serving: 0g
Fat per serving: 1g
Protein per serving: 4g
Sodium per serving: 160mg

Strawberries with Strawberry Cream

❖

Almost a "no-recipe" recipe, this simple dessert is quite elegant if jumbo strawberries with long stems are available. Diners either dip their share of scarlet beauties into a communal pot of strawberry cream or are given individual servings. Lacking long-stemmed strawberries, simply slice ripe berries into pretty glass bowls and top with a healthy spoonful of strawberry cream.

> 2 ounces Neufchâtel cheese, at room temperature
> 3 tablespoons orange juice
> ½ cup crushed (fresh or frozen) strawberries
> zest of 1 orange
> 1 tablespoon orange liqueur, such as Triple Sec or
>   Grand Marnier (optional)
> 1 pint fresh strawberries

1. In the bowl of a food processor or in a bowl with an electric mixer, combine the cheese, orange juice, and crushed strawberries until smooth. Stir in the zest and liqueur. (Cream may be made up to 8 hours before serving. Keep covered and chilled, but bring it to room temperature before serving.)
2. To serve, either spoon the strawberry cream over sliced berries, or arrange long-stemmed strawberries around a small glass bowl of the strawberry cream.

Yield: 4 servings
Calories per serving: 77
Carbohydrate per serving: 10g
Cholesterol per serving: 11mg

Dietary fiber per serving: 2g
Fat per serving: 4g
Protein per serving: 2g
Sodium per serving: 58mg

FAST TRACK

Chicken Breasts with Green Peppercorn Sauce
Herb Roasted Potatoes
Honey Glazed Carrots

Learning to cook lighter meals that don't skimp on flavor means changing some old habits. Throughout this book, you've been coached to reach for the chicken broth; to smatter, not slather the butter; to use cholesterol-free oils whenever possible; and to use arrowroot instead of flour for thickening. You've traded the sour cream container for one of yogurt, the cream carton for a milk carton, and all but thrown the mayonnaise away. Highly fatty meats have been replaced with skinless chicken and ocean-fresh fish. You've served more vegetable-rich meals with small servings of animal protein. You've seen the emphasis placed on fresh ingredients and found that good food is just that: it doesn't need a lot of doctoring. You've been cutting back on fats, but have still enjoyed delicious meals because you've made conscious choices when shopping and cooking.

"Fast Track," a menu for four, holds another little trick for the weight- and health-conscious cook. In the Chicken Breasts with Green Peppercorn Sauce recipe you'll learn how to make a "cream" sauce that never sees cream. Dishes that deep-fat fry or cover chicken with a cream and butter sauce obliterate the calorie advantage of skinned poultry while augmenting its somewhat bland flavor. Here is the best of both worlds—pound-saving chicken with a mouth-filling yet body-sparing sauce.

With the chicken are Herb Roasted Potatoes, a deliciously simple way to enjoy potatoes without the butter they absorb like sponges. Kids are particularly partial to these, so you might like to have the herb mixture on hand. Add some color with Honey Glazed Carrots and you'll have a meal that will help speed your way on the fast track to health.

Focus: Heart Disease Risk Factors

One result of all the research that has gone into determining the causes of heart disease is the identification of risk factors. It is important to remember that none of these factors *cause* the disease, rather they happen in association with it. They are:

• Elevated blood cholesterol and triglyceride concentrations,
• High blood pressure,
• Cigarette smoking,
• Diabetes mellitus,
• Obesity,
• Lack of physical activity.

Chicken Breasts with Green Peppercorn Sauce

Here is a peppery, piquant sauce for those who'd rather eat a bowl of cereal than a bland, plain chicken breast. The sauce preparation is a snap, but if you'd rather, it can be prepared several hours ahead and held, covered, in the refrigerator. Green peppercorns are packed in brine and sold in specialty food shops. An opened jar or can will keep for weeks in the refrigerator, or months in the freezer.

For the Chicken Breasts

4 chicken breasts, boned and skinned
juice of half a lemon
⅛ teaspoon salt
freshly ground black pepper to taste

For the Green Peppercorn Sauce

4–6 raw spinach leaves
1 tablespoon unsalted butter
1 tablespoon all-purpose flour
½ cup homemade chicken stock or canned chicken broth
2 tablespoons low-fat cottage cheese
¼ teaspoon salt
1 teaspoon or to taste drained green peppercorns

1. Preheat the oven to 450 degrees (unless you prefer to microwave the chicken). Place the chicken breasts in an ovenproof dish just large enough to hold them. Season them with the lemon juice, salt, and pepper. Cover the dish with foil and bake in the lower third of the oven until chicken is firm when pressed, but still juicy, about 12 to 16 minutes. To cook the chicken in a microwave oven: Season it as described above, cover with plastic wrap, and cook it at high power for about 3 minutes.

2. While the chicken cooks, prepare the sauce. Rinse the spinach and place it in an 8-inch skillet with the water that clings to its leaves. Cover and bring to a boil over high heat. Boil just until the spinach is wilted, about 1 to 2 minutes. Scrape the spinach into a food processor.

3. Over high heat melt the butter in the same skillet until foamy, about 1 minute. Stir in the flour. Cook, stirring, over medium-high heat until very lightly browned, about 45 seconds to 1 minute.

4. Remove the skillet from the heat. Whisk in the chicken broth until smooth. Return the skillet to medium-high heat and stir until the sauce thickens, about 2 to 3 minutes. Scrape the sauce into the food processor with the spinach.

5. Add the cottage cheese, salt, and peppercorns to the food processor. Process until flecks of spinach remain in a light green sauce. (If you decide to make the sauce several hours ahead, hold it, covered, in the refrigerator, and reheat over low heat, stirring often, just before serving.)

6. Remove the chicken from the oven. Pour the cooking juices into the sauce and pulse the machine to combine. Place a chicken breast on each plate, and spoon the sauce on top.

Yield: 4 servings
Calories per serving: 185
Carbohydrate per serving: 3g
Cholesterol per serving: 81mg

Dietary fiber per serving: 0g
Fat per serving: 6g
Protein per serving: 28g
Sodium per serving: 349mg

Herb Roasted Potatoes

You might like to double or even triple the herb mixture and keep it handy in the refrigerator—making this pleaser even snappier to prepare.

1 tablespoon freshly grated Parmesan cheese
1 tablespoon sesame seeds
1 tablespoon minced fresh parsley
1 teaspoon minced garlic
1/4 teaspoon paprika
1/4 teaspoon dry mustard
1/4 teaspoon salt
freshly ground black pepper to taste

2 large baking potatoes (1 pound), scrubbed but
   not peeled
1 tablespoon safflower oil

1. Preheat the oven to 400 degrees. Combine the cheese, sesame seeds, parsley, garlic, paprika, mustard, salt, and pepper.
2. Cut the potatoes in half the long way, then cut each half in quarters, also the long way. Place the potatoes in a 7- by 11-inch baking dish. Brush the potatoes with half the oil, and sprinkle with half the herb mixture.
3. Bake in the upper third of the oven for 20 minutes. Turn potatoes over, brush with the remaining oil, and sprinkle with the remaining herb mix. Bake another 20 minutes or until potatoes are tender when pierced with a fork. Broil 4 to 5 minutes to brown, if necessary.

Yield: 4 servings
Calories per serving: 140
Carbohydrate per serving: 20g
Cholesterol per serving: 1mg

Dietary fiber per serving: 0g
Fat per serving: 5g
Protein per serving: 3g
Sodium per serving: 175mg

Honey Glazed Carrots

❖

Rich in vitamin A and ever-present in many a refrigerator, carrots are as handy a fresh vegetable as you'll find. Buy carrots with the tops attached, if possible, for they are infinitely tastier, but twist off and discard the tops before storing them. For variety, add a teaspoon of chopped fresh mint or dill.

4 to 5 carrots, peeled
5 tablespoons homemade chicken stock or canned
   broth

1 tablespoon unsalted butter
2 teaspoons honey
½ teaspoon salt
a few gratings fresh nutmeg
freshly ground black pepper to taste

1. Slice the carrots into thin sticks or rounds either by hand or in a food processor. Place them in a 1-quart saucepan and add the remaining ingredients.
2. Press aluminum foil right on top of the carrots, then cover the pan. (Carrots may be prepared to this point and held 1 to 2 hours at room temperature.)
3. Place the pan on high heat. When steam escapes, lower the heat to medium-high. Cook 18 to 20 minutes, shaking the pan by the handle from time to time. Serve the carrots hot.

Yield: 4 servings
Calories per serving: 78
Carbohydrate per serving: 13g
Cholesterol per serving: 8mg

Dietary fiber per serving: 1g
Fat per serving: 3g
Protein per serving: 1g
Sodium per serving: 328mg

❖ Eggplant, a.k.a. the mad apple, was once believed to cause insanity. ❖

TURKEY REDUX

Curried "Cream" of Turkey Soup

Whole Wheat Bread Sticks

Strawberry Parfait

More than other dishes, a bowl of hot soup always seems to equal more in taste than the sum of its parts. Nowhere is this truer than with a sparse turkey carcass and a few humble carrots and onions. Simmered together with a judicious drift of herbs, a pinch of this, and a dab of that, and you've got a bowl of good eating, nearly one hundred percent fat free plus chock-full of the foods nutritionists champion.

And what's more appropriate with soup than hot homemade bread? "Turkey Redux" offers a simplified breadstick recipe that requires only one rising and has a rich whole wheat taste.

Unlike most other menus in *The Enlightened Gourmet,* both the soup and bread recipes serve more than the standard four, six, or eight persons. It makes good use of time to work in big batches here, for the leftovers freeze very nicely. The finish is a cool and smooth Strawberry Parfait, a gelatin-thickened dessert that needs an hour's chilling time before it is served. It serves four generously and is easily doubled for eight.

Curried "Cream" of Turkey Soup

❖

The Yankee thrift in me used to cringe when I threw out a turkey carcass, yet I long ago tired of traditional turkey soup. This soup is a little variation with my ever popular curry powder. It is thick and rich but not fattening, and looks spectacular when served from a hollowed out pumpkin. A carcass from a 12-pound turkey yields 10 to 12 cups of stock. Freeze the remaining turkey stock for another soup or use whenever a recipe calls for chicken stock. Leftover soup may be frozen up to 2 months or chilled up to 3 days. Chilled soup will thicken, so thin it with a little stock or milk.

For the Turkey Stock

1 meaty turkey carcass, without skin
water to cover
4 medium onions, chopped
3 celery ribs, chopped
2 carrots, chopped
½ cup minced fresh parsley
1 teaspoon salt
freshly ground black pepper to taste

For the Soup

6 cups turkey stock
4 small onions, chopped
3 carrots, chopped
3 celery ribs, chopped
½ cup minced fresh parsley
¾ cup brown or white (not instant or converted) rice

1 medium apple, cored, peeled, and chopped
1 bay leaf
1 teaspoon salt
freshly ground black pepper to taste
2 cups low-fat or skim milk
1½ tablespoons or to taste curry powder
1 cup fresh or frozen peas

To Prepare the Turkey Stock

1. Roughly chop the turkey carcass into fourths. Place the bones in a 15-quart stockpot and cover with fresh, cool water. Add the remaining ingredients listed under turkey stock.
2. Cover and bring to a boil over high heat. When a boil is reached, reduce the heat so the liquid just simmers. (Stock should not boil or it will be cloudy.) Half cover the pot and simmer for 3 to 4 hours.
3. In the sink place a strainer over a bowl large enough to hold the stock. Pour the stock through the strainer. Cool the solids in the strainer until you can pick the meat from the bones.
4. Add the meat to the stock. Hold the strainer over the stock and press the solids with the back of a wooden spoon to extract the juices. Discard the solids in the strainer. The stock is now ready to use. Or it may be chilled and held up to 24 hours before using, or frozen up to 4 months before using. Boil chilled or frozen stock 5 minutes before using it.

To Prepare the Soup

1. Combine the turkey stock, onions, carrots, celery, parsley, rice, apple, bay leaf, salt, and pepper in a 12-quart or larger stockpot. Cover and bring to a boil over high heat.
2. When a boil is reached, half cover the pot and reduce the heat so the liquid just simmers. Simmer 1 hour, stirring occasionally. Remove the bay leaf.

3. Puree the soup in batches in a food processor or blender. Return the pureed soup to the stockpot.
4. Stir in the milk and curry powder over medium heat. Whisk until well blended. Taste for seasoning adjustment.
5. Stir in the peas and simmer until they are tender, about 15 minutes. The soup is ready to serve, or it may be kept warm up to 1 hour before serving.

Yield: 8 to 10 servings
(analysis based on 10)
Calories per serving: 129
Carbohydrate per serving: 26g
Cholesterol per serving: 2mg

Dietary fiber per serving: 3g
Fat per serving: 1g
Protein per serving: 5g
Sodium per serving: 295mg

Whole Wheat Bread Sticks

Making bread sticks needn't be a chore. These are table-ready in about three hours. Leftovers wrapped tightly in plastic and then in foil stay fresh in the refrigerator up to 3 days or up to 6 months in the freezer. For variety, brush the risen breadsticks with an egg wash just before baking, then sprinkle with sesame, poppy, or caraway seeds.

2 packages (¼ ounce) dry yeast
3 tablespoons warm (105–115 degrees) water
½ teaspoon sugar
1 cup skimmed buttermilk
2 tablespoons honey
3 tablespoons margarine
1 teaspoon salt
1½ cups all-purpose flour
1½ cups whole wheat flour
additional whole wheat flour for work surface

1. Put the yeast, water, and sugar in a glass measuring cup. Let rest about 10 minutes or until foamy and at least doubled in volume.
2. Scald the buttermilk and honey in a small saucepan on the stove over high heat or in a microwave oven. Set aside to cool slightly. Melt the margarine in a small saucepan over medium heat on the stove or in a microwave oven. Set aside to cool slightly.
3. When the liquids are still warm but not hot and the yeast has doubled, sift the salt and white flour into a large bowl. Mix the liquids into the flour with a wooden spoon. Mix in enough whole wheat flour to make a stiff dough. (You may use slightly more or less than the 1½ cups specified. Let the consistency of the dough be your guide, not the recipe.)
4. Sprinkle the work surface with whole wheat flour, and turn the dough out onto it. Knead the dough until smooth and elastic, about 3 minutes.
5. Shape the dough into a ball. Return it to the bowl and cover the bowl with a kitchen towel. Leave the bowl in a warm place for about 10 minutes.
6. Turn the dough out onto the work surface and knead again for about 3 to 4 minutes.
7. Spray 2 large baking sheets with cooking spray. To shape the dough into breadsticks follow one of the following methods. For twisted breadsticks: Roll, stretch, and pat the dough into a rough rectangle about 7 by 11 inches. Cut the dough crosswise into ¼-inch-wide strips. Twist two strips together to form a breadstick. Pinch the ends together and place the breadstick crosswise on the baking sheet. Continue until all the dough is formed. Place the breadsticks 2 inches apart on the baking sheet. The dough may be rerolled as often as necessary. For twirled breadsticks: Follow the twisted breadstick instructions but cut the dough into ½-inch-wide strips. Hold either end of the breadstick in your fingers. Twist the dough in opposite directions, which will make the stick twirl. Place the breadstick on the prepared baking sheets. Repeat until all the dough is formed. The dough may be rerolled as often as necessary.

8. Cover the breadsticks loosely with a kitchen towel. Place the sheets in a warm spot to rise until the breadsticks have about doubled in size, which will be roughly 2 hours. (They may be held as long as 4 hours before baking, if desired.)
9. Preheat oven to 375 degrees. Bake the breadsticks in the middle of the oven for 12 to 15 minutes or until golden brown and cooked through. Serve warm.

Yield: about 19 breadsticks
Calories per breadstick: 94
Carbohydrate per breadstick: 16g
Cholesterol per breadstick: 1g

Dietary fiber per breadstick: 4g
Fat per breadstick: 2g
Protein per breadstick: 3g
Sodium per breadstick: 160mg

Strawberry Parfait

❖

Neufchâtel cheese is much like cream cheese but with lowered fat and more protein. It combines beautifully with strawberries and orange in this do-ahead dessert.

1 package unflavored gelatin
2 tablespoons orange juice or water
3 ounces Neufchâtel cheese, at room temperature
1 6-ounce can orange juice concentrate
½ cup skimmed evaporated milk
12 ounces fresh or frozen strawberries, no sugar added
4 tablespoons orange liqueur, such as Grand Marnier or Triple Sec
2 tablespoons sugar
finely grated rind (zest) of an orange (optional)

1. Soften the gelatin in the 2 tablespoons of orange juice in a 1-cup measure. Place the cup in a 1-quart saucepan filled with 2 inches water and place the saucepan over high heat. Stir the gelatin frequently until it has dissolved, about 2 to 3 minutes. Remove the pan from the heat.
2. Combine the cheese with the orange juice concentrate and the evaporated milk in a food processor or blender. Process until smooth. Add the gelatin and process until well blended. Scrape the mixture into a bowl.
3. Coarsely puree the strawberries with 3 tablespoons of the liqueur, leaving the fruit slightly chunky. Fold half the berries into the cheese mixture in the bowl.
4. Divide the cheese-strawberry mixture among 4 parfait or champagne glasses. Cover and chill until set, about 1 hour. They also can be held chilled up to 24 hours.
5. Combine the remaining berries with the sugar and the remaining tablespoon of liqueur. Chill, covered, until serving time.
6. To serve, top each parfait with a tablespoon of the strawberry sauce, garnish with the orange zest, and pass the remaining sauce at the table.

Yield: 4 to 6 servings
(analysis based on 6)
Calories per serving: 189
Carbohydrate per serving: 30g
Cholesterol per serving: 12mg

Dietary fiber per serving: 1g
Fat per serving: 4g
Protein per serving: 5g
Sodium per serving: 83mg

❖ A single kiwifruit has twice as much vitamin C as several types of oranges. ❖

INDEX

A

À la Grecque, mushrooms, 54
Al Forno restaurant, 466, 471, 484
Almond angel food cake, 309
Almond cream, 285
Amino acids, 472
Angel hair pasta with chévre, 451
Appetizers, 39–65
  beef with broccoli, 41
  chévre-stuffed artichokes, 41
  chicken and pork skewers, 47
  clam and sausage, 46
  curried clam fingers, 58
  crudités and dips, 28, 31, 49, 50, 51, 52,
    72
  duxelle melba, 52
  eggplant caviar, 270
  fresh mozzarella and tomato pizza, 65
  mushrooms à la Grecque, 54
  mussels in remoulade sauce, 56
  Roquefort skinny dip, 52
  sauce verte dip, 50
  seviche, 62
  shrimp-stuffed mushrooms, 63
  sole and crab peppers, 60
  sun spread, 51
Apple(s)
  artichoke salad with Hollandaise, 109
  baked slices with bourbon sauce, 365
  and cabbage stuffing, 138
  with cider and pork medallions, 324
  in nutted fall fruit tarts, 326
  with pork cutlet and cider cream sauce, 141
  sauce, cranberried, 180
  tart, hot, 298
  in tossed green salad, 358
  in walnut and Roquefort salad, 477
  in zucchini pancakes, 318
Arrowroot
  about, 7
  calories in, 460
  in cooking, 337
Artichoke(s)
  in apple salad with Hollandaise, 109
  chévre-stuffed, 41
  to peel, illus., 363
  in potato gratin, 362
  in veal ragout, 475
Arugula
  in tossed salad, 464
Asparagus, 231–34
  about, 231–32
  and maltaise sauce, 23, 233
  mimosa, 232
  and mousseline sauce, 23
  in red pepper pasta with vegetables, 436

roasted "Al Forno," 471
Avocado, in tarragon ice, 74
Avocado-pear salad with hot lime dressing, 405

B

Baked apple slices with bourbon sauce, 365
Balsamic-walnut oil vinaigrette, 97
Bananas Creole, 354
Barley and mushrooms, 325
Basil
  fillet of sole with, and tomato, 196
  in grilled Bermuda onion, 385
  in grilled vegetable salad, 339
  in herb vinaigrette, 436
  oil-dried, about, 64
  in oyster pan roast, 357
  in tomato slices with extra-virgin olive oil,
    429
Basil-walnut sauce, 32
  and paillards, 157
  and pasta salad, 112
Beans
  black, sauce, 60
  dried, in ham and bean salad, 490
  dried, in hoppin' John, 409
  dried, to quick soak, 490
  dried, and vegetable protein, 472
  green, 245–47
  green, in Bibb, tuna salad, 108
  green, with pecans, 334
  green, roasted, 484
  with red pepper puree, 262
  with tomato nuggets, 247
Béarnaise sauce
  about, 20–21
  direct heat method, 24
  food processor or blender method, 25
  variations, 26
Beef
  about, 121–22
  braised, with pineapple and papaya, 122
  with broccoli, 44
  consomme, gingered, 348
  and horseradish Béarnaise, 26
  and horseradish-parsley-mayonnaise, 28
  meat glaze, 15
  paupiettes with sausage and zucchini, 128
  roasted tenderloin of, 130
  stock, 14, 18
  stroganoff, 132
  and wine sauce, 34
Beets, 234–35
Berries and almond cream, 285
Bibb, tuna, and green bean salad, 108
Bisque, spinach and oyster, 85